Changing Fortunes

Changing Fortunes

Income Mobility and Poverty Dynamics in Britain

by Stephen P. Jenkins

OXFORD
UNIVERSITY PRESS

OXFORD

UNIVERSITY PRESS

Great Clarendon Street, Oxford OX2 6DP

Oxford University Press is a department of the University of Oxford.
It furthers the University's objective of excellence in research, scholarship,
and education by publishing worldwide in

Oxford New York

Auckland Cape Town Dar es Salaam Hong Kong Karachi
Kuala Lumpur Madrid Melbourne Mexico City Nairobi
New Delhi Shanghai Taipei Toronto

With offices in

Argentina Austria Brazil Chile Czech Republic France Greece
Guatemala Hungary Italy Japan Poland Portugal Singapore
South Korea Switzerland Thailand Turkey Ukraine Vietnam

Oxford is a registered trade mark of Oxford University Press
in the UK and in certain other countries

Published in the United States
by Oxford University Press Inc., New York

1006429842

© Stephen P. Jenkins 2011

British Library Cataloguing in Publication Data

Data available

Library of Congress Cataloging in Publication Data

Data available

Typeset by SPI Publisher Services, Pondicherry, India
Printed in Great Britain
on acid-free paper by
Clays Ltd, St Ives plc

ISBN 978-0-19-922643-6

1 3 5 7 9 10 8 6 4 2

To Lucinda

Preface

In the first half of the 1990s, most analysis of Britain's income distribution and the extent of poverty was concerned with the dramatic increases in inequality and poverty that had occurred between the mid to late 1970s and the late 1980s. But in the 1990s inequality and poverty rates flattened off—it appeared that there was little or no change in the income distribution from one year to the next. And much the same trend continued during the 2000s, apart from some more noticeable growth in inequality at the very top of the distribution.

From the mid-1990s onwards, I have been arguing that cross-sectional stability in the British income distribution hides longitudinal flux. Underneath the surface of an apparently little changing income distribution, there is substantial income mobility: households' incomes fluctuate between one year and the next, and there is substantial turnover in the membership of the low-income population. Although this picture of dynamics rather than stasis had been revealed earlier for countries such as the USA and Germany, the details of the British situation—based on the first few waves of data from the then new British Household Panel Survey (BHPS)—made headlines. Early findings received coverage in outlets ranging from the *Economist* to *Socialist Worker*. My research programme since has been devoted to documenting the nature of longitudinal flux and its correlates in more detail.

When I arrived at the Institute for Social and Economic Research (ISER) at the University of Essex in September 1994, only two waves of BHPS data were available and I had not begun to write the computer programs to produce the measure of net household income on which almost all of my income dynamics research is based. (BHPS 'net income' variables are available as a supplement to the main BHPS release: see the UK Data Archive pages at <http://www.esds.ac.uk/findingData/bhps.asp>.) Eighteen waves of BHPS data have been collected and, from 2009 onwards, the sample has been incorporated into Understanding Society, a new and very large household panel survey, also run from ISER (<http://www.understandingsociety.org.uk/>).

This book builds on my research on income dynamics in Britain over the last 15 years. I have taken the opportunity to update my work in several ways, in particular considering whether patterns of income mobility and poverty dynamics have been changing over time. Much of the book comprises new material which has not been published elsewhere. I hope that readers will see a benefit in looking at income dynamics in Britain in a relatively integrated fashion. Drawing out common themes, I hope to convey that the whole is greater than the sum of the various parts and to disseminate the findings to a broad audience.

I am grateful to my co-authors and collaborators for allowing me to draw on our joint work, especially Elena Bardasi, Nick Buck, Lorenzo Cappellari, Francesco Devicienti, John Ermisch, Sarah Jarvis, Horacio Levy, John Micklewright, John Rigg, and Philippe Van Kerm. They bear no responsibility for the way in which I have used, interpreted, or developed our work in this book.

My research on income mobility and poverty dynamics has been funded by the UK Economic and Social Research Council through the Research Centre on Micro-Social Change and the United Kingdom Longitudinal Studies Centre, both based at ISER, together with co-funding from the University of Essex. I am grateful for the ESRC's belief in the research value of household panel survey data and for funding and refunding ISER in its survey and research activities, and for the University's continuing support of the Institute. At various stages, additional research funding for my research on the topics covered in this book has come from the Joseph Rowntree Foundation, the Nuffield Foundation, the Department for Work and Pensions, the UK National Equality Panel, and the 2009 University of Melbourne Downing Fellowship.

I am grateful to the University of Essex and my ISER colleagues for granting me sabbatical leave during academic year 2009–10. Without this, this book would never have been written. I spent my leave in the congenial and supportive surroundings of the Melbourne Institute of Applied Economic and Social Research (October to December 2009), the Swedish Institute for Social Research, Stockholm University (March 2010), and the Institute of Economic Analysis, Barcelona (February to August 2010). I wish to thank their directors—Mark Wooden, Anders Björklund, and Clara Ponsatí—for their hospitality.

Many ISER colleagues have provided me with helpful comments and suggestions and have responded to my requests for assistance or information. Among these, Nick Buck has been a fount of knowledge about the BHPS, John Ermisch has provided sage advice from first principles on many topics, J. Gershuny (now at the University of Oxford) has provided encouragement and imaginative vision, Peter Lynn has taught me a lot about survey methods, and Steve Pudney has given much helpful econometric advice. Richard Berthoud, Lucinda Platt, and Holly Sutherland have generously shared their knowledge about Britain's income distribution and its relationship to social policy. IT staff Tom Butler and Paul Siddall have provided invaluable support that has saved me on several occasions.

Many people outside ISER have improved and inspired my research on income distribution issues over the years, especially Tony Atkinson, Martin Biewen, Andrea Brandolini, Rich Burkhauser, Lorenzo Cappellari, Frank Cowell, Greg Duncan, Gary Fields, Peter Gottschalk, John Hills, Markus Jäntti, Peter Lambert, John Micklewright, Brian Nolan, Lars Osberg, Tim Smeeding, Mark Stewart, Philippe Van Kerm, and Robert Walker. I continue to learn much from them, both directly and indirectly by their example.

All estimates shown in the tables and figures in this book have been produced using Stata (<http://www.stata.com>). The multi-disciplinary perspectives on statistical analysis and graphics provided by the worldwide community of Stata users have enriched my research over the last two decades. I thank Statalist contributors, User Group meeting attenders, and the developers at StataCorp. In the course of my research, I have written a number of Stata programs that are freely available. To get them, click on the links revealed after typing findit stephen jenkins at the Stata prompt. Chapter 5 uses, in part, some Stata programs written by Philippe Van Kerm (<http://www.vankerm.net/stata/stata.php>). Throughout the book, tables were processed using Stata programs written by Ben Jann (<http://repec.org/bocode/e/estout/>). I am grateful to them both.

This book was commissioned at the Press by Sarah Caro whose enthusiasm and support convinced me to take on the project. My thanks go to Aimee Wright who took over as my contact at Oxford University Press when Sarah moved on, and to her production staff as well. I also wish to acknowledge the astute comments of the anonymous referees on my proposal which I have done my best to address.

Finally, and above all, I wish to thank Lucinda Platt for not only her love and companionship but also her advice and sufferance throughout the long gestation of this book. To her, the book is dedicated with love and admiration.

Stephen P. Jenkins
September 2010

Acknowledgements

Chapters 1 and 9 re-use, in part, material published in 'Modelling Household Income Dynamics', by Stephen P. Jenkins, *Journal of Population Economics*, 13, December 2000, 529–67. Copyright material is used with the kind permission of Springer Science+Business Media.

Chapter 2 re-uses, in part, material published in 'The Measurement of Economic Inequality', by Stephen P. Jenkins and Philippe Van Kerm, Chapter 3, pp. 40–67, in *The Oxford Handbook of Economic Inequality*, W. Salverda, B. Nolan, and T. M. Smeeding (eds), Oxford University Press, 2009. Copyright material is used with the permission of Oxford University Press.

Chapter 2 re-uses, in part, material published in 'The Dynamics of Child Poverty: Conceptual and Measurement Issues', by Bruce Bradbury, Stephen P. Jenkins, and John Micklewright, Chapter 2, pp. 27–61, in B. Bradbury, S. P. Jenkins, and J. Micklewright (eds), *The Dynamics of Child Poverty in Industrialised Countries*, Cambridge University Press, 2001. Copyright material is used with the permission of Cambridge University Press.

Chapters 8, 9, and 10 re-use, in part, material published in *The Dynamics of Poverty in Britain*, by Stephen P. Jenkins and John A. Rigg, with assistance from Francesco Devicienti, Department for Work and Pensions Research Report No. 157, Corporate Document Services, Leeds, December 2001. Crown Copyright material is reproduced with the permission of the Controller, HMSO.

Chapter 11 re-uses material published in 'Modelling Low Income Transitions', by Lorenzo Cappellari and Stephen P. Jenkins, *Journal of Applied Econometrics*, 19, September/October 2004, 593–610. Copyright material is used with the permission of John Wiley and Sons.

Contents

Contents

Envoi

List of Figures

List of Figures

List of Tables

List of Tables

List of Abbreviations

ARMA	Autoregressive Moving Average Process
BCS70	1970 Birth Cohort Survey
BHPS	British Household Panel Survey
CAPI	Computer Assisted Personal Interviewing
CEX	Consumer Expenditure Survey
CNEF	Cross-National Equivalent File
DI	Dependent Interviewing
DINK	Double-Income-No-Kids
DWP	Department for Work and Pensions
ECHP	European Community Household Panel survey
EITC	Earned Income Tax Credit (USA)
Eurostat	Statistical Office of the European Union
EU	European Union
EU SILC	European Union Statistics on Income and Living Conditions
FES	Family Expenditure Survey (UK)
FRS	Family Resources Survey (UK)
HBAI	Households Below Average Income
HILDA	Household, Income, and Labour Dynamics in Australia Survey
IS	Income Support
LFS	Labour Force Survey
LID	Low Income Dynamics
LLMDB	Lifetime Labour Markets Database
MCS	Millennium Cohort Study
MG	Moffitt and Gottschalk model
MIG	Minimum Income Guarantee
MLD	Mean Logarithmic Deviation
NCDS	National Child Development Survey
NIC	National Insurance Contribution

List of Abbreviations

NLSY	National Longitudinal Survey of Youth
ONS	Office for National Statistics (UK)
OSM	Original Sample Member
PPP	Purchasing Power Parity
PSID	Panel Study of Income Dynamics (USA)
PSM	Permanent Sample Member
SIPP	Survey of Income and Program Participation (USA)
SLID	Survey of Labour and Income Dynamics (Canada)
SOEP	Socio-Economic Panel Survey (Germany)
SoFIE	Survey of Families, Income, and Employment (New Zealand)
TSM	Temporary Sample Member
UK	United Kingdom (England, Wales, Scotland, and Northern Ireland)
VC	Variance Components
WFTC	Working Families Tax Credit
WPLS	Work and Pensions Longitudinal Study

Introduction

1

Introduction: Longitudinal Perspectives on the Income Distribution

Britain's income distribution is like a multi-story apartment building with the numbers of residents on the different floors corresponding to the concentration of people at different real income levels in any particular year. The poorest are in the basement, the richest are in the penthouse, and the majority somewhere in between. But what are the dynamics of occupancy patterns? Snapshots of the building register at different times tell us nothing about these. Over time, how much movement between floors is there, and has the frequency of moves or the distance travelled been changing over the last two decades? In particular, is there much turnover in the basement, and do basement dwellers ever reach the penthouse? Who moves the most and how far? What are the factors associated with movements up and down the income tower over time?

This book addresses such questions using data from the British Household Panel Survey (BHPS). Income mobility refers to the movements from all income origins and to all income destinations (movements to and from all the floors of the income tower). For poverty dynamics, movement is registered only if a person's income changes from below a low-income threshold to above it, or from above a low-income threshold to below it (movements into and out of the basement).

I show that there is substantial movement between floors each year but most residents only make short-distance moves. Few take the lift from the basement directly to the penthouse and few make the reverse trip. Fewer than one in ten people are long-term residents of the basement, stuck at the bottom. About one-half of the basement residents in a given year move out the following year, but there is also a significant probability of returning there within the following one or two years. Getting a new job or higher pay is closely associated with transitions upwards from the bottom, and losing a job is closely associated with downward moves to the basement. Demographic

3

events such as divorce, death of a partner, or the birth of a child are also important correlates of changes in fortunes, though more relevant for downward moves than upward ones.

Why should we be interested in information about income mobility and poverty dynamics? As I now briefly discuss (and return to elaborate in later chapters), such information is relevant for assessing the importance of inequality and poverty and their trends over time. In addition, a longitudinal perspective enriches knowledge of the nature of the income distribution in a society and its determinants, and the formulation of policy.

Whether having more income mobility represents an improvement for a society is not clear cut, because mobility has multiple features. For example, income dynamics are related to equality of opportunity and the openness of a society; people may tolerate greater inequality and poverty if there is a lot of mobility. Concerning inequality, for example, in Britain, and other countries such as the USA, the share of income held by the very richest groups such as the top 1 per cent has risen sharply in recent years while the income shares of most other groups have remained relatively stable (Atkinson 2005; Atkinson, Piketty, and Saez 2011). This growing concentration at the top may be of less social importance if the membership of the very richest groups changes over time—though there is little information about this for contemporary Britain. Concerning poverty, for example, a former British Minister of Social Security discounted the relatively high poverty rates during the 1980s by making reference to data about income mobility:

> Social mobility is considerable. Discussion about poverty is often based on the assumption that figures for households on low incomes describe a static group of people trapped in poverty unable to escape and getting poorer. However, this picture has been blown apart by recent studies. They show that the people in the lowest income category are not the same individuals as were in last year, still less fifteen years ago. (P. Lilley, speech in Southwark Cathedral, 13 June 1996, cited by Hills 1998: 52)

Mr Lilley assumes that income mobility is a Good Thing because it reduces the association between income origins and destinations over time so that the underlying degree of persistent poverty is significantly lower than current poverty.

Income mobility is not necessarily desirable, however. Another interpretation of mobility is that it signals uncertainty about individuals' income prospects: longitudinal flux means volatility in income flows over time. Since people are generally risk-averse, mobility can be a Bad Thing; an increase in mobility makes thing worse.

In sum, the implications of different degrees of income mobility in a society, and hence also the appropriate trade-off between poverty and inequality on the one hand and mobility on the other hand, are not clear cut. There is no question, however, that informed debate about the issues requires a solid foundation of information about the facts. One of the principal objectives of this book is to provide that information.

In addition to the relevance of longitudinal perspectives to normative assessments, there are positive reasons for employing them. At one level, the issues are to do with better measurement and description of poverty. It has been persuasively argued that the passage of time is intimately connected with the nature of the poverty that individuals experience—there are important differences between persistent, recurrent, and occasional poverty, for instance, in terms of the experience itself and the types of people who experience them. (See, for example, Walker 1994, and Gardiner and Hills 1999.) At another level, the issues are to do with improving our understanding of the determinants of poverty. Decreases in the number of people who are poor can arise because fewer people are entering poverty or more people are leaving poverty, or both. Since the processes determining poverty exits and entries differ, a better understanding of poverty is gained by looking at entries and exits separately rather than at poverty itself. Poverty entries and exits and their correlates are the subject of several chapters in this book.

The enhanced understanding provided by longitudinal perspectives has benefits for the formulation of income distribution policies in general and for anti-poverty policies in particular. Researchers have long emphasized that the design of anti-poverty policy measures should depend on whether poverty is a short-duration event which many people experience at one time or a long-duration event concentrated amongst particular identifiable groups in the population. See inter alia Duncan, Coe, and Hill (1984) and Bane and Ellwood (1986) for the USA, Leisering and Leibfried (1999) for Germany, and Walker (1994), Gardiner and Hills (1999), and Jenkins and Rigg (2001) for the UK.

Indeed, a dynamic perspective leads to a different way of thinking about anti-poverty strategies altogether. This argument has been emphasized by David Ellwood, a leading US researcher recruited as welfare reform advisor by President Clinton.

> [D]ynamic analysis gets us closer to treating causes, where static analysis often leads us towards treating symptoms. . . . If, for example, we ask who are the poor today, we are led to questions about the socioeconomic identity of the existing poverty population. Looking to policy, we then typically emphasise income supplementation strategies. The obvious static solution to poverty is to give the poor more money. If instead, we ask what leads people into poverty, we are drawn to events and structures, and our focus shifts to looking for ways to ensure people escape poverty. (Ellwood 1998: 49.)

5

The reorientation of policy thinking to acknowledge the dynamic perspective has been embraced in the UK as well: '[s]napshot data can lead people to focus on the symptoms of the problem rather than addressing the underlying processes which lead people to have or be denied opportunities' (HM Treasury 1999: 5).

Turning longitudinal perspectives from theoretical concepts into empirical measures is predicated on having suitable longitudinal data. In Britain, as in many countries around the world, there has long been much more information available about the income distribution at a point in time, or for a sequence of years, than information available about the longitudinal dynamics of income. Cross-sectional perspectives on the British income distribution are provided by the official statistics produced annually for two decades by the Department for Work and Pensions and its predecessor. The *Households Below Average Income* (HBAI) publication provides information about the distribution for each year with coverage of rich as well as poor incomes despite the title, and also trends over time. (Department for Work and Pensions (2010) is the most recent edition at the time of writing.) The data have also been used by non-governmental researchers to supplement the official picture: see, for example, the monographs by Goodman, Johnson, and Webb (1997) and Hills (2004), and the reports of major committees such as the Inquiry into Income and Wealth (Hills 1995) and the National Equality Panel (2010). These studies are based on (repeated) cross-sectional data derived from the Family Resources Survey (FRS) and, for earlier years, the Family Expenditure Survey (FES). The FRS and FES are large household surveys of nationally representative samples of the private household population, with responses from nearly 30,000 families each year in the case of the FRS. Interviews are undertaken throughout the year when creating the data for a given year. But the individuals who were interviewed in one year are not part of the sample for another year. Different years of data contain different samples of individuals, and so you cannot track the fortunes of the same people over time nor, in particular, examine movements into and out of poverty or affluence.

It was only during the 1990s that longitudinal survey data on household income became widely available in Britain and in much of Europe. The first household panel survey, the US Panel Study of Income Dynamics, started in 1968 but it was not emulated elsewhere for more than a decade. Major household panel surveys began in 1984 in Germany, the Netherlands, and Sweden. The multi-country European Community Household Panel survey was established in 1995, with interviews annually until 2004 for samples in 15 countries. There are now longitudinal data being collected in every EU country to contribute to the EU Statistics and Living Conditions data set. The British Household Panel Survey (BHPS) began in autumn 1991 and carried out interviews with the same individuals from more than 5,000 households annually until 2008, and the household net income data I use in this book are available through to survey year 2006.

The upshot is that it is now possible to document and analyse the longitudinal dynamics of income in Britain in a manner that parallels the way in which cross-sectional data on inequality and poverty and their trends are analysed. Basic descriptive statistics about income mobility and movements into and out of low income can be supplemented with more in-depth analysis of their determinants. And one can also begin to look at changes over time in patterns of income mobility and poverty dynamics. The Department for Work and Pensions now produces a *Low Income Dynamics* (LID) supplement to the HBAI publication, the most recent of which is Department for Work and Pensions (2009*a*). This book takes a broader perspective than LID—it looks at income mobility throughout the income distribution, as well as at movements into and out of low income, and it examines their correlates from a number of perspectives, and in a more in-depth and extended way than is possible in official statistics publications. As with LID, the longitudinal perspective taken in this book is intended to complement and supplement cross-sectional perspectives, not to supplant them.

1.1. Distinguishing Features of the Book

There are several distinguishing features of this book. The first is that I focus on income rather than on wages or earnings or wealth.

My presumption is that income provides a good (albeit imperfect) measure of the resources available to individuals and hence of their potential living standards and economic well-being. By income, I mean the total money income of the household in which an individual lives. This total is adjusted to take account of differences in household composition because these affect how far a given money income will stretch—a given money income provides a family of four with a lower living standard than it provides to a single person. For comparisons of money income over time, incomes are also adjusted to account for the effects of inflation on purchasing power. Household income includes labour market earnings, investment income, benefits, and other sources, and in multi-person households potentially comes from more than one household member. At the same time, I also suppose that each person within a given household has the same income—the benefits derived from a particular needs-adjusted household income are assumed to be equally shared among all members of the same household.

There is widespread agreement that income defined in this way provides a fairly good measure of individual economic well-being relative to the alternatives available, though it is also widely recognized to be imperfect in a number of ways. The income definition is a very conventional and widely used one. It is used in Britain's official income statistics (the HBAI statistics mentioned earlier) and is in broad correspondence with the guidelines established by the international panel of experts known as the Canberra Group (Expert Group on Household Income Statistics 2001). I discuss the definition and measurement of income in detail in later chapters.

An important implication of the income definition is that everyone has an income, whether a child or adult; whether retired or of working age; or whether in paid employment, self-employment, or not working. This is relevant because one of the main rationales for documenting patterns of income mobility and poverty dynamics is to inform assessments of social welfare and, by definition, social welfare refers to society as a whole rather than to selected groups within it.

My focus therefore differs in an important way from the analysis of many labour economists. Their analysis of dynamics concentrates on the dynamics of wage rates or earnings for persons in full-time employment, and typically for men rather than women or children. One of the themes of this book is that income dynamics for all individuals are not the same as earnings dynamics for employees, drawing attention to the roles played by changes in labour earnings from spouses, changes in non-labour income (including benefits), and by changes in household composition. There are advantages to my more encompassing approach that looks at household income and all of society, but there is also a price. Because many more factors (income sources and people) are involved in income than in individual earnings, theoretical models of income dynamics are relatively under-developed. Empirical models of the dynamics of household income are inevitably more descriptive than models of the dynamics of employment earnings for prime-aged male household heads.

A second distinguishing feature of the book is recognition of the importance of the nature of the data and the measures constructed from them. It would be possible to write a book without detailed discussion of the sources used but that would have disadvantages. Measures need to be secure not only in their theoretical foundations but also in their empirical applicability. This book is an empirical study and it is important to communicate the nature of the data that are used—the nature of the survey design and the construction of key variables such as 'net household income'. Those who are not interested in these topics can of course skip over the chapters about measurement and data to the analysis. But I hope that the discussion of definitions and sources will prove of use to many others.

A third distinguishing feature of this book is that it is a single-country study and is the first such study of its kind for any country as far as I am aware: the BHPS provides information about all of the United Kingdom, with the exception of Northern Ireland (see Chapter 4). The single-country focus allows me to examine dynamics in greater detail than is possible in a multi-country study, and has the advantage of considering a population sharing a common tax-benefit system, albeit one that has changed over time. A potential disadvantage of a single-country focus is that it may limit the generalization of the findings. I refer to research about other countries in order to place the results for Britain in context and I attempt to draw out universal findings where possible, but the book is not intended to be a comprehensive cross-national comparative study.

A fourth distinguishing feature of the book is that it examines both income mobility and poverty dynamics. The research literatures on these topics do not overlap as much as one might expect. For example, academics have devoted more attention to developing measures of mobility than measures of poverty dynamics; policy-related research has examined poverty dynamics to a greater extent than it has studied income mobility. I believe it is useful to consider the topics together—they are both concerned with the longitudinal dynamics of income and they draw on the same data sources. Looking at mobility as well as poverty dynamics reminds us that longitudinal change in income is a fact of life for people of all income origins and not only those who are at the bottom at a particular point in time. There are social welfare implications of income mobility that are more general than those of poverty dynamics.

A fifth distinguishing feature of the book is that it examines trends over time in income mobility and poverty dynamics: I describe not only patterns within multi-year subperiods between 1991 and 2006 but also how patterns changed between subperiods. With a long run of panel data, it is possible to describe these changing patterns, and it is also of interest to seek explanations for them. During the period covered by my BHPS data, there were significant changes in the state of the British labour market and in the macro-economy more generally. There were also major reforms to the tax-benefit system. Because of the importance of labour income and cash benefits to household income packages, these two contextual changes are obvious explanations for any changes over time in income mobility and poverty dynamics that I find. Because of the centrality of change over time to the book as a whole, it is worthwhile reviewing these contextual changes at this stage so that I can refer back to them.

1.2. Changes in the State of Britain's Economy and in its Tax-Benefit System, 1991–2006

The household net income data used in this book cover from 1991 through to 2006. This period began with a major recession with almost continuous economic recovery from 1993 onwards until the mid-2000s. There is no coverage in the book of the major recession that followed the financial crisis in late 2008, reflecting the lack of available data at the time of writing. The improvement in the state of the labour market and of the macro-economy as a whole for the 15-year period following 1991 is illustrated by Figure 1.1. The chart shows claimant count and ILO unemployment rates and the annual GDP growth rate, by year. Unemployment rates were at a maximum of around 10 per cent in 1993 and 1994 but fell relatively rapidly thereafter, with the rate of decline slowing down from the end of the 1990s. In the first half of the 2000s, the claimant count unemployment rate was around 3 per cent, and the ILO rate was around 5 per cent. The growth rate of GDP was negative at the start of the period but increased year-on-year thereafter until 1994 after which it was without trend between 2 per cent and 4 per cent per annum.

During the period 1991–2006, there were also major changes in the tax-benefit system, especially the measures introduced by the Labour government in the late 1990s directed primarily at families with children and at pensioners.

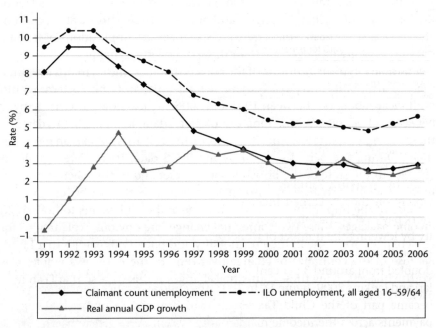

Figure 1.1. Claimant count and ILO unemployment rates (%), and GDP annual growth rate (%), by year

Notes: The ILO unemployment rate is for all adults (men aged 16–64, women aged 16–59), derived from the Labour Force Survey, and is a three-month average centred on the October of the year in question.

Sources: The GDP growth rate, claimant count unemployment rate, and ILO unemployment rate series are series YBEZ, BCJB, and YBTI from the UK Office for National Statistics, available at <http://www.ons.gov.uk>.

Table 1.1. Principal changes to the UK system of cash benefits and tax credits, 1991–2006

Year of introduction	Change
1996	Job Seekers Allowance (JSA) introduced in October 1996 with 'income-based' and 'contribution-based' components. JSA replaced Income Support (IS) and Unemployment Benefit (UB) for unemployed jobseekers. Accompanied by more stringent job search requirements for those assessed as available for work, IS became available only to those not available for work.
1999	Working Families Tax Credit (WFTC) introduced in October 1999, and fully phased in by April 2000. This in-work benefit programme for low-income families was more generous and widened eligibility relative to its predecessor, Family Credit, introduced in 1988. Administered by the income tax authorities (HM Revenue and Customs) rather than the benefits authorities (Department for Work and Pensions, and Benefits Agency).
1999	Increased support for families with children, including increases in Child Benefit (a flat-rate payment per child, paid regardless of parental work status or income), and increases in the child allowances in other benefits.
1999	Minimum Income Guarantee (MIG) for pensioners introduced: a means-tested income supplement that is a form of IS for pensioners.
1999	National Minimum Wage introduced.
2001	MIG for pensioners increased in generosity and structure simplified, from April 2001.
2003	WFTC replaced by the Working Tax Credit (WTC) and Child Tax Credit (CTC) programmes from April 2003. WTC extended eligibility to single people and to families without children. CTC unified child allowances across benefits.
2003	MIG for pensioners transformed into the Pension Credit.

Note: See Brewer and Shephard (2004) and Waldfogel (2010) for more detailed discussions and overviews of the Labour government's changes in the tax-benefit system.
Source: Adapted from Cappellari and Jenkins (2009: table 2).

The changes are summarized in Table 1.1. Probably the most significant reform was the replacement of the existing in-work benefits programme, Family Credit (FC), by Working Families Tax Credit (WFTC), which was modelled more closely on the US Earned Income Tax Credit programme. Aiming to 'make work pay', WFTC had more generous payments than FC and extended eligibility by lowering the number of work hours required for qualification to 16. The proportion of working-age adults in families in receipt of in-work tax credits doubled from around 3 per cent in 1999 to around 6 per cent in 2002 (Cappellari and Jenkins 2009: figure 1). In 2003, the child allowance elements of WFTC became part of the Child Tax Credit, which aimed to unify child support payments across the income maintenance system more generally. The WFTC component supplementing earnings became Working Tax Credit, with increased generosity, including increases in the amounts of reimbursable child-care costs. Also, eligibility was extended to single people and to families without children, and this gave another fillip to the numbers of people in families receiving tax credits. By 2005, the proportion of working adults in families in receipt of in-work tax credits had doubled again to around 12 per cent (Cappellari and Jenkins 2009: figure 1).

Among other policy reforms introduced by the Labour government to make work pay was a national minimum wage rate per hour. And, as part of its aim to reduce child poverty, there was an increase in support for families with children through increases in Child Benefit (a universal non-income-tested benefit paid per child) and in the child-allowance element of other benefits. There were also a number of active labour market programs for specific groups, the New Deals for unemployed young people and for lone parents, providing individualized help to improve job readiness and job search (compulsory in the first case, and voluntary in the second).

Focusing on families with dependent children, Brewer and Shephard's (2004) summary assessment is that '[e]xamining outcomes of Labour's ultimate objectives would lead one to conclude that the make work pay policies have been a success. . . . Academic studies agree that government policies were partially responsible for these changes, at least among lone parents' (2004, p. vii). Further detailed analysis, again focusing on families with children, is provided by Waldfogel (2010). Her calculations of net incomes for a range of family types and various combinations of work hours and child-care costs for each year between 1998 and 2008 reveal that the incomes of working families with children increased markedly with the introduction of tax credits. Waldfogel points out that median income, and hence also a poverty line based on a 60 per cent of median threshold, also increased over the period. However, she also shows that, for these families, incomes increased relative to the poverty line (Waldfogel 2010: table 2.4) and there were also increases in the gap between incomes in work and out of work.

Older people benefited from the introduction of the Minimum Income Guarantee (MIG) from April 1999. The MIG was essentially a version of Income Support, providing means-tested support at specified rates to individuals aged 60 years or more. There was a marked increase in the MIG's generosity in April 2001, with increased payments and higher allowable levels of financial assets. Zantomio, Pudney, and Hancock (2010) provide further details of the changes and demonstrate that they led to higher entitlements and take-up. The MIG was transformed into the Pension Credit in October 2003. Like the MIG, the Pension Credit provides means-tested support to low-income people who have reached the qualifying age (the Guarantee Credit component), but also provides some additional income to people aged 65 or more who have a private pension or some other savings (the Savings Credit component).

In this book, tax-benefit policies and policy reforms are acknowledged as important factors characterizing the environment within which income mobility and poverty dynamics occur, and are referred to in discussions of changes over time in patterns of income dynamics. The labour market trends are treated similarly. However, this book is not a policy evaluation study; it does not provide estimates of the causal effects of specific macroeconomic and tax-benefit system changes on income mobility and poverty dynamics. This would require more narrowly focused studies of specific policy changes and of particular target client groups. There have been many studies of the various policy changes introduced in the late 1990s and 2000s. Examples include estimates of the impact of WFTC on labour supply, especially of lone mothers, by Blundell (2001), Blundell and Hoynes (2004), Brewer et al. (2006), Francesconi and van der Klaauw (2007), and Harkness, Gregg, and Smith (2009), and of the impact of the 1996 Job Seekers Allowance reform by Manning (2009) and Petrongolo (2009).

The book aims instead to document, at a more general level, the patterns of income mobility and poverty dynamics in contemporary Britain and how they have changed. The goal is to provide a better understanding of how people's economic fortunes vary over time and of the factors associated with these variations, and thereby to help with the formulation and evaluation of related social policies. Arnold Zellner's Presidential Address to the American Statistical Association enjoined us to always ensure that we 'GET THE FACTS' (1992: 2), and that is my goal. Put differently, this is primarily a book about the measurement and description of Britain's income distribution from a longitudinal perspective rather a book about policy. It is my firmly held belief that such social arithmetic is a necessary foundation for any discussion of the relationship between the income distribution and policy.

1.3. Outline of the Book

The book has three main parts. The first consists of three chapters about measurement and data. Part II contains three chapters that document the patterns of income mobility and their trends over time. The four chapters in Part III are about poverty dynamics and their trends over time, and also contain multivariate analysis of the lengths of time that people spend in poverty.

In Chapter 2, I take up issues previewed earlier, discussing how economic well-being should be measured when the perspective is a longitudinal one. I consider the relative merits of income and consumption expenditure, the sources that make up income, and the income unit. I distinguish between the household as the unit of account and the individual as the unit of analysis and point out that it is only individuals who can be followed consistently over time (households cannot, because they form and split over time). I give particular attention to the measurement of income over time, considering the related issues of the accounting period for income and various longitudinal concepts such as transitions, transition probabilities, and spells. I make the case for use of a current income definition (rather than an annual income definition), and also discuss in detail the nature and implications of measurement error in income data.

In Chapter 3, I discuss sources of longitudinal data on income, focusing on administrative record data and household panel surveys (of which the BHPS is an example) and comparing their strengths and weaknesses. I point to the variations in household panel survey designs using illustrations from around the world. The discussion also serves as an introduction to the longitudinal data sets that have been used to undertake the cross-national comparative analysis that is discussed in the book.

Against this general background, Chapter 4 introduces the BHPS, the data source underpinning the book. I describe its features in detail—the design, sample size and response (including attrition), imputation, and weighting. The second part of Chapter 4 explains how the net household income variable that is used in the analysis reported in the rest of the book is derived. As part of the data quality assessment, I show that BHPS cross-section distributions of income correspond well with distributions derived from the HBAI data that are derived from the Family Resource Survey, the UK's specialist income survey.

Part II of the book documents the patterns of income mobility in Britain and how mobility has changed since the beginning of the 1990s. Chapters 5 and 6 consider income mobility over the short run (from one year to the next). Chapter 5 begins with a discussion of what constitutes income mobility or the lack of it, differentiating between four dimensions—origin dependence, movement, income growth, and income risk. I contrast these in terms of whether they characterize mobility as representing a social improvement or a problem. The rest of the chapter presents data about income mobility in Britain from the first three perspectives; mobility defined as income risk is documented in Chapter 6.

Chapter 5 shows that there is much mobility from one year to the next in Britain for people of all income origins and regardless of how one summarizes mobility. However, most income changes from one year to the next are not very large and, even when incomes are longitudinally averaged, so that transitory variations are smoothed out, substantial permanent income differences are revealed. The analysis of mobility trends over time reveals the perhaps surprising finding that the degree of income mobility within various subperiods between the 1990s and early 2000s did not change over time, whether mobility is defined in terms of origin dependence, movement, or inequality reduction.

Chapter 6 examines mobility from the perspective of income risk, defined in terms of what economists have labelled the transitory variance of income and income volatility. These measures have received a great deal of recent attention in research about the USA. I show that, although US measures have trended upwards over the last two decades, there is no such trend in the UK. Given the changes in the macro-economy and the tax-benefit system described earlier, this finding is surprising. Further analysis suggests that the explanation is not that there are no changes at all; rather there are increases in longitudinal variability for some income sources (for example, income from benefits and tax credits) that are offset by decreases in variability for other sources.

In Chapter 7, the focus shifts to how an individual's income evolves over many years, and the shape of a person's income-age trajectory is considered. There is a long tradition of describing how income varies with age; for example, there is Seebohm Rowntree's (1901) famous description of life being 'characterized by five alternating periods of want and comparative plenty' (2000 [1901]: 136). I argue that most descriptions focus on some average experience (as Rowntree did). They do not reveal the diversity of income trajectories, even among groups of individuals with similar characteristics. A picture of how people's incomes vary with age looks like a plateful of strands of cooked spaghetti, but I argue that this spaghetti can be unravelled with the help of the statistical model: key features of income trajectories are summarized using a small number of parameters estimated from the data. The analysis is undertaken initially in terms of income defined in terms of wages but results are also presented for the needs-adjusted household income measure that is used throughout the rest of the book.

I show that differences across individuals in income-age trajectory shapes can be summarized in terms of individual-specific differences in income at the start of the working life, individual-specific differences in income growth rates, and a close association between initial incomes and income growth rates— those with a lower initial income experience greater income growth on average so there is a tendency for trajectories to cross. In addition, there is a role played by individual-specific income changes from one year to the next, representing the effects on income of genuine transitory variation, measurement error, or life-course events such as having children, or family formation or dissolution.

Part III is devoted to analysis of poverty dynamics. Just as there are different concepts of mobility, there are different ways to examine poverty from a longitudinal perspective. For instance, one can look at the length of time that people spend in poverty in terms of the number of years that people are poor over an interval of fixed length, or the extent to which people's longitudinally averaged incomes are below the poverty line (chronic versus transitory poverty), or take annual transition rate or spell-based approaches.

In Chapter 8, I document poverty dynamics in Britain from each of these perspectives and show that there is a consistent pattern across the measures. Although around a fifth of the population is poor in any given year, over a longer period many more of the population are touched by poverty. Persistent poverty, however it is defined, is experienced by a relatively small minority of individuals and, moreover, its prevalence has declined over time, especially for families with children and for single pensioners. I suggest that these trends reflect the impacts of the changes in the tax-benefit system and the labour market outlined earlier.

The subject of Chapter 9 is the diversity of routes into and out of poverty and the relative importance of various life-course events as triggers of poverty transitions. The starting point is the approach pioneered by Bane and Ellwood (1986) which classifies poverty-spell endings and poverty-spell beginnings according to the main event associated with the transition. I show that of all trigger events, changes in a household head's labour earnings account for the largest share of exits from poverty as well as of entries into poverty. Nonetheless there is a diversity of routes into and out of poverty. Demographic events are relatively more important for poverty entries than for poverty exits. Changes in labour earnings for individuals other than the household head account for almost as many poverty exits as do the earnings changes for household heads. (There are of course differences by household type, which I also document.) When I compare patterns in the period 1991–7 with those in the period 1998–2004, the Bane-Ellwood approach (which I label 'Method 1') suggests that there is virtually no change over time in the relative importance of different types of trigger event.

Chapter 9 also proposes a modification to Method 1. I argue that the Bane-Ellwood (1986) approach is over-restrictive in the way in which it defines a mutually exclusive hierarchy of events. Moreover, it is also useful to summarize the importance of trigger events for poverty transitions from an individual-level perspective. That is, rather than only look at the share of all poverty transitions accounted by different events (as with Method 1), it is also informative to look at individuals' chances of making a poverty transition if they experience a trigger event. A trigger event that is important at the individual level need not be important in aggregate share terms (because the latter also depends on how prevalent an event is). Implementing this second approach (which I label 'Method 2') reveals some changes between the 1991–7 and 1998–2004 periods in the chances of poverty among those people who experience various trigger events. These trends are most apparent for households with children and I argue that they can be explained by the changes in the tax-benefit system. For this group, the reforms led to greater cushioning of the impact of adverse life-course events such as a marital split, as well as a greater propulsion effect for those experiencing favourable events such as a move from unemployment to work.

The next two chapters employ multivariate models of poverty dynamics. Chapter 10 uses hazard regression models to examine differences in people's experience of poverty over a period of time. For individuals who enter poverty, the total length of time that they spend in poverty subsequently depends on both the chances of exit from poverty and the chances of re-entry to poverty. Model estimates are used to simulate and thereby compare poverty patterns for different types of individual. Few authors combine poverty exit and re-entry analysis in this way. Many focus on poverty exits alone, thereby missing an important feature of poverty—poverty recurrence—that increases the accumulation of poverty experienced over a period of time.

Of all the individuals who fall into poverty, most of those in working-age couple households have relatively short poverty spells. Relatively long spells are experienced by lone parents and their children, and by pensioners. Among those who finish a poverty spell, lone parents and their children stand out as a group that becomes poor again relatively quickly. Combining these sorts of findings generates predictions of poverty persistence for individuals with different sets of characteristics. For example, an individual from a double-income-no-kids household entering poverty is estimated to spend about 1.3 years poor over the next eight years. But for someone aged 60–4, and with no one working in the household, the average number of years poor over the next eight was predicted to be almost twice as long, about 3.5 years. And for a lone parent, the number of years poor is predicted to be 3.5 years if she has one young child and 4.2 years if she has two children.

Chapter 11 looks at similar issues as Chapter 9, but does so using a Markovian model of poverty transitions. In a Markovian model, the specification of how poverty exit rates and poverty entry rates vary with duration is not as sophisticated as that incorporated in the hazard regression models of Chapter 10. However, most applications of hazard regression models have assumed that the chances of being poor when first observed and the subsequent chances of poverty exit or entry are independent (the 'initial conditions' issue). Also, people who are always poor or never poor are typically excluded from the analysis (examples of the problem of 'left-censored' spell data). Moreover, sample dropout (panel attrition) has also typically been ignored in estimation of both types of model. Put another way, models accounting for all the various complications mentioned are rare. This is unsurprising given the apparent complexity of the issues, but I demonstrate that it is feasible to account for them using a Markovian approach. Markovian models therefore provide a complementary approach to the more commonly used hazard regression models. Their use allows us to gauge the extent to which our pictures of poverty dynamics patterns are robust to the approach used.

The Markov model's estimates confirm that initial conditions and sample retention issues are indeed relevant issues to take into account when examining poverty transitions. Nonetheless the results are also reassuring in that the patterns of differences across individuals in the experience of poverty are similar to those found in Chapter 9. For example, married couples have both lower poverty entry rates and lower poverty persistence rates than lone mothers, implying longer spells of poverty and shorter spells of non-poverty for the latter group. It is also shown that there appear to be non-trivial scarring effects of low income: even when differences in characteristics are controlled for, the chances of being poor this year are much higher if you were poor last year rather than non-poor.

Chapter 12 draws together the main themes and lessons of the book and proposes some topics for future research.

This book addresses many aspects of income dynamics, but not all of them. For example, it does not include detailed case studies of particular life-course events and the changes in income that are associated with them (other than the discussion in Chapter 9). For some BHPS-based case studies, I refer readers to analysis of the income changes associated with marital dissolution (Jarvis and Jenkins 1997; Jenkins 2009a), re-employment (Jenkins 2001a), retirement from the labour market (Bardasi, Jenkins, and Rigg 2002), and disability (Jenkins and Rigg 2004).

1.4. Income Mobility and Poverty Dynamics: A Preview

One of the major findings of this book is that, for people of all income origins, there is substantial change in their incomes between one year and the next, though much of the movement is short distance rather than long distance. This is illustrated in many ways in later chapters, but it may be useful to illustrate this basic fact right at the very start in order to set the scene and to illustrate issues that are examined in greater detail in the rest of the book. I do so using income data from the first two BHPS interview waves, that is, survey years 1991 and 1992. Substantially more detail about the BHPS and its income measure is provided in subsequent chapters.

The relationship between income in wave 1 (1991) and income in wave 2 (1992) is summarized in Figure 1.2. Each small circle in the scatter plot represents the wave 1 income and wave 2 income pair for one person in the longitudinal sample. The more people there are with the same pair of incomes, the greater the concentration of people and hence the darker the picture in the relevant location in the picture. Also drawn are lines representing a

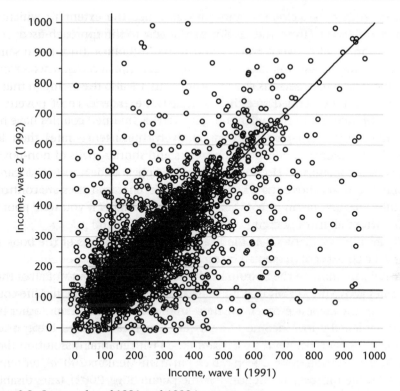

Figure 1.2. Scatter plot of 1991 and 1992 incomes

Notes: Sample of individuals (adults and children) present at BHPS waves 1 (1991) and 2 (1992) with incomes less than £1,000 per week. Each circle represents the incomes for the two years for each individual. The definition of income is given in the text (the adjustment for differences in household size and composition uses the Modified OECD equivalence scale). Incomes are expressed in pounds per week (January 2008 prices). The dark horizontal and vertical lines correspond to an income equal to 60% of contemporary median income (£123 per week for wave 1; £126 per week for wave 2).

low-income cut-off, defined as 60 per cent of the median income, for each year. (The median income is the income of the person in the middle of the distribution when individuals are ranked in order of income.)

From a cross-sectional point of view, there is little change in the income distribution between 1991 and 1992. In each year, most incomes are concentrated in the range between about £75 per week and £400 per week (January 2008 prices). The median income increases slightly from £205 per week to £209 per week. Overall inequality measured using the Gini coefficient is equal to 0.32 in both years. The fraction of individuals with an income below the low-income cut-off falls slightly, from 22 per cent to 21 per cent.

From a longitudinal point of view, there is a substantial year-on-year change in individuals' incomes. If each person's income in 1992 were the same as his or her income in 1991, that is, if there were no income mobility at all, then there would not be a cloud of points in Figure 1.2. Instead all points would lie along the 45° ray from the origin. At the other extreme, if there were no association at all between wave 1 and wave 2 incomes, then the points in the chart would be scattered evenly throughout the picture; there would be no specific areas where persons were concentrated. Clearly the picture of income mobility is not described by either of these two extremes. There is a concentration of incomes in the neighbourhood of the 45° line, meaning that most mobility over the one-year interval is relatively short range—but there is also a significant number of points which are distant from the line. The correlation between incomes in 1991 and 1992 is 0.73. There is evidence of both upward mobility (points above the 45° ray from the origin) and downward income mobility (points below the 45° ray). Moreover, mobility is experienced by people from all income groups, rich, middle-income, and poor.

Figure 1.2 also enables a first look at poverty dynamics. Taking the poverty line to be 60 per cent of median income, the people who are poor in both 1991 and 1992 are those in the bottom left-hand quadrant of Figure 1.2; those with incomes above the cut-off in both years are those in the top right-hand quadrant. The low-income escapers are those in the top left quadrant (7 per cent of the sample); the low-income entrants are those in the bottom right-hand quadrant (8 per cent). Of the total sample, 14 per cent are poor at both waves and 71 per cent non-poor at both waves. But at the same time, there is also some considerable turnover in the low-income population. To put things another way, over the two-year period, a substantial proportion of the sample, nearly one-third (29 per cent), had a low income during at least one of the two years, a rate that is 50 per cent greater than the cross-sectional poverty rate in either of the two years.

Two years is, of course, a relatively short period in people's lives and, in the chapters to follow, I track individuals and their incomes for up to 16 years. I describe the characteristics of the people who experience the various types of income change and the life-course events associated with movements into and out of poverty over time, and characterize the diversity of shapes of income trajectories.

A second major theme of the book concerns the sources of changes in fortunes, highlighting the role of demographic change and of changes in different types of income. Changes in one's own fortunes over time depend not only on one's own circumstances but also on with whom you live and how these arrangements change over time. Additional household members potentially contribute income to the household total, and also change the number of mouths to be fed (or household 'needs' more generally). Changes in the net disposable income of a household can arise through changes in not only earnings from employment or self-employment, but also income from benefits and credits, investments and savings, and deductions such as income and local taxes and National Insurance contributions.

If households did not change their form and composition very much over time, the potential for demographic change to affect household incomes would be minimal. But, in contemporary Britain, the reality is that demographic change is commonly experienced. This is illustrated by Jenkins (2000) whose analysis follows individuals over the first six interview waves (survey years 1991–6) of the BHPS. I show that almost one in ten individuals experienced a change in household head between the wave 1 and wave 2 interviews, and just under one in five individuals experienced some form of demographic change in their household over the same period (including arrivals and departures of household members). By the wave 6 interview, 23 per cent of the sample had experienced a change in household head and almost one-half (47 per cent) had experienced some form of demographic change. These statistics demonstrate that demographic change is pervasive and so cannot be ignored in any study of income dynamics.

The importance of longitudinal variation in different sources of household income is also illustrated by Jenkins (2000). If each person's household income stayed the same year on year (or grew at an equi-proportionate rate), there is no inequality in the incomes making up each person's income stream over time. As it happens, there is a marked degree of inequality in six-year income streams—the coefficient of variation (the standard deviation divided by the mean) is around 0.25 if averaged across the sample (Jenkins 2000: table 5), by comparison with the inequality of incomes across individuals at a point in time, which is at least 0.6 according to the coefficient of variation. However, the contributions of different income sources to the overall longitudinal variability of income are diverse (and also vary by household type). For example, for the population as a whole, variability in a household head's labour earnings accounts for only one-half of the total variability in income over the six-year period, which is about the same as the contribution to overall variability in labour earnings of other household members (Jenkins 2000: table 5). Variability in other income sources also contributes to overall variability, and the relative importance of the various sources differs by household type (changes in earnings are relatively unimportant for pensioner households, for instance). Changes in different income sources, and heterogeneity in patterns across different household types, are described in greater detail in the rest of the book.

Having set the scene with some preliminary illustrative results, it is important to discuss the building blocks of the analysis in greater detail before proceeding to the detailed findings set out in Parts II and III of the book. Part I of the book considers fundamental issues relating to the definition and measurement of income (Chapter 2), sources of longitudinal data in general (Chapter 3), and the BHPS and its income data in particular (Chapter 4).

Part I

Measurement

Part I
Measurement and Data

2

Income over Time: Measurement Issues

This chapter considers some of the measurement issues that arise when one looks at the income distribution from a longitudinal perspective. Although many of the issues are the same as those that are relevant to analysis of the income distribution at a single point in time, they often need to be seen in a new light when one looks at incomes longitudinally. And there are additional issues that arise precisely because of the dynamic perspective, such as the measurement of poverty spells. The chapter builds on discussions by Bradbury, Jenkins, and Micklewright (2001) and Jenkins and Van Kerm (2009). The issues discussed in this chapter are data-related ones. Discussion of definitions of 'mobility', 'poverty persistence', and related concepts, appears in later chapters, especially Chapters 5 and 8.

Choosing the concept of living standards is fundamental. As was flagged in Chapter 1, the focus of this book is on income defined as household income adjusted for differences in household size and composition. In Section 2.1, I revisit the definition of income, and discuss the relevance of money-based measures in contrast with non-monetary and multidimensional measures (several of which are also collected annually in leading household panel surveys), and whether an alternative measure such as consumption expenditure is able to provide a better measure of living standards. Other issues addressed are the distribution of living standards within households and the choice of the equivalence scale which is used to adjust observed money income (or consumption expenditure) to take account of differences in household size and composition, and the distinction between the observational unit for income (the household or family) and the unit of analysis (the individual).

Section 2.2 considers issues related to income and time. First, I discuss the period of time over which money-based measures of living standards are measured, contrasting 'current' and 'annual' measures in particular, and arguing that this distinction is sometimes overdrawn. Although the issue of the accounting period is important in all income distribution studies, there are additional issues concerning income and time in the study of dynamics, specifically how to measure income through time. The stance taken on the issues depends in part on the research goals, for example whether one is studying income mobility or poverty transitions between two points in time or individuals' patterns of poverty over time, in which case one needs definitions of poverty persistence and poverty spells. One also needs a definition of the poverty line but, for brevity, I do not discuss this issue at all. Throughout this book, I use a widely used poverty line equal to 60 per cent of contemporary median income.

In Section 2.3, I examine some additional data issues that arise with longitudinal data on incomes, specifically the problems of incomplete or missing data (which can arise from survey non-response and survey design), and measurement error. I discuss their nature and consequences, and how the problems might be addressed.

2.1. Income and Other Measures of Economic Well-Being

In Chapter 1, I stated that the definition of income used in this book referred to a household income total from all sources, adjusted by an equivalence scale to take account of differences in household size and composition and also adjusted by a price index to account for differences in price levels. I claimed that this was a relatively good measure, albeit an imperfect one. Candidates for alternative measures include multidimensional measures of well-being and material deprivation, direct measures of individuals' happiness, and unidimensional monetary measures such as consumption expenditure.

The principal claims in favour of income as a measure of economic well-being are as follows. (Some matters of detail are followed up in subsequent sections.) It has a high degree of validity, though with reference to a narrowly-defined concept. Related, its informational content is high in the sense of being able to discriminate between individuals to a fine degree. The measure is objective, in the sense of relating to individuals' circumstances which can be externally verified in principle, rather than relating to individuals' subjective perceptions of their circumstances. (The issue of measurement error is returned to below.) Related, the concept of income is relatively transparent and easily understood by most people (though adjustments for differences in household size and composition or for inflation may offset this). And there is a close connection between income, the measure of personal economic well-being, on the one hand, and the monitoring of social progress, and the formulation and evaluation of major social policy instruments, such as a country's system of taxes and cash benefits, on the other hand. This is the consequence of having a highly monetized economy. And there are other practical advantages: measures of income are regularly collected on a regular basis not only in cross-section surveys but also in panel surveys such as the BHPS. An additional reason for interest in income is an instrumental one. Arguably, variations in money income have causal effects on other outcome variables in a manner that other well-being measures do not, that is money itself matters. See the discussion of the relationship between income and child outcomes by Jenkins and Micklewright (2007).

Income is a narrowly focused measure. Economic well-being is only one aspect of individuals' well-being—there are many other aspects of people's lives that may matter for their well-being besides their money income, and multidimensional approaches offer the promise of encapsulating these. For example, drawing inspiration from Amartya Sen's (1979, 1985) 'capabilities' approach, the Equalities Measurement Framework of the UK's Equality and Human Rights Commission refers to ten dimensions of people's lives (health; physical security; legal security; education and learning; standard of living; productive and valued activities; participation, influence, and voice; individual, family, and social life; identity, expression, and self-respect), and considers not only differences in outcomes per se, but also processes (such as unequal treatment) and autonomy (Alkire et al. 2009).

Also multidimensional is the material deprivation literature pioneered by Townsend (1979) and developed by the Breadline Britain surveys (Mack and Lansley 1985; Gordon and Pantazis 1997), Gordon et al. (2000), and Nolan and Whelan (1996). This is more narrowly concerned with outcomes, though limited by the fact that the measures focus on variations at the bottom of the distribution. Living standards are assessed in terms of access to a particular set of goods and services or participation in particular activities.

Although multidimensional measures of well-being have the attraction of taking a broader and more comprehensive perspective on what matters for people's lives, they raise a number of issues. There are questions concerning, first, the choice of indicators. In the material deprivation literature, researchers usually choose a relatively small set of indicators, in many cases following Townsend's (1979) original work, and much the same set has been incorporated in subsequent surveys. This has also been stimulated by a European-wide demand for the collection of such data, and is related to EU agendas concerning measurement of social exclusion. The BHPS, for instance, has collected such data annually since the mid-1990s. Gordon et al. (2000) drew on the views of sample respondents, aiming to narrow down the list of potential deprivation indicators to those that had substantial support (their survey asked about 54 items and activities). The selection of indicators underpinning the Equalities Measurement Framework involved several rounds of deliberative consultation with the general public, 'at risk' groups, stakeholders, and subject specialists (Alkire et al. 2009). Such developments are likely to increase the legitimacy of the indicators chosen, but it is unlikely that such exercises will ever lead to a consensus about an indicator set to the same extent as there is about the primacy of income. In any case, second, given a set of indicators, there remains the issue of how indicators should be aggregated to form an overall assessment of a person's well-being. (Disaggregated information is useful in some circumstances, but there is a high demand for aggregate summaries.) For income or other unidimensional measures, the problem is solved by construction. Much of the material deprivation literature has given scant attention to this issue and simply used sum-score measures or ad hoc statistical criteria that lack transparency (Cappellari and Jenkins 2007). The literature on multidimensional inequality and poverty comparisons has pointed to many of the issues and made some useful progress on these issues, but the literature is still in its infancy and will always face an intrinsic complexity problem when there are multiple dimensions, especially if there are more than two. (See inter alia Atkinson 2003 and Bourguignon and Chakravarty 2003.) For the same reason, the direct usefulness of multidimensional information for policy purposes currently remains much less than that provided by income measures. There is, for instance, a much less transparent link between outcomes (especially if aggregated) and policy instruments.

Asking people about their happiness, or related concepts such as life satisfaction, has the seductive attraction of appearing to measure directly what is of interest. Moreover, responses are expressed on a unidimensional scale and so the problems that arise from having multiple dimensions per se disappear. In addition, panel surveys such as the BHPS collect this information regularly from respondent adults. The attractions of subjective happiness measures have led to increasing attention being given to them by economists: see the reviews by, for example, Frey and Stutzer (2002), Clark et al. (2008), Kahneman and Krueger (2006), and van Praag and Ferrer-i-Carbonell (2009). It remains the case, however, that the majority of economists are sceptical about the use of such measures for the sorts of assessments that can be provided by monetary measures such as income.

There are three major reservations (Kahneman and Krueger 2006). First, people's responses take the form of a global retrospective judgement provided at the time of the interview, but are sensitive to their current mood and the context. (Since all well-being measures, including income, may be subject to similar or related problems, this is a claim about the relevant importance of the issue in this context.) Second, there is the puzzle that although major changes in life circumstances of many kinds, for example onset of disability or divorce, lead to changes in measures of life satisfaction in the expected direction, there is a relatively quick return to the same or almost the same level as before (so-called 'adaption'), whereas one might expect a valid measure of well-being to exhibit relatively large and long-lasting changes. Third, respondents may use and interpret the response categories presented to them in surveys, and the labelling of them, in different ways (Conti and Pudney 2011). By contrast, an income of a particular amount is not open to difference of interpretation to the same degree, and can provide a more fine-grained description of circumstances than does a question with a small number of categories (11 is typically the maximum used).

It appears, then, that the main competitor with income is consumption or, rather, consumption expenditure—the monetary aggregate of spending on consumption items. A household's consumption expenditure over a given period is equal to net income (as defined earlier) minus the amount accrued as savings. For well-developed arguments in favour of using consumption expenditure rather than income measures of material well-being, see Meyer and Sullivan (2003). Although consumption expenditure measures are not in widespread use in official statistics in the way that income measures are for high income countries, they are commonly used in research about the distribution of economic well-being in developing countries. The argument there primarily concerns relative measurement errors. See, for example, Deaton (1997) for a discussion of this. I return to the issue of measurement error in income later in this chapter.

The choice between the two measures is a matter of balancing principle and practice. If one takes the conventional welfarist approach to measuring economic well-being, then consumption is arguably the more appropriate measure for distributional analysis, because it is consumption that is the argument that enters an individual's utility function, not income. However, the welfarist approach is not universally accepted. Economic inequality is often considered to be about differences in access to, or control over, economic resources rather the actual exercise of that power (Atkinson 1991), in which case income is the measure preferred to consumption. From this point of view, a miserly millionaire is considered rich rather than poor.

From the practical point of view, researchers interested in the dynamics of well-being are faced with the fact that existing household panel surveys for developed nations, such as the BHPS, focus their data collection efforts on income and its components rather than on consumption expenditure and its components. Collection of reliable data about consumption expenditure that is comprehensive in its coverage has, to date, been limited to specialist (repeated) cross-section surveys and has relied on data collection by means of expenditure diaries completed by respondents for frequently purchased items and additional questions for less frequently purchased ones such as durables. A leading example is the UK Expenditure and Food Survey (formerly the Family Expenditure Survey). A US example is the Consumer Expenditure Survey. The amount of time that diary methods require, and the associated respondent burden, have ruled these methods out from use in household panels. The BHPS, for instance, collects recall information and only about a limited range of items—essentially household expenditure on food, utilities, and housing costs, and the acquisition of consumer durables—from the household head. (The limited collection of data about savings and stocks of wealth also rules out derivation of consumption aggregates from income and savings data.) Browning et al. (2003) usefully review the limitations of deriving measures of total household expenditure from household survey questions. Pudney (2008) draws attention to other problems associated with the collection of consumption expenditure from household panel survey respondents and emphasizes how these lead to biases in estimates of the dynamics of expenditure.

An alternative way to derive panel data on consumption is to impute information from a specialist consumption survey to the members of a household panel survey. (Having both consumption expenditure and income information in the same longitudinal survey is rare: see Casado (2011) who uses the Spanish Household Budget Continuous Survey, a quarterly rotating panel.) The imputation route is the approach taken by Blundell, Pistaferri, and Preston (2008), who derive consumption expenditure measures for respondents to the US Panel Study of Income Dynamics (PSID) from the Consumer Expenditure Survey (CEX), using regression-based methods. They argue that their imputations work well in the (relatively narrow) sense that the trend in consumption inequality in the recipient data set (PSID) tracks that in the donor data set (CEX). For their specific analytical purposes, Blundell, Pistaferri, and Preston (2008) restrict their analysis sample to continuously married couples headed by a man aged 30–65, thereby excluding the old and the young and those who experience changes in a household head (a surprisingly large number: see Chapter 1). This book, focusing on income, is concerned with the dynamics of well-being for the population as a whole.

To summarize, there are good reasons for the use of an income measure to characterize the dynamics of individuals' economic well-being. This does not mean that the measures of income that are available in household surveys, including panel surveys, are perfect. Issues of comprehensiveness of coverage of income sources are one particular concern, and are considered now. Other issues, including measurement error, are considered later.

2.2. Coverage of Income Sources

Ideally, the measure of income should be as comprehensive as possible for, if one neglects to take particular sources into account, then one will get a biased picture of the distribution of economic well-being, and of how it changes over time for particular individuals. On the other hand, the more comprehensive a measure is, the greater the risk of incorporating components that are potentially measured with error, or components for which valuation methods are difficult or controversial, or that are inordinately costly to collect data about.

The treatment of non-monetary (non-cash) sources of income is a leading example of these problems. These can be major sources of economic resources and a substitute for money income; without them, households could have maintained consumption levels only by spending money income. In developed nations, examples include non-cash fringe benefits in employee remuneration, and publicly provided access to education and health care. Another often-discussed source of non-cash income is that derived from home ownership: relative to people who rent their accommodation, people who own their own home have an income advantage because they do not have to pay rent. In principle, imputed rental income from owner occupation is equal to the market rent of an equivalent home less the costs incurred with ownership (for example, maintenance, or mortgage interest payments). In practice, the definition is difficult to implement. For example, there may be no equivalent dwellings in the rental market to provide a reference point, and it may be difficult to collect information on all relevant costs of ownership. Other valuation approaches have also been used. Capital gains are another income source that is difficult to collect information about in a household survey context and to value. (Valuation issues also arise with consumption expenditure measures concerning expenditures on health care and durables, for example.) The AIM-AP (2009) project has examined issues associated with incorporating various non-cash income sources, with empirical illustrations for many European countries.

The difficulty of settling on robust practical methods is reflected by the fact that few countries include non-cash income receipts or capital gains in the compilation of their survey-based official statistics on the personal distribution of income. For the same reasons, the BHPS measure of income that I use throughout this book does not include non-cash sources either: see Chapter 3 for details.

2.3. Households and Individuals

So far, I have largely referred to household income (or expenditure) as if the household were the unit for which income or spending is collected or aggregated. And yet we wish to summarize the economic well-being of individuals. This raises two distinct analytical issues. The first concerns how income is distributed within each household, and the second concerns the comparability of incomes for households of different sizes and composition. Although the discussion is in terms of income, the same issues would arise were one to examine data on household consumption expenditure.

Income Sharing within Households

The first issue concerns the pooling and sharing of incomes within households. It is a problem that does not arise with analysis of employment earnings because there is a one-to-one relationship between income earner and income recipient in that case. This is no longer true when one moves to the household level. Some individuals may not receive any income in their own name, for example mothers not in paid employment, and dependent children, and yet the income of the household as a whole ensures some level of consumption or access to resources, via within-household sharing. The problem is that the actual within-household distribution is unobserved, and the sharing rule is likely to vary across households.

This book follows the practice, almost universally employed in distributional analysis, of assuming that, within each household, incomes are pooled and the total is equally shared among each household member. Thus, each individual within the same household, whether adult or child, is assumed to receive the same income. This allocation rule is likely to be wrong when considering multi-person households. Qualitative research on financial management within couple households (Pahl 1983) has drawn attention to the different allocation systems that couples use and, although not specifically about sharing rules, the results suggest there is a heterogeneity of arrangements including unequal sharing. (See also the survey-based research of Vogler 1989.) Other research, based on interviews with poor families, reveals how parents, especially mothers, may go without items or activities in order to provide for their children (Middleton, Ashworth, and Braithwaite 1997) Differences in income between parents and children are also revealed by Lazear and Michael (1986, 1988) who fit an economic model of household allocation to US expenditure data. Subsequent research on economic models of family decision-making has continued this tradition of deriving sharing rules, developing theoretical models that are fitted to survey data (see, for example, the overviews by Bourguignon and Chiappori 1992 and Chiappori and Donni 2009), though focusing on allocations between partners to a couple rather than parents and children. Although progress has been made in this area, it remains the case that the research has not yielded recommendations for income distribution analysis to use instead of the ubiquitous equal-sharing rule.

There are two ad hoc approaches to examining the sensitivity of conclusions to this assumption (Jenkins 1991). The first approach examines distributions of 'individual income' rather than household income, that is, each individual is allocated the income which he or she reports receiving from all sources, and hence is the polar case to the equal-sharing one (and again imposes the same rule rather than allowing heterogeneity in arrangements). As expected, this approach suggests much larger differences in incomes between men and women than the conventional approach—women are more likely not to be in paid work than men, and benefits that they may collect do not offset the relative lack of employment earnings. (See National Equality Panel (2010) for further discussion and some comparisons of distributions of individual income and household income.) To the extent that actual receipt of an income source is indicative of control over the allocation of the resource, this is useful information—recall the discussion earlier concerning income versus expenditure.

The second type of sensitivity analysis allows for unequal sharing within households, by instead assuming equal sharing within families. The distinction between a family and a household is that a household also includes individuals at the same address who are not part of the nuclear family, such as grandparents, adult children, or unrelated lodgers. These are individuals who are likely to have relatively low incomes, and so the alternative approach tends to raise the proportion of individuals who are poor and increase inequality. See, for example, Johnson and Webb (1989) who show that the proportion of the population with income below half the average is 11.1 per cent on a family basis but 8.1 per cent on a household basis. For further discussion of the definition of households and families, see Atkinson (1991) and also Chapter 3 for the different definitions employed in household panel surveys.

Equivalence Scales and Price Indices

In addition to the within-household allocation problems, there are issues of how to compare incomes across recipient units of different household composition in different time periods, and located in different geographical regions within countries or between countries. In each case, nominal amounts are usually made comparable using household-specific deflators, and hence there are questions concerning equivalence scales and price indices of various kinds.

Equivalence scales adjust for differences in household size and composition. They attempt to address the issue that an income of £5,000 per month is of much greater benefit to a single person than a family of four. One could instead examine the distribution of income per capita (in which case the nominal income of £5,000 is converted to £1250 for the family of four). However, per capita adjustments ignore the fact that adults and children have different needs and larger-sized units can benefit from economies of scale. For example, the extra cost of heating and light for a third person in a family of three may be negligible. Thus, most equivalence scales deflate household income (or expenditure) by a household-specific factor that is less than one for each extra household member, and typically differentiate between adults and children. There is a large literature concerning the appropriate choice of equivalence scale relativities, with Coulter, Cowell, and Jenkins (1992*a*) distinguishing five approaches: 'econometric scales (based on what people buy), subjective scales (based on what people say), budget standard scales (based on what experts say), social assistance benefit scales (based on what society pays), and pragmatic scales (which are precisely that)' (1992*a*: 79). Their review emphasizes the essentially normative aspects of equivalence scale specification: a 'correct' scale cannot be determined from observational data alone.

The 'McClements' scale that was formerly in Britain's official income distribution statistics is an example of a scale originally derived from econometric analysis. Pragmatic ad hoc scales include the 'modified OECD' equivalence scale for a given household, equal to $1 + (0.6 \times$ number of additional adults) + $(0.3 \times$ number of dependent children), now used by Eurostat and in the UK's official income distribution statistics. The 'square root' scale commonly used in cross-national comparative analysis (cf. Atkinson, Rainwater, and Smeeding 1995), is even simpler: it is the square root of household size. In this book, I use the McClements and modified OECD scales as these are the ones mostly used in the cross-sectional analysis for Britain that my analysis of dynamics complements.

Nevertheless, the potential arbitrariness in choice of equivalence scale relativities raises the issue of whether the conclusions of distributional analysis are sensitive to the choice of a specific scale. For analysis of this issue, see inter alia Buhmann et al. (1988), Coulter, Cowell, and Jenkins (1992*b*), and Jenkins and Cowell (1994). Perhaps unsurprisingly, marked changes in scale relativities can substantially affect estimates of the relative income position of single and multi-adult households on average and, related, the position of elderly people relative to married couples with children. The sensitivity of cross-national comparisons has also been demonstrated, though within-country trends over time appear less sensitive. Little research is available about the impact of using different scales on measures of income mobility or poverty dynamics. One study is by Cantó-Sanchez (1998) who investigates poverty persistence in Spain. Jarvis and Jenkins (1999) analyse the sensitivity of estimates of income change associated with partnership dissolution.

There is no examination of equivalence-scale sensitivity in the empirical analysis in this book. This is partly for brevity and partly because the analysis of Jenkins and Cowell (1994) suggests that the modified-OECD and McClements scales incorporate broadly similar scale relativities. Statistics published by the Department for Work and Pensions (2009*b*) confirm that, at least for cross-sectional analyses, conclusions about distributional shape, or trends over time, are relatively insensitive to moderate variations in equivalence-scale relativities.

For comparisons of real income (or expenditure) for households at different dates, one requires a suitable index of inflation so that the purchasing powers of nominal amounts received at different times are equivalized. The most commonly used approach, also adopted in this book, is simply to deflate incomes or expenditures by an inflation index that is common to all households, that is, ignoring the fact that different inflation rates may be relevant to households of different types. (On this, see Crawford and Smith 2002.) I also give little attention to an issue that has received greater attention in analysis of low-income countries—the choice of price deflators for geographical regions within a country or across countries—reflecting the often substantial differences in prices between urban and rural areas (see, for example, Deaton 1997). In high-income countries, between-region price variation is much less often considered due to more integrated markets nationwide, including transport networks. (But see the discussion of price variation in the USA considered by, for example, Citro and Michael 1995.) For cross-national comparisons of real income and expenditure distributions, the deflator required is a form of exchange rate. Currency exchange rates are widely thought to provide misleading pictures of true relative purchasing power of different currencies (and are often unduly influenced by foreign exchange market dealing). More appropriate are the exchange rates encapsulated in Purchasing Power Parities (PPPs). For further discussion of the issues, see, for example, Gottschalk and Smeeding (2000).

The Unit of Analysis

The preceding section has argued in favour of a measure of a person's economic well-being that depends on the circumstances of the household within which he or she lives. Put another way, the demographic unit of account for income is the household, but the unit of analysis is the individual. We are concerned with the well-being of individuals within the population. This is the almost universal convention in academic analyses and is adopted also in the UK's official statistics on the personal income distribution. The argument in favour of this convention is essentially a democratic one—each individual counts once in the assessment of social welfare.

It should be noted, however, that the case in favour of this procedure is not as straightforward as it might initially appear. The issues have been rigorously addressed by inter alia Ebert (1997) and Shorrocks (2004) who examine how individuals and their circumstances should be summarized in the social evaluation function that summarizes overall social welfare or inequality. Different weighting schemes (for example, weighting household incomes by the number of equivalent adults rather than household size) may arise depending on assumptions made about how to treat individuals with the same standard of living but different personal characteristics, and the impact of income transfers to those worse off. Ebert and Shorrocks also draw attention to the important role played by the assumption that the equivalence scale does not vary with income (as in all the examples cited earlier).

For analysis of income distributions from a cross-sectional perspective—for example comparisons of marginal distributions in terms of inequality or poverty—the conventional approach of examining distributions of (equivalized) household income among individuals is equivalent to examining distributions of (equivalized) household income among households within which each household is weighted by the number of individuals within the household (household size), a consequence of the equal-sharing assumption. By contrast, for longitudinal analyses of income mobility and poverty dynamics, there is no such correspondence between calculations based on households and calculations based on individuals as the unit of observation, nor is one possible. Duncan and Hill (1985) provide the authoritative statement of this case.

The only consistent approach in longitudinal research is to use individuals as the unit of analysis, because households cannot be followed over time in a consistent manner, whereas individuals can. Over time, households form, grow, shrink, and split apart. It might be possible to trace a household over time by focusing on one particular individual from that household over time, for example the head of the household identified in the first wave of a panel household. But this begs the question of what to do about the people not covered by such definitions of a 'longitudinal household', and the number of individuals is relatively large. Over a period, the number of people who do not experience changes in the composition of their household is surprisingly small: see Chapter 1. This is not a peculiarly British phenomenon. For example, Duncan (1983) notes that in the 13th year of the US PSID, only 12 per cent of the families originally sampled (in 1968) had not changed composition and as many as 57 per cent were headed by someone other than the original family head. Debels and Vandecasteele (2008: table 1) show that, for 13 European countries participating in the European Community Household Panel, the proportion of households experiencing some form of demographic change over one year ranged between 9.4 per cent (Greece) and 15.8 per cent (Ireland) on average, and the majority of the changes were accounted for by changes in the number of adults. To put things another way, focusing on households without any compositional change selects a group that is unrepresentative of the population as a whole, and therefore undesirable. This argument has been demonstrated in a developing country context by Rosenzweig (2003), who shows that focusing on households who do not experience any splits leads to 'substantial' biases in estimates of economic mobility.

Hence, the only consistent way to proceed in longitudinal analysis of incomes is to follow individuals over time, while assessing their circumstances in terms of the income of the household in which they live.

2.4. Income and Time

Income is a flow, referring to an amount per unit of time. What should that unit of time—the 'accounting period', or 'reference period'—be? (Many of the same issues also arise in the measurement of consumption. For example, spending over a shorter period may not measure consumption, because consumption may also be based on accumulated stocks. Spending may also reflect purchase of consumer durables that do not directly contribute to consumption.) I discuss the question in two parts, first starting with accounting period issues from the cross-sectional perspective and then, second, considering new issues that arise when one takes a dynamic perspective.

The Accounting Period for Income

Discussion of the choice of accounting period is often reduced to a comparison of a longer period such as a year with a shorter period such as a month or week. The standard argument is that the longer period is preferable because then transitory fluctuations (and measurement error in respondent reports) are smoothed out, thereby producing a more representative picture of household circumstances. In practice, however, a person's ability to transfer income over time, and hence to smooth consumption, depends on her income or assets (which may provide collateral or a source to draw on). For example, if poor people are less able to borrow or draw on savings than rich people, variations in their income on a week-to-week or month-to-month basis may provide a more accurate reflection of their access to resources than an annual income measure. If short-term transitory variations in income are purely random, and uncorrelated with income level, then it can be shown straightforwardly that the shorter-period income measure will lead to smaller estimates of inequality and larger estimates of mobility that does a longer-period income measure. (See the discussion of classical measurement error below.)

Two crucial issues are the extent to which individuals' incomes genuinely fluctuate within the year, and the terms on which they are able to borrow (or save). On both topics, there is little UK evidence. (The BHPS does not provide a measure of total household income on a month-by-month basis.) One important source is the research by Hills, McKnight, and Smithies (2006) who tracked the incomes of around 100 individuals from low- to middle-income families with children (all receiving Working Families Tax Credit) week by week over a full year (financial year 2003–4). Their report provides evidence of a high degree of variability of income over the short term that was not around any clear trend upwards or downwards. (The reliability of the findings is backed up by the relatively close correspondence between respondent's reports in the survey about their income and linked administrative record data for the same individuals.) Fewer than one-tenth of respondents had income that varied by less than 10 per cent either way from their annual average. Only a third had income in at least 11 four-week periods within 15 per cent of their mean, and within 25 per cent of it in any other four-week periods. A quarter of the cases experienced substantial variability in income, with at least four of the 13 four-week periods outside the range from 85 to 115 per cent of their annual average (Hills, McKnight, and Smithies 2006: 4). The authors conclude that their respondents appear to cope with variability by 'tailoring spending to match variable incomes, often with little margin for error. By implication, incomes received over relatively short periods, such as a month or four weeks, may matter considerably for their living standards at that time, rather than income averaged over longer periods, such as a year' (Hills, McKnight, and Smithies 2006: 7).

Evidence for Britain about the extent to which individuals are able to borrow when faced with an income drop is primarily qualitative. For example, there is Kempson's (1996) research that points to the use made by low-income families of both licensed and unlicensed moneylenders—sources charging higher interest rates than sources like bank overdrafts that higher-income families have easier access to. To be sure, borrowing can take place in a variety of other forms as well, including informal loans from relatives and friends and by delaying payment of electricity and fuel bills, but there is no reason to suppose that the terms on which low-income families are able to utilize these devices are better than those for middle- and high-income families.

There are other relevant issues too, concerning the ability of household surveys to collect information about income, including the need to vary the length of the accounting period according to the income source for which information was being collected.

The Canberra Group (Expert Group on Household Income Statistics 2001) recommends that a year be used as the reference period, on the basis that this is the natural accounting period for a number of income sources, for example profit and loss accounts for self-employed people, or employment earnings derived from administrative sources. However, the Group is also careful to note that different periods may be relevant in different contexts, especially when data are collected by using household surveys. For example, if sources such as wages and salary income, or social security benefits, are paid on a regular weekly or fortnightly basis, then the respondent burden may be lower and reporting accuracy higher if the shorter reference period is used. (For example, in Britain, unlike in the USA, the majority of the population does not complete an annual tax return.) For sources like investment income, or irregular bonuses or holiday pay for which receipts may be less frequent, a longer reference period would be more appropriate. To produce a total income measure for an annual period then involves some grossing up of shorter-period components; to produce a current total income measure involves scaling down of the longer-period components.

Using a mixture of reference periods to compile a total income measure is also recommended by Atkinson et al. (2002) in their substantial review of social indicators for Eurostat. Their preferred measure is 'current modified income', that is, aggregating 'annualized current regular components (wages, regular social benefits, pensions, multiplied by twelve if paid monthly) and, for irregular components or those best collected on an annual basis, figures for the most recent and appropriate period (for example self-employment income, capital income, annual bonuses)' (2002: 107). This is a 'grossing up' version of the Canberra Group's preferred measure.

The BHPS household income measure that I use in this book is also based on a mixture of several accounting periods for the various component income sources of total income, but is a 'scaling down' rather than 'grossing up' version of the Canberra Group's measure (see Chapter 4 for details). Although I use a 'current' income measure (income around the time of the interview) rather than an 'annual' income measure, I report on my earlier research that shows that the two measures provide very similar pictures of the income distribution (Chapter 4).

The use of a current measure of this type is standard in Britain's income surveys. This practice was most recently reviewed prior to the introduction of the Household Below Average Income (HBAI) series (Department of Health and Social Security 1988.) Four options were considered: annual, quarterly, normal, and current. (Normal income is a current income measure with imputations of previous income made for people recently moving out of employment.) Although quarterly income was ranked as best, it was ruled out in favour of current income on the grounds of impracticality within the constraints of the income survey used at the time (the Family Expenditure Survey). See Walker (1994: 13) for further discussion.

An example of a survey with an annual measure is the US PSID, in which the main questions about income sources ask respondents directly what the total amount received was for each source over a named calendar year.

Another consideration that is of particular relevance for longitudinal analysis, and which contributes to arguments in favour of a sub-annual measure, arises from the common requirement to analyse income (or consumption expenditure) with reference to the characteristics of the individuals or household to which the measure refers—whether simply to calculate an equivalence scale or to use household composition as a variable to explain money incomes. With a short period measure, the household's income sources and the membership of the household are closely matched. The longer that the reference period prior to the interview is, the more likely it is that the household itself may have changed composition in a way that may not be recorded (or precisely dated). It is difficult to collect information about individuals who were present at some time during the reference period, but who have left by the date of data collection.

These problems are illustrated by the European Community Household Panel (ECHP), in which the main household income variable is derived by summing the incomes for calendar year $t–1$ that were reported by members of a household at the survey year t interview (in the autumn). Calendar year $t–1$ includes the year $t–1$ interview date, at which time household composition differed from that at the year t interview for a significant minority of individuals. The same structure is incorporated in the longitudinal surveys used to derive the EU Statistics on Income and Living Conditions which replaced the ECHP. See Jenkins (2010b) for a critique.

The mismatch between income reference period and household composition and the problems it creates are discussed in detail by Heuberger (2003) and Debels and Vandecasteele (2008), who also propose modified income measures to work around these problems. For individuals present at wave t, Heuberger proposes creation of a wave t household income variable from the incomes for calendar year t reported by those individuals at the wave $t+1$ interview. Debels and Vandecasteele propose essentially the same measure, but modified to take account of potentially multiple changes in household membership between the wave t and $t+1$ interviews. Their 'change-adjusted' annual income variable involves an average over month-specific incomes, adjusted by a month-specific equivalence scale. As both sets of authors acknowledge, although their measures address the mismatch issue, they also have disadvantages. For example, they can be constructed consistently only for households for which all members at t were also respondents at wave $t+1$. These problems are obviated if a current income measure is available.

Income through Time: Transitions and Spells

The defining feature of a longitudinal survey is that it provides repeated observations on income (and other characteristics) for individuals over time, and so the researcher can build up 'histories' of income and other characteristics of a person and their household. But does a longitudinal perspective change how we should think about accounting period issues relative to the cross-sectional case? My view is that the answer depends in part on the type of longitudinal analysis is undertaken.

Dynamic analysis might be classified into two main types:

(a) transition analysis: analysis of income at two or more *dates*; and
(b) spell analysis: analysis of income *through* time.

Under the first heading falls most analysis of income mobility (including Chapters 5 and 6 of this book), and analysis of annual poverty entry and exit rates (Chapter 8) and the correlates of such transitions (Chapters 9–12). The focus is on a person's income (or poverty status) at a date in survey year *t* which is compared with his or her income at a date in survey year *t+s*. This *panel* approach is the direct longitudinal analogue of a repeated cross-section survey in the sense that the latter also provides observations on incomes at a succession of dates (though the observations are not of the same people in the second case).

The household panel situation can be represented like case (a) or case (b) in Figure 2.1. In both cases, there are repeated observations on income for each panel respondent, but whether the observations on income cover every part of the interval of time between the dates at which observations are taken depends on the accounting period used for income. The shorter the accounting period, the more likely there are to be 'gaps'—as in the case of data about current income collected at annual interviews. But this does not necessarily matter if the goal of analysis is only to look at income transitions between interview dates. Then the issues regarding the choice of accounting period are the same as for cross-sectional analysis, and as discussed earlier.

By contrast, spell analysis is interested in how long someone has had an income of some particular level (including whether it is below the poverty line), where the length of time is summarized in terms of the length of each

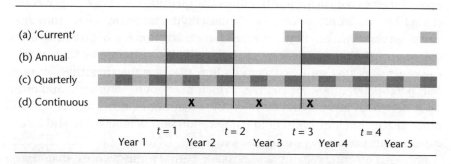

Figure 2.1. Accounting periods for income, and temporal coverage: examples

Notes: The width of each shadowed bar (dark or light grey) shows the period of time over which income was measured at the date of interview (*t*). 'X' marks a date within the year at which household income changed.

spell, or other summary statistics based on spells such as spell repetition, or the length of time spent poor over a fixed interval of time (three years, say). This perspective is much more data hungry. The most comprehensive spell-based perspective is gained by having information about every date at which each person's income changes, and the level of income prevailing between those dates. These dates need not coincide with the interview date, of course. See trajectory (d) in Figure 2.1 for an illustration of this case. Of course, if one had this type of information, it would also be possible to undertake panel analysis of the type discussed in the previous paragraph.

Unfortunately, longitudinal data of this kind do not exist in existing household panel or cohort surveys. It is simply infeasible to collect such detail for the many income sources that comprise household income and from all the potentially multiple income recipients per household. Income is likely to change much more frequently than, say, the employment earnings of one household member over a year. There are too many pressures on questionnaire time to collect all the information in any case and, even if there were questionnaire time, the process of collection would be much too burdensome for respondents, or the process of recall of all the details would be too error-ridden. (The BHPS contains spell information about employment earnings and how they change if there is a job change, which is dated. Monthly information about receipt of various cash social security benefits is also collected, but not the amount received. For more information about the BHPS, see Chapter 4.)

So, if we wish to provide complete coverage of the time axis, the only choice appears to be either to increase the frequency of observation (reducing the length of time between survey interviews), as illustrated by case (c) in Figure 2.1, or to lengthen the accounting period for income, which takes us back to case (b). The former choice is illustrated by the US Survey of Income and Program Participation (SIPP), which has interviews every quarter, and asks about incomes for each month within the quarter. The latter choice is illustrated by the annual measures of household income in some household panel surveys. Although these annual measures solve the problem of the coverage of the time axis—gaps are removed by construction—there remain the issues discussed earlier concerning how this measure smoothes (averages out) potentially important changes (which may not be desirable), and introduces potential mismatches between the accounting period for income and other factors, such as household composition and demographic and labour market events occurring within the period.

Although a contrast is sometimes made between the 'movies' that can be derived about respondents' lives from a longitudinal survey, and the 'snapshots' that are provided by cross-sectional surveys, in reality, household panel surveys provide snapshots too—repeated ones, with the shutter being opened at each interview date. Ideally, one would like continuous and comprehensive coverage of histories so that there is no 'jerkiness' in the movie produced from the sequence of snapshots, but, for household income measures, some degree of jerkiness in the sequence of pictures produced is inevitable.

Thus, in practice, the issues relevant to the choice of accounting period in the context of household panel data are largely the same as those in the cross-sectional survey context (as discussed earlier), with the new complications entering when analysis of spells is required. Repeated observations on a measure of current income have the disadvantage of yielding income histories containing gaps, so some short poverty spells may be missed altogether. Repeated observations on an annual income measure produce income histories without gaps, but within-year changes, including within-year poverty transitions, are not observed because of the income smoothing incorporated by construction in the measure. Both types of measure do not pick up short poverty spells.

Figure 2.2 illustrates these points further with reference to some of the types of poverty history that an individual might experience. (Similar arguments apply were one to analyse 'high income' or 'middle income' rather than 'low income'.) The chart shows, schematically, the poverty experience of eight people over a period of around three years. Calendar time is measured along

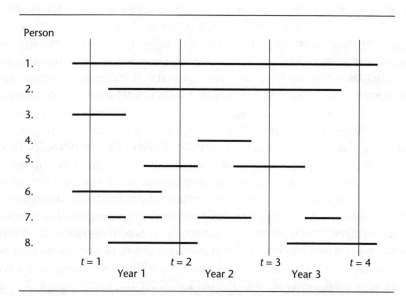

Figure 2.2. Spell data and patterns of time spent in poverty: examples

Notes: For each person, the horizontal line shows the timing and length of each poverty spell. Each date *t* refers to the date of an annual interview of a household panel survey.

Source: Adapted from Bradbury, Jenkins, and Micklewright (2001, Figure 2.1).

the horizontal axis and the duration of each poverty spell is represented by the length of a line. Suppose we have complete information about poverty histories—monthly income levels recorded on a month-by-month basis, and hence the months of poverty entry and exit. Persons who never experience a spell of poverty are not shown in the picture. And any issues of survey item non-response on income, or sample dropout are ignored. (These issues are considered later.)

Each of the individuals represented in the figure experiences poverty at least once, but their experiences differ considerably in terms of the length of each spell, the prevalence of multiple spells, and the time spent poor in total. Person 1 is poor throughout the three years, with the spell starting before the three-year 'observation window' and continuing after it finishes. Person 2 also has one long spell, but in this case the starting and finishing dates are within the three-year window. Persons 3 and 4, on the other hand, have one short spell each. Persons 5–8 have two spells or more (poverty repetition), with some long spells and some short, and some entirely within the three-year window and some straddling one end of it.

One straightforward way of accounting for such diversity would be to focus on the total number of months spent poor during some fixed interval of time. From this perspective, Persons 5 and 7 have the same experience if the period is taken to be the three years shown. However, their cases also illustrate that same total poverty experience may be consistent with very different patterns of entry and exit. The fact that patterns of poverty experience may vary greatly has led some authors to summarize them taxonomically. For example, Ashworth, Hill, and Walker (1994) classified poverty during childhood into categories such as 'transient' poverty, 'persistent' poverty, 'occasional' poverty, etc. See also Jenkins and Rigg (2001) and Chapter 8. (One complication, not addressed here, is that annual interviews do not occur at dates exactly one year apart.)

How would the poverty experiences shown in Figure 2.2 be described if one had current or annual income measures rather the monthly measures assumed? That is, suppose the accounting periods were as in cases (a) or (b) of Figure 2.1. The first thing to note is that the picture of poverty over time would be different. With a current income measure, poverty is only recorded around the time of the interview, and spells outside this period are missed altogether. If current income means monthly income around the date of the annual panel interview, then at least one spell could be missed for every individual, with the exception of Person 1 who is continuously poor. Indeed, for someone experiencing many short poverty spells (like Person 7), all spells might be missed.

Second, and related, poverty histories derived from measures of current income at the annual interview, have gaps in them, and one cannot talk about poverty-spell *lengths* using such data without making some additional assumption about what happened in the gaps. The standard assumption (also employed in this book) is to suppose that the poverty status recorded at the annual interview also describes what happened during the gaps—an imputation that may or may not be correct, depending on how much income fluctuates over a year.

Third, if an annual income measure were available, the picture of poverty experience would also differ from what is shown in Figure 2.2. Annual income is less variable than monthly income—because income is smoothed over a 12-month period—and so, at any particular date, fewer people will be found with an annual income below the poverty line than would be found using a current or monthly income measure. The difference between the estimates is not necessarily large however. Ruggles (1990: table 5.1) shows for the USA in 1984 that the annual poverty rate among persons in married-couple families with children was 7.4 per cent, whereas the average of the monthly rates was 10.2 per cent. For persons in lone-parent families, the corresponding figures were 40 and 43 per cent. Böheim and Jenkins (2006) show that, for the Britain of the early 1990s, the differences between current income and annual income estimates of the proportion of the population with low income differ by at most one or two percentage points. But our concern here is with poverty spells rather than point-in-time poverty prevalence. That is, the implication of the lower estimate of the point-in-time poverty rate is that short spells may not be recorded at all. For example, much of the poverty experienced by Person 7 in Figure 2.2 may be missed—but this is the exactly the same type of person whose experience may be poorly captured by the current income measure.

So, it appears that current income and annual income measures share some deficiencies for the analysis of poverty spells. The former uses an imputation for periods when there are gaps between the observations and thereby in effect smoothes income over the longer period. The annual income measure does not lead to gaps in histories, but incorporates income smoothing during the year by its very construction. So, the real issues concern not so much the accounting period of the income per se, but the extent to which incomes genuinely fluctuate over time, and the extent to which individuals are able to cope with such fluctuations if they experience them. Put another way, do very short poverty spells actually 'matter', and (related) can people maintain their living standards by saving or borrowing? As discussed earlier, there is not a lot of information available about very short-term income fluctuations and people's ability to cope with them.

The choice of an annual or current income measure also has implications for the estimates of income mobility between one year to the next and the corresponding poverty transition rates. One might expect that the estimates derived from data on current incomes from two consecutive interviews one year apart would be greater than estimates based on consecutive observations on annual incomes, on the grounds that there is more variability in the short-term measure. However, this is not the full story. If longitudinal income mobility is summarized using the Pearson correlation coefficient, then it is straightforward to establish that mobility estimates are larger for a short-term income measure than for a long-term income measure (Gottschalk and Huynh 2010). Allowing for income variability over time for individuals loosens the overall association between past and current incomes. What about poverty transition rates?

The annual poverty exit rate is the ratio of the number of movers out of poverty between this year and last year divided by the number of persons who were poor last year. Reflection suggests that current income measures provide higher estimates of the number of movers (the numerator of the exit rate calculation) than do annual income measures, but the previous paragraph indicated that current income measures also provide higher estimates of poverty rates at a point in time (the denominator). Hence, the poverty exit rate calculated on the basis of current income is not necessarily greater than the corresponding estimate based on annual income. However, the BHPS-based calculations of Böheim and Jenkins (2006: table 8) suggest that the annual poverty exit rate in the former case is about one percentage point higher (with exit rates of around 29 per cent), and the annual entry rate is less than one percentage point higher (with entry rates of around 10 per cent).

2.4. Further Data Issues: Household Surveys and Income

The earlier sections have shown that the measures of income available in household surveys including panel surveys are not ideal. A number of other issues in addition to definitional ones also arise with survey data. Inevitably, survey data on incomes are *incomplete* and they are likely to be *measured with error*. This section explains these issues. Examples referring to specific longitudinal surveys and the BHPS in particular are provided in Chapters 3 and 4.

Incomplete Data: Non-response and Censoring

Survey data, whether cross-sectional or longitudinal, can be incomplete because there is incomplete response by the respondents to the survey. There is the case of item non-response, which arises when a participating respondent does not provide a response to a specific question, either refusing to provide an answer or simply not knowing what the answer is. (These situations differ from the case where data are missing because a question is not relevant for a person. For example, someone who is not in paid work will have data missing on employment earnings.) Asking people about their income is often considered to be more intrusive than asking them about other aspects of their lives such as their health, or their values and opinions. And the level of detail associated with incomes is harder to remember and to report. Correspondingly, there is typically a higher prevalence of non-response to income questions than for other items. For similar reasons, income-related information may be missing because questions about some specific topics are deliberately not included because of potential burdens on respondents or pressure on questionnaire space. A leading example of this in household panel surveys is information about direct taxes (income tax and social insurance contributions) paid by household members.

A second type of non-response is unit non-response, which arises when a respondent refuses, or is unable, to participate in the survey altogether, so there are no data at all for that person. This type of non-response may occur in both cross-sectional and longitudinal surveys. In longitudinal surveys, there is an additional type of unit non-response—attrition—in which a current par-ticipant drops out of the survey at a later interview round, perhaps perma-nently. Because measures of household income are derived by aggregating across not only a number of income sources but also across all the adult members of a household, non-response on income items by any household member has a knock-on effects for the household as a whole. Missing data on any income source for any one person means that there are missing data on total household income for the household as a whole.

Non-response is important because it leads to smaller sample sizes and because responding individuals and households and their useable non-missing data may be unrepresentative of the underlying target population and hence any estimates derived from the data may be biased. The prevalence of these problems and strategies used to address them are considered in the following two chapters.

Finally, there is another type of data incompleteness that arises with longi-tudinal data, namely the *censoring* of spell-length data. This refers to the situation when information is missing about the start date or end date of a spell. It is not non-response that is the problem, but the temporal coverage of the survey.

Censoring arises either because a respondent's spell of poverty (say) is already in progress when the first panel interviews are undertaken (and there are no retrospective recall questions about incomes prior to the spell start date—infeasible given the nature of household income), or because the spell was still in progress when the person and their household were last observed in the panel. The first case is known as left censoring, and the second case as right censoring. Referring again to Figure 2.2, suppose that the longitudinal data on poverty spells is available from only time $t = 2$ onwards (year 2). In this case, the spells for Persons 1, 2, 5 (first spell), and 8 (first spell) are left-censored. Suppose also that the survey data do not cover beyond time $t = 4$ (year 3). In this case, there are right-censored poverty spells for Persons 1 and 8 (second spell).

There are no easily available options for dealing with poverty histories with start dates missing—left-censored spells are typically simply omitted from analysis of exit and entry rates using life-table and hazard rate regression methods. See Iceland (1997) for a review of the issues. He points out that dropping left-censored spells can lead to biased estimates because left-censored spells tend to be relatively long ones. An essential part of the specification of hazard regression models is allowing the poverty exit (or entry) rate at a point in time to vary with the length of time that the person has been poor. But if the spell start date is missing, then the analyst does not know the length of the poverty spell up to that date—which is required for the model specification. For sophisticated approaches that take account of left-censored spell data by modelling the chances of beginning a spell at different dates in the past, see Gottschalk and Moffitt (1994a), Moffitt and Rendall (1995), and Nickell (1979). But even these approaches can only be employed if the researcher is able to 'backcast' the values of respondent characteristics (used as explanatory variables) to the period prior to the survey. Where long runs of panel data are available, the effect of dropping left-censored spells can be checked by using data from the later interview waves of the panel and comparing the estimates derived dropping the left-censored spells in that sample with the estimates derived from the full set of panel data: see, for example, Stevens (1999). This method assumes stationarity: it may be unreliable if there are changes in the transition process over calendar time.

By contrast, right-censored spell data can be modelled straightforwardly. When a person is last observed in the panel, the spell length up until that time is known and that provides a lower bound on what the total spell length will ultimately be. This information can be used in model specification and estimation. The problem is not one of bias but of inefficiency in estimates. Compared to the situation when the analyst has data on the lengths of completed spells, right-censoring represents a reduction in information and so estimates are not as precise.

Measurement Error

Measurement error of various kinds is endemic in survey data, and can arise in many ways (Biemer et al. 1991). It is often thought to be more of a problem for longitudinal estimates than cross-sectional ones because measures of change are affected by the errors in two measures rather than one.

Thinking about income data, respondents may simply forget that they receive income from a particular source or be too busy to think carefully, or misremember amounts conditional on receipt, whether in a random way or by rounding exact amounts. Individuals may confuse one income source with another—this is a serious possibility in the British social security system where there are many different types of benefits whose names change quite often. Also benefit entitlements are made at the family level, though claims are by one individual on behalf of the family, which may lead to inconsistencies of reporting within the families if non-claimant respondents report receipt (Lynn et al. 2004, 2006). For some types of income, especially self-employment income, a clear-cut perception of what one's income is at a particular point in time may be hard to assess. Respondents may misreport income for reasons other than cognitive demands on them. If a society values material rewards highly, then individuals may over-report incomes. If receipt of particular types of benefit is perceived to have some social stigma attached, respondents might not mention the source at all or under-report their income. (This is more likely to be an issue at the bottom of the income distribution than at the top.) Even if the survey organization has no connection with the tax or benefit authorities, a respondent may suspect that there is a link, and also desire to minimize liabilities for taxation. (This may be more likely among the rich than the poor.) Measurement error may also be survey-produced, as for example with the use of imputations for missing data, or faulty transcription of data within the interview process, and its structure may change over time if the survey process changes in significant ways, for example a shift from pen-and-paper personal interviewing to computer-assisted personal interviewing as with the BHPS between waves 8 and 9, or the introduction of greater use of feeding forward information between one wave and the next (the BHPS introduced dependent interviewing in wave 16).

Measurement error in income is generally considered to introduce bias in estimates of income inequality, poverty, and mobility. It is commonly supposed that measurement error in income is 'classical', which is to say that it is assumed to be random and uncorrelated with income now or in the past, and that errors for a particular individual are not correlated over time. If this is the case, the error adds additional 'noise'—extra dispersion—into measured incomes, so that estimates of income inequality in the cross-section are greater than 'true' (error-free) inequality. This spurious variability also means that the association between this year's and last year's incomes based on data for measured incomes is less than the true association: measured mobility is greater than true mobility.

With classical measurement error and a distribution-independent poverty line, the bias in poverty rates depends on the level at which the poverty line is set and the number of individuals with incomes in the neighbourhood of this cut-off (Chesher and Schluter 2002). However, if the poverty line is less than the modal income (the typical case in western industrialized nations), the poverty rate estimated using observed incomes will be greater than the poverty rate estimated using 'true' incomes. If the poverty line is distribution-dependent (for example 60 per cent of median income), then there is an additional aspect since measurement error can affect the estimation of the median. Chesher and Schluter (2002) show that this factor may have an offsetting effect. Under the classical assumptions, the probabilities of correctly identifying poor people as poor, and non-poor people as non-poor, is assumed to be the same. If, instead, reliability is lower for poor people, then the observed poverty rate may underestimate the true one (Breen and Moisio 2004).

The effect of classical measurement error on estimates of annual poverty transition rates is less clear (Böheim and Jenkins 2006). Although error would be expected to lead to a greater prevalence of spurious income change that would be recorded as a poverty transition (the numerator of the transition rate increases), the denominator of the transition rate may increase or decrease. The denominator is the number of people poor (for exit rates) or the number non-poor (for entry rates). With classical assumptions about measurement error, the measured proportion poor is too high (see the previous paragraph), and so the overall bias in the poverty exit rate is unclear. Another type of measurement error is that associated with the reporting of histories, for example about circumstances on a month-by-month basis between annual interviews. A common problem with the spell data derived from these histories is that there is an implausibly large number of transitions reported at the 'seam', which refers to the months at which the monthly sequences from consecutive panel interviews are stitched together. This leads to biases in the estimation of spell lengths, and of the parameters of event history models estimated from such data. See Jäckle (2008a, 2008b) for a review of the causes of seam bias, and validation study evidence concerning its effects.

Most of the research by economists about measurement error in income data has focused on the earnings of men rather than on household income, and refers to US studies: see, for example, the comprehensive review by Bound, Brown, and Mathiowetz (2001). See also Atkinson, Bourguignon, and Morrisson (1992). Assessment of the nature of measurement error has been derived from validation studies—studies in which survey reports by respondents may be matched with reports by the same respondents in another source, usually administrative record data, which are treated as error free. These validation studies confirm that survey data on earnings contain substantial measurement error. But they, and later work for the USA, provide important information about the nature of the errors: specifically, measurement errors in earnings are distinctively non-classical. Errors are negatively correlated with earnings level: low earners tend to over-report their earnings and high earners tend to under-report (the case of 'mean reversion'). In addition, errors for the same person tend to be positively serially correlated: for example, those who under-report continue to under-report.

Measurement error with these properties has very different implications for estimates of earnings inequality and earnings mobility than classical measurement error does. This is demonstrated most clearly by Gottschalk and Huynh (2010). They develop a model of non-classical measurement error and fit it to annual earnings data for male respondents aged 25–62 years from the US Survey of Income and Program Participation, which is linked to tax-record data on earnings for the same set of people. Gottshalk and Huyn show that the survey estimate of the variance of log earnings is smaller than the record data estimate, because mean reversion in errors has an inequality-reducing effect that is sufficient to offset the inequality-increasing effect of the additional variability introduced by the error. In addition, the survey estimates of earnings mobility summarized by the elasticity of one year's log earnings with respect to log earnings in the previous year, and the corresponding correlation in log earnings, are little different from their counterparts derived from the tax-record data. There is a fortuitous combination of offsetting effects. In addition to the upward bias arising as in the classical case, there are the effects of mean reversion in both years, which are in opposing directions and so largely offset each other, and there is a bias-reducing impact of having errors positively correlated over time. Dragoset and Fields (2006) use the same linked data sources to examine the impact of measurement error on estimates of a wide range of other measures of earnings mobility and find that similar qualitative conclusions about mobility are derived from both survey and record data. From a quantitative perspective, the statistics often differed by quite a lot, but there was no systematic upward or downward bias. Kristensen and Westergaard-Nielsen (2007) present evidence about measurement error in earnings in Denmark, suggesting that it has similar properties to that found in the USA.

Not covered by this research is information about the impact of measurement error on measures calculated using household income data (rather than data for individual earnings) and for other sorts of statistics, including poverty transition rates. Also, empirical evidence from validation studies is rare outside the USA.

Assessing the impact of measurement error in household income is complicated, because the measure is derived by aggregating a potentially large number of different income sources. Measurement error in each source adds spurious variability to total income. This upward bias in inequality will be reinforced if errors in each source of household income are positively correlated, but offset if the errors are negatively correlated. The sign of the correlation is unclear a priori since the different sources are often derived from reports from different people in the household. You would probably not expect errors in a husband's reported earnings and his wife's reported earnings to be systematically related in panel surveys like the BHPS where the reports are derived from each adult separately, whereas, in the US PSID, one respondent reports about all income sources, in which case a positive correlation is more plausible. One might expect there to be a positive serial correlation in the errors for each source. Potentially offsetting this may be the effects of household demographic change: the persons contributing to household income may change over time.

Patterns of mean reversion may differ by type of income source, and there is the additional complication that the nature of income packaging varies with household income level. For example, at the bottom of the distribution, cash social security benefits are a larger share of total income than at the top. A recent UK validation study of social security benefits (Lynn et al. 2004, 2006) found evidence for under-reporting of receipt, but the differences in proportions reporting receipt in the survey and record data were not large (and there was also some over-reporting). US validation studies report similar findings for transfer income and also point to under-reporting of amounts conditional on receipt: see the review by Bound, Brown, and Mathiowetz (2001).

Other research has reported inconsistencies between the income reported by low-income families and other measures of family living standards, such as consumption expenditure and indicators of material deprivation. For example, Brewer et al. (2009b) show the households with children with the very lowest survey incomes do not have the greatest material deprivation—the lowest living standards are for households with children with incomes of between roughly 30 to 50 per cent of median income (2009b: 9). (The UK's official poverty line is 60 per cent of median income.) Brewer et al. (2009b) also find lower deprivation scores at the same total measured income for families with self-employment income compared to families reliant on employment income, particularly at the bottom of the income distribution, which is suggestive of under-reporting of self-employment income. Meyer and Sullivan's (2003) study of poorly educated lone mothers in the USA also suggests that income is poorly measured (under-reported) at the bottom of the distribution.

This evidence of under-reporting at lower incomes is consistent with—but not demonstration that—measurement error in total household income is mean reverting. Mean reversion also requires over-reporting among richer households, and the principal evidence for that is the evidence about mean reversion in employment earnings cited earlier (combined with the observation that employment earnings accounts for a large fraction of income for many households). Bound, Brown, and Mathiowetz's (2001) review indicates that there is little evidence available about measurement error in asset income (more likely to be held by richer households), though such evidence as there is suggests that such income is likely to be under-reported—which is consistent with mean reversion.

The most comprehensive validation evidence available about measurement error in household income is the study by Rendtel et al. (2004), comparing administrative register data with income reported by respondents to the Finnish sample of the ECHP. They provide evidence that measurement error in the survey data leads to upward bias in cross-sectional measures of inequality and poverty, for example the Gini coefficient for 1999 in the survey is 0.265 but 0.251 in the register data and the corresponding poverty rates are 0.084 and 0.059. The data also exhibit clear evidence of mean reversion: errors decline almost linearly with log income. The serial correlation of measurement errors in 1995 income and 1999 income is 0.03, which corresponds to a correlation for errors one year apart of around 0.4. Both these features are similar to those reported by Gottschalk and Huynh (2010) for US men's annual earnings; indeed, Rendtel et al. (2004) report that the measurement error structure for earnings is what underlies the structure for income. (See, however, the study for Norway by Epland and Kirkeberg 2002 which suggests there is mean reversion in household taxable gross earnings for individuals, but it is less obvious for household taxable income.) Rendtel et al. (2004) is the only validation study I am aware of with evidence about poverty transition rates. They find the greatest difference between survey and register estimates for poverty exit rates rather than entry rates (which are quite similar). For example, the poverty exit rate for the period 1995 to 1999 is 5.34 per cent according to the register data, but 8.66 per cent according to the survey data.

Aside from the studies based on validation studies, there have been model-based approaches to assessing the impact of measurement error on estimates of poverty transition rates: see Breen and Moisio (2004), Rendtel, Langeheine, and Berndtsen (1998), and Worts, Sacker, and McDonough (2010). The basic idea is that, if one has sufficient repeated observations on poverty status over time (at the minimum, three waves of panel data yielding two potential poverty transitions per respondent), and assume stability over time in the true transition probabilities, then one can estimate these rates and attribute the difference between true and observed transition proportions to measurement error. In technical terms, the statistical approach involves fitting latent class models with a Markov structure.

Application of these models leads to apparently dramatic findings. For example, Breen and Moisio (2004) use data from the first four waves of the European Community Household Panel, focusing on Denmark, the Netherlands, Italy, and the UK, and take a poverty line of 60 per cent of contemporary national income. They report that 'mobility in poverty transition tables is over-estimated by between 25 and 50 per cent if measurement error is ignored' (2004: 171). Rendtel, Langeheine, and Berndtsen (1998) report a large amount of misclassification too, for Germany. For all four countries considered in Breen and Moisio's study, the principal impact of error is on estimates of the poverty exit rate rather than the poverty entry rate. For example for the UK, the 'latent' and observed poverty entry rates are both around 10 per cent. However, the 'latent' poverty exit rate is around half that of the observed rate: about 16 per cent rather than 34 per cent for transitions between 1994 and 1995, or 1996 and 1997. Worts, Sacker, and McDonough (2010), comparing poverty dynamics in the USA and Britain, report that, according to their model estimates, '[p]overty is less temporary and risks are less widely dispersed than otherwise assumed, while cross-national differences are more pronounced' (2010: 419). There are a number of differences across countries, however, including estimates of how the reliability of reporting differs between poor and non-poor people. For the UK, Breen and Moisio (2004) estimate that reliabilities are much the same for the two groups, but, for the other three countries they study, it appears harder to accurately identify poor people than non-poor people.

Taken at face value, these studies suggest that measurement error may undermine the reliability of any study of poverty transitions, including this book's analysis. The studies may paint an overly bleak picture, however. First, and as Breen and Moisio (2004) and Rendtel, Langeheine, and Berndtsen (1998) emphasize, measurement error is identified not by comparison with an external source but by model assumption. Different models, with different assumptions made about heterogeneity in transition probabilities across individuals, lead to rather different results, as both sets of authors show. (On the identification issue, see also Hausman, Abrevaya, and Scott-Morton 1998: n. 1.) Second, the models do not account for important non-classical features of measurement error, especially mean reversion.

If there is mean reversion in household income, as Rendtel et al.'s (2004) work on Finnish data suggests, then the magnitude of income falls is under-reported and the magnitude of income increases is under-reported. Thus mean reversion may act to reduce the number of poverty entries and exits that are observed (that is, in an offsetting direction to the effects from the greater variability in the survey data). The overall impact will depend on the specificities of the relationship between error and income level, the location of the poverty line, and the relative concentration of individuals around the poverty line. At present, we know little about these aspects (apart from the Rendtel et al. (2004) validation study). The degree of misclassification has implications not only for estimates of poverty transition rates themselves, but also of their correlates. It is well-established that even a relatively small degree of misclassification in a binary dependent variable can lead to large biases in the estimates of the impacts of explanatory variables. See, for example, Hausman,

Abrevaya, and Scott-Morton (1998), who show that marginal effects are likely to be attenuated and provide Monte Carlo evidence about the magnitude of bias.

In sum, the current situation is that the impact of measurement error in household income is difficult to assess given the lack of suitable validation studies (which are hard to design in any case, as there are few administrative record data sets that combine all relevant income sources). Perhaps, at best, we can conjecture that the effects of measurement error for household income are similar to those for men's earnings, appealing to the fact that in most countries men's earnings form a large share of household income for a large fraction of households, and to the evidence for Finland on income from Rendtel et al. (2004). From a practical point of view, the literature also suggests that there is likely to be less measurement error in income data if one excludes those cases whose principal source of income comes from relatively unreliable sources such as self-employment income, or those for whom a large proportion of household is imputed. (Gottschalk and Huynh 2010 show that the impact of measurement error is less among their sample without imputed earnings.) Conversely, household income data are likely to be more reliable where there is some verification of amounts—of which the main example is where respondents consult a payslip or similar document when reporting earnings.

2.5. Summary and Conclusions

The study of longitudinal data on incomes raises a number of conceptual and measurement issues. This chapter has provided a general introduction to these issues, emphasizing aspects that arise when the income distribution is considered from a longitudinal perspective. Among the issues considered, I have argued that the case for using a current income measure in this context is stronger than is typically appreciated. Also the recent evidence about the nature of measurement error, and mean reversion in particular, raises the question that the existing conclusions about implications of error for estimates may be overly pessimistic. Providing more conclusive answers requires further research using validation data.

The issues discussed in this chapter provide a reference point for what follows—the next two chapters, which provide detailed information about longitudinal sources of data on income and the BHPS in particular, and the empirical work based on those data that follows in the rest of the book.

3

Sources of Longitudinal Data on Income: Household Panel Surveys in Context

This chapter is the first of two chapters about sources of longitudinal data. The analysis of this book is based on one specific source, the British Household Panel Survey (BHPS), which is a household panel survey. But there are other sources of longitudinal data, including cohort studies and linked administrative record data—what the advantages and disadvantages of household panel surveys relative to these? Also, there are different types of panel survey, including rotating panels and household panels. What are the main distinguishing features of these surveys and how does the BHPS compare with similar surveys around the world? By addressing these questions, this chapter aims to both provide a review of longitudinal sources of income in general and also place the BHPS into context in particular. Chapter 4 then provides many more specific details about the BHPS, especially the derivation of its income data.

This chapter draws on and extends Buck, Ermisch, and Jenkins (1996). For more extensive discussion of the topics addressed, see the volumes edited by Rose (2000), Kasprzyk et al. (1989), and Lynn (2009).

Income data are available in a number of different types of longitudinal data source. One important distinction is between administrative registers (information collected by linking over time administrative records on persons and their incomes) and panel surveys (information is collected from a sample of respondents who are followed over time). It is also possible to combine both features to have linked panel survey-administrative data: administrative record data on incomes are linked to other questionnaire data about respondents after administering the survey interview. In this section, I discuss each of these types of longitudinal data in turn.

Before contrasting panel surveys and administrative registers, note that retrospective surveys are another source of longitudinal data, but they are rarely used for collecting income information. Respondents are interviewed only once and they are asked about the past. The advantages of this method are its simplicity and cheapness (primarily because there is only a single interview; respondents do not have to be tracked etc.), and the immediate availability of longitudinal information (since one does not have to wait for a second interview to measure change). The principal disadvantages are that the information about the past is dependent on respondents' recall of events, and the accuracy of this is questionable for some variables. In particular, people are unlikely to remember earnings or income levels beyond the immediate past, or may do so in a biased way. On the other hand, the dates of significant low-frequency life-course events such as getting married or divorced, having a child, or changes in one's main job, are more likely to be remembered with reasonable accuracy. These events have therefore been the focus of retrospective social surveys to date.

3.1. Administrative Register Data

Longitudinal data on income can be collected by linking personal records from existing administrative data gathered for official purposes, for example income tax returns or social security benefit administration records. These data have some substantial advantages relative to the interview-based survey sources discussed in later sections. First, by not relying on interviews and hence respondent recall, there is no respondent burden and measurement errors arising from recall and reporting are much reduced. Indeed, as discussed in Chapter 2, administrative record data on incomes are often treated as being error free and used as a validation gold standard against which to assess measurement error in survey-based income data. Second, longitudinal register data usually have very large sample sizes, and so analysis can be undertaken for almost any population subgroup of interest, and sampling variability in estimates is minimized. Third, and related, there is no problem of sample dropout (attrition) as there is with panel surveys (see below). Whether data for an individual is included in the register is not a choice made by the individual.

However, there are also disadvantages with administrative register data. First, and most critically, the data simply may not exist in some countries, at least in a useable form, or the data may not be made available to researchers for technical reasons or concerns about data security issues such as privacy, confidentiality, and disclosure risk.

A second problem arises because the original registers are usually designed for a specialist purpose, for example to administer the tax-benefit system, rather than for research. The data may have restricted coverage of populations of interest, and include a limited set of variables—which constrains the topics that can be analysed or individual factors that can be controlled for. For example, tax records refer only to those who complete a tax return, and so may exclude many people from low-income groups who are of particular policy interest. Coverage in this respect depends on the nature of the country's social security system and whether cash benefits for low-income households are taxable or delivered through the tax system (as with the UK's tax credits or the US Earned Income Tax Credit). People may move into and out of coverage of the registers (again depending on the nature of the tax-benefit system), which gives rise to a form of longitudinal non-response on income which may be selective in the sense that respondent dropout from a longitudinal survey (attrition) is sometimes said to be.

Tax returns, by their very nature, contain quite a lot of information about various income sources, but the total income variables available may be less comprehensive than is possible in a sample survey. Also, tax returns contain relatively little other data about individual characteristics and family or household circumstances. A country with an independent (individual-based) tax system, for instance, may not collect basic information such as marital status. Educational qualifications are irrelevant for tax liabilities, but a variable commonly desired for analysis. Another important issue concerns the ability to link together records for individuals from the same family or household (which, again, may relate to whether the country has an individual- or family-based tax-benefit system). If within-family linkage is impossible, analysis is restricted to individual-level variables, such as labour earnings or total individual income, but total family income or equivalized total family income cannot be analysed.

Longitudinal data sources on income derived from administrative registers are most common in the Nordic countries—Denmark, Finland, Norway, and Sweden. These are countries in which there has been a shift towards using linked registers to replace national population censuses, which is facilitated by every person having a unique national identification number which is widely used in everyday life. Also facilitating this are national cultures which are less concerned with personal privacy issues related to income and taxation than are the cultures prevailing in most other countries. (This is not to say that data disclosure and confidentiality of individual data are treated as unimportant in the Nordic countries; rather it is that mechanisms have been developed for researchers to exploit the data while respecting national data security standards.) Another relevant factor is that tax thresholds are relatively low in these countries or there is an incentive for individuals to file returns in order to receive benefits. So, problems related to coverage of low-income populations are reduced.

The nature of the Nordic administrative register data sources is illustrated by, for example, Aaberge et al. (2002), who compare income inequality and longitudinal income mobility in Denmark, Norway, and Sweden with that in the USA. (For the USA, the data source is a household panel survey, the PSID; for Sweden, the administrative record data are linked to respondents to Level of Living Surveys.) The authors construct three cross-nationally comparable annual income variables: individual labour earnings, total market (gross) income, and total net (disposable) income. The authors explain that earnings also include work-related transfers such as unemployment insurance, sick pay, and part-time pensions (2002: 447). Market income is total income from all sources. Net income is market income plus non-work-related social transfers (excluding social assistance and income in kind), less taxes paid. Aaberge et al. point out that these definitions are 'data-driven' (2002: 447). And, although the gross and net income variables are each intended to represent the total equivalized income of the family of the relevant individual, this is not quite the case in practice. The totals they are able to calculate for each country represent the total for the individual and spouse (if the individual is legally married) and for the individual otherwise (that is, a cohabiting partner's income is not included), with any income from any other individuals in the family not included. For legally married individuals, total income is divided by two and the result allocated equally to each spouse. The authors are able to calculate longitudinal series up to 11 years long for individuals, but they also work with a shorter series to take account of intertemporal non-comparabilities in the Swedish data arising from a major tax reform in 1991 that changed the definitions of the income variables in the registers. When analysis is restricted to a single country, the administrative register data may allow a more comprehensive income definition to be used. See, for example, the research on Finland by Rendtel et al. (2004) on measurement error described in Chapter 2.

There are fewer opportunities for studying income dynamics in Britain using administrative register data than in the Nordic countries. Longitudinal administrative data exist, for example in the Lifetime Labour Markets Database (LLMDB), a source compiled from a 1 per cent random sample of individuals identified by their National Insurance numbers for each tax year. It contains information on annual earnings from employment, spells of self-employment and benefit receipt, date of birth, sex, home address postcode, and whether a migrant. Currently, LLMDB use by non-governmental researchers has been restricted to relatively narrow measures of income—labour market earnings—rather than a more comprehensive measure accounting for all sources of income, and without household income totals for all individuals belonging to the same household. Reflecting stringent data security concerns, securing access to the data is not straightforward. For one pioneering study based on LLMDB data, see Dickens and McKnight (2008), who study earnings inequality and mobility using data on more than 700,000 individuals followed for up to 25 years between 1978/9 and 2005/6. For earlier work on earnings mobility based on linked administrative records created from the annual New Earnings Survey, see Dickens (2000). Under development is a Work and Pensions Longitudinal Study (WPLS) which links benefit and programme information held by the Department for Work and Pensions on its customers with employment records from the department administering the tax system (Her Majesty's Revenue and Customs). See <http://research .dwp.gov.uk/asd/longitudinal_study/ic_longitudinal_study.asp> and <http:// www.eurim.org.uk/activities/pi/060223talk.pdf> for more information. This is a very rich source with much potential, but it is unlikely to provide income measures as comprehensive as those available from Nordic registers. Its coverage appears to be restricted to particular income sources at the individual level.

The situation for the USA is currently similar to the UK's. There are very rich longitudinal administrative data available on individual earnings and various other labour market variables from the Social Security Administration's records, but not more comprehensive household income measures. For a study of earnings inequality and mobility using such data right back to 1937, see Kopczuk, Saez, and Song (2010). See also Dragoset and Fields (2006) and Gottschalk and Huynh (2010), who used the administrative data to assess measurement error in survey responses on earnings (see the discussion in Chapter 2).

In panel surveys, a sample of persons (a 'panel') is selected, interviewed, and then followed up over time and re-interviewed. Each interview round is called a 'wave' or 'sweep'. Among the many variations under this general description, there are two main types of panel survey: cohort panels and household panels, which I discuss in turn. The 'following rule' specifying who is re-contacted and re-interviewed determines the nature of the longitudinal data. Another important feature of all panel surveys is the extent to which respondents are lost to follow-up—the process also known as sample dropout or attrition. I discuss this aspect after discussing the main features of household panel survey designs.

3.2. Cohort Panel Surveys

Cohort surveys are individual-level panels focusing on the persons comprising a specific birth cohort of the population (or some subsample of this). By construction, the definition of membership of this group is fixed by birth year, and so the 'following rule' for this survey type is simple: attempt interviews with all original sample members. Information might be collected about the persons in a sample member's household, but no attempt is made to follow these people: they cannot become sample members in their own right. Sometimes, however, depending on a survey's purpose, an original panel may be supplemented subsequently, for example by immigrants of the same birth cohort as the original sample members. Even in this case the focus remains on a specific set of individuals.

Britain has several birth cohort surveys for social science research. The National Child Development Survey ('NCDS' or '1958 Cohort') is based on more than 18,000 persons born in Britain during a week in March 1958, with some later supplementation with immigrant children of the same birth cohort. There have been interviews at birth, and ages 7, 11, and 16 (information collected primarily from the children's parents and schools), and at ages 23, 33, 42, 46, and 50 (information collected primarily from cohort members). There is the later 1970 Birth Cohort Survey (BCS70) with a similar design, sampling and following more than 17,000 children born during a week in April 1970. Follow-ups have taken place at ages 5, 10, 16, 26, 30, and 34. Third, there is the Millennium Cohort Study (MCS), again with around 18,000 births, but with coverage extended to Northern Ireland, and sampling births over a whole year (2000/1) rather than a single week. Follow-ups have occurred at ages 3, 5, and 7, with another wave of data collection planned for 2012.

These birth cohort surveys are rich sources of data about social and medical factors associated with child development and, as the studies mature, about the relationship between childhood experiences and outcomes and those in later life. But they are not well suited to examining income mobility and poverty dynamics over the short term: data are collected at a few selected points in time which are not evenly spaced, and the information on incomes is not consistent over time in most of the surveys. (The cohort surveys prior to the MCS reflected the interests of biomedical disciplines rather than social sciences, at least at the initial and early sweeps.) For example, in the NCDS, no income data were collected from the parents at the time of the child's birth and, at ages 7 and 11, only a binary indicator of 'financial difficulties' was collected. The interview sweep at age 16 was the first time that any attempt was made to measure total household income (using a set of banded income categories). For assessments of the quality of the NCDS income data, see Micklewright (1986) and Grawe (2004). When cohort surveys have more frequent interviewing and data are collected at each interview wave, analysis of short-run changes in income is possible. Thus, for instance, the US National Longitudinal Studies of Youth (NLSY) have annual interviews. The MCS early sweeps are at approximately two-year intervals and, for example, Platt (2009) uses these data to examine children's transitions into and out of poverty.

The target population for a cohort survey is defined by birth year, and the surveys may start sampling people during adolescence or later in life rather than at birth. The US National Longitudinal Surveys of Youth sampled adolescents and young adults, and the English Longitudinal Study of Young People sampled children in Year 9 of school (aged around 15). The US Health and Retirement Study and the English Longitudinal Study of Ageing sampled adults aged 50+ (and their partners if present).

3.3. Household Panel Surveys

Household panel surveys, like cohort surveys, follow individuals over time, but their design is necessarily more complicated because they aim to be representative of not only individuals but also the households within which they reside, and not only in the initial year but also in subsequent years. For most household panels, the population of individuals refers to the civilian non-institutional population. The initial wave is a sample from the households and individuals of this 'private household' population. To ensure proper representation of the population of persons and households as time passes thereafter, in particular for representing new entrants (persons and families) into that population, following rules are required that are more complicated than for cohort surveys.

The idea is to follow the original panel over time, regardless of whether they are still living with the same household members as in the initial year, and regardless of whether the individual is living at the same address, while also taking account of children (new entrants to the population). The following rule which aims to maintain the ongoing cross-sectional representativeness of the population initially sampled is as follows. Define all the adults and children in the representative sample of households in the first wave as 'original sample members' (OSMs). Then, at second and subsequent waves, attempt interviews with all adult members of all households containing either an OSM or an individual born to an OSM whether or not they were members of the original sample. If respondents move abroad they are not followed, but interviews are attempted with people who move out of the private household population into institutions (for example, care homes for elderly people). Versions of this following rule underlie the design of virtually all household panel surveys.

The same sorts of data collection instruments are common to most household panel surveys. Questions about the household itself (for example, type of dwelling, housing costs, household membership, and relationships between members) are answered by the household head or some other designated adult. Each adult household member answers an individual questionnaire which asks about personal characteristics and behaviour. Information is also derived from the administration of the panel itself (for example, addresses and response status), and from 'cover sheet' details filled in by the interviewer.

The number of household panels has increased significantly over the last few decades. The pioneer and longest-running is the US Panel Study of Income Dynamics, which began in 1968 (Hill 1992). Major household panel surveys began in 1984 in Germany (Socio-Economic Panel; ongoing), the Netherlands (Dutch Socio-Economic Panel, 1984–97), and in Sweden (Panel Study of Market and Nonmarket Activities, HUS, 1984–98, and the Level of Living Surveys, from 1968 onwards). Over the following two decades, household panels began in Australia, Belgium, Canada, Korea, Luxembourg, the Lorraine region of France, Hungary, New Zealand, Switzerland, and of course Britain (the BHPS, from 1991). The BHPS is now superseded by a new household panel survey called Understanding Society—the UK Household Longitudinal Study, which not only incorporates the BHPS sample, but adds a new large sample of respondents (from 2009). There is the multi-country European Community Household Panel (ECHP) survey, which used a cross-nationally harmonized instrument. In 1994, the first waves of surveys were fielded in 12 of the then member states, with two other pre-accession member states joining later (Austria, 1995; Finland, 1996). There were eight waves of fieldwork, with the final one in 2001. Comparable cross-national panel data have also been derived by harmonization of data after collection in each country. The most successful of these ventures is the Cross-National Equivalent File (CNEF), including data from the US PSID, German SOEP, Canadian SLID, the BHPS, and more recently also data from the Australian HILDA and Swiss Household Panel Surveys. See Frick et al. (2007) for a description of the CNEF. Both the ECHP and the CNEF are used in the cross-national comparisons of income mobility and poverty dynamics discussed in subsequent chapters of this book.

There are also a growing number of household panel surveys in other countries, including developing ones. Examples include the KwaZulu-Natal Income Dynamics Study (KIDS), the Russia Longitudinal Monitoring Survey (RLMS), and the Indonesia Family Life Survey. For a summary guide to household panel surveys around the world, see <http://psidonline.isr.umich.edu/Guide/PanelStudies.aspx>.

Although household panel surveys have common elements to their design, there are of course variations in this, which I now consider. I discuss elements such as sample size, sample refreshment policy, the time interval between interviews, and the number of interviews in total, the following rules, and methods of data collection.

Sample Size

Sample size matters because, other things being equal, larger samples lead to greater precision in estimated statistics. Larger samples are, however, more expensive to maintain. So, there is a delicate trade-off to be made, with choices complicated by the fact that household panel surveys are general-purpose instruments, rather than directed at one or more topics or hypotheses, as in many biomedical longitudinal studies for instance. The number of households included at the first wave of household panel surveys has typically been around 5,000–7,000, but with substantial variation around that. Some panel surveys have had smaller initial sample sizes, for example the Luxembourg panel PSELL-I had some 2,000 households (Luxembourg is a small country). Sample sizes have also been substantially larger, including New Zealand's Survey of Family, Income, and Employment (SoFIE), with individuals from around 11,500 households interviewed at the first wave. The new Understanding Society study is the largest household panel survey in the world, with the initial wave aiming to include a new general population sample of nearly 30,000 UK households (in addition to other samples such as the BHPS one). The rationale for Understanding Society's large sample size is the ability to study dynamics for relatively small-sized groups within the population (for example single age cohorts, lone parents, or relatively small geographical regions), or to study relatively rare events.

Over-Sampling, Extension and Refreshment Samples

Rather than increasing the overall sample size to ensure small-sized groups of special interest can be studied, panel study designs may instead over-sample such groups, either in the initial wave or by extending the sample at later waves. Thus, Understanding Society also has an 'ethnic minority boost' sample in addition to the main sample to facilitate ethnicity research. This is intended to provide samples of at least 1,000 adults in each of five ethnic minority groups (Indian, Pakistani, Bangladeshi, Caribbean, and African), plus as many members of 'other' minorities as are found through the screening process used to identify ethnic minority individuals. The US PSID and the German SOEP are older household panels which used over-sampling. In the case of the PSID, the main sample was supplemented by an independent sample of about 2,000 low-income families (the so-called 'SEO' sample). In the case of the SOEP, the over-sampling was of some 1,400 'guest worker' households—individuals in households headed by someone with Turkish, Greek, Yugoslavian, Spanish, or Italian citizenship. (There was a significant influx of migrant workers to Western Germany during the 1960s and 1970s.)

The BHPS did not use over-sampling in the initial sample of around 5,000 households. However, from wave 7 (1997), the BHPS was used to provide data for the UK component of the European Community Household Panel (ECHP), taking over this task from the established UK-ECHP sample. In order to extend coverage to all of the UK, specifically Northern Ireland, and to increase sample numbers in groups of particular interest, the BHPS sample was augmented by a subsample of the UK-ECHP sample, including all households still responding in Northern Ireland, and a 'low-income' sample from the rest of the panel. (The low-income sample was selected on the basis of characteristics associated with low income in the ECHP.) To save money, this additional sample was dropped after 2001, though utilized separately in other methodological work. (See the discussion of the ISMIE project by Jäckle et al. 2004.) The most substantial supplementation of the BHPS sample occurred in the late 1990s. The devolution of government to administrations in Scotland, Wales, and Northern Ireland in the 1990s led to increased research interest in analysis of each country and in cross-UK comparisons. (Although households from Scotland and Wales are included in the original 1991 main sample, their number is small.) To meet these needs, additional 'extension' samples of 1,500 households in each of Scotland and Wales were added in 1999 to the original main sample of some 5,000 households. A sample of 2,000 households from Northern Ireland was added in 2001. Extension samples were added to the German SOEP in 1998 and 2000 (samples E and F). In these cases, the primary motivation was to increase sample size to increase the reliability of analysis of small-sized groups in general rather than to address some specific research questions.

Over-sampling and extension samples can save money in the sense that increasing sample numbers for the specific target groups of interest is cheaper in terms of survey costs than boosting the total sample size to achieve the same target sample size for the subgroup. Against this substantial advantage, there is the problem that the differential sampling probabilities of the main and boost or extension samples means that weights need to be used for the derivation of population statistics. This complicates analysis of many research questions beyond simple descriptive statistics, and raises the chances of researcher error. Also, the panel length is short relative to that of the original sample drawn in 1991. For these reasons, the BHPS extension samples have primarily been used for single-country analyses, and only rarely otherwise. This is true in this book too: all analysis is based on the original sample. The extension samples are not used at all.

With over-sampling and extension samples, there is some risk that research interest in the specific group(s) may turn out to be relatively short-lived, in which case one is left with a panel with an unduly complicated design. An additional related issue is that over-sampling of a particular group is most effective if the characteristics that identify a subgroup of interest do not change over time. Ethnic minority group and country of birth are examples of such characteristics. However, poverty status is not fixed (as much of the rest of this book argues), and so defining a boost sample in terms of low-income status at one point in time (as with the PSID SEO sample) may be problematic.

Increasing the precision of estimates by using larger samples is not the only reason for adding a new sample. New samples may also be added to a household panel to improve its representativeness of contemporary society. The most common reason for this is to account for immigration after the initial sample year. New samples may also be added in order to maintain sample numbers more generally, especially if they are judged to be significantly depleted by sample dropout. (If there were no attrition, sample numbers would remain much the same size over time, or gradually increase, depending on the precise nature of the following rule.) In household panel surveys, the original sample is designed to be representative of the population in the first year of interviewing, and standard following rules (see above) are used to maintain sample size and cross-sectional representativeness subsequently. This will not be achieved if there is substantial attrition or immigration into a society over time. A rotating panel design may address these problems better than the standard household panel design: see below.

To account for immigration into the USA, the PSID in 1990 added an additional sample of Latino households consisting of families originally from Mexico, Puerto Rico, and Cuba—though the sample was dropped again after 1995 because it was felt not to sufficiently represent all immigrant groups and because of lack of funds. Instead, small numbers of immigrant families were added to the sample in 1997 and 1999. (See <http://psidonline.isr .umich.edu/Guide/Overview.html> for details.) The German SOEP added an immigrant sample in 1994/5, selecting individuals who had migrated to Germany between 1984 (when the SOEP began) and that year. By contrast, the BHPS has not added any immigrant samples, though there has been significant migration into Britain since 1991. The BHPS's ongoing representativeness therefore refers to the sorts of people who were living in Britain at the beginning of the 1990s rather than today. This was one of the reasons for the new Understanding Society panel study.

Interview Frequency

Interview frequency matters because it affects the nature and quality of the data that can be collected, and it also affects survey costs. More frequent interviewing means higher costs; less frequent interviews are less costly to run, but run higher risks of losing hard-to-follow individuals and their households. Closely related to the question of interview frequency is the issues of how often the underlying phenomena of interest are likely to change (frequent interviews, or repeating questions at every interview, are wasteful if a characteristic is fixed), the length of the reference period for the relevant measures (see Chapter 2), and how reliable are the data that might be collected from different designs. If respondent's recall concerning measures is considered unreliable when the recall period is long (as is often assumed for income), then data quality can be improved by more frequent contemporaneous collection, such as by interview. Again the design must strike a balance reflecting the general-purpose nature of household panel surveys. They aim to cover many topics and phenomena, but are constrained to use a single interview frequency.

The vast majority of household panel surveys use interviews at approximately annual intervals, though at least one has used biennial interviewing from the start (the Swedish HUS), and the US PSID switched to biennial interviewing in 1997. Analysis of income and poverty dynamics has motivated many panel studies and annual collection of income data from annual interviews addresses the fact that there is sufficiently frequent change in income that is of substantive interest. In addition, longer intervals between data collection would lead to data reliability problems for measures of income (and for most countries, there are currently no adequate substitute methods of collection, such as via linkage to administrative records). Annual data collection also helps maintain comparability with other, mainly cross-sectional, data sources in a country—these are typically undertaken on an annual basis. In more specialist surveys than general-purpose household panels, the interview frequency has been higher in order to track income dynamics in greater detail. The leading example of this is the US Survey of Income and Program Participation (SIPP) which has quarterly interviews. It is now the primary source of information about short-term income dynamics in the USA, supplanting the PSID which now focuses on other topics.

Like several other general-purpose household panel surveys such as the PSID, the BHPS supplements its extensive and detailed data collection at the interview with less detailed collection by retrospective recall of some information about income components on a monthly basis, typically concerning receipt but not amounts. It is therefore not possible to derive a monthly total household income variable of the sort that the SIPP provides (without substantial amounts of additional assumptions and modelling).

Although most household panel surveys interview respondents at approximately one-year intervals, the timing of the interviews during the year varies. For most surveys, interviews are concentrated in one season of the year because such concentration is efficient for survey organizations. (In countries in which most people have to personally file a tax return—which is not the case in Britain—the interview season may also be chosen to be close to the end of the tax year, so that income values are fresher in respondents' minds.) For example in the BHPS, interviews are conducted during the autumn, with October being the modal interview month. In the German SOEP and the US PSID, most interviews are undertaken in the spring. But interview concentration may also lead to capacity problems for the survey organization if a survey's sample size is large. New Zealand's SoFIE and the UK's Understanding Society both use continuous interviewing for this reason. In the latter case, each wave of interviews is undertaken over a two-year period: there are 24 monthly samples, with respondents in each sample re-interviewed after a one-year interval.

Following Rules

There are some variations in the following rules used. For example, practice differs in the treatment of new panel members who subsequently stop living with an OSM. In most surveys, these people are not interviewed again unless they have an important relationship with a sample member. (A BHPS example is someone who joins the panel after the initial wave because he or she forms a partnership with an OSM, and they have a child, who is an OSM.) By contrast, the German Socio-Economic Panel (SOEP) since wave 7 has followed and interviewed all panel members, regardless of their relationship to the OSM: once respondents join the panel for whatever reason, they are retained. Another variation in design concerns the age at which children are asked to complete the full adult individual questionnaire. In the BHPS, it is the year the child turns 16; in the Australian HILDA, it is 15, and in the SOEP, it is the year the child turns 17.

Number of Interviews, and Rotating Panels

Household panel surveys also differ in the total number of interview waves that form the study. There is a distinction between 'indefinite life' and 'fixed life' panels. In the former case, the most common one, the number of interviews is not fixed at the outset. Examples include the PSID, SOEP, and the BHPS. By contrast, the number of interviews is fixed in 'fixed life' panels. For example, the NZ SoFIE, which began in 2002, is scheduled to have eight annual waves only. The most important examples of fixed life panels are, however, 'rotating panels'. In this case, the number of waves for a given panel is fixed at the outset but, at any one time, there are multiple overlapping panel samples comprising the study because new samples are drawn at different times. Otherwise, the design features of indefinite life and rotating panels, for example following rules, are similar.

A rotating panel design has four features of note. First, the shorter interval between interviews relative to most household panels can be used to help reduce recall errors about relatively high frequency events and details of variables such as income. At the same time, the shorter period covered in total means that there may be fewer completed spells observed in the data and there is less opportunity to examine the antecedents of events or their consequences. Second, the survey as a whole can also provide better cross-section information at a point in time, using data combined from the constituent panels (in so far as the measurement periods for each of these overlaps). The increase in sample size reduces sampling errors. Ongoing representativeness of the current population is easier to maintain by revisions to the selection criteria for new panel samples. Third, by restricting the duration of each panel to a finite period (often only a few years), the likelihood of attrition is reduced (total respondent burden is less), and so too are potential problems of 'panel conditioning' (long-standing respondents become familiar with the questionnaire and its structure and may modify their responses accordingly). Fourth, rotating panel designs can be more expensive to maintain than single panel designs because of their greater complexity. Fifth, that same complexity also introduces difficulties when combining and merging data from the separate panels.

Two leading examples of ongoing rotating panel surveys for social science research are the US Survey of Income and Program Participation (SIPP), which began in 1983, and the Canadian Survey of Labour and Income Dynamics (SLID), which began in 1993, though they have exploited these design features in different ways. The SIPP has put greater emphasis on the first feature, emphasizing higher frequency of data collection than an annual interview design: interviews are every four months. The number of interviews has varied with different samples, with panels varying in length from 12 to 32 months (eight interviews). The increase in number of interviews reflected a desire to improve the study of long spells of poverty or welfare benefit receipt and multiple transitions (see the review of the SIPP by Citro and Kalton 1993). For more information on the SIPP's design, see <http://www.census.gov/sipp/intro.html>. By contrast, the SLID has put greater emphasis on the maintenance of cross-sectional representativeness (the second feature).

In Europe, the main rotating panels with detailed income data are those used in a number of countries to deliver national statistics about longitudinal dimensions of poverty and social exclusion over a four-year period as part of the EU Statistics on Income and Living Conditions (EU SILC). (See for example Eurostat 2007.) Other countries derive these statistics from longitudinal administrative register data, as discussed earlier for Nordic countries.

The rotating panels cited so far differ in design from the rotating panels that form the Labour Force Surveys in most European countries. These surveys are residence-based panels; the survey organization returns to the same dwelling at each interview wave and interviews those present. (The UK LFS re-interviews households each quarter, for five quarters in total.) Unlike in household panels, people who leave a sample dwelling are not followed. This substantially constrains the capacity of these surveys to study the association between income change and household change, and the selective nature of household change may also lead to problems of analysis of other topics. Another limitation of Labour Force Surveys for studying income dynamics is that their focus is usually, as their name suggests, the labour force behaviour of individuals, and the level of detail collected about all sources of household income is much less than for household panels. Even where, in some countries, surveys of the LFS design collect more detailed income information—as with the Encuesta Continua de Presupuestos Familiares (ECPF) in Spain—there remain the issues associated with the residence-based design. On this, see also the discussion dispelling the concept of the longitudinal household in Chapter 2.

Variations in Methods of Data Collection

There is variation across household panel surveys in from whom information is collected and especially in how information is collected (the issue of survey mode). On the first issue, the PSID is unique in using one adult respondent (the 'head') to provide information about all individuals in the family (for example, the earnings of his spouse), as well as providing information about the household as a whole (such as, for example, about the dwelling). By contrast, to collect information about each adult respondent, later household panels use interviews with each adult panel member directly. (Information about the household as a whole is collected from the 'head'.) Using multiple interviews increases survey costs but has substantial research pay-offs. Data collected directly from the person concerned rather than from a proxy are likely to more accurate—this is particularly relevant to income. Moreover, research scope is extended because the responses of respondents can be compared. For instance, the BHPS has regularly asked questions about how household finances are managed, and the similarities and differences between husbands' and wives' responses are of substantial research interest. Proxies are used in these later panels in cases of non-response within households (or if the target individual is simply absent or too old or infirm to complete the interview), in which case a minimal amount of information is collected from other household members. In the BHPS, no income information is collected by proxy, but, in any case, fewer than 3 per cent of interviews are with proxies (Lynn 2006: 32).

More substantive differences concern the modes of data collection—how the main questionnaires are administered. (Most panels supplement their main individual and household questionnaires with a short respondent self-completion instrument. The BHPS also has a separate self-completion questionnaire for children aged 11–15 years.) One important distinction is between personal interviewing, which is when questions are put to respondents by interviewers face to face in the respondent's dwelling, and when questions are asked by interviewers during a telephone interview. (Web interviewing is rarely used at the moment.) Telephone interviewing has long been used in the PSID, with a majority of interviews conducted thus since 1973, and at least 98 per cent since 1999 (<http://psidonline.isr.umich.edu/Guide/Overview.html>). The SOEP uses both personal and telephone interviewing. The former is the most common, but respondents are given the option to choose the latter and the fraction doing so has been rising over time. In the BHPS, personal interviewing is the rule (around 96 per cent of all interviews), with telephone interviews very occasionally used when a personal interview is not possible to arrange (fewer than 1 per cent of all interviews): see Lynn (2006).

Arguably, telephone interviewing can lead to reductions in survey cost without significant deterioration in the quality of the data collected. (Lepkowski et al. 2008 discuss telephone survey methods in detail.) However, it is currently unclear to what extent this is true outside the USA. Telephone interviewing is common in Britain and elsewhere in Europe, but only for one-shot cross-sectional and shorter surveys, not household panel surveys. Downward pressure on survey costs makes this an important question to resolve in the future. Additional complications are that individuals increasingly do not have a land-line telephone, and mobile telephone numbers are changed relatively frequently (making contact and re-contact more difficult as well). Also, there is increased interest in collecting physical measures data that require a face-to-face visit as part of household panel surveys. Web interviewing is another possibility for data collection which can reduce survey costs, but its advantages are likely restricted to particular sorts of questionnaire content, and there remains the issue of non-universal internet access. All these factors mean that, in the future, household panel surveys are likely to increasingly use a combination of different modes to collect different types of data from each respondent. This is 'mixed mode' collection, in contrast to the use of 'multiple modes', when different types of data collection methods are used either for collecting the same types of information from different groups of respondents, or from the same respondent (such as data collected by questionnaire and by nurse visit).

Another important aspect of data collection is whether interviewers record responses on a paper questionnaire that is subsequently converted to computer-readable form by data-entry staff or whether responses are entered directly onto a portable computer. All the major household panels have now converted to the latter approach—computer-assisted interviewing— to administer their main individual and household questionnaires. This improves the efficiency and quality of survey operations. For example, question-routing options are enforced automatically, the need for later data editing may be reduced, data transcription is reduced (lessening the chance of error), and data turnaround improved (results can be returned from the field to the survey organization more expeditiously, and user databases prepared and released more quickly). Survey costs can also be reduced substantially (after initial development costs). On the BHPS experience, see Laurie (2003).

Also, it is only with computer-assisted interviewing that is possible to introduce important structural changes to the nature of the questionnaire. The principal example of this is 'dependent interviewing' (DI), also known as 'feed forward'. This comes in several flavours, but the key feature is use of responses from a previous interview when collecting data at the current interview. DI has been shown to reduce the amount of spurious change over time in respondent characteristics and behaviour that is observed when conventional 'independent' interviewing is used. (For BHPS-related experimental work demonstrating this, and citations to other research, see Jäckle and Lynn 2007; Lynn et al. 2004, 2006; Lynn and Sala 2006.) With proactive DI for a specific item, respondents are presented with their response the previous year, and then asked whether circumstances have changed. With reactive DI, respondents receive the question first (as with conventional independent interviewing), but if their answer differs from that for the previous interview, the interviewer reminds them of their previous response and asks them to confirm or modify their current circumstances in the light of this.

Differences in the modes used, and in the reliance on computer-assisted interviewing and dependent interviewing, are aspects of survey design that have potentially important effects on the comparability of data from different household panels—even if the question wording for a particular item is fully comparable. But perhaps more important in practice is that these features are not always present from a survey's beginning, but introduced in stages over time, so the issue is: do such changes introduce non-comparabilities between data from different waves of the household panel survey in question?

The BHPS introduced computer-assisted interviewing for the main individual and household questionnaires from wave 9 (survey year 1999) onwards. According to Laurie (2003), the BHPS 'made the shift without adversely affecting ... response rates or introducing gross mode effects' (2003: 13). Dependent interviewing was introduced in wave 16 (survey year 2006) for various questions concerning current employment, job history, and income sources, but substantive investigations of comparability over time have not yet been undertaken. I report some simple checks in Chapter 4 regarding series based on household income variables.

Attrition in Household Panel Surveys

One of the undesirable but inevitable features of all panel surveys—cohort and household panels—is sample dropout over time. This attrition arises in several ways: respondents may no longer wish to participate in the survey (participation is voluntary) or it may be that, between one fieldwork period and the next, the survey organization is unable to trace a respondent, make contact, and arrange an interview—which is often associated with a respondent moving house. (In the BHPS, for example, around 10 per cent of respondents move in a given year: see Lynn, 2006: 39.) For a review of the reasons for sample dropout in panel surveys and of previous research on the topic, see Uhrig (2008: Section 3).

Attrition is not necessarily permanent. Respondents may indicate that they wish to have a break from participation, and they are re-contacted the following wave. As a result, survey participation for each respondent is not necessarily a sequence of interviews in consecutive waves, but may be intermittent. Initial dropout is a good predictor of later complete dropout, however.

Survey administrators are of course well aware of the problem of attrition and devote substantial resources to both minimizing its incidence and reducing its impact after data have been collected. Panel maintenance activities addressing the former aspect are wide-ranging, and include measures to maintain respondent interest in and engagement with the survey (for example, feedback about findings from research, freephone contact with the survey organization), measures to facilitate the passing on of changes of address, collecting contact details of a person who would know the respondent's whereabouts, etc. In addition, resources are devoted to 'refusal conversion'—trying to elicit participation from sample members who initially give a 'soft' refusal. These various activities are in addition to the (small) financial incentive provided to sample members. For example, the BHPS has, since wave 6, sent each adult respondent a £7 chain-store gift voucher in advance of the interview, so it is not conditional on taking part. See Lynn (2006) for more details about BHPS respondent incentives.

Attrition has two undesirable effects: it reduces sample size and it may harm the representativeness of the survey ('differential' attrition), thereby leading to bias in estimates. Whether the impact on sample size should be judged as large or small depends on research context. In most mature household panel surveys, attrition reduces sample size by around 5 per cent per annum, with a larger decline between the first and second waves (for more specific details on the BHPS experience, see below). Assuming 5 per cent is the dropout rate, after ten waves of annual interviewing, only about one-half of the original sample still participate ($0.95^9 \approx 0.63$) and, after 15 waves, the proportion remaining is less than one half ($0.95^{14} \approx 0.49$). Clearly this is substantial dropout, but its impact should not be exaggerated. The effects depend on how many waves of data the analyst requires and their temporal coverage, with the worst-case scenario being when there are research questions that can only be addressed with many waves of data and also with coverage of the most recent years of the survey. These conditions apply in only a minority of projects.

Differential attrition arises when sample dropout is not random but, instead, is associated with respondent characteristics and behaviour. For example, people who experience job changes, job loss, or divorce—factors which are also associated with residential mobility—may be less willing to continue to participate in the survey or be harder to trace. And these events are likely to be associated with income changes over time, including entry to or escape from poverty. Using the data only for the respondents who remain in the panel sample without taking account of these associations may lead to biased estimates.

Survey administrators are also aware of this issue and devote resources to helping researchers minimize the potential effects of attrition, notably by providing general-purpose weighting variables ('weights') to use in analysis. Longitudinal weights are intended to reduce bias in estimates derived from longitudinal data, such as the proportion of poverty entrants in a given year who are also poor when interviewed in the following two years. Cross-sectional weights are intended to reduce bias in estimates of cross-sectional estimates such as the poverty rate in a given year—after the initial survey year, these weights must include a component accounting for attrition as well, in addition to addressing cross-sectional representativeness per se. The nature of the weights supplied with the BHPS is discussed in Chapter 4.

As far as the US PSID is concerned, Fitzgerald, Gottschalk, and Moffitt (1998) report that although there is differential attrition—sample dropout rates are higher for those with lower socio-economic status or unstable earnings and marriage, for example—the proportion of the total attrition which is explained by factors such as low income is relatively small and, in any case, the effects of attrition are moderated over time. They conclude that 'despite the large amount of attrition [since 1968], we find no strong evidence that attrition has distorted the representativeness of the PSID through 1989, and considerable evidence that its cross-sectional representativeness has remained roughly intact' (Fitzgerald, Gottschalk, and Moffitt 1998: 251). Similar sentiments were expressed in other papers in the same *Journal of Human Resources* special issue devoted to 'Attrition in longitudinal surveys'.

The focus of these studies was on US panel surveys, especially the PSID. The similarities in the designs of the major household panels suggest that we might have some confidence in generalizing the conclusions. And, indeed, analyses of attrition in the household panel surveys comprising the European Community Household Panel have led to similar conclusions: see Watson (2003) and Behr, Bellgardt, and Rendtel (2005). Note that the BHPS was used as the British component of the ECHP and is analysed as part of both studies. When considering the impact of attrition on income-related summary statistics, Watson examined cross-sectional measures of inequality, whereas Behr et al. also examined estimates of quintile income group transition proportions between ECHP waves 1 and 2. Behr, Bellgardt, and Rendtel point to large cross-country variations in the nature of the attrition process, but also state that the 'attrition effects were found to be minimal' (2005: 504). Watson concludes similarly. Looking specifically at the BHPS, Cappellari and Jenkins (2008) show that estimates of the determinants of entry and exit from low pay in Britain are contaminated by differential attrition, but the size of the effect is small. Jones, Koolman, and Rice (2006), examining the socio-economic determinants of health using BHPS and ECHP data, compare estimates derived from weighted and unweighted data and conclude that 'on the whole, there are not substantive differences' (2006: 543).

Problems caused by attrition are not considered in detail in the research reported in this book, largely because my experience is that differential attrition appears not to have a large impact on the conclusions. (Estimates derived using unweighted and weighted data differ very little.) But it also has to be acknowledged that analysis of the impact of differential attrition on estimates derived from the BHPS has been less extensive than for the PSID. Why might differential attrition have relatively small effects? One answer is that the panel maintenance activities described earlier, and weighting or related modelling methods, are effective. Another is that the impact of differential attrition is likely to depend on the type of analysis. For instance, much of the analysis is of short-run transitions, only requiring relatively short sequences of observations for each respondent, and so there is less opportunity for the deleterious effects of attrition to cumulate.

3.3. Linked Panel Survey-Administrative Data

This linked panel survey-administrative data design is essentially the same as that for household panels, except that administrative register data on incomes are used to enhance data quality, notably by reducing measurement error. There is also the possibility of significant extension in temporal coverage if the linked longitudinal data is able to fill in gaps for periods between interviews or extend coverage back in the past before the survey. The Swedish Level of Living surveys have been enhanced in this way by researchers: see, for example, Björklund (1993) and Gustafsson (1994), who develop long series to study inequality and mobility trends. The Finnish component of the European Community Household Panel survey also used linkage with administrative register data on incomes (Rendtel et al. 2004).

Linkage in most countries outside the Nordic region is conditional on securing the informed consent of the respondent, which introduces issues of bias, since those giving consent may differ from those who do not. On this consent bias, see Jenkins et al. (2006) and references therein. On the other hand, if consent is secured, administrative data linkage also has the potential to reduce respondent burden substantially. For example, the Canadian Survey of Labour and Income Dynamics (SLID) offers respondents the choice of reporting earnings and other income data to the interviewer or instead providing consent for administrative record data about these sources to be linked to the respondent's survey responses (around 75 per cent choose the second option). This raises the additional issue of how to combine the different sorts of income data. On this and related issues, see Michaud and Latouche (1996).

Of course, whether one can have linked panel survey-administrative data also depends on the existence of register data in useable form, and a framework within which such data can be made available to outside researchers. Possibilities of linking administrative record data on incomes to respondents to UK panel surveys of all kinds are currently uncertain because of government concerns about data security. For a prototypic study of how to implement linkage of administrative data on income to survey respondents in Britain, see Jenkins et al. (2008).

3.4. Summary and Conclusions

Before considering specific details of the BHPS and its income variables, it is worthwhile summarizing the key advantages and disadvantages of household panel surveys relative to the main competing longitudinal designs. See Table 3.1, which highlights issues discussed in greater detail in the preceding sections. The assessment is from the perspective of a researcher undertaking analysis of household income mobility and poverty dynamics, as in the rest of the book, and the judgements about the relevant longitudinal designs might differ were other perspectives to be taken.

Comparisons across longitudinal designs are to some extent moot because often a researcher does not have a choice about which source to use: there is only one available. However, being aware of other design possibilities does highlight the features of the source that is available. This is particularly the case in Britain if one wishes to study the dynamics of household income—the BHPS is the only source currently available.

Drawing on the discussion of Chapter 2 as well, it appears that the main potential weaknesses of the BHPS for analysis of this topic are: the interview frequency (and, related, income reference period), implying that short poverty

Table 3.1. Relative advantages and disadvantages of a household panel survey design

Design feature	Advantage or disadvantage relative to other longitudinal designs
Sample size: cross-sectional	Small relative to linked register panel and rotating panel
Sample size: longitudinal	Small relative to linked register panel
Panel length	For indefinite life panels, depends on maturity, but longer than rotating panels in principle
Coverage and representativeness	Depends on target population underlying design but, unlike many linked register panels, does not depend on whether income is within limits defined by the tax-benefit system
Attrition	Potentially a greater problem than for a linked register panel or a rotating panel
Interview frequency	Annual interviews constrain definition of income reference period, and the ability to identify short-run income changes and poverty spells
Measurement error	Greater than for a linked register panel
Non-comparabilities over time	Depends if and when design innovations such as introduction of computer-assisted and dependent interviewing are made (may also affect linked register panel income variables if the tax-benefit system changes in major ways)
Availability and access	Much greater than for linked register data

spells are missed altogether, and measurement error. Small sample size is also an issue when studying some population subgroups such as lone parents (Jarvis and Jenkins 1999; Jenkins 2009*a*) and disabled people (Jenkins and Rigg 2004). But of course the BHPS also has many strengths, as illustrated in subsequent chapters.

4

The British Household Panel Survey and its Income Data

The aim of this chapter is to provide readers with information about the British Household Panel Survey (BHPS) that serves as a reference point for the research reported in the rest of the book. Much detail is provided about the BHPS, going well beyond the general features discussed in Chapter 3, but concentrating on aspects most relevant to the study of household income dynamics.

First, I discuss various BHPS design features, drawing on the BHPS Quality Profile (Lynn 2006). See also BHPS Documentation Team (2009) or, for a concise overview, Department for Work and Pensions (2008: Appendix 2).

In the rest of the chapter, I discuss how the data on equivalized net household income are derived, thereby explaining how many of the definitional issues that were discussed in Chapter 2 are resolved in practice. The BHPS net household income definition is modelled on that used in Britain's official personal income distribution statistics (*Households Below Average Income*, HBAI) based on the much larger and specialist cross-sectional income survey, the *Family Resources Survey* (FRS). The BHPS definitions are contrasted with those employed in the HBAI, and there are also comparisons of estimates of key cross-sectional summaries of the income distribution. I show that the BHPS distributions track the HBAI ones relatively well over time. (Analogous checks of longitudinal features such as poverty transition rates or income mobility are not possible because there is no comparable longitudinal data source.) By the end of this chapter, readers should have a good appreciation of the strengths and weaknesses of the BHPS income data used in the chapters that follow.

4.1. BHPS: Its Design and Other Features

As Chapter 3 shows, the BHPS is a classic example of a household panel survey designed to address a wide range of research topics. The dynamics of household income in general, and poverty dynamics in particular, were among the core research topics initially envisaged. Other topics include labour market behaviour, education and training, housing, household formation, dissolution and fertility, social and political attitudes and values, health. The general-purpose nature of the survey means that there is inevitably some degree of compromise in the specification of measures relating to any particular topic area, including household income.

The BHPS was originally designed as an indefinite life panel but has now ended, at least in its current form. There have been 18 waves of annual interviewing, with the last wave completed in survey year 2008. The BHPS sample is now incorporated into Understanding Society—the UK Household Longitudinal Study, providing a sample with a long run of panel data that will supplement data for new samples of respondents with whom interviewing began in 2009.

The first wave of the BHPS was intended to represent the private household population of Great Britain south of the Caledonian Canal. Great Britain consists of England, Wales, and Scotland. The United Kingdom is Great Britain plus Northern Ireland. (The Caledonian Canal traverses northern Scotland and, to its north, population density is very low.) Residential addresses were selected using a equal-probability clustered and stratified design from the Postal Address File (PAF), the source also used to select samples for major national cross-sectional surveys, and then all households at each address (with a selection of households for the 3 per cent of addresses with more than three households). As explained in earlier sections, additional samples drawn from Scotland, Wales, and Northern Ireland were added to the original sample in the mid to late 1990s. As data from these samples are not analysed in this book (for the reasons given earlier), I do not discuss the nature of these samples further. See Lynn (2006) for details.

The BHPS design means that individuals residing in institutions were not eligible for selection, for example residents of nursing homes, military barracks, or student halls of residence. The National Equality Panel (2010: Appendix 3) discusses the size and composition of the non-household population in the UK, and estimates its size to be around 2 per cent of the total population. The BHPS's design also means that people without a residential address are excluded from sample coverage. Since most homeless people are also destitute, it is clear that the BHPS—like all other national surveys in Britain—undercounts the number of people who are poor, but the numbers of homeless people are very small.

The National Equality Panel's conclusion is that, because of the wide range of incomes in the non-household population, 'the data ... on the household population, while incomplete, can still present a fair picture of the circumstances of the population as a whole' (2010: 411). I assume that this is the case in this book as well.

The BHPS definition of a 'household', and the unit to which 'household income' refers, is the same as that used in the UK's national statistical practice (Lynn 2006: 16), that is, 'one person living alone or a group of people who either share living accommodation, or share one meal a day and who have the address as their only or main residence'. Living together requires six months' continuous residence. This means that students are included if their term-time address was selected, unless they were living in a hall of residence.

The BHPS definition of the 'family' coincides with the definition in the British tax-benefit system (also known as the 'benefit unit'), that is, a single person or a couple living together with or without dependent children. A dependent child is aged less than 16 years, or more than 16 years but under 19 years and unmarried, in full-time non-advanced education, and living with his/her parent or parents. Parent status is defined by blood, adoption, or guardianship. A household may contain several benefit units. Examples of this are a non-dependent child living with his parents (two benefit units), or three single adults sharing a house (three benefit units). As the discussion of within-household income sharing in Chapter 2 showed, the choice of the household versus family as the income recipient unit can have marked differences on estimates of statistics such as poverty rates.

The BHPS definitions differ from those used in other panel surveys. In the PSID, for instance, the unit of focus is the 'family', defined to be 'a group of people living together as a family. They are generally related by blood, marriage, or adoption, but unrelated persons can be part of a FU if they are permanently living together and share both income and expenses'. (<http://psidonline.isr.umich.edu/Guide/FAQ.aspx#90>. See also Hill 1992.) Stated thus, the definition is close to the BHPS's definition of a household. But income distribution researchers using the PSID often focus on family income definitions using a narrower, US Census Bureau, definition of the family that excludes unrelated individuals—who are treated as one-person families. (See, for example, Gottschalk and Danziger 2005.) The definition of the income-receiving unit used in this book (and in most UK income distribution research) is therefore wider than in much US research on income distribution.

All individuals, adults and children, enumerated in BHPS respondent sample households at wave 1 became part of the longitudinal sample, and have been followed over time. Each person in this group is an Original Sample Member (OSM). New permanent members of the sample joining the longitudinal sample after the initial BHPS wave are either babies born to or adopted by OSMs after the initial wave, or the parent of a longitudinal sample member who joins the household of an OSM. So, if an OSM got married in 1994 and the couple had a child together, the spouse and the baby would both become permanent sample members (PSMs). If the partners subsequently divorced and lived separately, they and their baby would each be followed as part of the longitudinal sample. Otherwise, all persons joining the household of a longitudinal sample member are interviewed in the waves at which they are present in the sample household, but they are not followed if they leave that household—they are temporary sample members (TSMs).

The fieldwork for wave 1 was carried out between 1 September and 1 December in 1991. In subsequent waves, the fieldwork period was broadly the same, except that there was an extension running, in principle, through to the following May, in order to try and re-interview respondents who were difficult to trace or contact or to secure response from. But fieldwork remained heavily concentrated in the autumn: the modal interview month was October for waves 1–5, and September thereafter, with at least 80 per cent of interviews undertaken in either September or October (Lynn 2006: table 21). Wave 9 was the only exception, when around 12 per cent of interviews took place in the January–May period, arising because of the difficulties associated with the introduction of Computer Assisted Personal Interviewing (CAPI). The concentration of fieldwork has the advantage of helping to control for seasonal effects on response, including effects associated with Christmas. But, equally, these aspects cannot be studied.

The main survey instruments are an individual questionnaire answered by each adult member of a sampled household (lasting around 45 minutes on average), and a household questionnaire answered by one of these persons on behalf of the household (a further 15 minutes on average). There is also an adult self-completion questionnaire and, from wave 4 onwards, a self-completion questionnaire for children aged 11–15. (The repeated responses to this youth questionnaire are sometimes referred to collectively as the 'British Youth Panel'.) When children reach the age of 16, they become full sample members in their own right, and interviews are based on the instruments for adults. In addition, at the first three waves of the BHPS, there were a number of additional modules focusing on respondent life histories prior to the initial wave, using respondent retrospective recall to collect data about work and jobs, partnerships (legal and cohabiting), and fertility. All the information used to collect the various components of household income are derived, however, from the two main instruments (the individual and household questionnaires) and additional data about the household derived as part of the survey process (such as the enumeration of its members).

4.2. Sample Size

As Lynn (2006: 17–18) documents, the BHPS initial sample selection process yielded 8,167 addresses, with fieldwork identifying 13,840 persons at those addresses, including 10,751 aged 16 or older eligible for personal interviews. The number of personal interviews achieved at wave 1 (including proxy interviews) was 10,264, spread across 5,505 households. As the panel has matured, the number of achieved interviews with main sample OSMs has fallen gradually, reaching just under 8,155 at wave 7, and 7,120 by wave 13 (Lynn 2006: table 4). But, at the same time, the number of personal interviews achieved with PSMs has also increased gradually, from 10 at wave 2 to 240 at wave 7 and 299 at wave 13. The corresponding numbers of TSM personal interviews are 484, 1,071, and 1,236. Thus, the total number of achieved individual interviews went from 9,845 at wave 2, to 9,466 at wave 7, to 8,655 at wave 13 (Lynn 2006: table 4). These trends reflect attrition from the original sample, but the numbers themselves cannot be used to infer response rates. On these, see below.

Longitudinal sample sizes are more difficult to derive than cross-sectional ones because numbers depend on the particular research issue addressed, and because there are many ways of looking at the data longitudinally, including for example using long sequences of repeated observations on individuals or pooling year-on-year transitions from successive years. Numbers depend on initial sample sizes and subsequent attrition (Lynn 2006: 18).

Lynn (2006) provides six tables illustrating these points, including breakdowns by age. His table 5 shows, for instance, that of the 6,801 continuing OSMs with achieved interviews at wave 13, 5,481 provided a wave 1 response, and 4,648 provided interviews at all waves from 1 to 13. Lynn's table 6 provides information about the sequential response from wave 1 onwards. There were 4,653 respondents present at every wave from 1 to 13, but more than twice that who responded at one or more waves (9,912). Table 7 repeats the analysis, except that the calculations are for sequential wave response for those present at wave 5. 5,481 provided interviews at every wave, waves 3 through 13, but 8,162 provided one or more interviews. Table 8 summarizes the number of pairs of successive waves at which respondents gave a full interview—the sample size relevant to estimation of (average) transition rates such as proportions moving into and out of poverty (as later in the book). In this case, sample sizes are very large, over 110,000 (these numbers include the extension samples). Tables 9 and 10 show sample sizes for numbers of events. Table 9 shows that, over waves 1–13, the number of employment-to-employment transitions is very large (more than 60,000), but, for some transitions of particular policy interest, such as those from employment to unemployment, the numbers are much smaller (around 1,400). There is a similar issue with the numbers of respondents moving into or out of poverty being small relative to the number staying non-poor. Finally, Lynn's table 10 shows numbers of demographic events experienced by respondents over the 13 interview waves, referring to partnership formation and dissolution, and arrival and departure of children. Here the number of events is of the order of one to two thousand, that is, relatively small, especially once breakdowns by other characteristics are undertaken.

4.3. Response Rates, Including Attrition

Response rates can be calculated in many ways. A first approach is similar to that used for cross-section surveys, documenting wave by wave, data about field outcomes and response rates. Lynn (2006: tables 25–37) provides this type of information for waves 1–13 for the original BHPS sample. For example, at wave 1, there was complete coverage within 69 per cent of the 7,491 eligible households including proxies, and partial coverage with 74 per cent. In terms of individual adults ($n = 10,751$), 92 per cent provided full interviews, and a further 2 per cent provided proxy interviews. The most frequent reason for non-response was refusal (4 per cent), with reasons such as non-contact or absence, and age, infirmity, disability, or language difficulty being relatively unimportant. At wave 13 (individual adults $n = 9,956$), 87 per cent provided full interviews, and the refusal rate was 10 per cent.

The full 13 wave pattern is summarized in Figure 4.1, which shows that the cross-sectional response rate for individual interviews has hovered around 90 per cent after an initial fall and recovery as the panel settled in. A small downward trend in response rates is perhaps discernible towards the end of wave 13. Correspondingly, refusal rates typically fluctuate at around 10 per cent, with perhaps a slight upward trend towards the end of the period. Observe that there is no apparent change in response rates around wave 9 when CAPI was introduced. These rates (and trends) are in line with other leading household panel surveys such as the German SOEP and the Australian HILDA. For details of response in these surveys, see for example Kroh (2009) and Watson and Wooden (2006).

One-wave-at-a-time response rates are less useful for assessing household panel surveys because, for most analysis purposes (and in this book), it is longitudinal response or non-response and its cumulation over time that is relevant, whether for longitudinal statistics such as poverty transition rates, or cross-sectional statistics (after wave 1) such as poverty rates (Lynn 2006: 75). But, in this case, there is no single response rate calculation, as it depends on the combination of waves that the analyst wishes to use, and the number of

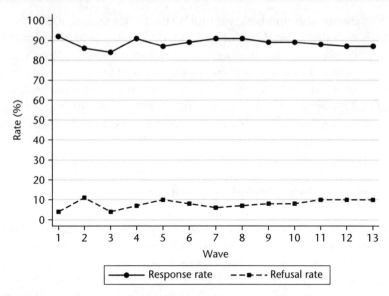

Figure 4.1. Individual interview response rate (%) and refusal rate (%), BHPS waves 1–13

Note: Calculations based on BHPS original sample.

Source: Author's derivation from Lynn (2006: tables 25–37).

possibilities is very large (Lynn 2006: 75). Inevitably, therefore, Lynn focuses on a small number of summary measures of response rates, which I now review.

Table 4.1 summarizes interview outcomes for individuals who were full respondents at wave 1. Ineligibility arises because, for example, sample members move abroad or die, and the rates have risen as the panel matures (remember the rates refer to wave 1 respondents only—an ageing cohort, by definition). The second column shows the fraction of those eligible (those alive, and in Britain south of the Caledonian Canal) who responded, and this rate has fallen as the panel matures from almost 88 per cent at wave 2 to around 65 per cent at wave 13. The final two columns summarize different types of longitudinal response rate. One shows the proportion of wave 1 respondents who also responded at every subsequent wave, wave on wave. This proportion has fallen markedly as the panel matured from around 88 per cent at wave 2 to 55 per cent at wave 13, but with the pace of decline decreasing over time (perhaps suggesting that there is a 'hard core' of compliant respondents). Although the decline in response rates over the period as a whole appears large, observe that requiring participation at every wave is unnecessary for many types of analysis.

The final column of Table 4.1 shows wave-on-wave response rates for individuals who have responded at each wave up to the previous one. After

Table 4.1. Interview outcomes for BHPS wave 1 respondents

Wave	% ineligible	% of eligible responding	% of eligible responding at all waves	Wave on wave response rate (interviewed all waves up to previous)
2	1.4	87.7	87.7	87.7
3	2.9	81.5	79.1	90.3
4	4.3	79.9	74.8	94.9
5	5.6	76.8	70.6	94.8
6	6.9	77.3	68.7	97.6
7	8.4	76.0	66.7	97.6
8	9.5	74.1	64.7	97.4
9	10.5	72.1	62.4	97.0
10	12.0	70.4	60.0	96.7
11	12.8	68.4	59.3	96.1
12	13.7	66.6	57.1	96.5
13	14.8	64.9	55.1	96.8

Source: Lynn (2006: table 67).

the initial fall-off—a phenomenon observed for all household panels—the wave-on-wave retention rate is very high, at around 95 per cent or higher. Again, this pattern and level is shared by other household panel surveys such as the German SOEP and Australian HILDA (Kroh 2009; Watson and Wooden 2006). If the calculations in Table 4.1 are repeated, but using numbers of people enumerated in wave 1 households (a group more relevant for household income distribution analysis) rather than respondents, then the trends in each column of the new table are the same, but corresponding percentages are slightly higher in the new table (Lynn 2006: table 68).

Lynn (2006) and Uhrig (2008) document which types of sample member are most likely to drop out of the BHPS. Uhrig (2008) fits multivariate discrete time hazard regression models to data from waves 1–14, modelling the hazard rate of dropout from the sample for wave 1 respondents, and hence the number of waves to first dropout from the sample. Respondents who become ineligible are treated as right-censored observations. Uhrig fits models of overall non-response, and also separate models for sample dropout due to non-contact and due to refusal, since the determinants are likely to differ. (Nicoletti and Peracchi 2005 demonstrate the importance of this distinction in the context of the ECHP.) Uhrig's estimates suggest that higher rates of non-contact are associated with physical impediments to contact (such as living in gated accommodation or apartment blocks), and characteristics associated with a respondent being more likely to be away from home or to be geographically mobile. Indicators of lack of interest in the survey and of a low motivation to participate are predictive of refusal per se. The study does not, however, examine the magnitude of the differential attrition associated with each characteristic.

Lynn (2006: tables 67–71) compares the distribution of characteristics among wave 1 respondents, with the distribution of characteristics of those who responded at some wave t but not at every wave from 1 to t, and those who responded at every wave from 1 to t, taking t = wave 5 or wave 13. Differences between the distributions are indicative of differential attrition. Lynn's summary of his findings states that those who failed to respond on at least one occasion included disproportionate numbers of people with the following characteristics at wave 1: aged 16–24 years; never married; unemployed; no qualifications; not active in any organizations; resident of Inner London, West Midlands conurbation, or Merseyside; tenant of local authority or housing association housing; and in the poorest 40 per cent of the income distribution. He also remarks, however, that 'although under-representation of these groups is statistically significant, the actual magnitude of under-representation is generally small. Furthermore, these differences apparent at the data collection stage are largely removed by the application of the weighting' (2006: 76). I discuss the BHPS weights below.

4.4. Item Non-Response

Even if sample members are counted as being respondents at a particular wave, they may not give complete responses to every question, either because they simply don't know the answer or because they are unwilling to provide the information. (Data may also be missing due to interviewer error such as skipping a question, though the introduction of CAPI should largely eliminate this problem.) This is the situation known as item non-response. Income details are examples of relatively sensitive items likely to be subject to this problem, though its prevalence may fall as the panel matures and respondents establish trust in the survey (Lynn 2006: 42).

Lynn (2006) provides information about levels of item non-response in BHPS waves 1–13. When non-response is considered in relation to all BHPS variables, its prevalence is relatively small, fluctuating around 2 per cent in both the individual questionnaire (table 50) and the household questionnaire (table 51). In the former case, and restricting attention to variables with more than 100 cases eligible to answer, item non-response ranges from 1.22 per cent (wave 7) to 2.46 per cent (wave 13), with no obvious trend over time or break points associated with the introduction of CAPI in wave 9. In the latter case, the range is from 1.78 per cent (wave 2) to 5.73 per cent (wave 10). The higher rates, apparent at waves 7–10, were associated with the introduction of additional follow-up questions concerning amounts spent on white goods. By wave 13, the item non-response rate was below 2 per cent again.

The BHPS and its income data

Of particular concern for the study of income dynamics are, not the overall rates of item non-response, but the rates associated with income and related items. Lynn (2006: table 51) reports that these rates are markedly higher than the overall rates. For example, a core component of the calculation of total household income is 'usual pay at last payment' for those in employment (see below for details). The non-response rate among employees for this variable was 15.1 per cent at wave 1 (the maximum among the rates at waves 1–13), 6.91 per cent at wave 9 (the minimum), and 11.03 per cent at wave 13, with fluctuation over time. For 'net profit' from self-employment, the rates of non-response are substantially higher, ranging between 32.8 per cent (wave 3) to 47.16 per cent (wave 9), again with fluctuation over time. (Note that the numbers of cases is much smaller: self-employment is much less prevalent than employment.) These rates can be contrasted with the rates for marital status, for which item response is near zero, or health status, for which the rate is always less than 1 per cent (Lynn 2006: table 51).

The discussion so far has been of item non-response on items provided by individual respondents on behalf of themselves (for example, their pay if an employee) or on behalf of the household as a whole (for example, questions related to the dwelling). But, for analysis of household income, it is non-response at the household level and on a combination of variables that is important. Data on total household income is incomplete if there is item non-response for any member of the household or, indeed, unit non-response by any one household member—even if there is complete response by all the other members.

In sum, item non-response is clearly an important issue for analysis of BHPS data on income. Researchers may simply omit cases with non-response, which may reduce sample numbers to unacceptable levels and introduce sample selection biases into estimates if not controlled for. Alternatively, researchers might use imputations for the missing data, thereby maintaining sample sizes, but run the risk of introducing measurement errors that will contaminate estimates. This second approach is what most analysts employ, and I do too for the most part. BHPS imputation procedures and the treatment of partial household non-response are discussed in this chapter shortly, and I return to examine the issue in later chapters as well.

4.5. Adjusting the Data after Collection: (i) BHPS Weights

The BHPS data release contains a large number of weighting variables that may be used to account for non-response in estimation, and which have been derived following conventional survey methodological practice. Here I discuss only those variables applicable to the original BHPS sample, and ignore the weights constructed for use with the extension samples. There are separate sets of weights for households, respondent individuals, and enumerated individuals (all persons within sample households). And there are cross-sectional weights for analysis of each wave taken separately, and longitudinal weights for longitudinal analysis.

The foundation of all the weighting variables for all waves is the set derived for wave 1, as these account for the unequal probabilities of selection of each address (determined as part of the design of the survey). These design weights are adjusted to take account of non-response at the household level, and non-response of individuals within households. There are then some 'post-stratification' adjustments to make the sample more representative of Britain's private household population, with the modifications aligning sample distributions with data on the distributions of housing tenure, household size, number of cars, age, and sex, available from the 1991 national Census. Finally, the resulting weights are trimmed in order that sampling variances are not unduly affected by outlier values, and then scaled so that their sum corresponds to the relevant achieved sample size. This procedure is used to derive wave 1 weights for households, respondent individuals, and enumerated individuals.

After wave 1, there are both cross-sectional and longitudinal weights for each of these groups, except that there are no longitudinal household weights because there is no valid concept of a longitudinal household (see the discussion in Chapter 2).

The BHPS longitudinal respondent weights for some wave t are non-zero for all individuals who gave a full interview at every wave up to and including wave t, and also for children at wave $t-1$ who became full sample members at t, but the weights are zero for TSMs. The longitudinal enumerated individual weights at t are non-zero for all those enumerated in respondent households at every wave up to and including wave t. For both sets of weights, the longitudinal weight at some wave s is the product of the initial wave 1 weight and weights adjusting for sample dropout between each successive pair of waves thereafter (wave 1 to wave 2, wave 2 to wave 3, and so on, up to and including wave s).

To derive the weighting adjustments, sample members were allocated to a large number of classes according to characteristics perceived as predictive of non-response or of particular interest to researchers. Within each class, that is, conditional on observed characteristics, it is assumed that response status is random. The inverse of the within-class response rate is used as the weight for all the responding cases who fall within the class (which is then further adjusted using post-stratification weights as described above). Clearly, the construction of the classes is crucial and, for this, the BHPS staff use an 'automatic interaction detection' procedure (as implemented in the SPSS

CHAID module), which facilitates derivation of a meaningful number of classes, while at the same time avoiding problems of small cell sizes. The procedure is analogous to running a probit or logit regression with response status as the dependent variable and a large number of explanatory variables and their interactions, and then using the inverse of the predicted response probability as the weight.

For the longitudinal respondent weights, the classification variables include: whether moved from the previous address; age, sex, employment status, income total and composition, race, level of organizational membership, and educational qualifications, and various household characteristics such as region, housing tenure, number of cars, and ownership of consumer durables (Lynn 2006: 51). Children reaching the age of 16 are allocated a longitudinal respondent weight equal to the minimum of that of their parents. A similar procedure is used to derive longitudinal enumerated individual weights, with the main difference being that weighting classes were mainly based on the characteristics of the household and the household head. Newborn children receive the average of the weights for their parents.

Derivation of the cross-sectional weights after wave 1 is complicated by the need to derive weights for new entrants after wave 1. A person marrying an OSM does not have a wave 1 weight or a longitudinal weight. Moreover, their initial sample inclusion or response probabilities are not known and so assumptions have to be made about these. The 'equal shares' method that the BHPS uses (in common with other panels like SLID) in effect derives the unknown initial sample probabilities by supposing that the new entrants are like the other members of their household and uses the information about the members who were present in wave 1 to derive these probabilities. At each wave, the 'average' of the weights for the original members of the household, adjusted for subsequent dropout, is shared with the joiners at that wave. Cross-sectional respondent weights can be derived by a similar procedure, and a household weight is set equal to the cross-sectional individual weight, re-scaled to correspond to the total number of households.

Although the rationale for weighting is relatively straightforward, it is clear from this discussion that the detailed derivation of the different types is complicated. Similar procedures are used across the major household panels. For example, the PSID has weights corresponding to the BHPS's longitudinal weights. The German SOEP, like the BHPS, has longitudinal and cross-sectional weights, except that the former are provided for each pair of successive waves up to and including wave t (unconditional on response prior to wave $t-1$), rather than the one set of weights for the full sequence of waves up to and including wave t. The Australian HILDA provides both types of longitudinal weights as well as cross-sectional weights.

Additional issues concerning the use of the BHPS weights are their general-purpose nature and the derivation for individuals with a particular type of response pattern. Particular outcomes of research interest may be associated with particular patterns of non-response and, ideally, one should take account of this. And the BHPS longitudinal weights are non-zero only for original and permanent sample members, with complete response at every wave up to and including the current one. Those with intermittent response are excluded and this is undesirable for some types of longitudinal analysis—a common example is analysis based on wave-on-wave transitions.

This discussion suggests several options. One might be to develop one's own set of specialist weights, appropriate to the research question under consideration. This is rarely done (but see, for example, Jenkins 2009a). Aside from the complications involved, there are also conceptual problems. For example, researchers (including me) commonly examine transitions between states between two consecutive waves, pooling transitions from multiple pairs of waves. In this case, it is unclear what population of interest the pooled transitions are intended to represent and hence how either to calculate suitable longitudinal weights or to combine the weights typically supplied. This is not a decisive argument against using the weights supplied; rather the lesson is that differential non-response can lead to biased estimates, and so analysts should check the sensitivity of their conclusions to different assumptions about non-response. An approach commonly used, also in this book, is to compare weighted and unweighted estimates and to claim robustness if they are similar.

Economists are sometimes resistant to using weights in estimation, especially in analysis based on multivariate regression modelling. Reasons for this view are rarely documented, but partly represent the idea that many of the variables included as explanatory variables in the regressions are the same as those that would be used to predict non-response and thence generate weights, and so there is a form of redundancy if weights are used. (On this, see Winship and Radbill 1998.) A contrary view would be that the interpretation of the impact of these variables is made more complicated (estimated coefficients reflect the impact of non-response as well as the substantive impact on the outcome) and, in any case, non-response related to survey design and which manifests itself via non-contact rather than refusal is typically not included as an explanatory variable. A second reason for economists' scepticism about weights is that the multivariate models of response used to derive them ignore the impact of unobservables.

The issue of whether to weight or not in the multivariate regression context has been helpfully clarified by Wooldridge (2002a), who shows that 'the weighted estimator is consistent if we have an appropriate ignorability assumption and if we either know or can consistently estimate the sampling probabilities' (2002: 11). Ignorability refers to there being no unobservable factors associated with both the outcome of interest and the probability of response (conditional on observable variables). This is untestable without further assumptions about the nature of the association, and the standard approach is to suppose a model in which the additive 'error' terms in the outcome and response equations that characterize unobservables are independent of observables, and distributed multivariate normally. Identification of model parameters relies on there being variables that explain response that do not also affect the substantive outcome ('instruments'). In this approach, the test for ignorability is a test of the statistical significance of a correlation. For an application to poverty transitions, see Chapter 11, and to low pay transitions, see Cappellari and Jenkins (2008). In both cases, attrition was found to be non-ignorable, but the magnitude of its impact is small.

4.6. Adjusting the Data after Collection: (ii) BHPS Imputation Procedures

Item non-response arises when a respondent is judged to have provided a full interview, but data are missing on some variables of interest. The issue, as with attrition, is whether the non-response is differential rather than random. If it is, then analysing data consisting of only non-missing cases—which is the default in most software packages—may lead to biased estimates. As an illustration of the scope for this, Frick and Grabka (2005) show, using German SOEP data, that income mobility estimates using only cases with non-missing data markedly understate estimates derived from all cases, including those with imputed income values. The differences may represent bias or the effects of measurement error introduced by imputation.

One approach to item non-response would be to develop suitable sample weights, exploiting the parallels with the case of non-response and attrition just discussed. The alternative, more commonly followed, and also adopted by the BHPS producers, is to make some specific assumptions about the item non-response process, and to use these to generate predicted values that are used to 'fill in' the missing values. At the same time, additional variables ('imputation flags') are created in order that researchers may identify cases with imputed values, and exclude them or derive alternative values if they wish.

BHPS imputation procedures focus on variables connected with income and housing costs (see the discussions of prevalence earlier). Two imputation approaches are used depending on the nature of the variable.

Hot-deck imputation is used for variables derived from questions with a limited number of valid responses—for example, banded income from investments and savings, or some cash benefits. The procedure is very similar to that described earlier for the derivation of weights. Cases are placed in classes defined by combinations of variables believed to predict item non-response and then, assuming that response is random conditional on class membership, a case with a valid value for the variable of interest is randomly selected and that value imputed to a case from the same class with missing data. Classes are constructed using the same automatic interaction detection methods as described earlier.

When monetary amounts are missing, a regression-based imputation method known as 'predictive mean matching' is used for a number of primary variables from which some other income-related variables are derived. Taking cases with non-missing values of the variable of interest, a regression model is fitted with this variable as the dependent variable and a large number of explanatory variables thought to be predictive of response and their interactions. Predictions of the amount are derived from the fitted model for all cases, including those with missing amounts. The closest valid value to the predicted value of a missing case is then determined, and imputed. Using the closest valid value rather than the closest predicted value of a non-missing case ensures that only possible real values are imputed, and that the imputation process does not reduce the variance of imputed values relative to valid values. The imputation regression used for a particular wave also makes use of information about the value of the variable in other waves for some key components of household income, including gross usual pay from employment. The idea is that past or future realizations of the variable are informative about the missing current value (in addition to current characteristics). The BHPS procedures use information from up to three waves—previous, current, and next (BHPS Documentation Team 2009: A5–24 and table 27). The result of this cross-wave imputation is that '[t]he imputed value should . . . imply a rate of change drawn from a randomly selected similar case. This approach will avoid introducing spurious change for panel analysis, which would be likely to arise if only single wave imputation was used' (Lynn 2006: 55).

These imputation procedures lead to non-missing values (and imputation flags) for individual-level income variables. For total gross household income, there is also the problem of household members who refuse to complete the questionnaire altogether. For these refusers, income totals are imputed using the methods described above. Total gross household income can then be derived for every household.

The BHPS imputation procedures are relatively conventional, but not the only possibilities. Multiple imputation methods (Rubin 1987) have not been used, for example. Other panels use different approaches. For example, the German SOEP mainly uses the row-and-column method proposed by Little and Su (1989): see Frick and Grabka (2005).

In the rest of this book, I use the BHPS imputations for the most part—as do the vast majority of BHPS analysts. In some chapters, however, I recognize that imputation may introduce a form of measurement error, and examine the sensitivity of estimates to inclusion or exclusion of cases with imputed values.

The discussion so far has focused on the data that are in the main public-release BHPS files, made available to any bone-fide researcher who is registered with the United Kingdom Data Archive (<http://www.data-archive.ac.uk>). The net household income variables that are analysed throughout this book are also made available in the same way, but have been created separately from the main release and on an ad hoc basis. Given the importance of the variables for the analysis presented in this book, I now turn to discuss their derivation in detail.

4.7. Derivation of the Net Household Income Variables

The BHPS net household income definition is modelled on the one used in the UK's principal official source of information about the personal income distribution—the so-called *Households Below Average Income* (HBAI) series prepared by the Department for Work and Pensions (formerly the Department for Social Security). The HBAI publication provides detailed information about inequality and poverty, using repeated cross-sectional data from the annual *Family Resources Survey*, a large specialist income survey. Some 20 editions have been produced to date; the most recent at the time of writing is Department for Work and Pensions (2010), covering the period between 1994/5 and 2008/9.

Since the early 1990s, my colleagues and I have derived net household variables to provide a longitudinal complement to the HBAI statistics. The first edition of our data was for BHPS waves 1 and 2 (documented in the appendix to Jarvis and Jenkins 1995), and the latest covers waves 1–16 (Levy and Jenkins 2008). The computer code required to derive the variables is extensive. The structure is designed to be as modular as possible in order to facilitate updating to take account of changes in the taxes and benefit system, but, inevitably, it remains complicated.

In the early 2000s, the Department for Work and Pensions began to create its own net household income variables from the BHPS, and to use them in its *Low Income Dynamics* (LID) statistics, first publishing these summaries along with the main HBAI statistics, but more recently publishing them separately on the internet: the latest edition is DWP (2009*a*). The definitions of net household income used in the LID and by me are broadly similar, but differ in matters of detail. The LID definitions are not documented, but the principal difference from my net income definition appears to be that the LID one does not include a deduction for local taxes.

Improvements and corrections have been made to the BHPS net income variables at every edition (and documented in the materials accompanying their release). These changes have been applied to every wave of data retrospectively (where relevant) in each new edition of the files. For brevity, the discussion that follows here refers to the definitions used in the latest edition, with little mention of the changes introduced earlier. All the analysis reported in this book is based on the 16-wave net income file release, with the exception of Chapter 9 (14-wave release), and Chapters 10 and 11 (nine-wave release).

The BHPS net income variable has three key features:

1. The reference period for the majority of income sources is the period round about the time of the interview, that is, it is a current rather than annual definition, with income converted pro rata to be expressed in terms of pounds per week. (Some comparisons between current and annual income are made later in this chapter.)

2. The unit over which incomes are aggregated is the household (as defined in the previous section).

3. The sources of income and deductions from income that are included in the definition of net income are summarized in Table 4.2. (Non-cash income from other sources, including imputed rent from owner-occupied housing, and capital gains, is not included.) *Gross* income is the sum of sources (a) to (g).

These three components define an income variable that corresponds to the 'before housing costs' (BHC) net household income variable used by

Table 4.2. The income sources included in net household income

	(a)	usual gross earnings from employment
+	(b)	earnings from subsidiary employment
+	(c)	profit or loss from self-employment
+	(d)	social security benefits and tax credits
+	(e)	private and occupational pensions
+	(f)	income from investments and saving
+	(g)	private transfers and other income
−	(h)	income tax (employees and self-employed)
−	(i)	National Insurance Contributions (employees and self-employed)
−	(j)	contributions to occupational pension schemes
−	(k)	local taxes
=		Total net household income

Notes: The income definition refers to net income before the deduction of housing costs, i.e. net income 'BHC' in HBAI terminology. Gross income is the sum of sources (a) to (g).

the DWP in the HBAI statistics. (Details differ because the BHPS does not collect as much detailed information as the *Family Resources Survey*.) Post-calculation adjustments to account for differences in household size and composition using equivalence scales, and adjustments to constant-purchasing power terms using prices, are summarized after discussion of the derivation of the nominal household net income variable.

The steps involved in constructing income components (a) to (k) are as follows:

1. Derive a measure of taxable income from employment and self-employment for each individual (components (a)–(c) in Table 4.2);

2. Estimate the income tax and National Insurance Contribution liabilities implied by this estimated taxable income, together with estimates of contributions to occupational pension schemes (components (h)–(j));

3. Add on the sources of non-labour income (components (d)–(g));

4. Estimate liabilities for local taxes (currently Council Tax; formerly the Community Charge).

Estimation of tax and National Insurance Contribution (NIC) liabilities is based on labour income only, reflecting the limited information available (see below) and, moreover, all such liabilities and also the deductions for occupational pension and local taxes are estimated rather than observed in the data. The use of simulation methods to estimate income deductions is common practice and employed by all UK tax-benefit microsimulation models, but may lead to the introduction of measurement error. However, estimated liabilities for wave 1 and 2 respondents who provided both gross and net amounts are remarkably similar to the difference between gross and net labour income (Jarvis and Jenkins 1995: tables A–9 and A–10). This suggests that the use of simulation does not lead to major problems. In any case, there are advantages of consistency in applying the same derivation procedure to all households. I now discuss steps 1–4 in more detail.

Income from Employment and Self-Employment

The BHPS asks employees to report their gross and net (take-home) pay at last payment, the time period it covered, and whether their last payment was equal to what they are usually paid. If last and usual pay differed, respondents are then asked to give their usual pay and to explain why the last amount was unusual. A majority of respondents provide both gross and net amounts. If possible, the interviewer checks a recent payslip and sees them in around one-third of the cases. A small minority of employees either refuse to give information or do not know the amount or time period of their last earnings.

The BHPS data include imputed values for these cases (see above), which are used. The survey also asks about earnings from second jobs, but this information is reported only as a gross figure.

Income from self-employment is difficult to measure in household surveys because the degree of non-response and under-reporting tends to be higher for the self-employed than for employees, and income from self-employment varies considerably over time, making it difficult for respondents to assess their incomes and for researchers to derive a measure of 'current income' from the data provided. Both of these problems occur in the BHPS. The survey asks the self-employed to provide details of their most recent accounts or (where this is not available) an estimate of their usual monthly gross earnings. Approximately one-fifth of self-employed respondents either refuse to give information or do not know how much they earn. The BHPS contains imputed values for these cases, and these are used as an estimate of gross earnings.

The data refer to the most recent period for which the respondent has either kept profit and loss accounts or has a record of his or her gross earnings. This information may be out of date by up to four years, and therefore under-estimated. To correct for this, the incomes are updated to allow for inflation, using the not-seasonally-adjusted Average Earnings Index (AEI) for the whole economy (Office for National Statistics series LNMM). Where earnings from self-employment have been imputed in the BHPS, the modal reporting period from the non-imputed cases is used, which is the financial year ending in the April before the interview.

Total gross earnings from all sources (employment, self-employment, and income from second or occasional jobs) are computed using the most recent *usual* gross payment received. There are a small number of respondents who are not employed or self-employed but who report income from occasional jobs in the month previous to the interview. It is assumed that this income is untaxed and net labour income is set equal to the gross amount reported for these cases.

Income Tax

The first step in estimating income tax payments is derivation of each individual's taxable income. This is defined to be equal to gross income minus certain tax allowances and tax-deductible contributions to employer pension schemes. The rules have changed over time, and the calculations take account of this. Other minor tax allowances which can be set against income are ignored as there is insufficient information collected by the BHPS. Under independent taxation (introduced in 1990–1), each taxpayer is entitled to a personal allowance, the value of which is higher for those aged 65 or over. A married man can also claim a married couple's allowance in addition to his personal allowance. If his income is insufficient to make full use of this allowance then the unused part can be transferred to his wife. It was only from the tax year 1993–4 onwards that couples could choose to allocate the whole allowance to the wife or split it equally between them.

Each individual's tax allowance is estimated using demographic information on age and marital status reported in the BHPS. Data for husbands and wives are matched in order to be able to use information on spouses' age and earnings when calculating the married couples' allowance (MCA). It is assumed that any unused MCA is transferred from the husband to the wife. (As Sutherland and Wilson (1995) point out, this transfer does not happen automatically, but depends on decisions made by the couple concerned. In cases where the husband's income level is likely to increase in the near future (for example, temporary unemployment) then the couple may decide not to transfer the allowance.) The procedure for computing the MCA was modified in the ten-wave release of the net income variables to take account of the fact that the part of the MCA that is age related has to go to the husband and cannot be transferred to the wife. However, the husband can transfer to the wife the part that he is not able to use (and it is sensible to do so). In practice, the old and the new procedure produced similar results, but the allocation between husband and wife is slightly different (in a few cases, even the total MCA the couple is entitled to). From 2000–1, the married couple allowance for people born after 5 April 1935 was withdrawn. Hence, the general MCA no longer exists and the MCA for older people will progressively disappear.

Having deducted the appropriate tax allowances and pension contributions from gross income, tax paid is calculated by applying the schedule of tax rates for the relevant year. Net labour income is equal to gross earnings minus estimated tax, NICs, and occupational pension contributions.

National Insurance Contributions (NICs)

Employees are liable to pay Class 1 NICs if they are aged 16 or over and earn more than the 'lower earnings limit'. All of the earnings of an employee who earns at least the lower earnings limit are subject to NICs up to the upper earnings limit. The rate of contribution is calculated as a percentage of gross earnings and depends on whether the employee is a full member of the state retirement pension scheme or whether their employer has contracted out of the earnings-related part of the state scheme and provides a separate occupational pension. Employees in contracted-out employment pay NICs at a rate 2 per cent lower than the non-contracted-out rate on earnings between the upper and lower limits. Prior to 1977, married and some widowed women could elect to pay NICs at a reduced rate of 3.85 per cent. This rate is the same for both contracted-out and non-contracted-out employment. Those who chose to do so (before 1977) could then continue to pay reduced rate contributions thereafter. Administrative statistics (Department of Social Security 1994) show that approximately 10 per cent of women paid reduced rate contributions in 1991/2 and this can be expected to have fallen after that, due to some of these women leaving the labour market.

Since the BHPS collects no information about NICs, they are estimated for employees using data on gross earnings and membership of occupational pension schemes. It is assumed that members of an employer's scheme pay NICs at the lower contracted-out rate, and that all others make full contributions. (Since there is no information to identify the women who opted to pay reduced-rate contributions, it is assumed that all are paying at the non-reduced rate.) This may overstate the number of contracted-out employees by approximately 10 per cent: see the discussion in Jarvis and Jenkins (1995).

Self-employed people are liable for two types of NICs. Class 2 contributions are paid as a flat-rate weekly amount, with exemption given to those whose profits fall below a specified amount. Class 4 contributions are calculated as a percentage of annual taxable profits between an upper and lower earnings limit. Half of Class 4 contributions can be offset against income tax. NICs for self-employed people are estimated using data about their most recent gross earnings or profit. There are insufficient data available to estimate lump-sum tax or NIC payments or refunds, and so these factors are ignored.

Occupational Pension Contributions

For the respondents who report making contributions to their employer's pension scheme, pension contributions are imputed at a rate equal to 4.7 per cent of gross earnings. This figure is the average of the figure reported by respondents to the *Family Expenditure Survey* in survey years 1991, 1992, and 1993. The average rate for 2003/4 according to *Family Resources Survey* data is not much different (4.9 per cent). The earlier figure has been retained simply for consistency. Clearly these estimates are an approximation of reality, but it was thought that the benefits of attempting to derive a more accurate individual-specific amount (for example, using occupation-specific data) were not justified by the time required.

Social Security Benefits and Tax Credits

Using respondents' retrospective recall at the interview, the BHPS collects detailed information on the type of social security benefit received by each member of the household on a month-by-month basis for the whole of the period from September of the previous year to the date of the interview. The survey also asks about the amount of the last payment of each benefit.

To construct the net income variable, the BHPS-derived variable, which measures the total benefit income of the household in the month before the interview (and therefore includes imputed values), is used, with one important caveat concerning the housing benefit component. A change in the wording between waves 1 and 2 of the prompt card used by BHPS interviewers to remind respondents of their various sources of income appears to have led to a large drop in the number of people reporting housing benefit receipt. Whereas in wave 1 the card referred to 'Housing Benefit (Rent Rebate and Allowances)', in wave 2 it referred to 'Housing Benefit paid directly to you'. This appears to have led some individuals who do not receive their housing benefit directly to fail to report it in wave 2. To deal with this discontinuity, an alternative measure of housing benefit is created, using information from the household questionnaire (following Webb 1995). Households are asked to report their rent as both a gross and a net amount, the latter taking into account housing benefits received. For households reporting a 100 per cent rent rebate, housing benefit is set equal to gross rent. For other households, the estimate of housing benefit is equal to gross rent minus net rent.

There have been revisions to the details of our calculations in different editions of the net income files, the most significant of which was in the most recent (16-wave) edition. There was a coding error, now corrected, which meant that, for households reporting a 100 per cent rent rebate, housing benefit was set equal to zero (rather than gross rent). The correction increases the income of low-income households and reduces measured inequality—though only for waves 2–8 is the effect particularly marked (Levy and Jenkins 2008).

The other notable modifications to the calculations have been related to the introduction of and reforms to tax credits. In October 1999, Working Families Tax Credit (WFTC) replaced the Family Credit and Disabled Person's Tax Credit (DPTC) replaced Disability Working Allowance. In April 2003, WFTC and DPTC were replaced by Child Tax Credit (CTC) and Working Tax Credit (WTC). WFTC, DPTC, and WTC can be delivered in two ways: through the employer in the payslip or as a benefit. It appears that the payslip amounts are usually also recorded in the BHPS's income grid, but not always. Also, in a few cases, there are discrepancies between the two sections. As a rule, calculations use the amount that is recorded in the income section, ignoring the discrepancies between this amount and the one reported in the employment section. When no amount is recorded in the income section (and only in this case), but some positive amount is recorded in the employment section, the household's benefit income is assumed to include the amount recorded in the employment section.

The annual amount of Tax Credit received through the employer is computed as follows. First, the weekly amount is computed using the amount and pay period variables. Second, the annual amount is computed using the reported number of weeks worked in the relevant year—therefore assuming that those who are currently receiving the Tax Credit through their employer have received the same amount in every week they were in work during the relevant year. Finally, the amount computed in this way (and summed across individuals within each household to derive a household figure) is set equal to zero for those households where somebody declared receipt of the Tax Credit as a benefit, in order to avoid double counting.

Income from Investments and Savings

Obtaining reliable information about income from investments and savings is notoriously difficult in household surveys. In the first few BHPS waves of the BHPS, the questions asked were not very detailed. At waves 1 and 2, only banded responses were sought, using four categories. At waves 3–8, the top band was split into three. From wave 9 onwards, respondents have been asked for an exact amount and banded amounts sought from those who do not provide one. For those with non-zero amounts or non-exact amounts, BHPS staff impute a value from the banded responses (common to all reporting the same band), and those imputations are also used in the net income calculations. The use of banding is likely to result in an understatement of income from this source, particularly for those with very high incomes. Unlike as for other income sources, the BHPS asks respondents about amounts received in the past 12 months, and this annual figure is then converted pro rata to a monthly or weekly amount as required.

Transfers and Other Income

This category includes educational grants, maintenance and alimony payments, foster allowances, payments from family members not living in the household, and any other payments received by household members. The derived BHPS variable, which gives the household total for these income sources, is used for the net income calculation.

Local Taxes

Local tax payments are estimated for all households using external data on average Council Tax levels by local authority. For waves 1 and 2, when the community charge ('poll tax') was in operation rather than Council Tax, data on the average community charge payment in each local authority district are

100

used. For waves 3–6, council tax payments are imputed using data on the average council tax payment in each local authority area. (See Redmond 1997 for details.) From wave 7 onwards, the BHPS has collected data on the council tax band of households, and these are used to estimate more precise council tax liabilities in conjunction with information identifying the local authority in which the household resides.

Partial Unit Non-Response: Non-Response by some Household Members

As mentioned earlier, the measure of net household income cannot be derived if one or more of the adult members of the household are not interviewed—the problem of partial unit non-response. Figure 4.2 summarizes its prevalence. The proportion of all households at each wave with all adults providing an interview fluctuated between 80 per cent and 90 per cent at the beginning of the panel, but, at the most recent waves, the fraction is around 80 per cent. The increase over time is mostly accounted for by a growing fraction of individuals who refuse to provide an interview and, at more recent waves, by a small but growing proportion who provide only telephone interviews.

There are a number of ways of accounting for the impact of partial unit non-response. They range from doing nothing (the approach adopted in the construction of the net income variables used in this book) through to

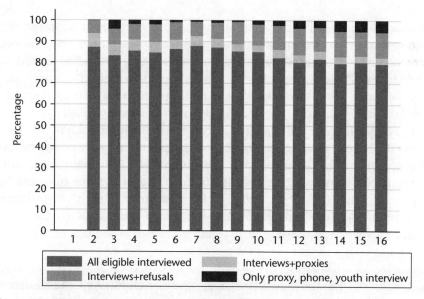

Figure 4.2. Full and partial response within BHPS households, rates (%) by wave
Note: The chart shows breakdowns of the BHPS variable wIVFHO (not available at wave 1).
Source: Author's calculations from BHPS Documentation Team (2009).

use of methods employing imputation of the missing data or re-weighting of the sample. Observe that partial unit non-response cannot occur within one-person households and the risk of occurrence is greater the larger the household.

The ECHP used a form of imputation in which there was a 'flat correction' method that re-scaled household incomes for households with partial unit non-response (Eurostat 2000). A range of methods are applied to German SOEP data and compared by Frick, Grabka, and Groh-Samberg (2009). Their results show that the importance of the issue depends on the context. For example, cross-sectional poverty rates estimated using the methods are very similar in any given year and follow similar trends over time (figure 7). Income mobility, including the probability of moving into or out of poverty, is greater for households with partial unit non-response, but arguably the differences in estimates from applying different methods is not large (figures 9–11). This may be because the prevalence of partial unit non-response, while non-trivial, is not large. In the following section, I show indirectly that partial unit non-response appears not to be a critical problem in BHPS net income data since estimated distributions match counterparts in the benchmark HBAI distributions remarkably well.

4.8. Equivalence Scales and Price Indices

In order to compare incomes for households of different size and composition, and to make comparisons of incomes in different years, each net household income value is adjusted by an equivalence-scale factor and by a monthly price index. These adjustments are standard ones that are commonly used. The particular choices employed in this book are ones that are used in Britain's official income statistics, *Households Below Average Income* (HBAI).

The equivalence scales I use are either the 'McClements' scale or the 'modified-OECD' scale (the 'before housing costs' versions in each case). In the late 1990s, Eurostat began employing the modified-OECD scale for its cross-national comparisons of income distributions and the UK has now adopted it for its headline statistics as well, switching over from the McClements scale. The modified-OECD scale distinguishes between individuals aged between 0 and 14 years, and those aged 15+ ('adult'). The scale equals 1 for the first adult and adds a weight of 0.5 for each additional 'adult' and a weight of 0.3 for each child. In addition, the Department for Work and Pensions normalizes scale values so that the (normalized) scale rate for a childless couple household is equal to 1.0 (rather than 1.5). This has the convenience of aligning the scale with the McClements scale, which is normalized to equal 1.0 for a childless married couple household. The weights used to construct the McClements scale take account of differences in household size and composition in finer detail (for example, with different weights for children of different ages or additional adults beyond the first two). However, the relativities for different household types are quite similar for the majority of households according to both the McClements and modified-OECD scales. For further details of the scales, see for example Department for Work and Pensions (2009*b*: appendix 2). Coulter, Cowell, and Jenkins (1992*a*, 1992*b*) and Jenkins and Cowell (1994) compare the McClements scale with other scales using parametric approximations, and their analysis also suggests that the choice between these two scales is not a major issue.

The price indices used to convert household net incomes from different time periods to constant price terms are the same as used in the official income statistics. The index is the 'all-items Retail Price Index excluding Council tax', created by the Department for Work and Pensions by the Office for National Statistics (ONS). Values of the index are reproduced in the appendices to Levy and Jenkins (2008). Earnings, analysed in Chapter 4, are deflated by the ONS's Average Earnings Index (series LNMM). Both indices are monthly indices (not seasonally adjusted), and are matched to respondents using data about the interview month in each survey year. The indices are national indices: as in the official statistics, no account is taken of potentially different inflation rates between different groups (such as low-income versus high-income households, or between young and old, or between different regions of Britain). See for example Crawford and Smith (2002).

4.9. Current versus Annual Measures of Income

The definition of net household income used in this book is essentially a measure of current income because it is mostly derived from respondents' reports about income received round about the time of the survey interview— as virtually all UK survey measures of income are. It is not a definition of annual income, as used by surveys for most other countries. As discussed in Chapter 2, use of a current income definition might be expected to produce estimates of inequality, poverty, and mobility that are larger than those derived using an annual income measure, other things being equal. In addition, the differences in types of measure may compromise comparisons between patterns for Britain and those of other countries.

Böheim and Jenkins (2006) show, however, that estimates of cross-sectional and longitudinal income distribution summary statistics derived from BHPS measures of current and annual income are remarkably similar. Almost all differences between corresponding estimates for the two measures are in the expected direction, but the magnitude of the differences is small both in

aggregate and also when looking at breakdowns by family type and employment status. Although our published paper is based on comparisons of gross
income measures rather than net income ones, our unpublished work shows
that similar results apply in this case too (2006: n. 8). The results suggest that,
for practical purposes, the distinction between current and annual income
measures is a minor one.

The reasons underlying this result have been foreshadowed in Chapter 2,
and mainly hinge on the fact that in Britain survey measures of income are
rarely purely current or purely annual in the sense of every constituent component having a current or annual reference period. Böheim and Jenkins
(2006) emphasize several specific factors related to this in the BHPS context.
First, the measure of employment earnings included in household income
refers to usual pay, and not the amount most recently received. Second, some
other income sources use a reference period that may often be as long as a year.
Self-employed workers who keep accounts report income (net profit or loss)
over a year, and the BHPS question about income from investments and
savings specifically refers to receipts over the previous 12 months. Third, at
the same time, the BHPS annual income definition is not derived from reports
of annual receipts for every source. Instead, it is a measure constructed using
information about incomes received at the current interview and at the previous interview, combined with information from retrospective monthly histories of employment and benefit receipt, and information from external
sources such as administrative statistics, in order to build up a picture of
incomes received between interviews. For each source, this information yields
a series of monthly income estimates that are summed to produce an annual
aggregate (see Böheim and Jenkins 2006 for more details). Total income is
derived by summing the annual receipts from each income source.

An additional reason for the minor differences between current and annual
income estimates is also investigated by Böheim and Jenkins (2006), namely
that the numbers of people moving into or out of jobs, or experiencing
changes in the demographic composition of their household, are relatively
small and hence consequential within-year income variability is relatively
small. To examine this hypothesis further, Böheim and Jenkins (2006) analyse
whether differences between statistics based on current and annual income
measures are larger for households which experience changes in labour market attachment or changes in household composition—but find that there
was no conclusive evidence one way or the other. Differences are relatively
small for most subgroups considered.

I conclude from this research that the distinction between the BHPS measures of current and annual income is unimportant relative to other issues. All
the analysis reported in this book is based on the current net household
income measure.

4.10. Comparisons of BHPS and HBAI Net Income Distributions from a Cross-Sectional Perspective

In this section, I compare BHPS net income distributions with their HBAI counterparts from a cross-sectional perspective, drawing on the more detailed comparisons provided by Jenkins (2010a). Ideally, one would like to have a longitudinal benchmark data set as well, but none is currently available for Britain. The cross-sectional comparisons are an important validation exercise, nonetheless, since getting the cross-sectional estimates for each year right is an essential part of getting right the estimates of the joint distribution for any pair of years. The HBAI distributions are taken as the reference point because they are derived from the Family Resources Survey, a specialist income survey that has a sample size almost six times larger than the BHPS samples used in this book (almost 30,000 households per year compared to about 5,000). The HBAI net income data are used to generate Britain's official income distribution statistics and are regarded as being of high quality.

The comparisons reported in this section are based on calculations using the 16-wave release of the BHPS net income files (Levy and Jenkins 2008) and the 2009 release of the HBAI files (Department for Work and Pensions 2009b). The latter cover financial years 1994/5 to 2007/8 and are the latest available at the time of writing. In both sources, the variable of primary interest is net household income (before the deduction of housing costs), as described earlier in this chapter, equivalized using the modified-OECD scale (with the HBAI variable re-normalized so that the scale rate equals one for a single-person household, as in the BHPS case), and expressed in January 2008 prices in pounds per week using the same monthly price index (see above). The BHPS calculations are based on the original sample only, and households from Northern Ireland have been dropped from the HBAI files, so that comparisons refer to Britain in both sources. All calculations for each series used the relevant sample weights.

An important difference between the HBAI and BHPS net income distributions is that the former include an 'SPI adjustment' in order to better measure incomes at the very top of the distribution. For each FRS year, the Department for Work and Pensions identifies a small number of rich households defined as being households containing a rich individual, with pensioner and non-pensioner households considered separately. The threshold defining 'rich' is set at a level above which it is considered that incomes are not measured reliably in the FRS because the sample size is too small.

'Year' refers to survey year in the BHPS (the modal interview month is October), and to financial year in the HBAI (interviews spread from April to following March). Because of the secular growth in incomes on average over the period, the financial year coverage of the HBAI may lead to lower incomes in the HBAI than the BHPS, ceteris paribus. However, the impact of this is likely to be relatively small.

Estimates of selected quantiles of the income distribution are shown for each source, by year, in Figure 4.3. Panel (a) summarizes differences in the top half of the distribution, showing the median ($p50$) and the 75th, 95th, and 99th percentiles ($p75$, $p95$, $p99$). Panel (b) refers to the bottom half of the distribution, showing the median ($p50$) and the 25th, 10th, and 1st percentiles ($p25$, $p10$, $p1$). There is a remarkably close correspondence between corresponding estimates from each source, with the notable exception of the very top of the distribution ($p99$), and also at the bottom of the distribution ($p1$).

The difference at the very top is readily explained by the use of the SPI adjustment in the HBAI data. (Estimates from unadjusted FRS data would be closer to the BHPS ones.) The SPI adjustment is also likely to explain why the $p99$ series for the two sources were relatively close in the mid-1990s but diverged thereafter. Atkinson, Piketty, and Saez (2011) report trends in the share of total income held by the richest 1 per cent in Britain for almost a century through to 2005, with their estimates derived from administrative record tax data on incomes, including SPI data for the most recent years. Their estimates (2010: figure 7A) show that, although the share was rising throughout the period 1990–2005, there was a step change upward round about 1995. Atkinson (2005) reports similar trends for income shares within the top 1 per cent. Although the definition of income and the income recipient in the tax data are not exactly the same as those employed here, the trends at the very top of the distribution are likely to explain what is shown for $p99$ in Figure 4.3(a).

Accurate measurement of very low incomes using household surveys is also a problem, and is reflected in the estimates from both sources of $p1$. For further evidence for Britain about this issue, see Brewer et al. (2009b). There is greater year-on-year fluctuation in the series for $p1$ compared to other percentiles, and more so for the BHPS (with the smaller sample size). Overall, the estimates presented in Figure 4.3 suggest that BHPS estimates of the net income distribution are relatively good, except at the very top and very bottom of the distribution.

What about summary statistics such as poverty rates and inequality indices? The similarities in estimates of quantiles throughout most of the income range mean that estimates of the proportion of persons with an income below 60 per cent of the median (Britain's headline poverty rate) are close for the two sources. This is shown in Figure 4.4. Even when the BHPS and HBAI series differ most (during the 1990s), the difference is at most about one percentage point.

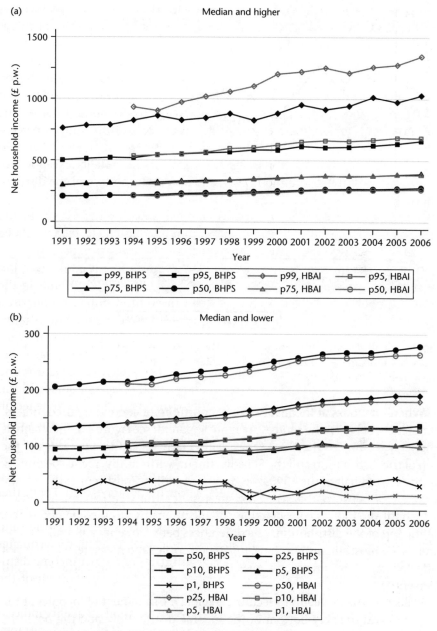

Figure 4.3. Selected quantiles of net household income, BHPS and HBAI, by year

(a) Median and higher

(b) Median and lower

Source: Jenkins (2010*a*).

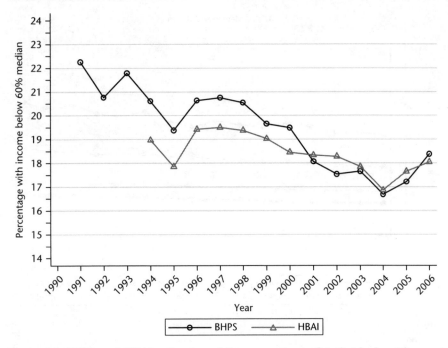

Figure 4.4. BHPS and HBAI estimates of the percentage of individuals with a net household income less than 60% of the median, by year

Source: Jenkins (2010*a*).

When one looks at inequality using a portfolio of commonly used indices, differences between the sources are more apparent: see Figure 4.5. Inequality is higher according to the HBAI series, particularly reflecting differences at the top of the distribution and the SPI adjustment, with the divergence beginning in the second half of the 1990s—as discussed earlier. Consistent with this, the differences between the series are greatest for the GE(2) inequality index which, of the indices considered, is the most sensitive to income differences at the top of the distribution. The differences between series are smallest (and trends are most similar) for the *p*90/*p*10 percentile ratio measure, which is not affected at all by incomes above the 90th percentile or below the 10th percentile.

Reflecting the problems of securing reliable measurement of incomes at the very top and the very bottom of the income distribution, and the potential lack of robustness of summary measures to outlier values at the top and the bottom of the distribution, it is often suggested that income data should be trimmed prior to analysis. Figure 4.6 shows what happens to the inequality estimates if this suggestion is implemented. Specifically, the bottom 1 per cent

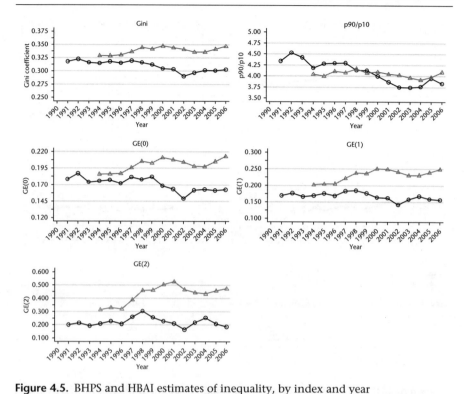

Figure 4.5. BHPS and HBAI estimates of inequality, by index and year

Notes: Within each chart, BHPS estimates are shown using round markers (and black lines) and the HBAI estimates using triangle markers (and grey lines). The inequality indices are the Gini coefficient (Gini), the ratio of the 90th percentile to the 10th percentile (*p90/p10*), mean logarithmic deviation (GE(0)), Theil index (GE(1)), and half the coefficient of variation squared (GE(2)).
Source: Jenkins (2010*a*).

and top 1 per cent of the distribution for each year and source are dropped prior to calculations of each index.

The result is that each BHPS index series is now much closer to its HBAI counterpart. There is a suggestion of a slight decrease in inequality up to around 2002 according to the BHPS but not the HBAI series. But both series suggest that inequality increased slightly after 2002 according to all indices. The trimming removes SPI-adjusted observations from the HBAI distributions, and note the impact on estimates of top-sensitive GE(2) in particular. The differences remaining between the series arise from the combination of relatively small differences throughout the income range, above and below the median (see Figure 4.3).

Of course, comparisons of the two sources need to consider potential differences at the level of population subgroups and specific income sources, not only for differences in the distribution of total net income among the

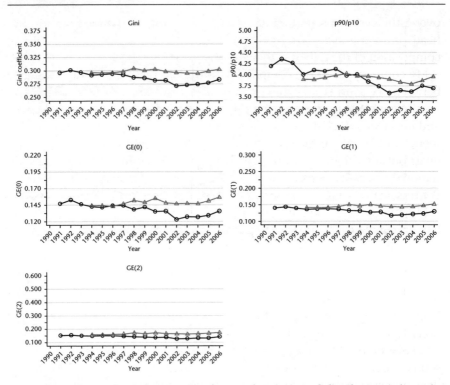

Figure 4.6. BHPS and HBAI estimates of inequality (trimmed distributions), by index and year

Notes: As for Figure 4.5, except that each inequality estimate is derived using a distribution from which the richest 1% and the poorest 1% of observations have been dropped.

population as a whole in a given year. In Jenkins (2010*a*), I show that BHPS estimates of the proportions of individuals in different family types or in different groups defined by the economic status of the family to which they belong are remarkably similar to those derived from HBAI data, using definitions of the subgroups that are the same as those employed by the Department for Work and Pensions (2009*b*).

Some differences between series appear when the focus is more detailed, however. For example, I also consider the subgroup composition of the poorest fifth and of the richest fifth of the distribution in each year according to the two sources (Jenkins 2010*a*). The family-type breakdowns suggest that BHPS produces an over-estimate of the proportion of single pensioners, especially women, in the poorest fifth of the distribution throughout the period as a whole. (For example, in 2006, the proportion of the poorest fifth who are female single pensioners is 14 per cent compared with 9 per cent in the HBAI.) Consistent with this, the economic status breakdowns indicate that the BHPS over-estimates the proportion of individuals in workless families containing a head or spouse aged 60+ in the poorest fifth. Estimates of the subgroup composition of the richest fifth are relatively close in both sources.

My comparisons of the composition of net household income distinguish between six sources for which comparable definitions in both sources are possible: income from employment, income from self-employment, benefits and tax credits (including the state retirement pension), income from investments and savings, other income (for example, transfers from private individuals outside the household), plus payments of income and local taxes and national insurance contributions (deductions which are 'negative' income). For this analysis, income is not equivalized.

My breakdowns (Jenkins 2010a) suggest that the BHPS under-records labour income relative to the HBAI. For example, for 2006, average household income from employment is £487 per week according to the BHPS, but £526 per week according to the HBAI. Deductions are also under-estimated, which most likely reflects the fewer details available in the BHPS to estimate them relative to the FRS/HBAI. For example, for 2006, deductions are £202 in the HBAI, but £166 in the BHPS. These two features offset each other, so that net household income totals are quite similar across sources (£551 in the BHPS and £571 in the HBAI in 2006, a difference of 4 per cent). Differences between sources do not appear as large if one summarizes income composition in terms of shares of the total. For instance, for 2006, the share of employment income in total net household income is 88 per cent according to the BHPS and 92 per cent according to the HBAI, and the shares of deductions are –30 per cent and –35 per cent, respectively. For other income sources, differences in corresponding shares of the total across sources is always less than two percentage points. When the focus is on income packaging for the poorest fifth or for the richest fifth of the distribution, there are similar offsetting patterns. And for both the distribution as a whole, and for the richest and poorest fifths, there is no apparent change in these patterns over the period 1994–2006.

Earlier sections raised the possibility that changes in the BHPS survey design may have affected income distribution estimates. Reassuringly, my analysis in Jenkins (2010a) reveals no obvious discontinuities in the BHPS series associated with either the introduction of CAPI (wave 9, survey year 1999) or of dependent interviewing (wave 16, survey year 2006).

Overall, use of the BHPS net income distributions data as a longitudinal complement to the HBAI appears to be valid, especially if the focus is not on the very poorest or the very richest incomes. Much of this book is concerned with movements into or out of poverty, and unlikely to be affected by the outlier values at the very bottom (or indeed the top) in the sense that poverty status is unlikely to be mis-measured. Also, the poverty lines I use are mostly fractions of median income, and these appear relatively well estimated according to HBAI benchmarks. In contrast, analysis of cross-sectional inequality and of longitudinal income mobility throughout the distribution is likely to more sensitive to mis-measurement of incomes at the extremes. My analysis suggests that trimming of observations at the very top or the very bottom of the distribution is a useful way to address this issue, and I do this in Chapters 5 and 6.

Part II
Income Mobility

Part II

Income Mobility
over Time

5

Income Mobility and How it has Changed over Time

The aim of this chapter and the next is to document the pattern of income mobility within multi-year subperiods between 1991 and 2006 and also to examine how mobility changed between subperiods. In general terms, mobility occurs when an individual's income changes over time, where the change may be defined in absolute terms (an increase or decrease of so many pounds) or in terms of a change in income position relative to other people in the population. I describe income movements throughout the income range, considering low, middle, and high-income origins and destinations. (Movements into and out of low income—poverty dynamics—are the focus of Chapter 7.) In this chapter, I argue that there are four ways to look at mobility, and provide evidence about three of the perspectives. The fourth perspective, referring to aspects of income risk and insecurity—as measured by transitory variability and volatility—is the subject of Chapter 6.

The analysis in both this chapter and Chapter 6 is of short-term mobility, that is, it is primarily about longitudinal changes in income between one year and the next or some later year. Longer-run mobility, specifically the shape of a person's life-course income trajectory, is examined in Chapter 7. Mobility over an even longer term, such as described by the association between the incomes of parents and children, is not considered in this book. Although intergenerational mobility is of much contemporary academic and policy interest in Britain (cf. Cabinet Office 2008), short-term mobility is also of interest, for the reasons I shall outline shortly.

Earlier work for Britain (Jarvis and Jenkins 1998), based on four waves of BHPS data, established that there is substantial income mobility from one year to the next, and for all income groups, but also found that most mobility is only short distance. This chapter and the next take the opportunity afforded by having 16 waves of BHPS data about net household incomes. I summarize income mobility using a broader portfolio of methods than the earlier research and also extend the analysis to examine how income mobility has changed over time.

This chapter and the next also focus on mobility assessed in terms of a relatively comprehensive measure of personal economic well-being (net household income) for the population as a whole, rather than using narrower measures of income for particular subgroups, such as employment earnings among men. As emphasized in Chapter 1, this book is concerned with aspects of social welfare assessment and that requires consideration of the experience of all individuals and using a broadly defined measure of living standards. However, in this chapter, I also contrast the experience of different groups within the population, differentiated by age, for example. There are further breakdowns by income source in Chapter 6. I also undertake analysis of men's earnings mobility in order to help explain the findings for household income (since labour earnings are the most important source of income for the vast majority of households of working age) and to compare my findings with previous research, much of which has been concerned with earnings mobility. The two chapters also include some cross-national comparisons with other European countries and North America in order to place the results for Britain in context. Comparisons with the USA receive most attention in Chapter 6, as this is a country for which transitory variability and volatility have been intensively studied recently.

The first section of this chapter discusses what income mobility is and discusses why the pattern of short-term mobility in a society is of public interest. The principal theme is that mobility has multiple features and the different dimensions relate to social welfare in potentially conflicting ways. From some perspectives, more mobility is a Good Thing; from others, it is a Bad Thing. It depends on whether one is interested in changes in relative position, individual income growth, reduction of longer-term inequality, or income risk. The task of this chapter is not to argue in favour of one position or another; rather it is to provide descriptive information relevant to such discussion, illuminating the nature of mobility patterns and trends using multiple perspectives. This analysis is presented in the remaining sections of the chapter and in Chapter 6.

The principal finding from the two chapters is that income mobility in Britain hardly changed at all over the period 1991–2006 according to almost all types of measure. This is in contrast to the situation in the USA where, as I discuss in Chapter 6, there is growing consensus that mobility in the shape of income risk has increased. The factors lying behind the lack of a trend in income mobility in Britain, and the transatlantic contrast, are explored towards the end of Chapter 6.

5.1. What is Income Mobility and Why is it of Public Interest?

Income mobility has many facets, as Gary Fields (2006) put it, and its various features have different, potentially offsetting, implications for social assessments. There is less agreement about what is meant by more or less mobility than there is agreement about what is meant by more or less inequality or poverty. Inequality and poverty refer to features of the distribution of income at one point in time. Inequality and poverty comparisons of 1991 and 2006 (say) do not require information about whether the individuals with low incomes in the initial year are the same people as those who have low incomes in the later year. Only relevant is the information about the change in overall dispersion or prevalence of low income. The concept of mobility is inherently more complex because the relationship between income origin and income destination is an essential ingredient of its measurement. Different ways of summarizing this longitudinal relationship, and of taking into account how it depends on the cross-sectional origin and destination distributions (if at all), are what lead to different mobility concepts.

Reviews of income mobility concepts and summary measures include Atkinson, Bourguignon, and Morrisson (1992), Fields (2006), Fields and Ok (1999a), and Jenkins and Van Kerm (2009). Drawing on this literature, I distinguish between mobility as positional change, mobility as individual income growth, mobility as reduction of longer-term inequality, and mobility as income risk.

Intrinsic to the concept of mobility as positional change is the idea that mobility for a specific individual depends on other people's positions as well. That is, the definition of each person's origin and destination depends also on the positions of everyone else in the society: it is these taken altogether that define a hierarchy of positions. (For specific measures, position can be defined in terms of income or the rank implied by that income.) Positional change mobility then refers to the pattern of exchange of individuals between positions over time, while abstracting from any change in the distribution of positions in each year—that is, 'structural mobility' rather than 'exchange mobility' (see, for example, Markandya 1984). Mobility for a person depends not on whether his or her income has increased or decreased but on how the change alters his or her position relative to others. Equi-proportionate income growth for everyone raises all incomes but there is immobility in the positional sense: the relative chances of moving to the top rather than bottom are unchanged. With positional change mobility, not everyone can be upwardly mobile.

Measures of positional change encapsulate the situation of maximal or 'perfect' mobility in two different ways. One view is that perfect mobility occurs when one's income destination is completely unrelated to one's income origin ('origin independence'). For example, the chances of being found in the richest tenth in 2006 are exactly the same for people who were in the poorest tenth in 1991 as for the people who were in the richest tenth in 1991. Another view is that perfect mobility occurs when destination positions are a complete reversal of origin positions ('rank reversal'), emphasizing positional movement per se. For example, the poorest person in 1991 is the richest person in 2006, and the richest person in 1991 is the poorest person in 2006. Summary measures of (the lack of) positional change between incomes in a pair of years include the correlation of incomes or the income rank correlation. Another commonly used measure is the proportion of persons who remain in the same tenth of the income distribution, or other measures derived from transition matrices classifying individuals into categories according to their origin and destination incomes.

Individual income growth refers to measures summarizing the change in income experienced by each individual within the society between two points in time. The change might be a gain or a loss, and can be summarized in absolute terms (an increase or decrease of so many pounds per week) or in proportionate terms (expressed as a percentage of original income). Income growth is defined for each individual separately and income mobility for society overall is derived by aggregating the mobility experienced by each individual. This mobility concept contrasts sharply with the positional change measure: positive income growth for everyone counts as mobility even if relative positions are preserved. An example of a summary measure is the simple arithmetic average across all persons of each person's income growth between a pair of years. This belongs to the family of 'directional' mobility indices proposed by Fields and Ok (1999*b*). They also proposed 'non-directional' mobility measures, which are calculated from absolute values of an income change (for example, a change of –£100 and of +£100 are each counted as £100). Non-directional indices summarize the degree of income movement in a society rather than of mobility as it is usually understood. I do not discuss these measures further for that reason.

The third mobility concept links income mobility with its impact on inequality. Income mobility means that, between one year and the next, income varies for most people. So, in any given year, the income for that year for an individual will differ from the average of his income taken over several successive years. Averaging across time smoothes the longitudinal variability in each person's income and, in addition, differences across individuals in these longitudinally averaged incomes will be less than the dispersion across individuals in their incomes for any single year. Mobility can therefore be characterized in terms of the speed at which inequality is reduced as the reference period for income is lengthened from one year to a longer period (Shorrocks 1978, 1981). More mobility corresponds to a greater reduction in inequality over a reference period of given length. The amount of mobility—the degree of the inequality reduction—depends on which inequality index is chosen to summarize income differences (Schluter and Trede 2003).

Related to the mobility-as-inequality-reduction idea is the decomposition of inequality in a given year into 'permanent' and 'transitory' variance components. Suppose each person's income in a given year is the sum of an unobserved 'permanent' component that is fixed over time and an uncorrelated unobserved transitory component that fluctuates randomly over time. Mobility from one year to the next arises from transitory variation in income according to this model: idiosyncratic random shocks lead to divergence between current-year income and 'permanent' income. If the model of income generation is correct, and the permanent component is estimated well by the longitudinal average of a person's income, there is a correspondence between the inequality of longer-period income described in the previous paragraph and inequality of the permanent component described in this paragraph. The inequality reduction that arises from lengthening the reference period, as described earlier, represents the smoothing out of transitory income variation.

The concepts of mobility as inequality-reduction and transitory variation diverge when the process describing income generation is not a simple sum of permanent and transitory components. (Strictly speaking, they diverge even in that case because such models are typically written in terms of the logarithm of income rather than income itself and so the inequality measure is the so-called 'variance of the logs'. For this index, it is possible for extensions to the income period not to reduce inequality: see Shorrocks 1978.) As I discuss in Chapter 6, models have been developed with more complicated descriptions of how the permanent and transitory components evolve over time. However, the distinction between relatively fixed elements of income and random (and hence unpredictable) shocks is maintained, and the focus remains on the transitory variance of income, motivated by its connection to the concept of income risk.

Mobility and the Public Interest

In what ways are these various mobility concepts of public interest? If there is greater mobility in the sense of less association between origins and destinations, society is arguably more open and there is greater equality of opportunity. More mobility is therefore a Good Thing since equality of opportunity is a principle that is widely supported, regardless of attitudes to inequality. This is relevant because independence of origins and destinations is consistent with inequality of outcomes being relatively equal or unequal. The argument just rehearsed is, however, typically made in the context of intergenerational mobility rather than intragenerational mobility, and origins refer to parental circumstances ('family background'). The appeal to fairness in this context is based on the meritocratic idea that someone's life chances should depend on their own abilities and efforts rather than on who their parents were. But, in the intragenerational context, the income origin is measured within a person's life and the outcome for an adult already reflects these abilities and efforts (as well as family background and other factors). To the extent that this is so, it might be argued that initial positions are 'fair' on the grounds of desert and hence, correspondingly, that independence between origins and destination has less appeal as a principle of social justice. This book is not the place to adjudicate on the issue; my intention is simply to point out that assessment of within-generational mobility is more complicated than is sometimes assumed.

Perhaps less controversial are views about mobility and inequality. It is commonly assumed by economists that having lower inequality improves social welfare (holding average income constant). Greater inequality at a point in time is more tolerable if accompanied by significant mobility because mobility smoothes transitory variations in income so that 'permanent' inequality is less than observed inequality. From this perspective, more mobility is also a Good Thing. (See Gardiner and Hills 1999 for further discussion of this interpretation of mobility.) Overall, social verdicts about mobility, and the emphasis put on observed versus 'permanent' income variations, are likely to depend on the extent to which intertemporal income smoothing is feasible. The usual view is that the terms on which people can borrow or save favour the rich rather than the poor. If you do not have assets to draw on, and cannot borrow except at very high rates, it is current income that matters rather than some (hypothetical) longer-term average income.

The relationship between individual income growth and social welfare is ambiguous. At the individual level, an income rise is a Good Thing and an income fall is a Bad Thing. Income growth universally experienced clearly corresponds to upward mobility from this perspective; indeed, it is possible for everyone to experience upward mobility and no one to experience downward mobility. (This view appears to form part of recent UK government thinking about social mobility: see Cabinet Office 2008, 2009; Panel on Fair Access to the Professions 2009.) This cannot be the case with mobility-as-positional-change. In practice, it is always the case that over time some people gain and some lose, even when average income is growing strongly. Evaluation of the impact of individual income growth on the welfare of society as a whole therefore requires a weighing up of the gains and losses for different people, and opinions are likely to differ about how to do this. What is important is who experiences the income growth. An egalitarian may weight income gains for the poor greater than income gains for the rich because this will contribute to reducing income differences between them. But arguments to the contrary, appealing to principles of desert or incentives, might also be made. It might be argued, for instance, that, if income gains among the rich reflect appropriate returns to their entrepreneurial activity (which is to be encouraged), differential mobility is of less concern. The argument is harder to make in the case of, say, the rise in bankers' bonuses in the manner observed in Britain in recent years.

Income mobility is more clearly a Bad Thing if the mobility-as-transitory-variation view is taken. In this case, mobility is a synonym for income fluctuation and also economic insecurity. Fluctuating incomes are undesirable because most people prefer greater stability in income flows to less, other things being equal, if only because it facilitates easier and better planning for the future. But, more than this, by definition, transitory income variation is an idiosyncratic shock which cannot be predicted at the individual level: greater transitory variation corresponds to greater income risk, and this is undesirable. How undesirable it is depends on the extent to which individuals are insured against such risks.

In this assessment, it is important to distinguish between transitory variation in an individual's labour earnings and transitory variation in a more comprehensive measure of economic well-being, such as equivalized household net income. Insurance against labour income risk is provided by social insurance against income loss due to unemployment, ill-health, and retirement because of old age, and by public and private schemes covering income loss through accidental injury or sickness. Individuals may also self-insure by accumulating stocks of assets that can be drawn on in bad times, by adjusting their labour supply, or by income sharing within families (for example, a spouse might work more hours if her partner is laid off). A comprehensive household income measure is intended to include income from these sources, and income accrues to all persons in the population (whereas earnings only go to individuals in paid work). Thus transitory variations in measures of household income are more plausibly associated with income risk that is of social consequence than transitory variations in the labour earnings of an individual.

The argument that transitory variation in income is a good measure of risk needs to be tempered because household income outcomes (as well as labour income outcomes) partially reflect choices made voluntarily and hence of less social concern. Income falls arising from choosing to work shorter hours are less socially worrisome than falls arising from lay-offs associated with firm closures, and it is moot whether changes in income associated with changes in household composition, such as family formation or dissolution or the birth of a child, should be treated as wholly voluntary (Burgess et al. 2000). For a model-based approach to identifying earnings uncertainty, see Cunha, Heckman, and Navarro (2005).

121

Because it is difficult to distinguish variations arising from these types of income change from variations arising from involuntary and unpredictable sources, and also because there are practical problems with estimating transitory income variation, changes in transitory variation over time are imperfect measures of changes in income risk. For this reason, there is a growing US literature which supplements estimates of transitory variation trends with estimates of trends in income 'volatility'—which can be interpreted as descriptive summary measures of the mobility-as-fluctuations dimension referred to earlier. Other US researchers have estimated how the prevalence of a large income fall has been changing over time. The idea is that it is negative rather than positive income shocks that contribute to the dimension of economic insecurity of social concern. That the relevant summary statistic is straightforward to calculate and communicate is also seen as a virtue. These issues are illustrated in the empirical analysis for Britain that follows in Chapter 6.

The discussion so far demonstrates that the relationship between intragenerational income mobility and social welfare is a complicated one. Whether an increase in mobility corresponds to a social improvement depends on which concept of mobility is emphasized. This conclusion is underlined by the theoretical analysis of Gottschalk and Spolaore (2002). Using a relatively general specification for the social welfare function to assess the joint distribution of income at two points in time, they show that whether an increase in income mobility corresponds to a net social improvement depends on the relative sizes of three parameters encapsulating social preferences—the degrees of inequality aversion, aversion to intertemporal income fluctuations, and aversion to future income risk. Gottschalk and Spolaore's (2002) comparison of intragenerational income mobility in the USA and Western Germany illustrates how different social preferences—represented by different combinations of parameters in their model—lead to different conclusions about which country has the greater mobility.

Because income mobility has conflicting implications for social welfare, it is important to present information about income mobility from multiple perspectives. This is the approach taken in the sections that follow and Chapter 6. Regardless of the normative implications of the findings, they are also of interest for their descriptive content, documenting aspects of social structure in the same way that information about income inequality does.

5.2. BHPS Samples and Income Measures

The empirical analysis for this chapter is based on waves 1–16 (survey years 1991–2006) of the BHPS, using data for individuals belonging to the original sample that began in 1991. The principal measure of income used for individuals is their real equivalized net household income, computed using the modified-OECD equivalence scale and expressed in pounds per week (January 2008 prices) pro rata. For further details of the sample and the income measure, see Chapters 2 and 4. I also employ two further measures to facilitate comparisons with earlier research. I use a less broad measure of household income for all individuals, namely real equivalized gross household income, which is the same as net income except that income tax, national insurance, and local payments have not been deducted. In Chapter 6, I also consider transitory variability in real monthly labour earnings for male employees aged between 25 and 55 years.

All calculations have been undertaken using data that are weighted to address potential issues of non-response, including attrition. For the most part, the longitudinal analyses employ the cross-sectional enumerated individual weight for the most recent wave used in a particular calculation rather the longitudinal enumerated individual weights, as these exist only for survey members with complete response sequences since panel entry (see Chapter 4). However, most calculations were repeated using the longitudinal weights and also with no weights at all, and the results are insensitive to the choice made.

All income distributions are trimmed to inoculate estimates against the adverse effects of outlier income values and changes: the bottom 1 per cent and the top 1 per cent of observations are dropped prior to the calculation of all longitudinal measures. (See the discussion of trimming in Chapter 4.) Preliminary investigations suggested that this was important. On the lack of robustness of mobility measures to rogue outlier values, also see Cowell and Schluter (1998). Trimming to avoid these problems is common practice in research on this topic: see, for example, Gottschalk and Moffitt (2009) and references therein.

In this chapter (and others to follow), I do not routinely report standard errors for estimates or undertake formal tests of statistical inference, though I provide indicative estimates of sampling variability when drawing conclusions about mobility trends. The aim is to focus the discussion on substantive findings, while communicating awareness of their reliability. In this respect, non-sampling error is also likely to be particularly relevant, including measurement error (for the reasons discussed in Chapter 2). I adopt several strategies to address this problem. First, a number of mobility measures are estimated using three-year longitudinally averaged incomes rather than single-year income, on the grounds that this may average out measurement error (to the extent that it is 'classical—see Chapter 2). I also re-estimate mobility measures using subsamples for which measurement error is expected to be less of a problem. That is, I drop observations from households in which at least one individual is in full-time self-employment, or if household gross income contains imputed data (see Chapter 4). More details are provided later, but the headline finding is that the conclusions drawn about mobility trends are robust to these adjustments.

In the subsequent sections of this chapter, I provide information about patterns of income mobility in Britain and how they have changed since 1991. I consider, in turn, mobility in terms of changes in relative position and as individual income growth. Income risk, as measured by transitory variation and volatility, is considered in Chapter 6.

5.3. Mobility as Change in Relative Position and Individual Income Growth

I begin with positional change. For 1991 BHPS sample members classified in terms of their income position, we can ask where they are located in subsequent years—in the short term (one or two years later) and up to almost half a generation (15 years) later. A series of transition matrices summarizing

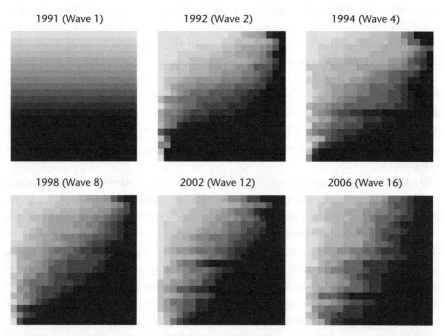

1991 (Wave 1)   1992 (Wave 2)   1994 (Wave 4)

1998 (Wave 8)   2002 (Wave 12)   2006 (Wave 16)

Figure 5.1. Changes in relative position over a 16-year period from 1991 income origins

Notes: Weighted estimates of vingtile transition matrices derived from a balanced sample of all individuals (adults and children) with valid household income data at BHPS waves 1, 2, 4, 8, 12, and 16. The poorest 20th of each year's distribution are at the top of each chart, and the richest 20th are at the bottom. The poorest 20th in 1991 are shaded light grey; the richest 20th in 1991 are shaded black. See text for further explanation of the charts.

the movement (or lack of it) between 1991 origins and later-year destinations is the conventional way of answering this question. I employ this device as well but represent it in terms of pictures rather than presenting a mass of statistical detail that is harder to digest.

I line the 1991 sample up in ascending order of income, and split them into 20 equal-sized groups. This defines the poorest 20th, the next-poorest 20th, and so on through to the richest 20th of individuals. This parade is shown in the '1991' picture of Figure 5.1. There is a strip for each income group, with the poorest group at the top of the picture and the richest group at the bottom. Different shades of grey are used to tag people in terms of their relative position in 1991: the poorest in 1991 with the lightest shade of grey, through to the richest in 1991 with black. For later years, the same conventions are maintained: the poorest group in each year is shown in the top strip of that year's picture and the richest group for that year in the bottom strip, and 1991 income group membership is indicated by shades of grey.

Movement between groups over time is shown by the extent to which the 1991 groups—identified by the different grey scales—are found in different strips from their original one. If there were no changes in relative position over time, the picture for a later year would be identical to the 1991 picture. If there were maximal mobility, defined in terms of a complete reversal of positions, then the later-year picture would look like the 1991 picture turned upside down (the original poor would be at the bottom and the original rich at the top). If there were maximal mobility, defined instead as complete independence of destination from origin, then the later-year picture would be a 90-degree rotation of the 1991 one: there would be equal numbers from each origin group in each destination group.

Figure 5.1 shows the changes in position at intervals from one year after 1991 through to 15 years later. It is immediately apparent that there is a lot of mobility even over a one-year interval, but the mobility is primarily short distance. Just over one-half (54 per cent) of those in the poorest tenth in 1991 moved out of the poorest tenth within a year, and nearly one in four of those in the richest tenth (37 per cent) moved down to a lower income group. Long-range mobility is rare: most of the movement is to nearby groups. Between 1991 and 1992, less than 2 per cent from the poorest tenth moved up to the richest tenth, and vice versa. As the period of observation is lengthened, there is a noticeable increase in the extent to which destinations differ from origins. (This mobility does not simply reflect the systematic variation of income with age: the mobility picture based on age-adjusted incomes looks similar.) It is also remarkable that about half a generation later, in 2006, there remains a substantial association between where people started in 1991 and where they ended up in 2006. This is indicative of significant differences in income that persist over time—an aspect that I focus on in the next section.

Table 5.1. Positional change over a 16-year period, by summary index and year

Summary index	Immobility index (association between incomes in 1991 and incomes in a later year)				
	1992	1994	1998	2002	2006
Correlation (income), %	80	69	64	43	37
Correlation (log income), %	75	67	63	44	38
Rank correlation, %	78	67	62	44	38
Percentage remaining on leading diagonal of decile transition matrix	37	28	24	18	17
Percentage remaining on leading diagonal of decile transition matrix or one cell either side	73	62	54	45	39
Average absolute change (£ p.w.)	4.3	5.9	17.7	52.3	66.7
Average percentage change (%)	1.7	3.2	8.1	20.7	24.6

Notes: Weighted estimates from a balanced sample of all individuals (adults and children) with valid household income data at BHPS waves 1, 2, 4, 8, 12, and 16.

The pictures of mobility here are not simply the consequence of income changes associated with life-cycle earnings growth—the same patterns appeared when I looked at changes in incomes that had been adjusted for the effects of variation with age beforehand.

The story told by the pictures is underlined by the numerical summaries presented in Table 5.1. The correlation between people's incomes one year apart is about 80 per cent. After three years, the correlation between 1991 and 1994 incomes falls to 69 per cent and then continues to decline. The correlation for incomes 15 years apart is down to 37 per cent, less than half the two-year correlation, but still a long way from the value of zero corresponding to origin independence. Differently defined correlations, between log incomes or income ranks, tell the same story. The degree of immobility is also summarized by the proportion of individuals who remain in the same income group, where origin and destination income groups are defined in terms of tenths of the income distribution. Between 1991 and 1992, 37 per cent remain in the same tenth of the income distribution, which is a long way from both total immobility (100 per cent remaining) and origin independence (10 per cent). The short-distance nature of most mobility is underlined by the fact that almost three-quarters of the 1991 sample are in the same income group or one group higher or lower in 1992. Clearly, the association between origins and destinations declines with time according to these measures as well. After 15 years, only 17 per cent of individuals remain in the same tenth of the income distribution as in 1991.

The final two rows of Table 5.1 provide information about mobility in the form of individual income growth, summarizing average growth in income levels and average percentage income growth respectively, both of which increase the longer the interval considered. The average difference between a person's 1991 income and their 1992 income was just over £4 per week, but after 15 years the average is an increase of nearly £67 per week. These correspond to average proportional increases of nearly 2 per cent and 25 per cent for the two time intervals, respectively.

The data can also be used to shed light on mobility trends. In Figure 5.2, I summarize trends in the association between incomes one year apart (years t and $t+1$, where t runs from 1991 to 2005). At the top of the picture are the estimates for the three correlations used in Table 5.1, and at the bottom of the picture are the estimates of the proportion of persons remaining in the same tenth of the income distribution between one year and the next. The correlation estimates tell a similar story: there was a slight increase in the year-on-year association over the first half of the 1990s, followed by a gradual decline so that the final estimate is much the same as the very first one. It is difficult to claim, however, that these statistics provide substantial evidence of changes in mobility rates over time. The maximum difference between estimates for different years of the correlation in incomes is about five percentage points, while the standard error for any one estimate is between one and two percentage points, implying that even the maximum difference is on the borderline of being statistically significant from zero. Also, there is little trend in the proportion remaining in the same tenth: it fluctuates within a narrow range

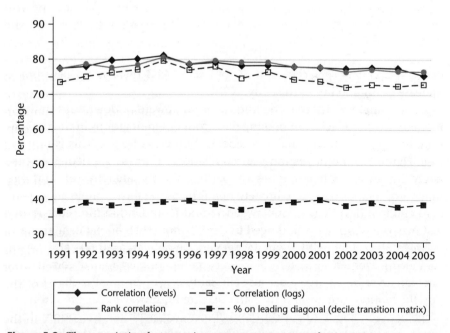

Figure 5.2. The association between incomes one year apart, by year

Notes: Statistics refer to associations between incomes for years t and $t+1$ in per cent. Weighted estimates from samples of all individuals (adults and children) with valid household income data for each pair of years.

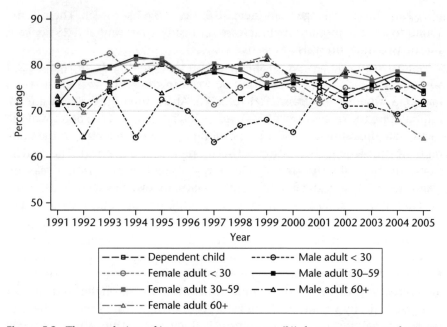

Figure 5.3. The correlation of incomes one year apart (%), by person type and year

Notes: Statistics refer to correlations between incomes for years *t* and *t*+1 (multiplied by 100). Weighted estimates from samples of all individuals with valid household income data for each pair of years. Person type refers to status in year *t*.

between about 37 per cent and 40 per cent. And there is no perceptible increase in immobility in the early 1990s.

Readers might worry that the finding of no upward or downward trend in mobility is an artefact from pooling data from different groups in the population, each of which may have experienced different trends. This is not the case. Figure 5.3 shows year-on-year correlations in incomes calculated separately for seven different types of person differentiated by sex and age (measured at year *t*). Approximately one-fifth of the total sample are dependent children (less than 16 or between 16 and 19 and in full-time education), just over one-tenth are adults aged under 30, more than 40 per cent are aged between 30 and 59, with about 10 per cent being men aged 60+ and 14 per cent being women aged 60+. For every group, the estimated correlations fluctuate over time, largely because the sample sizes are smaller than before. The fluctuations are around no particular trend, however. All the estimates range between about 70 per cent and 80 per cent, with the exception of the correlations for young male adults which are somewhat lower (that is, income mobility is greater for this group).

Mobility as positional change has also been documented for the USA in the 1970s, 1980s, and 1990s by Hungerford (1993, 2008), using decile transition matrices for family income calculated from PSID data. The results are similar to those for Britain in the sense that '[f]or the most part there was considerable movement within the distribution during the two observation periods (1969–76 and 1979–86), but the movement generally is not very great in either direction. The rags to riches success stories are fairly rare as well as riches to rags sob stories.' (Hungerford 1993: 414). Hungerford (1993, 2008) also suggests (as did Gittleman and Joyce 1999) that aggregate mobility in the USA did not change much between the 1970s and 1980s, but fell slightly between the 1980s and 1990s (when cross-sectional family income inequality increased). He reports that, between 1990 and 1999, around 73 per cent of individuals were in the same tenth or located within two decile groups (2008: 14). This corresponds to less mobility in the USA than in Britain (cf. Table 4.1).

My results about mobility trends in Britain are corroborated by the cross-national comparisons with Canada, Germany, and the USA undertaken by Chen (2009), also using a measure of equivalized household net income. He used data from the Cross-National Equivalent File (CNEF), which includes harmonized income and other variables from the BHPS, US PSID, German SOEP, and Canadian SLID (see Chapter 3). Chen also finds no systematic trend over the period 1991–2002 in the proportions of individuals who remain in the same tenth of the distribution between two consecutive years (2009: figure 1). He also shows that Britain was more mobile during the 1990s than Canada or Germany according to this measure. For example, the proportion for Britain is about 40 per cent or just below (as in Figure 5.2), but around 42 per cent or greater in Germany, and between 45 per cent and 50 per cent in Canada. Britain appears to have much the same level of mobility as the USA over the first half of the 1990s, with comparisons more difficult after 1996 (when the PSID moved to biannual interviewing). Chen (2009: figure 2) also calculates the proportion remaining in the same tenth for distributions five years apart. Britain appears to be slightly more mobile than the other three countries, with stayer proportions of around 25 per cent (with no upward or downward trend), compared with proportions of nearer 30 per cent elsewhere. I return to discuss Britain's mobility from a cross-national perspective at several points later on.

Accounting for the Effects of Measurement Error

Another potential issue concerns measurement error. To the extent that this adds random noise to income, and hence greater apparent movement over time, one would expect estimates of mobility from observed incomes to be biased upwards. That is, the degree of 'true' immobility is under-estimated if there is 'classical' measurement error. (See Chapter 2 for further discussion of the 'non-classical' nature of measurement error.) Measurement error is less likely to lead to bias in the estimates of mobility trends, however, as there is no reason to expect the structure of measurement error to have changed over time (the source composition of family income packages has not changed much over the period considered here), and its effects would cancel out.

One way of accounting for measurement error is to work with longitudinally averaged incomes on the grounds that this will smooth out the errors. To implement this idea, I compute three-year longitudinally averaged incomes and consider measures of positional mobility between '1992' and '1996' (each year label refers to the mid-year of the three years), and between '1999' and '2003'. As expected, the averaging reduces the estimated degree of mobility between any pair of years (correlations are larger). For example, the correlation between '1992' and '1996' incomes, that is, for incomes approximately four years apart, is 79 per cent, which compares with a correlation of around 69 per cent between non-averaged incomes for 1991 and 1994. The correlation between '1999' and '2003' incomes is 81 per cent, and so differs little from its counterpart for the earlier period. There are similar negligible increases in the correlations between log income and income ranks, from 80 per cent to 82 per cent and 78 per cent to 82 per cent respectively. The proportion of individuals remaining in the same tenth of the income distribution also remained much the same, falling very slightly between the two periods from 33 per cent to 31 per cent.

My overall conclusion is therefore that there is no trend for Britain in positional change mobility over the period from the beginning of the 1990s to the middle of the 2000s.

Individual Income Growth and its Progressivity

There is also no trend over time in mobility in terms of average individual income growth over a one-year interval: see Figure 5.4. Whether defined in terms of absolute changes in income or percentage changes, the average change fluctuates over the period 1991–2006. There is perhaps some general tendency for the indices to rise over the 1990s, and fall thereafter, but it is difficult to state this with confidence, especially given the outlier estimates for 2002. (The standard error for the absolute growth measure is typically between £1 and £2 and that for the proportionate growth measure about one percentage point, and so confidence bands are relatively wide.)

The no-strong-trend conclusion also emerges from estimates derived from three-year longitudinally averaged incomes as described above. For example, the average of individual income changes in absolute terms is £10 per week between '1992' and '1996' and only slightly higher at £13 per week between '1999' and '2003'. The corresponding estimates for income growth in proportional terms are 4 per cent and 5 per cent. These various estimates are

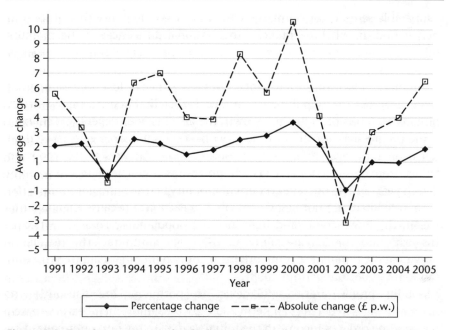

Figure 5.4. Trends in average individual income growth over a one-year interval

Notes: Statistics refer to the average of individual income changes between years *t* and *t*+1: the dashed line shows the average income change (£ per week); the solid line shows the percentage change (change in log income times 100). These are directional mobility indices proposed by Fields and Ok (1996, 1999*b*). Weighted estimates from samples of all individuals (adults and children) with valid household income data for each pair of years.

consistent with the gentle increase in average income over the period as a whole (see Chapter 4), but not exactly the same. Shown here is an average of changes rather than a change in average income or average log income.

From a cross-national perspective, Britain appears to be relatively mobile in terms of average individual income growth. Three studies have used income measures and samples broadly similar to those employed in this chapter. Van Kerm (2003) pools panel data for the 1990s for 16 European nations. Britain lies in the mid-range of countries ranked in terms of average proportional income growth. Ayala and Sastre (2008) use five waves of data from the European Community Household Panel to compare mobility in the UK, Germany, France, Italy, and Spain. Whether one looks at the 'short term' (1993–4) or the medium term (1993–7), average proportional income growth over the interval is similar in the UK and France, and greater than in Germany and, in turn, greater than in Italy and Spain, where the averages are close to zero (indices calculated from Ayala and Sastre 2008: table 2.) Chen (2009: table 1) presents some estimates of individual income growth over five-year intervals between 1991 and 2002 for Britain and three other countries. The most comparable series is for Germany, which has lower mobility than Britain in each period. In all three studies, cross-national differences of the mobility indices are difficult to assess because the countries were at different stages of the business cycle.

Summaries like Figure 5.4 do not show who gained or lost because they are averages across the population. I argued earlier that social assessments of mobility in terms of individual growth are also likely to depend on changes in the progressivity of the income growth—do poor people gain more than rich people, or vice versa, over a period of time? Answers to this question derived from cross-sectional data focus on groups of people defined separately in each year, and do not take account of mobility between income groups. The same individuals are not being compared in each year because there is turn-over in the low-income (and high-income) populations. To assess whether this year's poor (or rich) are gainers or losers, one has to track the fortunes of individuals of different income origins using longitudinal data (Jenkins and Van Kerm 2006; Hungerford 2008).

Mobility profiles are a useful device for portraying the distribution of income changes in detail (Van Kerm 2003, 2009). Sample members are ranked in ascending order of income in the initial year, with the ranks normalized by the population size, so that they run from zero through to one. Against these normalized ranks is then plotted the average income growth at each point. The average is plotted because people located at similar points of the base-year distribution experience different growth rates. This heterogeneity is not the primary focus here; rather the focus is on the differences across the whole of the income range. Estimation of the average at each point uses a smoothing process that gives greater weight to observations located close to the point and less weight to those further away.

The pattern of progressivity of income growth in Britain, and how it has changed over time, is shown in Figure 5.5. The horizontal axis shows normalized ranks, with the poorest in the initial year to the left and the richest to the right; the vertical axis shows the expected (average) income growth, in pounds per week, at each position. The solid line represents the pattern of income change for a period during the early to mid-1990s and the dashed line represents the pattern for a period spanning the late 1990s to early 2000s. Estimates are based on incomes longitudinally averaged over three-year periods, and each year label refers to the mid-point of a three-year period. The two horizontal lines (other than the line representing zero growth) show the average change for the two periods—the estimates of £10 and £13 mentioned earlier.

Figure 5.5 shows that, for both periods, income growth is negatively associated with position in the income parade: income growth is 'progressive' in the sense of reducing income differences. Those starting off at the bottom

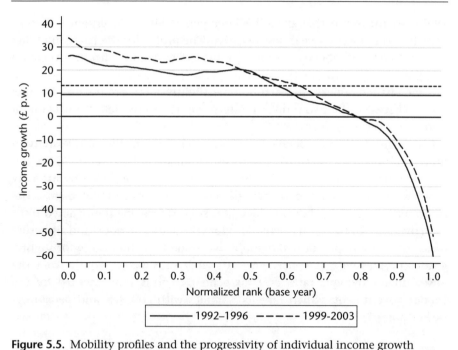

Figure 5.5. Mobility profiles and the progressivity of individual income growth

Notes: Estimates are based on incomes longitudinally averaged over three years. Year refers to the mid-point of three years. For example, '1992' incomes are longitudinally averaged incomes for 1991, 1992, and 1993. Weighted estimates from samples of all individuals (adults and children) with valid household income data for each set of six years. Normalized rank is defined in the text. Mobility profiles estimated using a local polynomial regression smoother of degree 1, bandwidth 0.05.

experience the largest income gains (on average), with the gain smaller the further you go up the distribution, and the richest fifth experience income falls. In part, these patterns reflect what is known as regression to the mean. Regardless of systematic changes associated with changes in the labour market or the tax-benefit system, if you have a low income, pure chance makes it more likely for an income change to be positive and also, if you have a high income, it is more likely that an income change is negative.

Although regression to the mean may induce a negatively sloped mobility profile, it does not determine its precise shape. For example, Figure 5.5 shows that profiles for Britain are approximately linear over the bottom four-fifths of the distribution. Broadly similarly shaped profiles arise if one instead plots (average) proportional income growth rather than absolute growth, except that the profiles are approximately linear over the middle 70 per cent of the distribution, with steeper sections at both ends (profiles not shown). Moreover, regression to the mean does not account for changes over time in the shape and location of mobility profiles. Figure 5.5 indicates that the pattern of income growth after 1999 represents a better situation than that for the early

1990s, in the sense that over the later period almost everyone's income change was more positive or less negative. The profile for the later period lies almost everywhere above the profile for the earlier period (with the exception being a crossing around the median person). In addition, the pattern of income change appears to have become slightly more progressive, because the gap between the two profiles is larger over the lower half of the distribution than over the upper half.

For further and more detailed analysis of changes in the progressivity of individual income growth in Britain, see Jenkins and Van Kerm (2011). We discuss how the picture of individual income growth provided by mobility profiles complements the picture derived from conventional approaches based on cross-sectional data (which also suggest that the poor gained more than the rich). Drawing on calculations for several time periods, and also using breakdowns by population subgroups, we argue that the finding of slightly greater progressivity is consistent with what one would expect from the lower unemployment rates and tax-benefit reforms implemented by the Labour government, which targeted families with children and pensioners (see Chapter 1).

5.4. Mobility as Inequality Reduction

This section documents the degree of mobility from the perspective of inequality reduction, and how it has changed over time, using the methods proposed by Shorrocks (1978). Shorrocks proposed an index of income rigidity or immobility, $R(m)$, equal to the inequality of m-year incomes divided by the weighted sum of the inequalities within each of the m years, where the year-specific weight is proportional to mean income of the period. The impact on inequality of lengthening the accounting period is summarized by the sequence of $R(m)$ values calculated for consecutive values of m up to some maximum. $R(m)$ declines as m increases because the averaging process smoothes out transitory fluctuations, and convergence to a limiting value is indicative of 'permanent' income differences. $R(m)$ lies between zero, the perfect mobility case in which extending the accounting period removes all longer-period inequality, and the case in which there is complete rigidity in relative incomes. For a variant on the Shorrocks index emphasizing inequality in the initial year as the reference point rather than a weighted sum of years, see Fields (2010). For a review of other generalizations, see Maasoumi (1998).

Figure 5.6 shows estimates of $R(m)$ for m varying from one up to the maximum number of years (16) that the BHPS net income data permit. The solid line shows estimates derived using the Gini coefficient as the inequality index and the dashed line shows estimates derived using the Theil index. It is

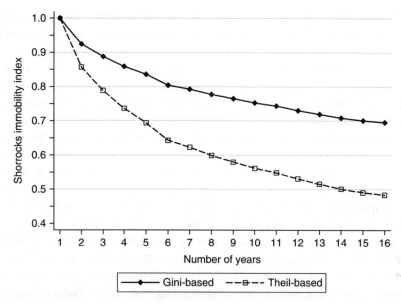

Figure 5.6. Income mobility and inequality reduction over a 16-year period

Notes: Weighted estimates from samples of all individuals (adults and children) with valid house-hold income data for all 16 years. Year 1 refers to 1991, year 2 to 1992, etc. Estimates derived using the mean logarithmic deviation (MLD) and half the coefficient of variation squared were very similar to those based on the Theil index.

important to use more than one inequality index because each one uses a different way of aggregating differences between smoothed and single-year distributions, and so leads to potentially different conclusions. Schluter and Trede (2003) show that most commonly used indices give greater weight to income smoothing at both the bottom and the top of the distribution relative to smoothing near the mean, but, among these indices, the variation in weights across the income range has a shallower U-shape for the Gini coefficient than for other indices. Calculations were also undertaken using the mean logarithmic deviation (MLD) and half the coefficient of variation squared—like the Theil index, members of the generalized entropy class of inequality indices. For brevity, results are not shown, because the estimates were numerically very similar to the Theil-based ones.

The estimates for both indices show that inequality declines steadily as the income reference period is extended, but, even after extending m from one to 16 years, significant persistent income differences remain. Lengthening the reference period to five years reduces the Gini coefficient by almost 15 per cent and the Theil index by about 30 per cent: $R(6) \approx 0.85$ and 0.70 respectively. After a further ten years, the longer-period Gini coefficient is about 30 per cent lower, and the Theil index 50 per cent lower, than their respective averaged single-year values: $R(16) \approx 0.70$ and 0.50 respectively. The smaller values for the Theil-based estimates of R arise because they give greater weight to mobility in the tails of the distribution than Gini-based estimates do.

To assess whether either series is indicative of a large or small degree of mobility, we can contrast its effect on inequality with the increases in income inequality in Britain that occurred during the 1980s—widely acknowledged to be large. Inequality measured using a similar income definition to that employed here was around 70 per cent lower in 1978 than in 1992 according to the Gini coefficient and 48 per cent lower according to the MLD (Brewer et al. 2009*a*). These numbers coincide with the estimates of $R(16)$, remembering that the MLD-based estimate is almost identical to the Theil-based one. Thus, over a similar-length interval, income mobility leads to an inequality reduction of the same magnitude as a historically large change in cross-sectional inequality.

Has the extent to which mobility reduces inequality changed over time? My estimates suggest not. Shorrocks immobility indices for ten six-year windows beginning in 1991 and ending in 2001, calculated using the same four inequality indices as before, are summarized in Figure 5.7. These estimates of

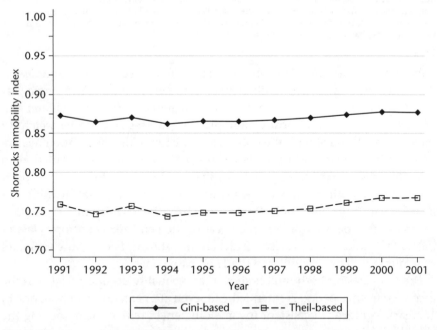

Figure 5.7. Income immobility (Shorrocks indices), by year

Notes: Weighted estimates of the Shorrocks immobility measure, $R(6)$, from samples of all individuals (adults and children) with valid household income data within six-year moving windows. Year 1 refers to 1991, year 2 to 1992, etc. Estimates derived using the mean logarithmic deviation (MLD) and half the coefficient of variation squared are very similar to those based on the Theil index.

$R(6)$ show no clear upward or downward trend. Arguably, immobility decreases slightly according to both indices in the middle of the period and then increases slightly from the mid-1990s onwards. However, this conclusion is hard to sustain because the changes are so small and unlikely to be statistically significant given that an approximate standard error for the Theil-based index, for instance, is approximately one percentage point.

When I focus instead on earnings for male employees aged between 25 and 55 at the start of each six-year period, I find that $R(6)$ also has no trend over time according to a Gini-based index (estimates not shown). According to a Theil-based index, there was a slight increase from the end of the 1990s onwards, but it is small and not statistically significant (the standard error is around one percentage point). In comparison, Dickens and McKnight (2008) report trends in estimates of R over the period 1978/9 to 2005/6 using large samples from administrative record data on British men's and women's earnings. There was a secular decline in men's earnings mobility over the 1980s which slowed at the start of the 1990s, that is, mobility fell as cross-sectional inequality rose. Unfortunately, a change in survey methodology in 1997 makes assessment of trends from the 1990s through to the mid-2000s difficult. Dickens and McKnight report a small decline in R (a small rise in mobility) at the very end of the period (figures 8–10), but it is only by at most a couple of percentage points. A claim that there has been no substantial change in mobility as inequality-reduction between the mid-1990s and mid-2000s seems safe to make.

Cross-national comparisons provide a benchmark against which to assess the British situation. Chen (2009), using CNEF data for Britain, Germany, Canada, and the USA over the period 1991–2002, provides the most directly comparable estimates for equivalized household income. According to MLD-based estimates of the immobility index R, Britain is distinctly more mobile than Germany which, in turn, is distinctly more mobile than Canada. For instance, taking 1993 as the initial year, $R(5)$ is 0.80 for Canada, around 0.75 for Germany, but about 0.70 for Britain. (The USA's position is similar to Germany's, but is difficult to assess because of the change to biannual interviewing in 1997 by the PSID. For an earlier study finding lower mobility in the USA than Germany during the 1980s according to R measures applied to earnings and household income, see Burkhauser and Poupore 1997.) When Chen (2009) extends the reference period to ten years, Britain remains distinctly more mobile than Germany: the $R(10)$ estimates are 0.61 and 0.71 respectively. Using inequality indices other than the MLD to calculate R does not change the country rankings. Leigh (2009) calculates estimates of $R(2)$ and $R(3)$ using CNEF data for Britain, Germany, and the USA, plus data for Australia (HILDA data were not included in the CNEF at the time). He finds that '[a]round 1990, the US was more immobile than either Britain or

Germany... During the 1990s, Germany became somewhat less mobile, and the US somewhat more mobile' (2009: 16) and that Australia was more mobile than all three other countries in the early 2000s.

Gangl (2005) compared income mobility between the USA and 11 European countries including the UK, using European Community Household Panel data covering 1994–9. His income definition is similar to mine but his sample is restricted to individuals aged 22–55 years. Gangl emphasizes similarities across countries rather than differences: for example, using a Theil-based index, 'about 75% to 80% of observed income inequality has been permanent over the 6-year observation period in most countries' (2005: 149–51). Nonetheless Germany, Ireland, and the USA are relatively immobile countries and the Netherlands and Denmark the most mobile. Interestingly, 'low-inequality countries... also tend to be the countries exhibiting the lowest degree of persistence in income inequality over time' (Gangl 2005: 151). Germany is an exception to this description: it is a relatively low-inequality country, but also has relatively high immobility. ECHP-based analysis by Gregg and Vittori (2009) comparing the mobility in labour earnings of individuals aged 20–64 across five countries provides rankings consistent with this. Inequality reduction is greatest in Denmark, followed by Italy, and Germany is the least mobile, with the UK and Spain in between.

5.5. Summary and Conclusions

I have argued that income mobility can be examined from four perspectives and provided information using three of them in this chapter. There are several clear findings.

First, there is a substantial degree of longitudinal flux in incomes between one year and the next, resulting in changes in relative position and a reduction in the inequality of longer-term incomes. It is also clear, however, that most income changes are relatively small and substantial inequalities in longer-term incomes remain after many years.

Second, the degree of longitudinal flux has remained remarkably constant during the period 1991–2006. It is only when one views mobility in terms of income growth and its progressivity that there appears to be some change over time. In particular, there appears to be a small increase in the extent to which longitudinal income growth benefits the poor rather than the rich after 1997. This can be explained by the lower unemployment rates and the redistributive reforms introduced by the Labour government.

Third, from a cross-national perspective, despite the increasing availability of comparable longitudinal data, it is difficult to draw clear-cut conclusions about income mobility in Britain relative to other countries. One of the issues is that research to date has tended to employ only one mobility concept and to analyse different selections of countries. The most secure conclusion is that Britain is more mobile than Germany. In terms of average income growth and inequality reduction, Britain appears to be a mid-ranking country relative to the EU nations included in the ECHP. Mobility in Britain appears to be much the same or slightly greater than in the USA in terms of positional change, but Chapter 6 shows that the reverse is the case for mobility defined in terms of transitory variation and volatility. Let us turn to examine this mobility concept in more detail.

6

Transitory Variation and Volatility in Income

This chapter continues the analysis begun in Chapter 5, examining mobility from a fourth perspective to add to the three perspectives considered earlier. According to this fourth mobility concept, longitudinal variability in income is indicative of economic risk and insecurity and summarized using measures of transitory variation and volatility of income. As argued in Chapter 3, these are imperfect and indirect measures of income risk, but useful all the same. Although household income risk is of greater social consequence than earnings risk for an individual (Chapter 3), most empirical studies have analysed men's employment earnings rather than household income. In this chapter, I present estimates using both types of income variable in order to check whether the conclusions drawn are sensitive to this choice and also to facilitate some cross-national comparisons, especially with the USA, a country for which the fourth dimension of mobility is receiving substantial attention.

In Sections 6.1–6.6, I consider transitory variation and volatility in turn, first defining the measures and then presenting BHPS-based estimates of them and their trends over time, together with some cross-national comparisons. I show that income mobility defined as income risk changed little in Britain over the period between the start of the 1990s and the mid-2000s, a result that echoes the no-change findings reported in Chapter 5. In Sections 6.7 and 6.8, I summarize the evidence about income mobility in Britain according to the four perspectives and consider explanations for the finding of no change in mobility over time.

6.1. Models of the Transitory and Permanent Variance Components of Income

To fix ideas, suppose that the dynamics of income can be described using the canonical random effects model:

$$y_{it} = u_i + v_{it}. \tag{6.1}$$

The logarithm of income for person i in year t, y_{it}, is equal to a fixed 'permanent' random individual-specific component, u_i, with mean zero and constant variance σ_u^2 (common to all individuals), plus a year-specific idiosyncratic random component with mean zero and variance σ_{vt}^2 (common to all individuals) that is uncorrelated with u_i. Thus total inequality as measured by variance of log income is equal to the sum of the variance of 'permanent' individual differences plus the variance of 'transitory' shocks:

$$\sigma_t^2 = \sigma_u^2 + \sigma_{vt}^2. \tag{6.2}$$

Assuming that permanent differences are relatively fixed over time, changes over time in income inequality arise mostly through changes in the variance of the transitory component. The interpretation of this latter component as idiosyncratic unpredictable income change leads to the association of changes in its variance with changes in income risk.

This canonical model is patently unrealistic in several respects and three types of extension have been incorporated. The first additional factor allows the relative importance for overall inequality of the permanent and transitory components to change with calendar time. For example, if there is an increase in the demand for skilled labour, and the permanent component of income represents relatively fixed personal characteristics related to skills (for example, human capitals of various kinds), then greater inequality resulting from widening differences over time in returns to skilled versus unskilled labour can be represented as the growing importance of the permanent component. In contrast, a secular trend towards greater labour market flexibility can be represented as a growth in the importance of transitory variations.

First, to allow for calendar time changes, equation (6.1) is modified to suppose instead that

$$y_{it} = \kappa_t u_i + v_{it}, \tag{6.3}$$

where κ_t is a year-specific 'factor loading' on the permanent component of income. Inequality trends and the permanent/transitory variance decomposition now also depend on trends in this weighting factor:

$$\sigma_t^2 = (\kappa_t)^2 \sigma_u^2 + \sigma_{vt}^2. \tag{6.4}$$

The second additional feature is persistence in transitory variation. The factors leading to a temporary fall (or rise) in income in one year are likely to have effects that last longer than a year: a transitory shock persists but with diminishing impact and eventually dies out. An example might be an accidental injury leading to a reduction in work hours that diminishes over time. This is characterized using a so-called autoregressive moving average process (ARMA) for v_{it}, labelled ARMA(p, q), in which parameters p and q characterize the nature of the persistence over time. For example, an ARMA(1, 1) process has the form

$$v_{it} = \rho v_{it-1} + \theta \epsilon_{it-1} + \epsilon_{it}. \tag{6.5}$$

If $\theta = 0$, then the variance of the transitory component this year is equal to a fraction—the square of the autoregression parameter (ρ^2)—of its variance in the previous year, a fraction ρ^4 of the variance two years ago, and so on. Transitory shocks die out quickly if ρ is small ($0.3^4 = 0.0081$ but $0.9^4 = 0.6561$). If $\rho = 0$, then the variance of the transitory component this year is equal to a weighted average of the variance of shocks this year and last year, with the latter receiving less weight (the weight is the square of the moving average parameter θ). Whereas we expect ρ to be positive (but no more than one), θ may be positive or negative. If someone is struck by bad luck two years in a row (ϵ_{it-1} and ϵ_{it} both negative), a negative value for θ implies that the effect of the past bad luck is dampened. The larger that p or q is in the ARMA(p, q) process, the longer the shadow that past shocks cast over present outcomes.

The third modification to the canonical model is to allow the fixed individual component to change over time. Two main approaches have been followed, originally distinct but now commonly combined. One is to allow u_i to vary over time via a 'random walk': this year's value is equal to last year's value plus or minus a random element. Instead of u_i, the 'permanent' component in (6.1) becomes

$$\mu_{it} = \mu_{it-1} + \pi_{it}. \tag{6.6}$$

Consider, for example, the case of a low-skilled car assembly plant operative who is laid off when the plant is closed and assembly transferred abroad (Gottschalk and Moffitt 2009). Although the worker may get another job later, this is likely to be at a lower wage—the change in earnings represents a permanent difference. Major health changes may have similar long-lasting impacts on income. The second approach allows for individual-specific rates of growth in income. The expression for the permanent component in (6.1) is modified so that it varies directly with time. Instead of u_i, we have

$$\mu_{it} = \mu_i + \beta_i a_t. \tag{6.7}$$

This is a 'random growth' model: β_i is the growth rate in income with age a_t (or work experience), equal to zero on average, but varying across individuals. Both a random walk and random growth lead to a fanning out of the income distribution over time, other things being equal. Rankings are preserved: those at the bottom stay at the bottom, but fall further behind those at the top, who stay at the top. It is increases in the transitory variance that increase mobility in the sense of reranking.

Using the terms 'permanent' and 'transitory' to label the components of income variability is potentially confusing if 'permanent' components vary over time and 'transitory' components persist. (Adoption of the more complicated specifications for the dynamics of income also makes it more difficult to straightforwardly identify the components of income variability that constitute idiosyncratic unpredictable risk.) The main distinction is between variations that do not change a person's long-run average income—they are mean-reverting shocks ('transitory')—and those that do ('permanent'). The permanent/transitory terminology remains in common use, largely through inertia and the convenience of familiarity and brevity, and so I follow custom in this book.

6.2. Estimation of the Transitory Variance: Econometric Methods

How are the transitory variance and its contribution to the overall variance of income estimated from longitudinal data? There is a long tradition of fitting econometric models to specifications incorporating one or more of the three extensions to the canonical model that have just been discussed. Applications of these 'variance components' (VC) models to the dynamics of men's earnings include Abowd and Card (1989), Baker (1997), Baker and Solon (2003), Chamberlain and Hirano (1999), Haider (2001), Gottschalk and Moffitt (2007), Guvenen (2009), Hause (1980), Lillard and Willis (1978), Lillard and Weiss (1979), MaCurdy (1982), Meghir and Pistaferri (2004), and Moffitt and Gottschalk (1995, 2002, 2008a, 2008b). Extensions include Browning, Ejrnæs, and Alvarez (2010) and Geweke and Keane (2000). All this research fits models to US or Canadian data for men. Two applications to British men's earnings data are Dickens (2000) and Ramos (2003). Daly and Valletta (2008) compare earnings dynamics in Britain, Germany, and the USA. An excellent review of VC modelling and recent extensions is provided by Meghir and Pistaferri (2010). There have been few applications to broader measures of household income: notable exceptions are Biewen (2005) for Germany, and Duncan (1983) and Stevens (1999) for the USA. The only studies applying these methods to British data on household income that I am aware of are Devicienti (2001) and Blundell and Etheridge (2010).

Although VC models have advantages for estimating transitory variances and their trends because of their sophisticated specifications to account for the complexities of income dynamics, they also have their weaknesses. These have been stated trenchantly by Shin and Solon, who write that 'the parametric models used ... are arbitrary mechanical constructs and the resulting estimates of trends can be sensitive to arbitrary variations in model specification' (2009: 4). To illustrate this point, they refer to Baker and Solon (2003), who fit general VC models to Canadian tax record data on men's earnings. The large sample facilitates more thorough specification checking than is possible with the smaller US (mostly PSID-based) data sets used in most previous studies. Shin and Solon report that Baker and Solon (2003) 'strongly rejected the restrictions of Moffitt and Gottschalk's (1995, 2002) preferred model and found that imposing those restrictions substantially biased the estimation of Canadian trends in components of earnings variation' (2009: 4–5). Guvenen (2009) also draws attention to the difficulties of differentiating between different VC specifications from the panel data sets on earnings that are typically available.

6.3. Estimation of the Transitory Variance: Descriptive Methods

Given these issues, simpler descriptive methods remain popular ways of estimating transitory variance trends. There have been three main approaches and, in this chapter, I report BHPS-based estimates for each of them. The first and simplest method, which I label MG1, was introduced by Moffitt and Gottschalk (2002) to complement their VC model estimates. It is used in Jacob Hacker's (2008) book, *The Great Risk Shift*, which received widespread coverage in the US press. (See also Hacker and Jacobs 2008.) The rationale for the MG1 method is that, if the canonical model set out in equations (6.1) and (6.2) is correct, the covariance between (log) incomes a sufficiently large number of years apart will estimate the permanent variance, and the transitory variance can be derived as a residual. The longer the interval, the less likely it is that the covariance will be contaminated by associations between persistent transitory shocks.

Shin and Solon (2009) use a prototypic VC model to show that the MG1 method provides biased estimates of the transitory variance and its trend if the permanent component's contribution changes over time: their result follows from equation (6.3) with variation in κ_t over time. Moffitt and Gottschalk are, of course, well aware of these issues, and acknowledged them in their 2007 paper. In subsequent work, they have used other descriptive methods (alongside their econometric ones).

Moffitt and Gottschalk's second descriptive method, which I label MG2, was applied by them in Gottschalk and Moffitt (1994b, 2009) and Moffitt and Gottschalk (2008b), and has also been used by several other authors including Gosselin (2008), Gosselin and Zimmerman (2008), and Keys (2008). These studies are all based on US data. Bartels and Bönke (2010) is an application of method MG2 to German household income and earnings data. Beach, Finnie, and Gray (2010) use the method to study men's and women's earnings in Canada.

The MG2 method works by first calculating the longitudinal average of each person's log income over a time window of fixed width, say T years. This provides an estimate of the person's 'permanent' income for that period. (If equation (6.1) describes the income generation process, the longitudinal average is an estimate of u_i.) The transitory incomes for each individual within the window are derived as a difference between this permanent income and observed log income, from which can be calculated the individual-specific transitory variance. The overall sample transitory variance is the average of these variances. The sample permanent variance for each window is calculated from the differences between each person's permanent income and the sample grand mean of these, with an adjustment to account for the fact that the mean contains a proportion of the transitory component that has not been fully averaged to zero over the T-year window. See Gottschalk and Moffitt (2009: 7) for full details of the formulae defining the MG2 method. Repetition of the calculations over a set of moving windows provides estimates of variance trends.

The MG2 method also provides biased estimates of the transitory variance and its trend if the permanent component's contribution changes over time. If (6.3) describes the income generation process rather than (6.1), a person's longitudinally averaged income is an estimate of their permanent income scaled by the longitudinal average of the κ_t, which may differ from one, and the transitory variance is over-estimated by a factor related to the variance in κ_t over the window. Using shorter-width windows for the calculations (smaller T) reduces the potential impact of this problem, but at the cost of reducing the statistical reliability of the estimate of each person's permanent income.

Without fitting sophisticated VC models—which brings its own problems, as discussed above—it is inevitable that measures derived using methods like MG1 and MG2 will reflect the variability from permanent shocks not just from transitory ones. Shin and Solon (2009) argue that this is a virtue of such measures:

> The recent interest in volatility trends stems in large part from a concern about whether earnings risk has increased. Because permanent shocks, such as those experienced by many displaced workers, are even more consequential than transitory ones, it makes good sense to include them in the measurement of earnings volatility. (Shin and Solon 2009: 9)

Their own calculations are based on a third measure, 'volatility', which has also been used by researchers including Dahl, DeLeire, and Schwabish (2007), Dynan, Elmendorf, and Sichel (2008), and Dynarski and Gruber (1997).

6.4. A Measure of Income Volatility

Volatility in a given year t, V_t, is measured by the sample standard deviation of the distribution of individual changes in log income between one year and an earlier year:

$$V_t = \text{sd}(y_{it+s} - y_{it}). \tag{6.8}$$

Changes are typically measured over a one- or two-year horizon: $s = 1$ or $s = 2$. The Fields and Ok (1996) directional index of individual proportional income growth (for which estimates were provided in Chapter 5) is the mean of the distribution of log income changes. Volatility is a measure of dispersion of the same distribution using one specific index of inequality. Of course, one could also look at trends in the complete distribution of year-on-year changes: see, for example, Shin and Solon (2009) who track percentiles of the US earnings-change distribution over time.

Shin and Solon (2009) argue that, although V_t also reflects both permanent and transitory variability, it is less susceptible than methods like MG1 to the impact of changes in κ_t over time. Specifically, they show that, if similar values of κ_t arise close together in time (which I view as a plausible assumption), V_t is a less biased measure of the transitory variance than MG1, and bias is minimized if income changes are taken over a one-year interval. There is another implication of having similar κ_t values occur close together that Shin and Solon do not comment on: the more this is so, the smaller is the variance of the κ_t within a fixed-length time window and hence the smaller the bias in an MG2 measure of the transitory variance. In my view, it is reasonable to assume that the variance of κ_t is relatively small for Britain in the 1990s. It is common to associate changes over time in the permanent component of earnings with changes in the rates of return to human capitals of various kinds. Walker and Zhu (2003) provide evidence that the average rate of return to wages of an extra year of education changed little between 1993 and 2001.

6.5. Trends in the Transitory Variance

I present BHPS-based estimates, derived using all three descriptive methods, both as a robustness check and because all have been used in the literature. I compare them with other estimates for Britain and the USA where possible. Following common practice, all the estimates presented are based on income variables adjusted in advance to remove the systematic variation of income with age. The idea is that such variation is predictable and hence less relevant to the concept of mobility as income risk. Thus, for each sample, income is first regressed on a fourth-order polynomial in age, and the analysis is of the residuals from the fitted equation. As it happens, analysis of unadjusted incomes leads to very similar conclusions. Estimates of the transitory variance are based on balanced samples of individuals with valid incomes for each year of a seven-year moving windows, with seven-year lags used in the case of MG1 and seven-year averaging in the case of MG2 (all estimates weighted). The sample sizes are around 4,000 persons from about 2,000 households for each window's sample. Repetition of the calculations using five-year windows does not change the conclusions.

Estimates derived from income data for all individuals are presented in Figure 6.1. Panel (a) shows the MG1 estimates and the total variance (using a long-dashed line) is the one-year variance. The MG2 estimates are shown in panel (b), and the total variance in this case is the sum of the permanent and transitory variances. The MG1 estimate of the transitory variance is a couple of percentage points larger than the MG2 estimates (as expected—see the earlier discussion), but the trends are the same. Both methods lead to the same conclusion: there has been no increase in the transitory variance of income in Britain between the mid-1990s and the mid-2000s.

A downward trend is perceptible for the period as a whole and this is consistent with US findings that the transitory variance changes counter-cyclically (Moffitt and Gottschalk 2008*b*; Shin and Solon 2009). Unemploy-ment rates in Britain were falling throughout the period (Chapter 1). Succes-sive MG2 estimates of the transitory variance are similar, but the decline from the beginning of the observation period to the end is from 0.048 to 0.040, a decrease of 17 per cent. Correspondingly, the fraction of the total variance that is transitory fell from around 37 per cent through the 1990s to 33 per cent by 2003. With an approximate standard error of around 0.001 for each MG2 variance estimate, year-on-year changes are not statistically significant, but the change between the mid-1990s and the mid-2000s as a whole is.

The conclusion that the transitory variance was constant over the period or fell slightly is robust to checks against the effects of measurement error. The estimates presented in Figure 6.1 were recalculated, first dropping all indivi-duals in households with income from self-employment and, second, dropping these individuals plus all those in households with an imputed gross income (estimates not shown). These are groups expected to have in-comes that are less reliably measured. In both cases, the effect was, as ex-pected, to reduce the magnitude of the estimated transitory variance of income (and its fraction of the total variance was also smaller). For example, in the first case, the MG2 estimate was about one percentage point smaller throughout the period than its Figure 6.1 counterpart—but there was still a slight downward trend. Restricting the sample further led to estimates that fluctuated noticeably over time—a consequence of the smaller cell sizes—but, again, there was no sign of an upward trend.

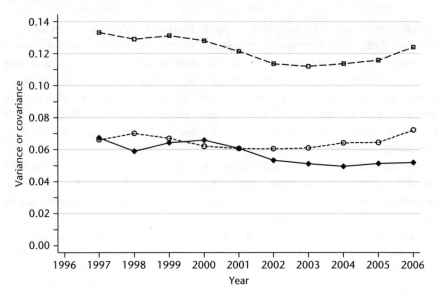

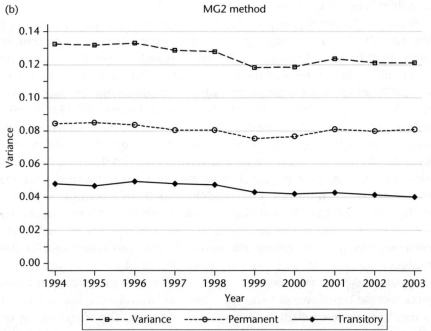

Figure 6.1. Transitory and permanent variances of log net household income, by estimation method and year

(a) MG1 method

(b) MG2 method

Notes: Weighted estimates using seven-year balanced panel samples of all individuals. See the text for explanation of the MG1 and MG2 estimation methods. For the MG1 method, year and total variance refer to year *t*, with the permanent variance estimated from the covariance between year *t* and year *t–6* incomes. For the MG2 method, year refers to the mid-year of each seven-year moving window, and the total variance is the sum of the permanent and transitory variances.

There are few estimates for Britain to compare these with. Perhaps the closest are those of Devicienti (2001), who fitted several VC model specifications to BHPS data for 1991–8, using the same income definition as mine. There is consistency in our estimates in the sense that Devicienti finds little change in the variance loading factors (cf. κ_t above) over the period. Blundell and Etheridge (2010) fitted a VC model to the net household incomes of a sample of household heads aged 25–60. Among household heads with positive labour earnings, their model parameters imply that the transitory variance was relatively constant from 1991 through to 2003. However, when they also include household heads without labour income in their sample, the predicted transitory variance is slightly U-shaped over the same period. It is unclear whether this trend, which differs from that derived from MG1 and MG2 estimates, does so as a consequence of the different modelling approaches used or due to different sample selections. (It is unclear who is followed over time in Blundell and Etheridge's longitudinal samples, for instance.) I recalculate MG2 estimates using different income definitions and subgroups in order to further check the robustness of my results.

An advantage of a gross income measure is that it allows closer comparisons with recent estimates for the USA derived from the PSID. (Recall that net household income equals gross household income less direct tax payments and employee social security contributions: see Chapter 4.) When the MG1 and MG2 methods are applied to data for (equivalized) gross household income rather than net income, but using the same samples and also adjusting for age in the same way, I derive the same conclusions about trends as for net income—a slight fall over the period as a whole. The main difference is that the estimates for each year of the transitory variance are slightly larger, by almost two percentage points. The MG2 estimates decreased from around 0.058 to 0.047 over the period as a whole (a 19 per cent decline compared to the 17 per cent decline for net income). The larger estimates for gross income are to be expected: one of the roles of the tax system is to smooth out the consequences of adverse income shocks, and the gross income measure does not pick up this aspect (since it is a pre-tax measure). The difference in estimates is not larger, however, because much of the income smoothing work is done by social security benefits rather than the tax system.

For the USA, Gottschalk and Moffitt (2009) report MG2-based estimates of the transitory variance for 'log annual family income', using nine-year moving windows covering from the beginning of the 1970s through to around 2000. The family income definition is similar to the BHPS gross income definition in that it is also a 'pre-tax post-transfer' definition (to use the US phrase), and both are equivalized (Gottschalk and Moffitt use the US official poverty line). The main difference is that income from the principal US in-work benefit, the Earned Income Tax Credit (EITC), is not included in the

PSID income definition, nor are receipts from in-kind benefits, of which the most important is Food Stamps (now called Supplemental Nutrition Assistance Program). Income from tax credits is included in the BHPS definition and there is no British counterpart to Food Stamps.

Gottschalk and Moffitt (2009: figure 5) report estimates of the transitory variance that increased over the 1990s, continuing a secular rise that had been in progress for the previous two decades. Although the rise was not continuous, it was marked, with the estimated transitory variance going from below 0.120 in 1994 to above 0.140 in 2000, which is a rise of at least 16 per cent. Gosselin and Zimmerman (2008) also use PSID data to estimate trends in the transitory variance using MG2 methods with six-year moving windows and find, by contrast with Gottschalk and Moffitt (2009), that the transitory variance rose over the first half of the 1990s but did not increase further in the second half of the 1990s (figures 5 and A1). Some of the differences may arise from the use of different methods: Gottschalk and Moffitt (2009) consider all individuals in families whereas Gosselin and Zimmerman focus on adults aged 25–64, and it may be the variability of circumstances for young adults and old people that has increased. Consistent with this view, Hacker and Jacobs (2008) find using the MG1 method that, for adults aged 26–61, the transitory variance rose in the first half of the 1990s but fell slightly thereafter.

It is not only the upward trend for the US transitory variance that differs from the British experience, but also the magnitude of the variance itself. Gottschalk and Moffitt's US estimates are roughly twice as large as the MG2 estimates for Britain reported above. This differential is likely to be an overestimate because of the exclusion of EITC income and Food Stamps from the PSID definition of family income—one would expect this to have a stabilizing impact. But, all in all, the comparison suggests that income risk is substantially larger for US families than British ones. On the other hand, the transitory variance for household income for Germany appears to be substantially smaller than Britain's but, as for Britain, the variance changed hardly at all over the 1990s, though the one for men's earnings did (Bartels and Bönke 2010).

There is only one explicitly cross-national comparison of the transitory variance in household income, by Gangl (2005), who used PSID data for 1992–7 for the USA, and ECHP data for 1994–9 covering 11 countries including the UK. Considering individuals aged 25–64, and using a variant of the MG2 method, Gangl reports that the transitory variance for the UK is around one-half of the US figure: 0.065 compared with 0.127 (Gangl 2005: table 2). According to this measure of income variability, the UK is a middle-ranking country along with the Netherlands, Belgium, and France. Denmark, Germany, and Ireland have substantially lower transitory variances, and the high transitory variance countries aside from the USA are Portugal, Greece, Italy, and especially Spain.

One noticeable feature of several of the studies cited above is their focus on samples of individuals that exclude young people and old people. It is therefore of interest to explore the differences between subgroups not only for their intrinsic interest, but also to see whether this may account for some of the differences in findings. Figure 6.2 shows MG2 estimates of the transitory variance in gross household income for each of seven person types differentiated by age and sex. The corresponding chart for net household income is very similar and not shown for brevity. The trend downwards in the overall transitory variance is driven by the downward trend for the most numerous groups, that is, men and women aged 30–59 and dependent children. The variances for these three groups are similar, which is unsurprising as they are mostly couples with children sharing a household. Men and women aged 60 years or more have substantially lower transitory variances than the other groups (though they have a downward trend as well) and the transitory variance is also a smaller fraction of the total variance. The vast majority of people of this age have retired from the labour market and state, occupational, or private pensions are the main sources of income, most of which are

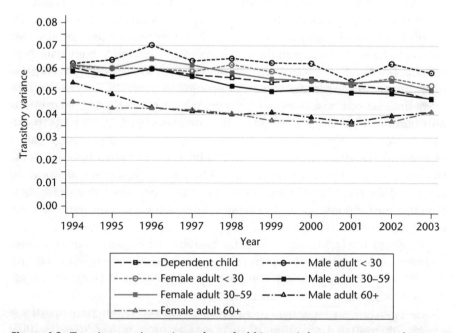

Figure 6.2. Transitory variance (gross household income), by person type and year

Notes: Weighted estimates based on the MG2 method using seven-year balanced panel samples of all individuals. Year refers to the mid-year of each seven-year moving window. Person type is defined by status in the first year of each seven-year window.

relatively fixed. (This is before the financial crisis at the end of 2008 when interest rates fell substantially.) Also consistent with expectations, the groups with the largest transitory variances of gross household income are adult men and women aged below 30, that is, those likely to have the highest rates of movement between paid work, education, and non-employment, and also making transitions between their parents' household and their own (which affects their total household income and the equivalence scale).

Transitory variance estimates were also derived separately for groups differentiated by their permanent income position within each seven-year window. For both gross and net household income, the transitory variance is substantially lower for individuals in the richest quarter of permanent incomes than in the rest of the distribution. For example, for gross income in 2000, the transitory variance for this group was 0.034 compared with 0.043 for the poorest quarter of the permanent income distribution and 0.056 for the middle half of the distribution. This result differs from that of Gangl (2005: figure 3), who reports that for the UK, as well as for ten other European countries and the USA, the transitory variance is highest for the poorest tenth and declines in magnitude across the next eight decile groups. Part of the difference relates to differences of definition. In my data, older people are over-represented in the poorest tenths of the permanent income distribution, and these are groups with the lowest transitory variances (see above). By focusing on people aged 25–65, Gangl (2005) excludes those groups, but also includes some young adults—a group with a relatively high transitory variance but also a low permanent income. I return to the British-US contrast again shortly in the context of men's earnings.

My final set of transitory variance estimates, also MG2 based, refer to the distribution of labour earnings for male employees aged 25–55 years at the start of each seven-year window. One reason for looking at prime-age men's earnings is that this is the group that has been studied most in research on volatility and so there are more possibilities for comparisons of findings. Second, since men's employment earnings form the largest share of household income for households of working age on average, transitory/permanent variance patterns for individual earnings and household income can be informative about the factors underlying the patterns for household income. The variance decomposition is shown in Figure 6.3, and this suggests that the transitory variance remained constant between the mid-1990s and mid-2000s, though the overall variance increased.

Decompositions by permanent earnings group reveal different trends for groups differentiated according to their permanent earnings. Some caution needs to be exercised because sample numbers are relatively small—around 180 men in each fourth of the permanent earnings distribution. Figure 6.4 suggests that the transitory variance was smallest for those in the top fourth of

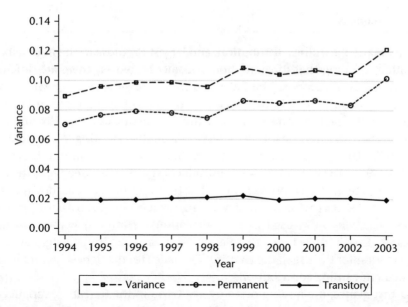

Figure 6.3. Transitory and permanent variances of gross earnings for prime-aged male employees, by year

Notes: Weighted estimates based on MG2 method using seven-year balanced panels of male employees aged 25–59 years at the start of each window. Year refers to the mid-year of each seven-year moving window, and the total variance is the sum of the permanent and transitory variances.

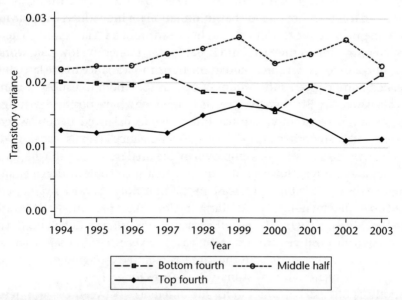

Figure 6.4. Transitory variance of gross earnings for prime-aged male employees, by permanent earnings group and year

Notes: Weighted estimates based on MG2 method using seven-year balanced panel samples of male employees aged 25–59 years at the start of each window. Year refers to the mid-year of each seven-year moving window.

the permanent earnings distribution, and largest for those in the middle half, a pattern echoing that for household income. Moreover, there are different trends across the groups. The flat trend in aggregate appears to reflect two offsetting factors: there is an increase in the transitory variance in the late 1990s for the richest three-fourths of the permanent earnings distribution, coinciding with a decline for the poorest fourth. It is tempting to attribute the decline for this group to the introduction of the National Minimum Wage in April 1999, on the grounds that the introduction of a more effective wage floor would reduce the transitory variance. (The timing of the decline shown in the chart is consistent with the policy change when one notes that a moving seven-year window is used in the calculations.) However, without further research, this is conjecture and, in addition, there is no immediately obvious explanation for the rise in the transitory variance for the richest quarter of the permanent earnings distribution.

At first glance, my finding of no overall trend in the transitory variance of men's earnings conflicts with that of Dickens (2000), who used large samples from administrative records on earnings for British men aged 22–59 years covering the period 1970–95. On the basis of VC model estimates, he finds that that both the transitory and permanent variances increased over the period for most birth cohorts. One explanation for the different findings concerns the coverage of the data sets. Dickens used the New Earnings Survey panel, and this does not include pay information for individuals with earnings below the income tax threshold (and hence without a PAYE record). There is no such restriction in the BHPS and it was for (permanently) low-paid workers that I find a small downward trend in the transitory variance in the late 1990s. A related point concerns the groups of earners for whom transitory variances are calculated. My BHPS analysis refers to men who have positive earnings at each of seven consecutive annual interviews (a balanced panel), whereas Dickens and many other VC modellers use unbalanced panels: earnings data for men with non-continuous employment are used from years in which their earnings are positive. However, it is unclear that such compositional changes would be responsible for an increase in the transitory variance over a period when unemployment rates were falling and jobs likely to be more stable rather than less. Moreover, when I repeat the calculations using an unbalanced panel (only requiring positive earnings for at least two years within each seven-year window), I find that trends are the same as pictured in Figure 6.3. The only change is a reduction in the estimated variances for each year.

Another potential explanation for the differences between Dickens' results and mine is that the specific periods covered differ—my estimates refer to a period beginning in the mid-1990s, which is when his sample ended. To be convincing, this argument requires additional evidence that the transitory variance stopped rising in the late 1990s. The studies by Ramos (2003) and

Daly and Valletta (2008) are relevant to this. Both fitted VC models to BHPS data on men's employment earnings, for the period 1991–9 and 1991–8 respectively, with some differences in specification and sample selection. Both papers suggest that the transitory variance fluctuated over the period, though on a slightly rising trend for several birth cohorts according to Ramos (2003: figure 3). My results are therefore not entirely consistent with those of the VC models.

On the one hand, this might be interpreted as suggesting that the MG2 and related descriptive methods provide biased estimates. (In this connection, I note that MG1-based estimates of the permanent and transitory variance may be derived from Dickens (2000: figure 3), and the growth in the transitory variance is not as apparent from these as from the VC model estimates.) On the other hand, there is the earlier argument that estimates of trends from VC models may be sensitive to the choice of model specification. For example, despite only relatively minor differences in model specification, the estimated time path of the transitory variance is quite different in the Ramos (2003) and Daly and Valletta (2008) studies. This sensitivity was one of the arguments for also examining estimates of volatility, and I turn to those shortly. Before doing so, however, I compare the British estimates of the transitory variance in earnings with those of other countries.

The leading estimates of the transitory variance in US men's earnings are those of Gottschalk and Moffitt (1994b, 2007, 2009) and Moffitt and Gottschalk (1995, 2002, 2008a, 2008b), derived using both MG2 and VC-based methods. As in research by others using PSID data, they find that the transitory variance for men's earnings rose over the 1970s and 1980s, but then stopped growing around 1990. From then until 2003—the period for which there are BHPS estimates—the transitory variance fell slightly and then rose again at the end of the period: see, for example, Gottschalk and Moffitt (2009: figure 1). Moffitt and Gottschalk (2008a) report the same trend between 1991 and 2003, using administrative record data rather than PSID data as in the other studies. The authors conclude that 'the transitory variance did not show a trend net of cycle over this period' (2008a: i) and draw attention also to the close association between changes in the transitory variance and changes in the unemployment rate (also see 2008b: figure 4). Beach, Finnie, and Gray (2010) also point out this association in their study of earnings in Canada.

The US findings throw up several contrasts with the research for Britain. First, there is consistency in estimates of trends in the transitory variance for men's earnings, regardless of which estimation method is applied. Second, there are differences in substantive findings. The U-shaped trend in the US transitory variance over the 1990s is not suggested by my findings or any of the other British studies cited earlier. However, the US result about trends is largely accounted for by cyclical factors. If these work in the same way in

Britain, then the steady decline in the unemployment rate in Britain over the 15 years starting 1993 suggests that the transitory variance would also not have increased substantially in the decade from the mid-1990s.

Second, the transitory variance for men's earnings is smaller in Britain than in the USA. For instance, around 2000, I estimate the British figure to be 0.02, compared to the corresponding US estimate, 0.14 (Gottschalk and Moffitt 2009: figure 1; MG2 method). The British estimate is closer to the estimate for West German men's monthly gross earnings for the early 2000s that is reported by Bartels and Bönke (2010: figure 1; MG2 method with five-year windows). For most of the 1990s, the estimate of the German transitory variance was smaller, a period when the unemployment rate was also lower. The British estimate also differs from that of the two other countries. When the transitory variance is expressed as a proportion of the total variance, the British figure is between 25 per cent and 30 per cent over the 1990s and 2000s, compared to around 40 per cent for Germany over the same period (Bartels and Bönke 2010) and around one-third in the USA during the 1970s and 1980s (Gottshalk and Moffitt 1994b). A third cross-national contrast is between the experiences of men in different locations of the permanent earnings distribution. Gottschalk and Moffitt (2009: figure 3) show that from the 1970s through to the early 2000s, men in the poorest quarter of the distribution had a transitory variance that is two to three times larger than the variances for the men in the middle half or top quarter (which are relatively similar). Bartels and Bönke (2010) also report larger transitory variances for the bottom quarter, with the differential about the same as those for the USA.

6.6. Trends in Volatility

I now consider estimates of volatility in household income among all individuals and in earnings for prime-aged male employees: see Figure 6.5. Volatility is measured by the sample standard deviation of the distribution of individual changes in log income between one year and the following year: equation (6.8) applies with $s = 1$. Incomes are age-adjusted, as before, but the adjustment makes virtually no difference to the estimates derived. One advantage of taking two distributions just one year apart is that potential selectivity issues associated with requiring survey participation over longer periods (as with the MG2 method) are minimized.

The estimated trends in volatility are similar to those for the transitory variance. Variability is greater for household income among all individuals than for earnings among prime-age male employees according to both types of measure. In addition, there is no clear trend upwards or downwards over the

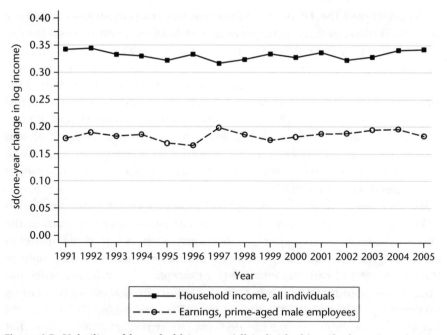

Figure 6.5. Volatility of household income (all individuals) and of earnings (prime-aged male employees), by year

Notes: Weighted estimates of volatility measure $V_t = \text{sd}(y_{it+1} - y_{it})$. Year refers to year t. Prime-aged male employees are those aged 25–59 years in year t.

period as a whole. There are fluctuations from one year to the next, but they generally lie within the bounds of sampling variability (the standard error for each measure in a given year is about 0.01). Calculations of volatility in household income for subgroups (not shown) reveal that volatility is greatest for adults aged less than 30 years compared to other age groups, and for the second and third poorest fifths of the year t income distribution. Excluding individuals with self-employment income or with imputed gross income components does not change the picture concerning trends either.

All other estimates of volatility that I am aware of refer to the USA. There is only one paper that has considered the volatility of household income: Dynan, Elmendorf, and Sichel (2008) report estimates for a family income measure that is not equivalized. Their samples are rather specific, being restricted to individuals who are household heads aged 25 or more and not retired and who remain the head of their household in the two distributions compared (these are two years apart to reflect the PSID's biannual interviewing from 1997). For this group, Dynan, Elmendorf, and Sichel report a discontinuous rise in income volatility between 1990 and 2004, with most of the rise in the first five years of the period (2008: figure 3). This follows a steady rise

157

in volatility over the 1970s and 1980s. For the volatility of the earnings of household heads (mostly men), there are similarities and differences. Dynan, Elmendorf, and Sichel's (2008: figure 1) estimates imply a rise in volatility over the 30-year period, but changes are more discontinuous than for household income. In particular, earnings volatility is estimated to rise at the start of the 1990s, fall back, and then rise again at the start of the 2000s. Some of the fine detail in the year-on-year changes may be obscured because Dynan, Elmendorf, and Sichel (2008) smooth the series they present, showing three-year moving averages. In any case, the US volatility estimates for the early 2000s are markedly higher than those for Britain: between 0.45 and 0.50 compared with around 0.35, respectively.

For US earnings volatility trends, the leading paper is by Shin and Solon (2009), also using PSID data, and with extensive sensitivity analysis of the effects of using different earnings definitions, examination of the impact of accounting for men with zero earnings, and more detail about dispersion in the distribution of earnings changes (for example, presenting quantiles and not only the standard deviation). Shin and Solon find that earnings volatility rose over the 15 years after the turn of the 1970s, and declined over the next five years. Over the first half of the 1990s, volatility was flat or fell slightly, but then from the mid-1990s started to rise again through to 2004. At this time, earnings volatility was around 0.5, which is substantially larger than the British estimate of around 0.20 shown in Figure 6.3. Rather than pointing to any secular trends in volatility, Shin and Solon emphasize that earnings volatility is highly correlated with the US civilian unemployment rate (2009: figure 1). This point echoes Moffitt and Gottschalk's (2008a, 2008b) finding that there is a close association between the transitory variance and the unemployment rate.

6.7. Trends in the Prevalence of a Large Income Fall

The final statistics related to income risk and economic insecurity that I present concern the prevalence of large income falls between one year and the next, and how this prevalence has been changing over time in Britain. The motivation is that some discussions emphasize that it is negative shocks to income that give rise to economic insecurity (if they are uninsured) rather than negative and positive shocks. Both the measures of income risk considered so far in the chapter—the transitory variance and volatility—treat income gains and losses symmetrically. Hacker (2008) draws attention to this point, also referring to the concept of 'loss aversion' from behavioural economics to argue that an income loss of a given size makes people feel worse off by more than an equal-sized income gain makes them feel better off. In addition, he

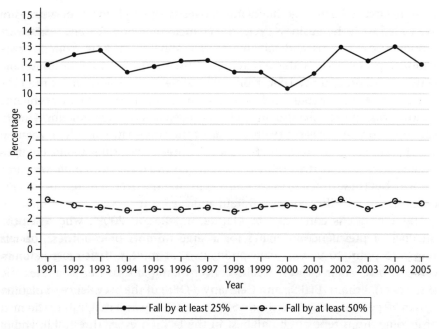

Figure 6.6. Percentage of individuals with a large income fall over a one-year interval, by year

Notes: Weighted estimates of prevalence of large income fall between year *t* and *t*+1, for all individuals with valid household incomes in both years. Year refers to year *t*.

argues that income-fall prevalence measures are useful because they are more transparent and easily understood than the other measures.

Estimates of the prevalence of a large income fall between one year and the next are shown for Britain in Figure 6.6. Once again, there is evidence of little trend over the 15-year period after 1991. The proportion experiencing an income fall of at least one-quarter over a one-year interval fluctuates over the period around a figure of about 12 per cent, but there is no clear trend, especially once sampling variability is taken into account. (The standard error for a year's estimate is about one percentage point.) A substantially smaller fraction, around 3 per cent of all individuals, experiences a halving of their income between one year and the next and, again, there is no upward or downward trend in this figure over the period. (The standard error of each estimate is about 0.3 percentage points.)

These British estimates contrast sharply with those for the USA. Hacker and Jacobs (2008: figure C) present estimates of the proportion of individuals aged 25–61 experiencing a fall of at least 50 per cent in size-adjusted family income between one year and another year two years later. They show that there has been a general rise in this proportion since the 1970s through to 2004, but there have also been large fluctuations over the period, many of which are associated with the business cycle: the chances of a large income loss rise in economic downturns and fall in upturns. What is striking from a cross-national perspective is the difference in prevalence of large income falls between Britain and the USA. From 1990–2004, the proportion for the USA fluctuated between about 7 per cent and almost 9 per cent—a figure which is almost twice the British estimate. (A fraction of 3 to 4 per cent describes the US situation only in the early 1970s.) Some of the cross-national difference may arise because of different definitions, for example calculating income changes over a two-year gap rather than a one-year gap and different sample selection choices. But these differences are unlikely to alter the overall picture of a major difference in volatility between Britain and the USA.

This contrast is confirmed by Hacker and Rehm (2009), who assemble income-fall prevalence estimates for a large number of countries, though they also point to various data problems that muddy their cross-national comparisons. Their clearest results concern comparisons between the USA (PSID data), Britain (BHPS), and Germany (SOEP) of the prevalence of income falls of 10 per cent, 25 per cent, and 50 per cent. They find that '[t]he incidence of income drops tends to be highest in the U.S. (at every threshold), and it tends to be lowest in Germany. The U.S. displays a marked secular upwards trend (and remarkable spikes in recessions), while the degree of realized risk tends to go down over time in the U.K. Germany (West Germany only) is characterized by—fairly strong but—trendless fluctuation' (2009: 11). Although Hacker and Rehm do not state it, for all three countries, the changes over time that they report appear to correspond with different stages of each country's business cycle. I do not find a slight decline for Britain as Hacker and Rehm do, a difference that is likely due to use of different sample selections (not stated in their paper). Repeating my calculations for only individuals aged 25–29 years in the initial year leads to similar findings to those shown in Figure 6.6. The main difference is that there are greater fluctuations in the two series, attributable to the smaller sample sizes (estimates not shown).

6.8. Mobility Trends: Summary and Explanations for the Findings

However one looks at income mobility in Britain from one year to the next, there is a lot of it—but most of the mobility is short distance. This chapter and the previous one have shown that this finding, highlighted by Jarvis and Jenkins (1998) when looking at Britain in the first half of the 1990s, remains an accurate description of the subsequent decade as well. Income destinations become less associated with income origins the longer the time that passes but, after half a generation, about one person in six remains in the same tenth of the income distribution that they started out. If people were to fully average their income flows over time, this would reduce inequality quite substantially. Over a 16-year period, this inequality-reduction impact of mobility is equivalent in magnitude (but of the opposite sign) to the historically large increase in cross-sectional inequality that occurred over the 1980s. Large differences in these smoothed incomes remain, however. Mobility does not fully offset inequality.

Both this chapter and Chapter 5 also emphasize that there are many concepts of mobility, drawing a distinction between mobility as positional change, inequality-reduction, individual income growth, and income risk. The British situation underlines the importance of these distinctions. From the perspective of positional change and inequality-reduction, Britain is more mobile than the USA, and middle-ranking relative to many EU nations. But from the perspective of income risk, Britain is clearly less mobile than the USA—the transitory variance of income and income volatility are much smaller, even though the definitions of family income in the USA exclude assistance through the EITC and Food Stamps programmes. (Comparable European data on this dimension of mobility are rare.) Moreover, trends in mobility in Britain appear to differ from those in the USA according to measures based on some mobility concepts but not others. For Britain, the degree of mobility remained much the same throughout the period from the start of the 1990s through to the mid-2000s, whatever the measure of mobility used. In contrast, US mobility appears to have stayed relatively constant over the 1990s according to measures of positional mobility and inequality-reduction, whereas measures of the transitory variance and income volatility fluctuated but increased over the period as a whole (following a more clear increase over the previous two decades).

Britain Compared to the USA and Other Countries

What explains these cross-national differences in mobility levels and trends? And how is it that different types of mobility measures provide different country rankings? It is useful to first distinguish between mobility as positional change and inequality-reduction on the one hand, and the other mobility concepts on the other hand. The first two concepts are based on relative income positions and how they change. In the case of positional mobility, relative position is defined relative to everyone else in the relevant population; in the case of inequality reduction, position is defined more indirectly, in terms of income relative to the relevant population's mean income. The potential for changing one's relative position depends, in both cases, on how much inequality there is in the first place.

As has also been said about international differences in intergenerational income mobility, 'moving up a ladder is harder if its rungs are further apart' (National Equality Panel 2010: 328). This provides a prima-facie explanation why the degree of mobility in Britain, according to these two concepts, is lower than in the USA: income inequality is significantly higher in the USA (OECD 2008). Gangl (2005) also points out, as mentioned earlier, that estimates of mobility as inequality-reduction and inequality are positively correlated among 11 EU nations and the USA (with Germany as an outlier case with high mobility but low inequality). The relationship with inequality also provides a prima-facie explanation why mobility measured as positional change or inequality-reduction hardly changed over the 1990s in Britain. It was a period when income inequality did not change very much, except for marked income growth at the very top of the income distribution (which is poorly covered by the BHPS). On this, see Chapter 4 and National Equality Panel (2010).

For mobility defined as individual income growth and measures of income risk, it is changes in individuals' income levels per se that count (in different ways), rather than changes in relative positions. Income differences between individuals at a point in time are not a direct input into the construction of the various measures. This helps explain why changes over time in transitory variance and volatility appear to be closely related with the economic cycle rather than with the level of inequality. As the state of the economy improves and unemployment rates fall, average individual income growth rises, and the transitory income variance and volatility appear to fall. This result is most apparent for the USA, where, with panel data covering almost three decades, there is sufficient intertemporal variation to observe such a correlation. This is not the case in Britain. BHPS data span only a decade and a half and, for virtually all this period (except the first two years), the economy was on an upswing and unemployment rates were falling (Chapter 1). This is a 'smoking gun' explanation for the constancy of measures of transitory variance and volatility in Britain between 1991 and 2006. An interesting test of this hypothesis, awaiting new data, would be to examine whether these measures increased with the onset of the economic crisis in 2008.

Britain's lower transitory variance of income and income volatility compared to the USA is straightforwardly explained by the differences in the comprehensiveness and generosity of their welfare states. (For a comprehensive comparison of these, see Walker 2005.) For people of working age in Britain without a job, there are means-tested social assistance benefits that are universally available and available indefinitely (subject to work-availability conditions) and supplementing social insurance unemployment benefits that have increasingly low coverage. These include means-tested assistance with high housing costs. The gap between the total income that the average person can get when working and the total income gained if not working has increased in Britain over the last two decades, especially with the introduction of tax credits for low-income working families (reflecting the Labour government's goal to 'make work pay': see Chapter 1). Nonetheless, the decrease in household income associated with job loss is substantially greater on average in the USA than in Britain. This is illustrated by the income replacement rates derived for an 'average production worker' by the OECD (2004). These show (for 2002) that in the initial phase of unemployment, an average worker with unemployment insurance coverage is slightly better off in the USA than the UK. But a long-term unemployed person who has exhausted his unemployment insurance entitlement (and also presumably someone who had no entitlement in the first place) is markedly worse off in the USA than in Britain, especially if he is single rather than married. The US replacement rate for a long-term unemployed married worker with a non-earning spouse and two children is 41 per cent compared with 73 per cent for his British counterpart. For a single worker, the corresponding rates are 7 per cent and 41 per cent (OECD 2004 in CESifo 2005: 81). Differences in welfare states have also been advanced as the explanation for differences in mobility between Germany and the USA: see for example Fabig (1999) and Bartels and Bönke (2010).

Given this evidence, it is interesting to speculate whether there is a more general systematic relationship across countries between income risk (as measured here) and welfare state 'generosity' or some other welfare state classification of the type popularized by Esping-Andersen (1990). Lack of suitable longitudinal data constrain the possibilities of examining this issue. Hacker and Rehm (2009) are among the first to address it, heroically assembling data from 20 panel surveys, including long-running panels such as the US PSID, German SOEP, and the BHPS, together with shorter panels for Australia and countries in Europe. They examine the association between the incidence of income falls of 50 per cent or more and measures of welfare state generosity, including derived indices and expenditures covering a number of domains (for example, health, unemployment, retirement pensions, incapacity and family benefits). With the exception of pension expenditures, they find a negative association between 'realized income risk' (the chance of a large income fall) and welfare state generosity, and they classify countries into four groups according to whether they are high or low realized risk countries and high or low inequality countries. They place the USA in the 'unstable, unequal' cell and tentatively put Britain in the 'stable, high inequality' cell, while noting various difficulties of allocating countries. As they put it, '[k]eeping in mind the limited time frame of the panel income data available for most nations, the preliminary conclusion to be taken from our data is that risk privatization is predominantly a U.S. phenomenon' (2009: 16). Further investigation of this topic would be fruitful.

Although differences between Britain and the USA in levels of income risk are plausibly explained by differences in their welfare states in particular, what explains the differences in the trends? In particular, why was there no significant change over the 1990s in Britain? Arguably, differences in trends can be explained partly by the differences in the economic cycle referred to earlier and, again, partly by differences in welfare states. The case is that, not only does Britain provide a more comprehensive and universal social safety net than the USA, but its safety net is better able than the US one to cope with change and continue to offset the impact of adverse income shocks on families and individuals. This argument is plausible but needs verification. Another argument is simply that the USA is an exceptional case: note Hacker and Rehm's (2009) remarks in the previous paragraph, and also see the extensive discussion of the privatization of risk in the USA by Gosselin (2008) and Hacker (2004, 2008), a phenomenon which does not appear to have a British counterpart. Again, this argument has plausibility. Nonetheless, it remains surprising that no significant changes in mobility are apparent in Britain during the 1990s, especially when there were major changes to the tax-benefit system introduced by the Labour government from the late 1990s onwards. If the nature of the welfare state changed, should this not have had impacts on the dynamics of income over time and not only on cross-sectional features such as poverty rates which motivated the policies? I hypothesize that these points can be reconciled if one acknowledges that there was change over the period, but various underlying factors had offsetting influences.

6.9. Offsetting Influences on Overall Mobility?

I examine this hypothesis in two ways, first, looking at trends in the transitory variances of income components, and second, looking directly at changes over a period in the contribution of different income sources to longitudinal variability in income itself. Total income is broken down into the same income sources in both cases: labour income (from employment or self-employment) of the household head, labour income of the spouse (if present), benefits and tax credits (including the state retirement pension), other income, such as receipts from investments and savings, and private transfers, and deductions of income tax, employee National Insurance Contributions, and local taxes. See Chapter 3 for more detailed definitions.

The examination of transitory variances for income sources follows analysis for the USA by Gottschalk and Moffitt (2009: Figure 6). Transitory variances are computed for each source using the MG2 method, as before, except that incomes values are used rather than log incomes, given that families may genuinely have zero income from several income sources. Incomes are

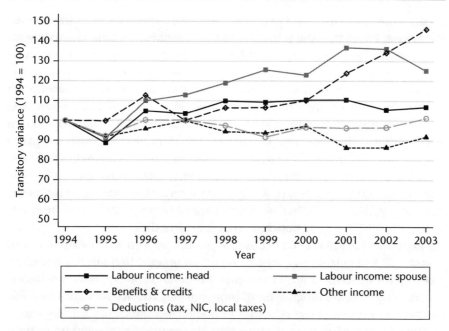

Figure 6.7. Trend in transitory variances of income sources

Notes: Weighted estimates based on MG2 method using seven-year balanced panel samples of all individuals aged 25–55 years at the start of each window. Year refers to the mid-year of each seven-year moving window. Transitory variance of each source refers to variance of income (not log income). Calculations restricted to individuals aged 30–59 at the start of each window provide a similar picture. Values for each income source are benchmarked relative to their value in the initial year (1994), which is set equal to 100. Values for other years show the trend relative to 1994.

expressed in January 2008 prices but not equivalized. Deductions from income are treated as positive values for this exercise. Following Gottschalk and Moffitt, I express estimates for each source relative to their value in the initial year (1994), which is itself normalized to equal 100. Values for other years show trends relative to the 1994 value. Figure 6.7 shows the results. These refer to samples of individuals aged 25–55 years in the first year of each seven-year window.

There is some evidence of offsetting forces in action: some transitory variances increased over time and some decreased. Increases over time are apparent for spouse's labour income throughout the period, and for 'benefits' from around 1999 onwards. It is tempting to link the former with the secular increase in women's labour force participation, which was perhaps also accompanied by instability in job holding. It is also tempting to link the trend in the transitory variance for benefits with the introduction of Working Families Tax Credit in 1999. Job instability of the sort just mentioned could also have knock-on consequences for tax credit eligibility and, in addition, income instability may arise from imperfect administration of the tax credits programme. (On this, see House of Commons Treasury Committee 2006.) Otherwise, I note that the transitory variance for principal income source for households of working age, head's labour earnings, has a relatively flat trend over the period, and is most likely the principal driver of the flat trend in the transitory variance for total income. A complete decomposition would also need to examine changes in correlations across transitory components, and changes in the shares of each source in total income. (I provide information about the latter shortly.) I repeated the analysis using all individuals (estimates not shown), and this leads to a picture about trends that differed in only two respects. One is that the transitory variance for benefits was closer to its 1994 value throughout the 1990s (but then also increased), and the other is that the transitory variance for 'other' income decreased below its 1994 value from the end of the 1990s, and it is unclear what is behind this.

The results for Britain echo those for the USA reported by Gottschalk and Moffitt (2009: figure 6), as they also report an upward trend in the transitory variance for benefits ('transfer income of head and spouse', which is largely income from welfare programmes), though it was also accompanied by a rise in the transitory variance of 'other nonlabor income of head and spouse'. Gottschalk and Moffitt conjecture that the results for benefits may have resulted from the welfare reforms which began in the early 1990s, and which led to higher welfare exit rates and shorter welfare spells.

For my second decomposition, I draw on methods that I have proposed for examination of longitudinal variability in income (Jenkins 2000). For each person, this variability is summarized by the dispersion of the incomes received over a period of fixed length—taken to be seven years here. One can then ask how much of this dispersion is accounted for by the income from different sources received over the period—an inequality decomposition by income source where the sources are the same five as before (measured in real terms and not equivalized). For each time window, these contributions are calculated for each individual using methods originally developed for decompositions of cross-sectional inequality by Shorrocks (1982, 1983), and then the statistics are averaged across individuals to provide an overall picture. I supplement the estimates with information about the shares of each source in total income, and how they have changed over time, as it is often found that variability contributions are closely related to income shares. The other determinants of the source contributions are the longitudinal dispersion of each of the sources, and the correlations between each source and total income (Jenkins 2000).

Before considering the estimates, observe that average longitudinal dispersion in equivalized net income among all individuals changed very little over the period, falling from 0.19 in 1994 to 0.17 in 2003 and from 0.19 to 0.17 among individuals aged 30–59 at the start of each window. The corresponding estimates for net income unadjusted for household composition are 0.21 and 0.19, and 0.20 to 0.19. The average longitudinal variability in household size or equivalence-scale factor did not change over time for either sample, suggesting that changes in household structure played no role. But what role did each income source play? See Table 6.1. The top panel provides results for all individuals and the bottom panel provides results for individuals aged 30–59 (and so excludes most retired people for instance). For each period, the source contributions (C_f) add up to 100 per cent, and so too do the shares of each source in total income (aside from rounding).

Table 6.1 shows that labour income of household head is the most important component of household income packages for both samples and, unsurprisingly, more so for adults aged 30–59. This explains why head's labour income makes the largest contribution to longitudinal variability of total household income. Taxes and National Insurance Contributions have a large variability-reducing influence—hence the negative contributions. Labour income of a spouse, and other income (mainly investment income), also have relatively large contributions to longitudinal variability.

Looking at trends over time, there is evidence of offsetting factors at work again. Specifically, there is little trend in the variability contribution estimates for taxes and NIC, or for other income. However, the share of the head's labour income in total household income declines between 1994 and 2003 and its contribution to variability falls from 45 per cent to 42 per cent among all individuals, or from 54 per cent to 49 per cent among those aged 30–59 years. Change is most apparent for benefits and credits. Among all individuals, its contribution increases from around 10 per cent to 16 per cent between 1994 and 2003. Among those aged 30–59, the increase in contribution is from around 6 per cent to 10 per cent. For both samples, change is not continuous throughout the period; rather there is a step-change upwards round about 1999 to 2000. The timing of these changes is similar to that found for the transitory variance of benefits, and provides corroborative evidence that the introduction of the Working Families Tax Credit was associated with an increase in income variability. The estimates of the contribution to variability of spouse's labour income also echo the findings for transitory variances. Among individuals aged 30–59 years (and hence excluding most retired people of both sexes), this source's contribution rose over the period as a whole (albeit only slightly), when its share also increased.

Gosselin and Zimmerman (2008) apply the same decomposition method to US PSID data on family income for individuals aged 25–64 years for periods covering the 1970s, 1980s, and 1990s. Their results are not fully comparable with mine because taxes are not deducted from their income measure. However, it is interesting to note that they also report a steady secular decline in the share of family income from head's labour income, accompanied by a

Table 6.1. Income sources and incomes over a seven-year period: contributions to variability (%) and shares of total (%), by year

Year	Labour income (head)		Labour income (spouse)		Benefits and credits		Other income		Taxes and NIC	
	C_f	Share	C_f	Share	C_f	Share	C_f	Share	C_f	Share
All individuals										
1994	46	57	33	32	10	15	39	24	−27	−28
1995	44	56	34	32	10	16	40	24	−28	−27
1996	45	54	32	32	10	17	39	24	−27	−27
1997	46	54	31	33	10	16	39	24	−26	−27
1998	46	55	29	33	12	16	38	23	−24	−27
1999	44	54	30	32	12	16	37	24	−24	−27
2000	43	54	33	31	13	17	37	25	−25	−27
2001	43	54	33	31	15	18	35	23	−25	−27
2002	43	54	31	32	17	18	35	23	−26	−27
2003	42	54	32	33	16	18	37	22	−26	−27
Individuals aged 30–59 years at the start of each seven-year window										
1994	54	61	35	36	6	10	37	23	−32	−30
1995	50	61	37	36	6	10	39	23	−32	−30
1996	54	59	33	36	5	11	39	23	−31	−29
1997	54	61	32	36	5	10	39	23	−30	−29
1998	55	61	30	36	7	11	36	22	−28	−30
1999	50	61	35	35	8	10	35	23	−28	−29
2000	49	61	37	35	9	11	34	23	−29	−29
2001	49	61	38	36	10	11	33	22	−30	−30
2002	48	62	37	37	11	11	34	20	−30	−30
2003	49	62	38	38	9	11	36	20	−32	−31

Notes: Longer-term income refers to the longitudinal average of seven-year incomes for balanced panel samples of individuals. Year refers to mid-year of seven-year interval. C_f is the contribution of source *f* to longitudinal variability in longer-term income; share is the share of source *f* in total longer-term income. Statistics refer to averages over individuals within each sample. Benefits and credits include state retirement pension.

secular rise in the share of spouse's labour income. They also report relative stability over time in the variability contributions of all but one of five income sources, namely 'transfer income' (2008: figure 10). From the mid-1980s to the mid-1990s, there was a marked increase in this source's contribution to longitudinal variability of income. The change in importance of this factor and its timing is consistent with the changes in the transitory variance of transfer income reported by Gottschalk and Moffitt (2009) and discussed earlier.

In summary, although the aggregate picture for Britain is one of little change in income mobility over the decade and a half since 1990, this does not mean that the underlying structures of income dynamics also remained constant. The decompositions by income source reveal that there were various influences at play over the period and with offsetting roles.

Interestingly, changes to the tax-benefit system—usually examined in terms of their cross-sectional redistributive effect—also appear to have effects on the longitudinal distribution of individuals' incomes. This is most clearly revealed when mobility is thought of in terms of individual income growth (and there appear to have been changes to its progressivity) or in terms of longitudinal variability (rather than positional change) where benefits and credits appear to have increased their contribution.

There is substantial scope for further research in this area, much of which awaits further longitudinal data not only for Britain but also for other countries. It is too early to judge, for instance, how differences in welfare states between countries are associated with differences in income 'risk'. The quotation marks are a reminder that the evidence about this presented here, and in other studies, is indirect—based on observations of longitudinal variability ex post. Further research is needed on the connections between income mobility, risk, and economic insecurity, taking account of the extent to which families can transfer resources across time and their ability to insure against adverse shocks.

7

Spaghetti Unravelled: A Model-Based Description of Differences in Income-Age Trajectories

This chapter provides new evidence for Britain about how income varies with age and how the shapes of people's trajectories differ between individuals. Most of the chapters in this book examine changes in income over a relatively short period of time, from one year to the next or over the course of a few years. Now I take a longer-run perspective, and analyse how incomes change over people's working lives. The emphasis is on the shapes of lifetime income profiles as a whole. That is, changes in income over the life course are not seen as the sum of series of short-term changes (mobility in the sense analysed in Chapters 5 and 6). Instead, 'mobility' refers to the fact that people have differently shaped income-age trajectories. For some people, income tends to rise and then fall with age; for others, income profiles are rather flat, and so on.

Most of the evidence currently available about the relationship between income and age is derived from cross-sectional data. The pictures of income-age trajectories are derived from survey data for a given year about a large sample of individuals of different ages. By contrast, my research uses longitudinal data that tracks the same people over time and accumulates information about the income-age trajectory for each person in the sample as each person ages. Data about how income varies between the age of 30 and 40 years (say) is derived by following 30-year-olds over a decade until they are 40 rather than comparing today's 30-year-olds with today's 40-year-olds. If one is interested in documenting the nature of individuals' income-age trajectories, including how income varies between one year and the next for each person, while also describing the heterogeneity across individuals in income-age trajectories, then a longitudinal approach is essential.

Knowledge of how income varies with age on average, and how individual trajectories differ from an average profile, is relevant to many aspects of social policy-making. How your income varies over your life is an important determinant of your spending possibilities (and hence consumption and economic well-being) at different ages and your ability to save for old age, whether privately or through company, occupational, or state pension schemes. The life-cycle pattern of earnings is also relevant to major borrowing decisions, such as taking out a mortgage to buy a house or a loan to finance tertiary education. It is important to identify not only the characteristics of the groups who, on average, have persistently low incomes and hence low abilities to save or borrow, but also whether a 'group average' is potentially deceptive. Even if income increases with age on average, this is consistent with there being considerable year-on-year fluctuation in the incomes of a minority, or a mixture of subgroups with rising income and subgroups whose income is falling. These features complicate the design of effective policies for fostering saving by all and for the design of social insurance schemes for income replacement, mortgage, and other borrowing plans.

It should be stressed, however, that this chapter provides evidence relevant to policy discussion rather than an evaluation of policy alternatives per se. The chapter develops a framework to summarize individuals' income-age trajectories in a tractable manner, and applies it to data for Britain. I use the word 'summarize' intentionally, for the shapes of income-age trajectories in contemporary Britain are complex, as I show below. A chart plotting income against age looks like a plateful of cooked spaghetti, with each strand corresponding to a profile for a particular person. A statistical model is essential for summarizing the key features of income-age trajectories and their diversity of shapes.

The key ideas are as follows. First, I differentiate 12 'social groups', with group membership defined in terms of similarity of birth year, educational qualifications, and sex. Then, second, within each group, I summarize income-age trajectories in terms of an average group profile, combined with individual-specific divergences from the group average. Figure 7.1 helps explain the idea (the formal statistical model is presented later).

The dashed lines show stylized income-age trajectories for two individuals from the same social group (men born in the same year who both left school with GSCEs but without any A-levels, say). The first profile is summarized by a relatively low income at the beginning of the working life (taken to be 25 here), combined with a relatively large growth rate in income with age (long dashed line). The other profile (short dashed line) combines a relatively high initial income but a relatively low growth rate in income with age—the slope of the trajectory is less steep than in the first case. Think of the first situation as characterizing John, who qualified as plumber. The starting salary is relatively low but increases over the working life, reflecting the return to the investment in training. The second situation represents Mike, who instead trained as a

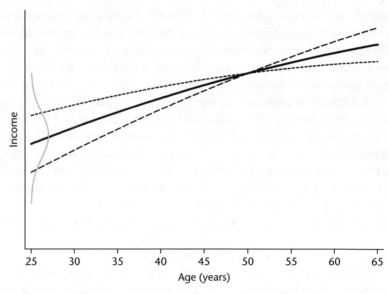

Figure 7.1. Stylized income-age trajectories for two individuals and the average trajectory

Notes: Chart shows stylized income-age trajectories for two individuals (dashed lines) and an average trajectory (solid line). The grey line illustrates variation in income at age 25. See text for further explanation.

motor mechanic. Mike's initial earnings are higher than John's and remain so until both individuals are nearly 50, at which point Mike's earnings are overtaken by John's. The solid line represents the average of the two individual profiles.

The main differences between John's and Mike's trajectories are, first, the difference in the initial incomes (one is below the average trajectory initially; the other is above the average initially) and, second, the difference in income growth with age (again, one rate is above the average and the other is below it). A third feature is that initial incomes and income growth rates are negatively correlated: John has a lower income than Mike to start with, but experiences greater income growth. Their trajectories cross.

Now suppose that we wish to summarize the trajectories for all of the many individuals in this group, not only those for John and Mike. Given the average trajectory for the group as a whole, we can think of there being a distribution of initial incomes around the average and also a distribution of income growth rates, and some correlation between initial incomes and growth rates. Although most individuals within the group are located relatively close to the average, there are a few outliers with relatively low (or high) initial incomes or growth rates. The relative frequencies of high and low deviations from the average initial income are illustrated in Figure 7.1 using the grey line to indicate the relative concentration at different values. Most people are located close to the average value at age 25 (the grey curve is higher), with relatively small numbers with extreme values (where the curve is lower). In the analysis below, the joint distribution of initial incomes and growth rates with age is characterized using a bivariate normal distribution. The advantage of this is that the distribution is completely characterized using only three numbers—the standard deviation of initial incomes around the average, the standard deviation of growth rates around the average, and the correlation between initial income and growth rate—and these parameters can be estimated from longitudinal survey data along with the parameters that describe the group average income trajectory. This characterization is consistent with both the trajectories increasing with age for a majority within the group, and declining with age for a minority.

The model implies that not only is there within-group inequality in income at each age, but also that this inequality varies with age. Intuitively, the less dispersion there is in initial incomes, or in income growth rates, the lower the within-group inequality at any age. Substantial dispersion in the income growth rate will tend to increase age-specific within-group inequality levels as the group members age. The cumulative effect of persistent differential income growth is to magnify initial income differences, providing an impetus for profiles to fan out with age.

The framework can also be used to illustrate differences in income trajectories between groups. It is straightforward to compare average income-age profiles using the estimated group average trajectories. One can also compare income dispersion at each age across the groups, examining for example whether at a given age, inequality among men is more or less equal than among women with similar educational qualifications and birth year. In addition, one can explore the extent to which income levels at each age overlap across groups, examining for example whether, at a given age, even the poorest men earn more than the richest woman with similar educational qualifications and birth year, or whether there is substantial overlap in income levels.

There are two features added to the model to make it more realistic. First, the group average trajectory is allowed to have more 'wiggles' than the stylized trajectories shown in Figure 7.1. Second, an additional year-by-year source of idiosyncratic variation in an individual's income from the group average is introduced to account for the substantial longitudinal variability in incomes that arises in real life. This variation might conceivably arise from several sources, including genuine transitory variation, measurement error in income, or might reflect the impact on income of major life events such as the birth of a child or divorce (as discussed in previous chapters).

As the famous statistician George Box once said, 'Essentially, all models are wrong, but some are useful' (1979: 202). My models are definitely wrong in some of their details, but I believe they usefully summarize the main features of income-age trajectories. Later, the strengths and weaknesses of the modelling framework are discussed further.

The rest of the chapter unfolds as follows. In Section 7.1, I discuss the longitudinal data drawn from the BHPS that are used in the study. In particular, I discuss the measures of income that I employ (hourly wages and equivalized net household income), as well as the definitions of the 12 social groups. Section 7.2 looks at raw data on income-age trajectories and shows that they look like cooked spaghetti. The rest of the chapter is concerned with unravelling that spaghetti.

I set out the statistical model of income-age trajectories in Section 7.3. I also discuss a number of statistical issues that arise when fitting the model and interpreting the estimates. Model estimates are discussed in Section 7.4, with the focus on trajectories of hourly wages for employees. All the analysis was repeated using income defined instead as total individual income and as equivalized net household income, and the most significant differences in results for the different measures concern the shapes of average trajectories rather than within-group differences around the average. I discuss the differences in average trajectories for household income in this chapter, but refer readers to Jenkins (2009*b*) for the full set of results for all three income measures. Section 7.5 provides a brief summary and conclusions.

7.1. Longitudinal Data from the BHPS

The analysis is based on longitudinal data from interview waves 1–17 of the BHPS, corresponding to survey years 1991–2007. I use the original sample, but not data from the extension samples for Scotland, Wales, and Northern Ireland, which began in the late 1990s, because of issues concerning how to combine the data with those for the original main sample: see Chapter 4.

Two Measures of Income

The two measures of income used in this chapter are the hourly wage and equivalized net household income, both of which are expressed in January 2008 prices. (Jenkins 2009*b* also considers a third measure: total individual income.) The hourly wage refers to current usual employment income from a main job divided by the number of hours worked, assuming hours of overtime work are paid at time-and-a-half, and is expressed in pounds per hour pro rata. The measure exists only for employees; it is not defined for self-employed workers or for those who do not currently have a job at all. It does not differentiate between wages derived from a full-time job and those from a part-time job. In order to compare income levels across years taking account of inflation, all hourly wages are converted to January 2008 prices using information about the month and year of the interview and the monthly all-items Retail Prices Index.

Equivalized net household income is a broader measure because it covers all money income sources, not only employment income, and in principle has non-zero values for all individuals rather than only employees. The measure used is the same as used in the rest of the book, with differences in household size and composition accounted for using the 'modified OECD' equivalence scale. Income is expressed in pounds per week (pro rata) in January 2008 prices using information about the month and year of interview and a modified monthly all-items Retail Prices Index. At the time of writing, this measure is currently available only for BHPS waves 1–16, whereas wage rates can be calculated for 17 waves. See Chapter 4 for full details of the household income variable's derivation.

The individuals included in the analysis differ according to the income variable considered. When describing trajectories in hourly wages, I consider only individuals of working age, that is, aged at least 25 and less than 60 (women) or 65 (men). The analysis of equivalized net household income is based on individuals aged 25 or more, but with no upper age limit imposed. Age 25 is used to demarcate the start of the working life to ensure that dispersion and variability of initial incomes are not unduly affected by the relatively high turnover among new labour market entrants. In addition, I sought an age by which educational careers had been completed for the vast majority of individuals. As explained shortly, I classify individuals into groups according to their highest educational qualification, seeking a definition such that group membership is fixed throughout the life course. Age 25 fits this requirement, as explained below.

Twelve Groups Defined by Birth Cohort, Educational Qualifications, and Sex

The research for this chapter was commissioned by the National Equality Panel (2010), for whom differences within and between social groups were a primary focus, with characteristics such as age, sex, household or family type, ethnic minority group, social class, religion, and region of residence used to define group membership. To define social groups for my analysis, I aimed to use similar characteristics, but there was an additional constraint. Since the analysis is intrinsically longitudinal, I want individuals to retain the same group membership regardless of their age. This rules out use of characteristics such as family type or residential location which change over time. Some other characteristics are ruled out because either the BHPS does not collect the information (for example, about religious affiliation) or because sample sizes are prohibitively small (for example, for almost all ethnic groups apart from white British).

As a result, the characteristics used to define social groups are restricted to birth cohort, educational qualifications, and sex. For birth cohort, I distinguish two groups: individuals born before 1955, and those born in 1955 or later. Three levels of education qualification are distinguished: 'none': having no qualifications at all; 'some': having some educational qualifications but below A-level standard; and 'A-level(s)+': having at least one A-level or equivalent (for example, Highers in Scotland), or a tertiary qualification such as a degree. A-level exams are usually taken around age 18, and provide qualifications for university entry. Those who gain an undergraduate degree typically do so by the age 25. By choosing to examine trajectories only from age 25 onwards, I ensure that virtually all individuals remain in the same educational qualifications group throughout their life. By also distinguishing between the sexes, 12 social groups are defined. Sample numbers in each group are shown in Jenkins (2009b: table 1).

The number of groups and their definitions represent a compromise between seeking to explore fine detail in between-group differences (leading to more groups) and maintaining reliability (leading to fewer groups, each with larger sample numbers). An additional factor is that there has been a marked increase in average educational qualification levels in Britain over the period covered by the BHPS: the proportion with no qualifications has fallen significantly, while the proportion with A-levels or more has risen. This prevents me using a larger number of birth cohorts because, if the number of cohorts is increased, it is difficult to maintain sufficient numbers of individuals in groups defined by sex, birth cohort, and educational level. A similar problem arises if more qualification levels are distinguished, in which case the numbers of individuals from earlier cohorts with high qualification levels becomes too small.

The birth year used to define the two birth cohorts is chosen to maintain the spread of sample numbers across groups. I experimented with different definitions (for example cut-offs of 1950 or 1960), but the general patterns of between-cohort results that are reported later did not change. The cohort of individuals born in 1955 or after includes birth years from 1955 through to 1982, and the respondents range in age between 25 and 52 years over the period of the panel (1991–2007). For the analysis of wages, the cohort of individuals born before 1955 includes birth years from 1927 (men) or 1932 (women) through to 1982, and the respondents range in age between 37 and 64 (men) or 59 (women) over the period of the panel. For the measure of household income, the cohort includes earlier birth years as well and hence some men aged 65 or more and women aged 60 or more.

7.2. Income-Age Trajectories Look Like Cooked Spaghetti

In this section, I summarize raw data on individuals' income-age trajectories and argue that the pictures look like cooked spaghetti. With BHPS data for thousands of individuals, it is infeasible to show the raw data for everyone and so, instead, I focus on the experience of men and women born in just one year (1966) who have educational qualifications to A-level or more. Similar graphs for other groups are shown by Jenkins (2009b: figure 2) and confirm the spaghetti-like features of trajectories for them as well. After completing this chapter, I discovered that other researchers have labelled a diagram like Figure 7.2 a 'spaghetti plot'. For a review of spaghetti plots and related graphical devices, see Swihart et al. (2010).

Figure 7.2 has four panels. The two on the left plot income trajectories for men; the two on the right plot those for women. The top two graphs refer to hourly wages, whereas the bottom two refer to equivalized net household income. Within each chart, there is a separate line connecting the raw income values for each individual. The length of a line shows the number of years for which there are valid data. (A very small number of outlier profiles are not shown.) The data do not cover the complete working life for any individual, only a maximum of 17 years (the length of the BHPS panel).

For the cohort of individuals born in 1966, the data cover the beginning of the working life. Over this period, wages appear to rise with age on average, with the growth rate greater for men that for women. Wage levels appear greater for men than for women on average, but, for both sexes, there is also substantial dispersion around the average. In other graphs not shown here (Jenkins 2009b), I show that, for individuals born in 1966 but with no education qualifications, wages are lower on average than for the more highly qualified group shown here (for both men and women), though there are overlaps in trajectories across groups.

It is clear that there is substantial dispersion in wages at the start of the working life, with a high prevalence of small year-on-year fluctuations experienced thereafter for most individuals, combined with occasional very large temporal variation for a small minority. In general, trajectories cross and intertwine. This is what I call spaghetti.

The patterns can also be seen in the two charts for equivalized net household income. The principal difference between the profiles for wages and household income is that there appears to be greater dispersion at each age for income than for wages.

The ubiquity of trajectory spaghetti and the similarities in patterns for the two income variables are chart features that I wish to emphasize. The first feature is important because it emphasizes the potential role that a statistical

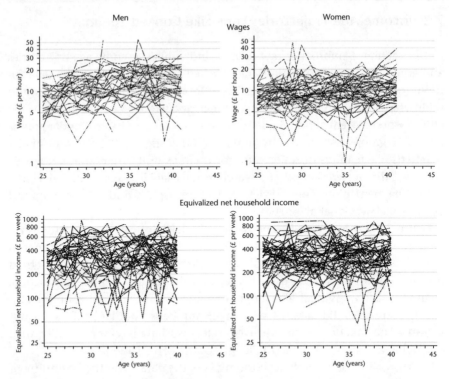

Figure 7.2. Income-age trajectories for hourly wages (£ per hour) and equivalized net household income (£ per week), logarithmic scale, for men and women born in 1966 who have A-level+ educational qualifications

Note: Author's derivation using data from BHPS waves 1–17.

model can play in summarizing these apparently complex patterns. The second feature is important because it suggests that the same statistical approach can be applied to each income variable and to each group. Echoing the quotation from George Box in the introduction to this chapter, these models are likely to be wrong in detail, but there are substantial advantages in having a unified common framework for comparisons across groups and variables. The statistical approach to unravelling spaghetti is set out in the next section.

7.3. A Statistical Model to Describe Individuals' Income-Age Trajectories

My statistical model of income-age trajectories draws on previous research. There are differences between approaches in the extent to which they consider the evolution of income over the short run or longer run (such as the whole life course) and the extent to which they focus on the average experience or variations across individuals.

The literature on income mobility referred to in Chapter 5 emphasizes the universal but heterogeneous experience of income change over time, but short-term income changes rather than life-course income trajectories are the object of study. Trajectories are central, however, to research that builds on the celebrated portrayal of the life-course variation in needs-adjusted income by Seebohm Rowntree, who characterized the life of a labourer as 'characterised by five alternating periods of want and comparative plenty' (2000 [1901]: 136). Rowntree's schematic summary related the shape of the income trajectory to important life-course stages such as childhood, marriage, the arrival and departure of children, and retirement. Rigg and Sefton (2006: figure 1) provide a late-20th-century update to this picture, drawing on ten waves of BHPS data. The pictures are not fully comparable because one is a stylized summary for a particular type of worker inspired by a pioneering cross-sectional survey (Rowntree) and the other is derived from representative panel survey data (Rigg and Sefton). Nonetheless it is interesting that both charts point to a quasi-M-shape in trajectories of needs-adjusted income in the middle of the life course and a clear decline after retirement.

What is missing from both pictures is characterization of the individual heterogeneity in profiles: the focus is on the average trajectory but not divergences from them. This task was beyond Rowntree's purpose, but Rigg and Sefton (2006) recognize the issue of heterogeneity as something that needs to be addressed. After relating their six trajectory types first to life-course stages, and then to life-course events, they ruefully acknowledge that '[a]lthough many of these events are related to specific income trajectories in the way we might expect, there is a large amount of heterogeneity in people's income trajectories following each of these life-cycle events... Typically, each life-cycle event increases the probability of experiencing a particular trajectory by a factor of approximately two, but most individuals will still follow one of the other trajectory types' (2006: 406). The message is that summaries of income-age profiles need to recognize heterogeneity in whole profiles. See also Gardiner and Hills (1999), who distinguish five types of trajectory shape using four waves of BHPS income data.

Heterogeneity is integral to the literature on variance components models that is reviewed in Chapter 6. These models are closely related to the one that I use in this chapter, but applications to date have had quite a different focus. Virtually all studies have modelled the dynamics of labour market earnings of men employed full-time and life-course demographic events are ignored because they are less relevant. Even more relevant for my current purposes, the implications of the models for income-age trajectories are rarely drawn out in any detail. (Chamberlain and Hirano 1999 is one exception.) I wish to place the variation with age centre stage when characterizing both average trajectories and divergences from them, while also making comparisons across groups and for several income measures.

My model is therefore a compromise. On the one hand, it is inspired by the variance components literature, but it uses a simplified specification relative to most contemporary applications. On the other hand, it also provides a framework for summarizing not only average income-age trajectories but also the individual-specific divergences from the average. A model similar to mine is that used by Gangl (2005) to compare income profiles across countries rather than social groups within a country. The analysis that is perhaps closest to mine in spirit is that reported in a series of papers by Creedy (1985, 1992, 1998). The relationships between average income and age, and income dispersion and age, are of central interest to Creedy, as they are to me. However, he does not draw out model implications for complete profiles as I do later in this chapter. There are also dynamic microsimulation models that produce estimates of life-course earnings and income profiles for large samples of individuals: see, for example, Statistics Canada (n.d.). These models are sophisticated but remarkably resource intensive in terms of the data and time required to develop them. My model is much less resource intensive, but captures many of the important features of the raw data.

To explain my model, I refer to 'income' in the generic sense; in the empirical work, I fit the same type of model to longitudinal data on each of the two measures of income described earlier. By contrast with the variance components literature, I do not first control for systematic observed differences in income by running regressions of (log) income on personal characteristics. Instead, I assume that the same model specification applies to each of the 12 social groups separately, but with different values of the model parameters applicable to each group. Both the regression and group approaches are ways of controlling for differences in characteristics. Using a group approach facilitates the between-group comparisons that I wish to do and is more flexible than the regression approach because all parameters including error variances and covariances are group-specific rather than homogeneous. On the other hand, whereas I identify 12 groups, regression-based approaches typically define many more, at least implicitly, because they use a large number of explanatory variables.

The outcome variable is the logarithm of income rather than income because this leads to better fitting models. The estimation method assumes that the residual error terms have a normal distribution and, because the distribution of income is skewed in shape, taking logs makes the normality assumption more appropriate. (I report checks on its suitability below.) The cost is that any observation with a non-positive income is dropped from the analysis, but this was rare.

Individuals in each group are differentiated by their age and their income. For person i in calendar year t, let age be represented by A_{it} and the logarithm of income by y_{it}. The model for y_{it} is described by:

$$y_{it} = (\alpha_t + \alpha_i) + (\beta_o + \beta_i)A_{it} + \gamma(A_{it})^2 + \delta(A_{it})^3 + \phi(A_{it})^4 + v_{it}. \qquad (7.1)$$

Equivalently, rearranging terms,

$$y_{it} = [\alpha_t + \beta_o A_{it} + \gamma(A_{it})^2 + \delta(A_{it})^3 + \phi(A_{it})^4] + \{\alpha_i + \beta_i A_{it}\} + (v_{it}). \qquad (7.2)$$

So, the model has three main building blocks.

The terms in [...] characterize the average trajectory for the group. This is a fourth-order polynomial function of age, hence allowing a flexible variety of shapes for the average profile. If parameters γ, δ, and ϕ are each equal to zero, then $\beta_0 + \beta_i$ shows the proportional rate of growth in income for each extra year of age for individual i, which may be negative. In general, the growth rate of income varies with age as well.

The model allows for a period-specific intercept, α_t, and so the whole income-age trajectory may shift up or down depending on the calendar year. Without such a term, increases in an individual's income arising from secular growth in the economy are attributed to age: the slope of the income-age profile would be over-estimated. I discuss issues related to the specification of α_t in more detail below.

The terms in { ... } characterize individual-level deviations from the group's 'average' profile. These deviations arise from differences in initial income (α_i) and differences in how income grows with age (β_i).

It is assumed that α_i and β_i each have a mean of zero—they represent deviations from an average—and follow a bivariate normal distribution. Thus individual-specific variation in income is captured by three parameters—two standard deviations and one correlation. There is the variation in 'intercepts' captured by standard deviation σ_α; the variation in 'slopes' captured by σ_β; and the correlation between slopes and intercepts, $\sigma_{\alpha\beta}$. These moments are fixed; they do not vary with age or calendar year. With a negative correlation, trajectories for different individuals may cross (as shown schematically in Figure 7.1 and in the raw data displayed in Figure 7.2).

The term in (...) introduces another source of individual-specific deviation from the average profile, that arising from idiosyncratic year-by-year variations from the average. This term is also assumed to be normally distributed with mean zero and dispersion summarized by σ_v, which does not vary with age or calendar year. These idiosyncratic deviations are assumed to be uncorrelated with α_i and β_i. In variance components modelling of wages, v_{it} is the 'transitory component', and discussed as arising from transitory variations per se or from measurement error (see Chapter 6). Examples of transitory variation are an occasional increase in wages negotiated in a collective bargaining agreement or occasional overtime working leading to a change in the wage rate. For a measure of income such as equivalized net household income, the v_{it} component may also reflect shocks to income arising from major life-course events, including job loss or gain and changes in household composition. Assuming that income changes arising from these sources have a normal distribution with a smooth symmetric distribution of deviations around the average is potentially questionable, and so some tests of normal fit based on quantile plots are reported by Jenkins (2009b). As it happens, the assumption appears remarkably good in the sense that the normality assumption appears consistent with at least 95 per cent of the observed data—it is only at the extreme tails of the implied v_{it} distribution that the fit is noticeably poor.

More important is my working assumption that these transitory shocks do not persist beyond the year in which they first occur. This assumption conflicts with the assumptions of and findings from the variance components literature. When I referred earlier to the necessity for compromises in modelling specification, this is the principal example of what I meant. In principle, persistence in transitory shocks could be incorporated in an extension of my modelling framework, but a lack of suitable software and time ruled out explorations of this kind for this chapter.

Underlying Explanations

A number of theories suggest that wages increase over the working life but at a decreasing rate. The conventional human capital story (Mincer 1974; Becker 1993) is that investments in education and training are largely financed by earnings foregone at the beginning of the working life and rewarded by faster-growing earnings subsequently. Even among groups with similar educational qualifications, one would expect configurations of trajectories as shown in Figure 7.1 because of differences in human capital investments other than in educational qualifications, for example on-the-job training. Differences in initial earnings may also represent genuine differences in 'ability', work readiness, and other factors affecting earnings. If these differences are observed by employers, one would expect trajectories to be higher for employees with greater 'ability' throughout the life course. But if 'ability' is not observed initially by employers, trajectory crossings may arise as a result of employer learning: 'ability' is revealed with the passage of time and pay is adjusted upwards or downwards accordingly. Personnel economics provides different arguments for upward-sloping wage profiles: an employment contract combining relatively low pay earlier in the working life with higher pay (including pensions) later provides incentives to employees to reduce shirking behaviours that might lead to dismissal and hence loss of the higher pay deferred until later in the working life (see, for example, Lazear 1995).

Various other matters complicate these stories and may lead to different average trajectory shapes for men and women, and for different birth cohorts. For example, women are more likely than men to work part-time, and part-time work is less well-rewarded. This is likely to produce slower-growing earnings for women relative to men over childbearing ages. Individuals from different birth cohorts may have the same level of educational qualification in name, but the knowledge and skills encapsulated in them may change over time and, correspondingly, the labour market rewards associated with them.

Since earnings are the principal income source for the majority of households, one would expect trajectories for wages and broader measures of income to be similar. Many of the differences in shape are likely to relate to periods when children are more likely to be present, not only because of the effects on labour force participation as discussed, but also because many social security benefits are child-related. For equivalized net household income, there is an additional effect: changes in the number of children (or adults) change this income measure via changes in the equivalence-scale factor, even if household money income remains the same.

Some Additional Issues

The 17 years of panel data do not span a complete working life, let alone a complete lifetime. For respondents who were 40 in 1991 (born in 1951), the panel covers the 17 years from age 40 until age 57; for respondents who were 25 in 1991 (born in 1966), the panel covers the 17 years from age 25 until age 42. So, if one wishes to describe income-age trajectories over the full working life, one has to assume some commonality of experience between people from different birth cohorts—which may not be appropriate. Alternatively, one allows for differences in trajectories between groups with similar birth years, and concedes that inference about complete life-cycle trajectories is constrained, which is the approach followed here.

A related matter is that the 17 years covered by the BHPS cover a particular period of economic history. At the beginning of the 1990s, Britain's economy was at the bottom of the economic cycle and the unemployment rate peaked in 1992/3 at around 10 per cent. (See Chapter 1.) Over the subsequent decade and a half, the state of the economy improved and by the peak of the cycle in 2007, the unemployment rate had halved. Incomes rose with economic growth and, as the labour market improved, more people previously without work took a job and those who might otherwise have lost their job or left the labour force (for example, by retiring) remained in work. This raises two potential issues.

The first arises from the association between the passage of calendar time and age, meaning that it is hard to prevent estimates of the relationship between income and age from being contaminated by the effects of period. Identification is secured by exploiting the fact that the panel contains individuals born in different years: for each calendar year, the panel contains individuals of different ages. But this in turn constrains the extent to which differences in income-age trajectories across birth cohorts can be identified, since age equals calendar year minus birth year. (For more discussion of age-period-cohort identification issues, see for example Deaton and Paxson 1994.) The approach taken here is to eschew estimation of fine-grained birth cohort effects, distinguishing only two groups, defined by whether a respondent's birth year was before 1955 or 1955 and afterwards. With a small number of broadly defined birth cohort groups, there is independent within-group variation in income by calendar year and age. The cut-off year of 1955 is arbitrary to some extent and chosen to ensure there are sufficient sample numbers in each group. I experimented with alternative cut-off years, and also with three groups rather than two, but this analysis did not change the broad tenor of the conclusions reported below. My allowance for calendar time (period) effects is relatively crude, and the empirical analyis simply distinguishes between the 1990s and the 2000s. (This choice was based on inspections of estimates from a series of preliminary ordinary least square (OLS) regressions of income against a fourth-order polynomial in age and a full set of binary indicators for survey year.) In terms of (7.1), α_t is specified as a binary indicator equal to one if the survey year is 1990–2000, and zero otherwise. Generalizing across income measures and groups, incomes were about 5 or 6 per cent lower during the 1990s than during the 2000s.

The second issue concerns changes in the composition of the labour force with the economic cycle or with age and other characteristics. Estimation of income-age profiles is based on data about those currently earning, but one would expect labour force attachment propensities to be positively associated with earnings potential, other things equal. For example, when the economy is in the doldrums, as it was at the start of the 1990s, there may be an under-representation of those with low earnings potential relative to boom periods. This 'selection' issue may be of particular relevance when estimating the average income of those at either end of the working life—young people entering the labour force, and older people approaching retirement age— relative to those aged in between, and also in comparisons between women and men, especially over parenting ages, since women with low earnings potential may be less likely to work or return to work. See Blundell, Reed, and Stoker (2003) for discussion of related selection issues in the context of estimating aggregate wage growth. In the discussion of empirical estimates in Section 7.4, I attribute some apparent anomalies in the shapes of income-age trajectories to selection issues.

Implications of the Model

The model implies that, within each group, log(income) is normally distributed at each age, and hence the shape of the distribution is characterized by the mean and variance of income at each age. This allows me to use the parameter estimates to summarize both the average trajectory for each group and the variation in income among people of the age within each group.

The average income-age trajectory for a particular group is given by the expected log income of a person at each age a:

$$E[y_{it} \mid A_{it} = a, t = \tau] = a_\tau + \beta_o a + \gamma a^2 + \delta a^3 + \phi a^4. \tag{7.3}$$

Thus the average trajectory is described by a fourth-order polynomial in age. The profile is period specific because the intercept α_τ is year specific.

The variance of log(income) at age a is:

$$\sigma^2(a) \equiv V[y_{it} \mid A_{it} \equiv a, t = \tau] = \sigma_\alpha^{\,2} + a^2 \sigma_\beta^{\,2} + 2a\sigma_{\alpha\beta} + \sigma_\nu^{\,2} \tag{7.4}$$

where $\sigma_\alpha^{\,2}$ ($\sigma_\beta^{\,2}$) is the variance of α_i (β_i), and $\sigma_{\alpha\beta}$ is the covariance between α_i and β_i. Thus, at each age, there is greater dispersion of income—a larger prevalence of deviations from the average group trajectory—the greater the dispersion of initial incomes or in income growth rates or in the dispersion of transitory income shocks. A negative correlation between intercepts and slopes is an inequality-reducing influence.

Assuming $\sigma_{\alpha\beta}$ is negative, the inequality-age relationship is U-shaped, that is, first declining with age and then increasing with age. More specifically, income inequality increases with age if $-\sigma_{\alpha\beta}\,\sigma_\alpha/\sigma_\beta < a$, and inequality decreases with age if $-\sigma_{\alpha\beta}\,\sigma_\alpha/\sigma_\beta > a$. Thus incomes are more likely to fan out as age increases, the larger is the dispersion in income growth rates and the less dispersion there is in incomes at the start of the working life.

For a lognormal distribution, as here, there is a one-to-one relationship between the variance of logarithms inequality index and other Lorenz-consistent inequality measures. For instance, the Gini inequality index is given by the expression

$$G(a) = 2\Phi([\sigma^2(a)/2]^{0.5}) - 1, \tag{7.5}$$

where $\Phi(.)$ is the normal probability distribution function. A U-shaped graph for $\sigma^2(a)$ against age a implies a U-shaped graph of $G(a)$ against age, with inequality changing from falling to rising at the same age. I do not examine inequality in the population as a whole, that is, for all groups combined, at each age. Overall inequality depends on three factors: inequality within each group (greater inequality in a group raises overall inequality); the mean income of each group (the greater the spread in the means, the greater is overall inequality); and the relative numbers in each group (the larger a group's population share, the greater the contribution to overall inequality of that group's inequality).

The normality property also enables me to summarize the whole range of incomes at each age. I focus on two specific ages, one at the start of the working life (age 25) and one in the middle (age 40), and use estimates of the lower and upper quartiles (the 25th and 75th percentiles) for each group to examine the extent to which the distributions of income for different social groups overlap.

The model could also be used to examine short-term mobility in incomes— the extent to which individuals may move up or down the distribution relative to others of the same age (as in Chapter 5). If (im)mobility is summarized using the correlation in log incomes between the two ages, its magnitude is intimately connected to the evolution of age-specific inequality with age. For example, there is greater mobility when inequality is rising with age. I eschew discussion of year-to-year income mobility, however. As discussed earlier, my model assumes that transitory shocks only have an effect on income in the year in which they occur. So, any income mobility predicted by the model is likely to be over-estimated. I focus instead on other aspects, in particular the shapes of age-income trajectories.

7.4. Estimates of Income-Age Trajectories: Group Averages and Individual Divergences

This section discusses the shapes of income-age trajectories on average and how they differ across individuals within and between groups. The discussion focuses on the estimates for hourly wages, with a comparison with the estimates for equivalized net household income at the end of the section. The presentation and interpretation of the results is done almost exclusively using graphs. For the parameter estimates, and discussion of the estimation method, see Jenkins (2009*b*).

Average Trajectories, by Group

The average trajectories for wages for employees of working age are shown for the 12 groups in Figure 7.3, and derived using equation (7.3), assuming the period corresponds to the 2000s. The trajectories are plotted using a logarithmic scale, so the slope of the trajectory shows how the proportionate growth rate of wages changes with age. (If wages increase at the same percentage rate for each additional year of age, the profile is a straight line.) The trajectories are shown only for the age ranges covered by the various estimation samples, so the pictures for the 1955+ birth cohort cover the age range 25–52 and those for

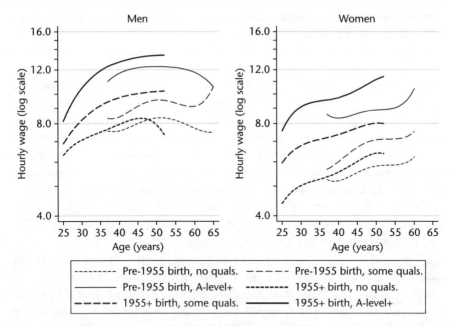

Figure 7.3. Average wage-age trajectories, logarithmic scale, by group, for employees of working age

Notes: Predictions of group average trajectories derived from estimates of statistical model discussed in the text. Estimates derived using data from BHPS waves 1–17.

the pre-1955 birth cohort cover ages ranging from 37 to 64 (men) or 59 (women). This is a reminder that conclusions based on extrapolations outside these age ranges (as in some later graphs) should be treated with caution.

Some clear patterns emerge from the estimates, and are in line with expectations. First, hourly wages increase with age from the beginning of the working life, but at a decreasing rate (with some anomalies that I return to shortly). On average, and regardless of group, men's wages grow continuously from the start of the working life but at a decreasing rate, peak in the late 40s and fall thereafter. In contrast, women's profiles do not have such a distinct peak—wage growth declines up until the late 30s, but then appears to rise again. The growth slowdown for women is consistent with a greater prevalence of part-time work, which is less well paid, particularly over the ages when many have children.

Second, for both men and women, and for both birth cohorts, having higher educational qualifications is associated with higher wages, with the return to additional qualifications greater for women than for men up until middle age (women's trajectories appear more parallel than divergent). But, third, among persons with similar educational qualifications and birth cohort, men are paid more on average than women at every age. Fourth, individuals from the later-born birth cohort are on higher trajectories than those from the earlier-born cohort, other things being equal.

The returns to different levels of education and differences between the sexes are substantial. For example, for men aged 40 from the 1955+ birth cohort, the difference on average between those with no qualifications and qualifications of at least A-level standard is a difference of around 50 per cent (just over £12 per hour, compared with just under £8). For women, the corresponding difference is around 55 per cent. But the difference between the hourly wage of a 40-year-old man and a 40-year-old woman, both from the younger cohort, is more than one-third in his favour on average (around 35 per cent). The average trajectory for women with at least A-level qualifications lies below that for men with some qualifications. The average trajectories for men with no qualifications lie almost everywhere above the average trajectories for women with some qualifications.

There are some potentially anomalous aspects to some profiles at the beginning and end of the working life, notably for the pre-1955 birth cohort: observe the upward twists in these cases. My explanation is that they reflect the impact of the selection effects cited earlier. For instance, arguably the women most likely to remain in the work force as the state retirement age (60) approaches are those for whom the pay rates are relatively high; those with relatively low pay rates retire. So, the pay rates used to estimate average trajectories over that age range are an over-estimate relative to the average that would be calculated were all women to have remained in work. Similar arguments can be made concerning older men, but it is a puzzle why the increase in the average is so pronounced for men with some qualifications but not for those with no qualifications. There is also a slight decline in average wages for men and women just prior to age 40 among the pre-1955 birth cohort. Arguably, this reflects a period effect. For this group, these years correspond to the recession years of 1991–3 and, again, men with relatively low earnings propensities were less likely to work, thereby raising the average calculated from those who were in employment.

Differences between Longitudinal and Cross-Sectional Estimates

Average income-age trajectories derived from longitudinal data look different from those derived from cross-sectional data. Figure 7.4 illustrates this point for hourly wages. The cross-sectional data used as the reference point are drawn from the UK Labour Force Survey (pooled data for 2006–8). I plot median wages (in 2008 prices) by age group, using the same age range as in Figure 7.3.

Longitudinal and cross-sectional data both point to some common features of trajectories, specifically that, on average, they have a 'hump' shape with

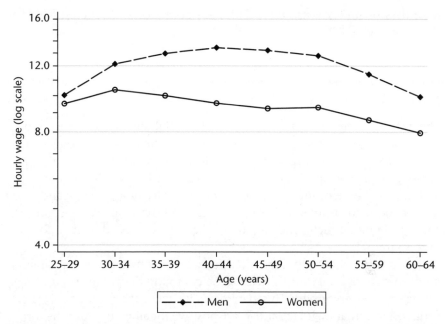

Figure 7.4. Cross-sectional pictures of 'average' wage-age profiles differ from longitudinal pictures

Notes: Data derived from UK Labour Force Survey, pooled data for 2006–8. Estimates refer to age-group medians. Logarithmic scale.

Source: Author's calculations from National Equality Panel (2010, table 3.2).

age, at least for men, and men are paid more than women at each age. However, there are some important differences. First, trajectories at the beginning of the working life are steeper—wage growth is greater—according to longitudinal data. And, second, wages continue to grow after age 40, whereas, according to the cross-sectional data, hourly wages peak during the 40s. Third, and related to the first two points, wage-age trajectories for women differ quite markedly between the two types of data source, and by more than for men. According to the Labour Force Survey (LFS) estimates, women's wage rates are fairly flat or decline from age 30 onwards (on average). By contrast, the BHPS longitudinal data suggest that women's earnings continue to increase throughout the working life on average, albeit with a dip in earnings growth rates associated with childbearing ages.

Part of the income growth associated with the longitudinal estimates may reflect the impact of secular growth in income—this is the issue of identification of age effects separately from cohort and vintage effects cited earlier. Illustrating this point, note that when I make no allowance for period effects when estimating average trajectories (that is, constraining α_t to be the same regardless of survey year), the profiles are even steeper (less concave) than shown in Figure 7.3.

Deviations from the Average Trajectory within Groups and Overlapping Group Distributions

The estimates reveal that there are substantial difference across groups in average income-age trajectories. But how much dispersion is there within groups around the average, and to what extent do the distributions across groups overlap? Table 7.1 provides a first look at the prevalence of within-group heterogeneity. It shows the estimates of σ_α, σ_β, $\sigma_{\alpha\beta}$, and σ_v for women born in or after 1955 with at least A-level qualifications, and the corresponding estimates for the other 11 groups expressed relative to those of this group.

The statistics shown in Table 7.1 illustrate the obvious but fundamental point that there is substantial heterogeneity around the group average trajectory and for every group. This heterogeneity takes the form of substantial variation in initial wages (σ_α and σ_v are positive for all groups, but the former is generally larger than the latter), combined with substantial variation differences in slopes ($\sigma_\beta > 0$). Moreover, there is a strong tendency for within-group

Table 7.1. Between-group differences in variance component parameters

Educational qualifications	Men		Women	
	Pre-1955 birth	Born 1955+	Pre-1955 birth	Born 1955+
sd(intercept): σ_α				
None	1.24	0.81	1.47	0.92
Some	1.75	0.84	1.36	0.92
A-level(s)+	1.63	0.90	1.66	1.00
sd(age coefficient): σ_β				
None	0.73	0.71	1.02	0.86
Some	1.07	0.80	0.91	0.80
A-level(s)+	1.06	0.89	1.07	1.00
corr(intercept, age coeff.): $\sigma_{\alpha\beta}$				
None	1.05	1.02	1.06	1.04
Some	1.07	1.02	1.05	1.02
A-level(s)+	1.05	0.99	1.05	1.00
sd(error): σ_v				
None	0.78	0.88	0.90	1.02
Some	0.90	0.79	0.85	0.95
A-level(s)+	0.86	0.86	1.08	1.00

Notes: Table shows estimated parameters of the statistical model discussed in the text. Estimates derived using data from BHPS waves 1–17. The parameters for each group are expressed as a ratio of the parameters for women born 1955+ with A-level(s)+. For this group, the parameters estimates are: $\sigma_\alpha = 0.993$, $\sigma_\beta = 0.030$, $\sigma_{\alpha\beta} = -0.919$, and $\sigma_v = 0.278$.

trajectories to cross: the negative estimate for correlation $\sigma_{\alpha\beta}$ means that employees with lower (higher) initial wages tend to have faster (slower) growth rates.

There are also some marked differences across groups, though there are few clear-cut patterns. The sharpest difference is between the earlier- and later-born birth cohorts. For both men and women, and for each educational group, the estimates of σ_α, σ_β, and $\sigma_{\alpha\beta}$ are notably smaller for the 1955+ cohort relative to the pre-1955 cohort, implying less within-group deviation from the average profile. But this impetus is offset for some groups by a rise in the transitory variance between earlier and later cohorts, and observe that the estimates of $\sigma_{\alpha\beta}$, vary little (all the ratios are close to 1.00).

The nature of the within- and between-group differences in income levels at different ages is illustrated by Figures 7.5 and 7.6. Figure 7.5 refers to the start of the working life (age 25); Figure 7.6 refers to nearer the middle of the working life (age 40). For each group, I show, using filled circles, the income of the person in the middle of the distribution (the median, which is also the mean given the normality assumptions). These are the income differences at

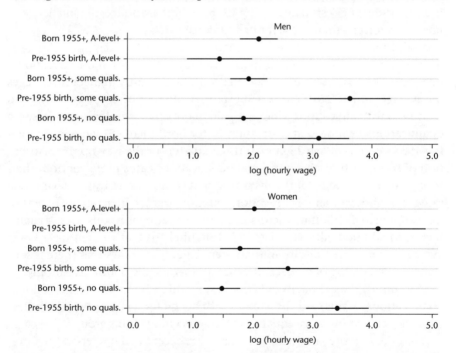

Figure 7.5. The distribution of log(hourly wage) at age 25, by group

Notes: Predictions derived from estimates of statistical model discussed in the text. The line for each group shows the group-specific inter-quartile range (distance between the 25th and 75th percentiles). The filled circles show the group medians (50th percentile), which is the same as the mean. The estimates for the pre-1955 birth cohort are less reliable because they are based on out-of-sample predictions: see text.

age 25 that are shown in Figure 7.3. The lines extending from each filled circle show the within-group dispersion in terms of a range of real income levels, specifically the distance between someone one-quarter of the way up from the bottom of the group distribution and someone three-quarters of the way up from the bottom (i.e. one-quarter of the way down from the top)—the difference between the 25th and 75th percentiles, otherwise known as the inter-quartile range. The chart shows that these correspond to substantial within-group differences in income. For example, for the 1955+ cohort, the inter-quartile range for both men and women regardless of education group is about 0.5, that is, the 75th percentile is some 50 per cent greater than the 25th percentile. The estimates for the pre-1955 birth cohort are less reliable because they are based on out-of-sample predictions, and so I give them less emphasis. The anomalous upward twists in the average profiles for this group discussed earlier imply an average income at age 25 that is implausibly large.

Figure 7.5 illustrates how the finding reported in Table 7.1 of smaller heterogeneity parameters for the later birth cohort relative to the earlier one translates into differences in the within-group spread of incomes. The sets of inter-quartile range estimates for the 1955+ cohort are noticeably smaller—the lines are shorter—than those for pre-1955 cohort.

In addition, Figure 7.5 shows that there is substantial overlapping in income distributions for the different groups. Even though having more educational qualifications, for example, is associated with significantly higher initial wages on average, at age 25 there is a substantial number of employees with no educational qualifications who are paid more than employees with some qualifications or indeed at least A-levels, for both men and women. Among the 1955+ cohort at age 25, a man three-quarters of the way up the distribution of those with some educational qualifications earns more per hour than someone in the middle of the distribution of those with at least A-levels. The same is true for women of this cohort, but note that, in general, the extent of overlapping in distributions across women's educational groups is less than for men's. In addition, although Figure 7.3 highlighted that women have lower average income-age trajectories than men, Figure 7.6 shows that there is substantial overlapping of men's and women's income distributions. Among the 1955+ cohort, the overlapping is smallest among those with no educational qualifications. In this case, the woman with her group's median wage earns less than the man whose wage equals the 25th percentile for his group.

Figure 7.6 is in the same format as Figure 7.5 except that it refers to the inter-quartile range for those aged 40, by group. (These are within-sample predictions for both birth cohorts.) The graph shows the same rankings of average wages at this age as reported in Figure 7.3, confirming for example that, on average, men are paid more than women, and having more educational qualifications is associated with higher wages. But, again, as at age 25, there is substantial dispersion of wages within each group, and this implies substantial overlapping in the wage distributions of different groups. Among those born in or after 1955, the man at the 75th percentile of the group with no qualifications earns slightly more than the man at the middle of the group with some qualification. But the man at the middle of the no qualifications group earns more than the woman at the 75th percentile of the group with no qualifications.

The model estimates can also be used to show how within-group inequality varies right across the age range covered by the working life. (Again remember that it is the middle age ranges for which there are within-sample predictions that are more reliable.) Figure 7.7 charts the inequality-age relationship, by group, using the Gini coefficient measure of inequality. The figures indicate large differences in inequality by age. For reference, observe that the Gini coefficient for wages among all employees increased from around 0.30 to 0.35 between the late 1970s and the mid-1980s—an increase widely regarded as historically large for Britain. (See, for example, Wren-Lewis, Muriel, and Brewer (2009: figure 2). Their report also provides inequality decompositions by age group based on cross-sectional rather than longitudinal data.) The

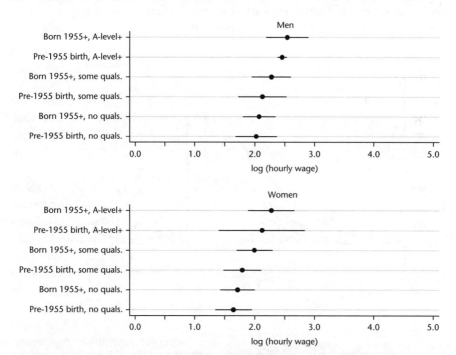

Figure 7.6. The distribution of log(hourly wage) at age 40, by group

Notes: Predictions derived from estimates of statistical model discussed in the text. The line for each group shows the group-specific interquartile range (distance between the 25th and 75th percentiles). The filled circles show the group medians (50th percentile), which is the same as the mean.

differences between the age-specific Gini coefficients for the beginning and end of the working life are of even larger magnitude according to Figure 7.6.

Two cross-group differences stand out from Figure 7.6. The first is the contrast between the profiles for the earlier-born and later-born birth cohorts. For those born in or after 1955, wage inequality increases with age throughout the working life after about age 35; before that age, there is little variation with age. By contrast, for those born before 1955, inequality declines with age until the mid-50s (men) or late 40s (women) and only then increases. (The reasons for the different age turning points in the profiles are not obvious.) The cross-cohort differences are related to differences in the ratio of the dispersion in initial wages to the dispersion of income growth rates ($\sigma_\alpha/\sigma_\beta$). Not only is each parameter smaller for the later-born cohort than its counterpart for the earlier-born cohort (Table 7.1), but so also is its ratio.

The second contrast is between those with A-level(s) or higher qualifications and the other two groups. In all but one case (men, pre-1955 cohort), those with A-levels experience distinctly greater inequality at each age throughout the working life than do those with fewer qualifications. There is a straightforward explanation for this. The other two groups are each relatively homogeneous in terms of formal educational qualifications, but the group with qualifications to A-level(s)+ includes not only people for whom A-levels are

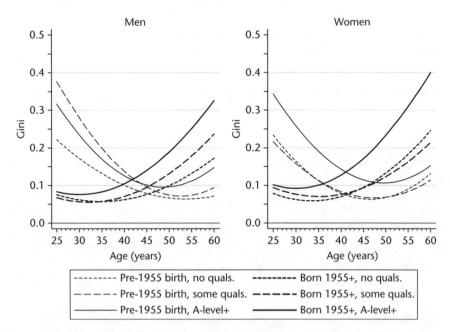

Figure 7.7. Inequality and age: Gini coefficient of hourly wages, by group

Notes: Predictions derived from estimates of statistical model discussed in the text. Out-of-sample predictions should be treated with caution.

their highest qualification but also people with undergraduate and postgraduate degrees, and one would expect there to be earnings differences associated with these differences in qualifications.

More about Within-Group Differences in Trajectories

The discussion so far has emphasized the importance of individual deviations from average trajectories in terms of the income differences within groups at each age, but the discussion has not described the shapes of complete trajectories for different individuals nor shown how these profiles differ from the average trajectory. I now do this, in two ways.

First, I use the model estimates to simulate complete trajectories for a set of individuals with the same observed characteristics. Within-group heterogeneity is summarized by the joint distribution of the individual-specific differences in intercepts, slopes, and transitory errors. These are fully characterized by σ_α, σ_β, $\sigma_{\alpha\beta}$, and σ_v for the relevant group, and so I randomly draw several sets of values—one for each hypothetical individual—from a joint distribution characterized by the estimated parameter values. Then, combined with the estimates of β_0, γ, δ, and ϕ (common within the group), I plot the wage-age trajectory that is implied for each of the hypothetical individuals.

Figure 7.8 shows the results of this exercise. It refers to men and women born in or after 1955 with A-level(s)+ qualifications, and the simulated trajectories refer to three men and three women. The average within-group trajectory is shown in Figure 7.3, and increases with age for both men and women (albeit at different rates). In Figure 7.8, there is a pair of trajectories shown for each person. The solid line shows the trajectory implied were there no transitory variation in wages (random values for v_{it} were not used in the simulation), and the accompanying dashed line shows the trajectory including simulated transitory variation.

The graphs show substantial differences in complete trajectories even within the same group. Features emphasized earlier such as the dispersion in initial incomes and dispersions in income growth rates are readily apparent again. But the diagram also brings out other features. In particular, the model is consistent with within-group trajectories crossing as well as not crossing: there are examples of both scenarios for men and for women in Figure 7.8. In addition, individual trajectories can be negatively sloped over most of the working life, even though the group average trajectory increases with age over the full age range.

Figure 7.8 also shows that transitory variation plays a major role in generating trajectory 'spaghetti'. Without the simulated transitory error term, profiles are relatively smooth. I emphasize the amplitude of the transitory variations, and not the temporal pattern of the errors for a given individual, because the

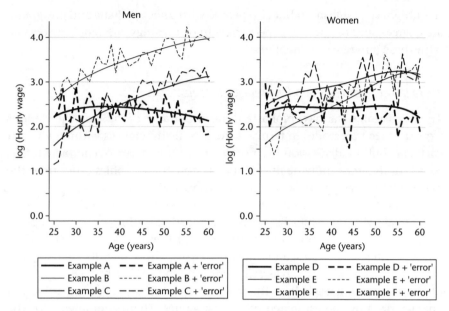

Figure 7.8. The heterogeneity of individual trajectories: simulated data example

Notes: Trajectories simulated using model estimates for men and women born in or after 1955 with A-level(s)+ educational qualifications. See text for further details.

model specification does not allow transitory shocks to have effects on wages that persist beyond the year in which they initially occur (see the earlier discussion).

A second approach is to examine the model's predictions of the complete trajectories for individuals observed in the analysis sample. Moreover, by comparing these individual-level predictions with the actual trajectories, we get an additional perspective on the role of transitory errors. To make the example more manageable, I focus on men and women born in 1966 (that is, who belong to the later-born cohort) and with A-level(s)+ qualifications—these are the employees whose trajectory spaghetti was summarized in Figure 7.1. The 'fitted' curves for each individual show predicted log wages, taking into account observed characteristics (age and the period-specific intercept in this context) and the best linear unbiased predictors of the individual-specific error components (α_i, β_i). These fitted values do not include the effects of transitory variation.

The graphs shown in Figure 7.9 highlight that there is substantial variation in individual income-age trajectories. Even with the smoothing of profiles incorporated into the derivation of the predicted profiles for each individual, there is substantial variation in complete profiles. There are large differences in

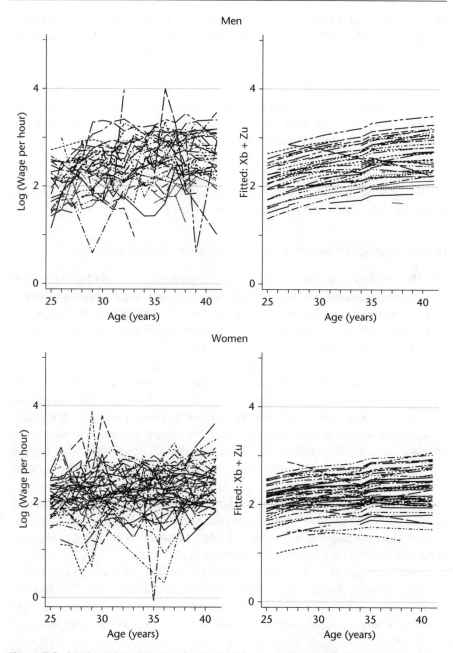

Figure 7.9. Log(wage) trajectories for men and women born in 1966 with A-level(s)+ qualifications: observed (left-hand side) versus fitted (right-hand side)

Notes: Charts refer to men and women born in or after 1955 who have A-level(s)+ educational qualifications. The two left-hand charts show the trajectories observed in the raw BHPS data. The two right-hand charts show trajectories fitted using model estimates. See text for further details.

fitted log wages at the start of the working life, and thereafter the fitted profiles for many move broadly in parallel, increasing with age. (The shift upwards in the middle of the fitted profiles arises from the allowance for a period effect—a different intercept for the 1990s and the 2000s.) But there is a relatively high prevalence of fitted profiles that cross over, and there is a minority of individuals for whom the fitted trajectory slopes downwards (wages fall with age), in contrast to the average pattern for the group (the prevalence of the latter feature appears greater for women in this case).

Figure 7.9 also underlines that it is the transitory component to income that cooks the spaghetti, introducing many of the year-to-year wiggles in trajectory shapes. Without transitory variation, trajectories are similar to what uncooked spaghetti looks like when it comes out of the packet.

How do Findings Change If Broader Measures of Income are Used?

All of the analysis reported so far for hourly wages was replicated using each of two income measures, namely individual income and equivalized net household income (Jenkins 2009b). I do not discuss all of these results because the main conclusions about the nature of the heterogeneity of income-age trajectories were broadly the same as for wages, including the diversity of shapes of complete profiles, with some rising and some falling.

The results that were most different across the measures concerned the shapes of the average trajectories. Figure 7.10 shows the average trajectories estimated for equivalized net household income, plotted using a logarithmic scale. There are several similarities with the results for hourly wages. For example, other things equal, higher trajectories are associated with having more educational qualifications, and being a member of the 1955+ birth cohort rather than the pre-1955 one. And as with wages, profiles are higher for men rather than women of the same educational level, though the sex differential is less than for wages—which is what is expected. The assumption of equal income sharing within households ensures this among couples and they form a large proportion of households.

However, there are noticeable differences across the measures in the shapes of the profiles for women, especially but not wholly those from the pre-1955 birth cohort. Whereas wages for women do not tend to fall as the state retirement pension age approaches, there is a clear decline in equivalized net household income. Equivalized net household income reaches a life-course peak in the 45–50 age range on average.

In addition, compared to the wage trajectories, there is a more marked dip in income growth rates over child-raising ages for wages (this result is derived from the data for the 1955+ birth cohort). The impact on the most educated group of women is pronounced: average income is predicted to fall in real

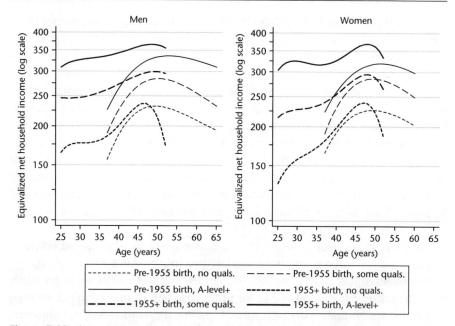

Figure 7.10. Average income-age trajectories for equivalized net household income, logarithmic scale, by sex

Notes: Predictions of group average trajectories derived from estimates of statistical model discussed in the text. Estimates derived using data from BHPS waves 1–17.

terms before rising again at around age 40 rather than to simply grow at a slower rate. In addition, there is a dip in the 30s for the two less qualified groups of women. A dip is perceptible for men too, especially for those with no qualifications. An explanation is that the partners of men without qualifications need to work to maintain family living standards much more than do partners of men with more qualifications. So, if the partner stops work or reduces work hours for child-related reasons, this also affects the household income share that men are assumed to get.

7.5. Summary and Conclusions

Most descriptions of the income-age relationship are based on comparisons of income across age groups in a particular year and are based on cross-sectional data. In contrast, this chapter takes a longitudinal approach, deriving trajectory estimates using 17 waves of BHPS data. My modelling framework provides summary descriptions of not only the way in which incomes among groups of similar individuals change with age on average, but also the way in which trajectories for individuals diverge from the average trajectory of their group.

The analysis draws attention to the cooked spaghetti nature of income-age trajectories. I have argued that this pattern can usefully be summarized in terms of a number of factors. Looking at groups of individuals with similar observed characteristics, one can distinguish an average income-age trajectory for each group. Within groups, one can summarize differences across individuals in terms of differences in incomes at the start of the working life, differences in income growth rates, and the association between initial incomes and income growth rates. (I find that those with lower initial incomes experience greater income growth on average.) In addition, income-age trajectories differ because of substantial individual-specific transitory income changes from one year to the next.

There are some clear differences in group average income-age trajectories, regardless of the income measure used. Other things being equal, an average profile for men lies above that for women; the average profile for individuals born in or after 1955 is above that for those born before 1955; and the average profile for individuals with educational qualifications to A-level or higher is above that for individuals with some qualifications, which, in turn, is above the profile for individuals with no educational qualifications. There is a distinct dip in income growth for women on average over the age range when many have children. These average income-age trajectories derived from longitudinal data look different from those derived from cross-sectional data. For hourly wages, trajectories at the beginning of the working life are steeper—wage growth is greater—according to longitudinal data. For household income, the picture for contemporary Britain is not exactly as Rowntree pictured it—but the flattening out of income profiles over the ages when children are likely to be present remains a reality.

Regardless of the pictures for the 'average' person in a group, there are substantial within-group differences in the shapes of complete income-age trajectories, with each of the sources identified above—differences in intercepts, slopes, and their correlation, and transitory variation—playing a role. Not everyone's income rises at the beginning of the working life; for some, income growth is minimal or even negative. As suggested in the introduction to this chapter, such heterogeneity is a reality that complicates the design of a number of social policy programmes. So, it is important to improve our statistical modelling of incomes over the life course, going beyond the approach employed in this chapter.

The chapter has argued that it is the transitory error component of income that cooks the spaghetti. These transitory changes may represent genuinely transitory effects on income, measurement error, or, for broader measures of income, the effects of life-course events, such as having children, and family formation or dissolution. A task for future research using models like mine is to incorporate more sophisticated assumptions about its nature and persistence over time. This is likely to be facilitated by access to even longer panels than used here. Long panels are necessary to help study the nature of income persistence in all its complex detail and to differentiate permanent changes from transitory variation.

Part III
Poverty Dynamics

8

Poverty Dynamics and How They Have Changed over Time

This chapter is about poverty dynamics in Britain. I document their nature and how they changed over periods covering from the beginning of the 1990s through to the mid-2000s. Chapters 5 and 6 examined income mobility throughout the whole of the income range; in this chapter and the next three, specific attention is given to movements above and below a low-income threshold—the poverty line.

To many people, poverty dynamics are of greater interest than income mobility. Governments and citizens tend to give greater weight to the reduction of poverty than to the reduction of inequality. Britain's former Labour government is no exception. (For recent evidence about attitudes to poverty and inequality in Britain, see Sefton 2009.) When asked in 2001 whether it was acceptable for the gap between rich and poor to get bigger, the then Prime Minister (Tony Blair) stated that 'the issue isn't in fact whether the very richest person ends up becoming richer. The issue is whether the poorest person is given the chance that they don't otherwise have', and 'the most important thing is to level up, not level down' (Blair 2001). The promise to reduce child poverty by one-half by 2010 and eradicate it altogether by 2020 is an important example of the Labour government's emphasis on poverty reduction. General principles were set out, for example, in the initial *Opportunity for All* (Department of Social Security 1999), and a range of initiatives were introduced to further poverty-reduction aims, targeted principally at families with children and pensioners: see Chapter 1.

At the same time, and following a similar shift in US policy discourse, much policy discussion of poverty reduction shifted emphasis from static to dynamic perspectives—this is the 'hand-up' rather than the 'hand-out' approach to those with low incomes. (See Gardiner and Hills 1999 about the UK, and Ellwood 1998 about the USA.) Summarized baldly, the old approach focused on the people who were currently poor and developed policies based on income supplementation. The new emphasis became the routes out of poverty for those who are poor and the routes into poverty for those becoming poor, together with the idea that policies should aim to support escapes from poverty and prevent entries into poverty.

The growing interest in this longitudinal perspective has also been accompanied by changes in how poverty is monitored in Britain. The annual *Opportunity for All* document, which summarizes progress on a wide range of indicators of poverty and social exclusion, includes a measure of 'persistent poverty' for children, working-age adults, and pensioners. More detail is provided annually in the Department for Work and Pension's *Low Income Dynamics* (LID) publication, of which the 2009 edition is the most recent at the time of writing. In both publications, persistent poverty is defined as being poor 'three or four years out of four', and rates are estimated from the BHPS (more on this below). A similar persistent poverty measure is also one of the European Commission's 14 Primary Indicators of social exclusion, with estimates produced using EU Statistics and Living Conditions data for every member state: see European Commission (2009).

Although there is general agreement about the importance of the longitudinal perspective on poverty, no single best way of characterizing poverty dynamics has emerged—just as there is no single best way of characterizing income mobility (Chapter 5).

Classification of people according to their experience of poverty persistence or repetition over a fixed period of time is an easily understood and transparent measure of poverty dynamics. For this reason, this measure has been commonly used since it was pioneered in applications to US poverty dynamics (see, for example, Duncan, Coe, and Hill 1984). But it also has disadvantages. First, the amount of time poor over a period does not tell us how long poverty spells are or how long people stay out of poverty if they have been poor. A person poor in the first year of a four-year window may have just entered poverty or been poor for five years already. Similarly, a person poor in the last year of the window may remain poor another year or another two years, or leave poverty. Information about spell lengths is incomplete: there are left- and right-censored spells, respectively (see Chapter 2). Second, and related, differences in the time spent poor, or in the time spent non-poor, reflect differences in individuals' poverty exit and entry rates—these are the more fundamental building blocks. So, it is informative to also examine these rates explicitly and to consider their correlates.

In this chapter, I describe poverty dynamics in Britain from all three perspectives: time spent poor over a multi-year period, lengths of poverty and non-poverty spells, and annual exit and entry rates. I also supplement these with a fourth perspective, one that distinguishes between chronic and transitory poverty. Chronic poverty measures are calculated by computing the longitudinal average of each person's income over a number of years, and comparing this average with the poverty line: someone is chronically poor in a given year if this averaged income is below the poverty line for that year. The approach has the advantage of taking some account of the intertemporal income transfers by individuals that smooth out transitory fluctuations—the idea that was also exploited in Chapter 6 when distinguishing between permanent and transitory variations in income.

The research reported here builds on previous research for Britain, notably that of Jarvis and Jenkins (1997), Jenkins (2000), and Jenkins and Rigg (2001). (For a systematic review of poverty dynamics research in Britain, see Smith and Middleton 2007.) The 2001 report provides a comprehensive picture of poverty dynamics based on nine waves of BHPS data (survey years 1991 to 1999). This chapter extends the description through to 2006 and, exploiting the longer run of panel data, provides more information about changes in the nature of poverty dynamics over time and about the prevalence of long poverty spells. Some comparisons with the experience of selected other European countries are also included in this chapter.

Since the Jenkins and Rigg (2001) report, the LID publication has provided valuable information about poverty dynamics using BHPS data, much of which is in formats that we developed. Compared to LID, the analysis in this chapter is more comprehensive in the sense of providing additional perspectives, notably on spell lengths and chronic poverty, and also gives greater emphasis to description of changes over time. On the other hand, the DWP report provides information for both 'before housing costs' and 'after housing costs' measures of household net income—only the former is considered in this book. In addition, LID utilizes several low-income thresholds, whereas I focus on one—a poverty line for a given year is equal to 60 per cent of median income for that year. A need for brevity is the main reason for this.

The justification for focusing on the 60 per cent of contemporary median income cut-off is that it is the principal poverty line used in Britain's official income distribution statistics and, related, is also the threshold focused on in official EU reports on poverty and social exclusion; indeed, it is the basis of the poverty persistence Primary Indicator cited earlier. This poverty line has increased over time from around £123 per week for BHPS survey year 1991 to £167 per week for 2006, in January 2008 prices. (The growth in median income over this period was shown in Chapter 4.) For poverty dynamics analysis using thresholds defined in terms of incomes equal to a constant fraction of 1991 average income—a line fixed in purchasing power terms—see, for example, Jarvis and Jenkins (1997) and Jenkins (2000).

There are other caveats. First, the analysis is based on a measure of current income, specifically net household income equivalized using the modified-OECD scale, the same measure as employed in Chapters 5–7 on income mobility and the construction of which is discussed in detail in Chapter 4. (The measure used in LID is very similar, the main difference being that local taxes are not deducted from income.) In this chapter, what is referred to for brevity is poverty status in a particular survey year, or poverty entries and exits between years Y and Z, but what is actually measured is poverty status round about the time of the interview in survey year Y and changes in poverty status between the annual interviews in survey years Y and Z. As discussed in Chapter 2, the combination of current income measures and annual interviews means that short spells of poverty that start and finish between interviews are missed entirely.

Second, there is little accounting for the effects of measurement error and potentially erroneous classifications of individuals as poor or non-poor arising from this. Small income changes—for example from £1 below the line to £1 above, or vice versa—may simply represent measurement error (or transitory variation) rather than a genuine transition out of or into poverty. One commonly used way to investigate the impact of these threshold effects is to count as a genuine poverty transition only those transitions that also involve an income change of a particular size or an income change taking a person some minimum distance above or below the poverty line. See, for example, Bane and Ellwood (1986) and Duncan et al. (1993). My experience with BHPS data is that such adjustments make little difference to the conclusions drawn: see Jenkins (2000) and Jenkins and Rigg (2001: 35–6). Analysis of chronic and transitory poverty is another approach to this issue and results based on it are presented below.

Third, the analysis reported in this chapter takes no account of how poor individuals are when they are poor (the shortfall of income below the poverty line) and no account of the extent to which income is above the poverty line during periods that individuals are not poor. How indicators of poverty severity should be introduced into longitudinal measures of poverty is not clear cut, and is the subject of current research: see, for example, Bossert, Chakravarty, and D'Ambrosio (2008), Duclos, Araar, and Giles (2010), and Foster (2007). In this chapter, I stick with measures that simply record whether or not someone was poor ('headcount' measures). For some analysis using longitudinal measures of poverty that account for the size of income shortfalls from the poverty line, see Hill and Jenkins (2001).

This chapter shows that patterns of poverty dynamics differ substantially from the patterns of income mobility, both across groups and over time. Income movement relative to a low-income threshold is different from income movement in general. The headline finding of Chapters 5 and 6 is that income mobility, however measured, hardly changed in Britain between 1991 and 2006, and this was so for most subgroups within the population as well. In this chapter, I show that there have been marked changes in the longitudinal experience of poverty in Britain, with reductions in the persistence of poverty, especially for dependent children and for single pensioners. These are groups for which it is relatively well-known that cross-sectional poverty rates have fallen (see, for example, Department for Work and Pensions 2010 and Joyce et al. 2010), but the longitudinal aspects are less well-known.

As a reference point for what follows, Figure 8.1 shows trends in poverty rates in Britain between 1991 and 2006, broken down by population subgroup. The rates are estimated using the BHPS income data that are used in the remainder of the chapter, and correspond well with those reported in *Households Below Average Income* statistics (Department for Work and Pensions 2010). The proportion of the population with an income less than 60 per cent of median income falls slightly over the 15-year period as a whole from just over 22 per cent in 1991 to around 18 per cent in 2006, but including fluctuations in the 1990s, followed by secular decline, and a small rise in the final two years when unemployment increased slightly (see Figure 1.1 in Chapter 1). This pattern describes the trends over time for most groups as

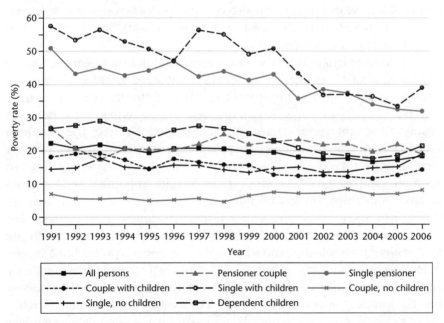

Figure 8.1. Poverty rates, 1991–2006, by family type

Notes: Estimates derived from weighted data for BHPS waves 1–16, and refer to distributions of equivalized household net income among all persons (see Chapter 3 for details). The poverty line is 60% of contemporary median income. The population shares of each group stayed relatively constant over the period, as follows: pensioner couple, 13%; single pensioner, 9%; couple with children, 36%; single with children, 7%; couple with no children, 18%; single with no children, 17%; and dependent children, 21%.

well. The main difference between the groups is their poverty rates, not the trends. For example, for dependent children, poverty rates are between 25 per cent and 30 per cent at the beginning of the 1990s, and around 21 per cent in 2006. The groups with the highest poverty rates are individuals in lone-parent families ('single with children') and single pensioners with rates around 55 per cent and 45 per cent in the early 1990s, but rates also decline over time to 'only' about 35 per cent in the mid-2000s. In what follows, I often highlight the experience of children or families with children, and single pensioners, as these are the groups for whom changes in poverty dynamics have been the most apparent.

8.1. Poverty Persistence and Recurrence: Number of Times Poor over a Period of Time

I begin by documenting the persistence and recurrence of poverty in Britain as summarized by the number of times an individual is observed poor over a period of time, and how these patterns have changed since 1991. I focus on a period of four years initially, but also consider periods of a nine-year length. Seven-year periods were also used in preliminary work but provide similar conclusions to nine-year periods.

What the best length is for the observation window is not clear cut. On the one hand, a relatively long window better enables us to judge whether, for example, a short spell of poverty represents a temporary phenomenon, or whether it forms part of a pattern of recurrent or long-term poverty. But there are also disadvantages of longer observation windows. First, the sample of individuals for whom a full set of nine waves of data is available may be less representative than the samples with data available for shorter windows. In addition, samples for longer windows are smaller in number and estimates derived from them are less reliable. Non-representativeness may arise for several reasons, for example, with a nine-year window, children aged less than 9 are excluded because they would not have lived long enough. By similar arguments, older pensioners may also be under-represented. A second potential problem is sample dropout that varies by income (existing evidence suggests that attrition is greater for poorer individuals than richer ones), but this problem is to a large extent addressed by using sample weights. All the calculations reported below are based on weighted data, but I find that unweighted data yield similar results. Third, with a long window, there is a greater likelihood that individuals change their characteristics during the window—over time, family formation and dissolution lead to changes in family type, and gain or loss of a job can change family economic status—thereby making it more difficult to undertake meaningful subgroup

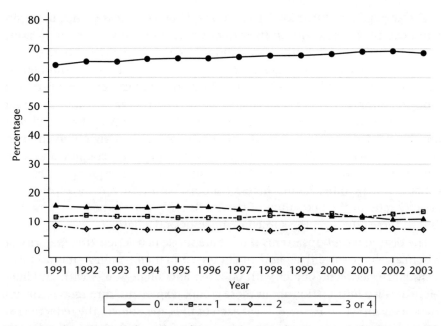

Figure 8.2. Distribution of number of times poor over a four-year period, all persons, by year

Notes: Estimates derived from weighted data for BHPS waves 1–16. Year refers to the first year of each four-year period. The poverty line is 60% of contemporary median income. Individuals are classified into groups according to their characteristics in the first year of each four-year period.

decompositions. Fourth, with long windows, the scope for examining change in poverty persistence patterns over an interval of one or two decades is constrained. Using four-year windows reduces these problems, and they also have the advantage that they are used in official British and EU statistics. In sum, nine-year windows provide a complementary perspective, subject to greater doubts about the reliability and interpretation of the estimates.

The distribution of the number of times poor over a four-year period is summarized in Figure 8.2. The chart shows the percentage of all individuals that was observed poor at no interview out of four, poor at one interview, and poor at three or four interviews ('persistently poor'). Just under two-thirds of all individuals are never observed poor over a four-year period at the beginning of the 1990s, with the fraction increasing over time to reach just over two-thirds in the mid-2000s. Expressed differently, around one-third of individuals in the population are 'touched' by poverty over a four-year period, which is a fraction about 50 per cent larger than the proportion poor in any given year. About one in seven individuals are persistently poor at the beginning of the 1990s (poor three or four times out of four), with the fraction falling to nearer one in nine by the mid-2000s.

The aggregate picture hides substantial differences across groups in persistent poverty rates and also in their trends over time. This is shown by Table 8.1, which summarizes the distribution of number of times poor, broken down by family type, for three four-year periods between 1991 and 2006—those beginning in 1991, 1997, and 2003. (Individuals are classified into groups according to their characteristics in the first year of each four-year period.) On the one hand, there are groups with relatively low persistent poverty rates and correspondingly high rates of never being observed poor: these are primarily individuals aged 30–59 years, childless couples, and individuals in families with one or more full-time earners (these groups overlap of course). On the other hand, there are groups with relatively large persistent poverty rates at the beginning of the 1990s and which experienced marked falls in these rates over the subsequent decade and a half.

The distinctive groups in this respect are single pensioners (the majority of whom are women), and dependent children and their families—it is useful to distinguish between couples with children and single adults with children. More detailed information about these groups' experience throughout the full 16 years is shown in Figure 8.3. For each of the cases shown, the reduction in the persistent poverty rate is accompanied by a rise in the proportion of the group who are never observed poor in a four-year period: there is relatively little change in the proportions observed poor once or twice.

Among dependent children (Figure 8.3(a)), the persistent poverty rate almost halves, falling from 20 per cent for the four-year period starting in 1991 to 11 per cent for the period starting in 2003, with decline most apparent for periods beginning around 1997, and hence covering the years when the Labour government changed the tax-benefit system to help families with children (Chapter 1).

Even more striking patterns are apparent when one compares the experience of couple families with children and lone-parent families: see Figures 8.3 (b) and 8.3(c). Among the former group, the proportion of families with a full-time earner is much higher and this is reflected in a substantially larger percentage of individuals who are never observed poor over a four-year period (rising from just below to just over 70 per cent over the full period), and a substantially lower percentage of individuals who are persistently poor—but their persistent poverty rate halved from 12 per cent to 6 per cent nonetheless. For individuals in lone-parent families, persistent poverty rates are very high—between 40 per cent and 50 per cent at the beginning of the 16-year interval—but also fell dramatically to around 26 per cent for the four-year period beginning in 2003. At the same time, the proportion never observed poor in a four-year interval increased by more than 50 per cent, from 26 per cent to 42 per cent. (The greater year-on-year variability in estimates for this group reflects relatively small sample numbers.) The distinct change in trends from

Table 8.1. Distribution of number of times poor over a four-year period, by year and family type

Percentages	None			One			Three or Four		
	1991	1997	2003	1991	1997	2003	1991	1997	2003
All individuals	64	67	68	12	11	13	15	14	11
Person type									
Dependent child	58	60	65	12	13	17	20	17	11
Male adult aged < 30 years	73	80	76	11	11	10	8	6	6
Female adult aged < 30 years	66	69	68	10	12	15	16	11	8
Male adult aged 30–59 years	78	80	78	10	9	11	7	5	5
Female adult aged 30–59 years	75	75	75	11	10	12	8	9	7
Male adult aged 60+ years	55	59	62	14	12	13	19	19	18
Female adult aged 60+ years	40	46	52	14	12	15	32	32	23
Family type									
Pensioner couple	61	60	64	13	12	12	17	17	17
Single pensioner	32	38	46	16	12	17	38	40	26
Couple with children	68	72	73	11	11	14	12	9	6
Single with children	26	25	42	13	18	21	49	42	26
Couple, no children	84	86	83	8	7	8	3	3	4
Single, no children	71	74	71	14	12	13	8	8	8
Family economic status									
One or more self-employed	60	61	55	18	15	21	10	11	14
Single/couple all in full-time work	91	92	91	5	5	6	1	2	1
Couple, one full-time, one part-time	86	87	84	7	9	11	2	1	2
Couple, one full-time, one not working	75	72	72	12	12	13	7	8	8
No full-time, one or more part-time	45	48	62	19	18	15	23	21	12
Workless, head or spouse aged 60+	42	47	53	14	13	15	30	30	23
Workless head or spouse unemployed	18	22	23	15	18	17	52	44	37
Workless, other inactive	29	34	34	14	19	28	45	37	22

Notes: Weighted estimates from BHPS waves 1–16. Year refers to the first year of each four-year period. The poverty line is 60% of contemporary median income. Individuals are classified into groups according to their characteristics in the first year of each four-year period. Table reads: 64% of all persons were not poor at any of the four annual interviews for survey years 1991–1993; 15% of all persons were poor at three or four interviews over the same period.

Poverty dynamics

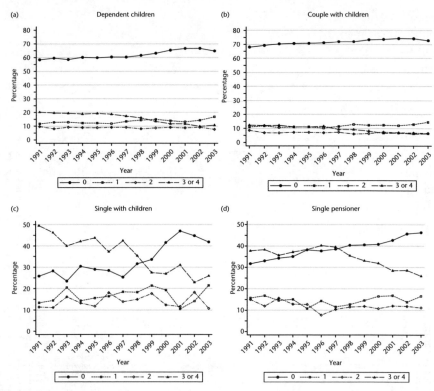

Figure 8.3. Distribution of number of times poor over a four-year period, by family type and year

Note: As for Figure 8.2.

around 1997 onwards is also more apparent when looking at each group of families with children separately.

For single pensioners, there are similar trends. There is a substantial fall in their persistent poverty rate of almost one-third, from 38 per cent to 26 per cent, with a sharp drop apparent from around 1997. Compared to families with children, however, the rise in the proportion never observed poor over a four-year period appears to have been steady throughout the whole of the 16-year period.

To investigate the sensitivity of the estimates to variations in the low-income cut-off, I repeated all the calculations for Table 8.1 and Figure 8.3, using the lowest quintile for each year instead of the 60-per-cent-of-median poverty line. (This poverty line is slightly less than the lowest quintile at the start of the 1990s and slightly less in the early 2000s: see Figure 8.1.) The conclusions about trends are much the same. The main difference is that the persistent poverty rates for lone-parent families and single pensioners are larger at the beginning and fall by more, reflecting the fact that these two groups are concentrated at the bottom of income distribution. (However, recall from Chapter 3 that the BHPS appears to have an over-representation of single pensioners in the poorest groups compared to HBAI benchmarks.)

Cross-National Differences in Poverty Persistence

Is poverty persistence in Britain larger or smaller than in other countries? The most comparable estimates are those of Fouarge and Layte (2005) for the four-year period 1993–8, derived from European Community Household Panel data for 11 European countries. They use a similar equivalized household income definition (except that they use annual rather than current income) and the same poverty line (60 per cent of median income). They show that the UK has the eighth-highest proportion of persons poor at least three years out of four, 14.1 per cent—slightly larger than the proportion in France (13.3 per cent) and slightly smaller than the proportion in Ireland (14.9 per cent). The degree of persistent poverty is substantially higher in Britain than in Denmark and the Netherlands, for which the persistent poverty rates are only 3.5 per cent and 6.4 per cent respectively. The third-smallest proportion was for Germany (7.8 per cent). The highest rates were in Greece (15.2 per cent) and Portugal (18.1 per cent), and the simple 11-country average was 11.7 per cent. These persistent poverty rankings are almost the exact reverse of the rankings according to the proportions of persons never poor over a four-year period.

Fouarge and Layte (2005: 412–13) suggest that the persistent poverty rankings accord with the rankings expected from classifying countries into welfare-state types in the Esping-Andersen (1990) sense, with 'social democratic' nations having lower rates and 'liberal' and 'residual' nations having higher rates. It is certainly true that social-democratic countries have lower persistent poverty rates, but the relationship with welfare-state type is not entirely straightforward. For instance, analysis by OECD (2001) suggests that the choice of poverty line can make a difference to conclusions.

OECD (2001: table 2.1) presents estimates of the proportion of persons poor in three years out of three for the period 1993–5 for the same set of countries as Fouarge and Layte (2005), but also adding Luxembourg, and data for Canada and the USA from the Cross-National Equivalent File. As before, among the European nations, Denmark has the lowest rate (0.8 per cent) and Greece and Portugal have the highest rates (6.5 per cent and 7.8 per cent), but now the two 'liberal' welfare-state nations, Ireland and the UK, also have relatively low rates (1.3 per cent ranking second, and 2.4 per cent ranking fourth, respectively), and Germany slips down the rankings. The most likely explanation for the differences in rankings is that OECD (2001) used a poverty line of 50 per cent, not 60 per cent, of median income, and there are cross-country differences in where most people are concentrated along the income range. Related to this, OECD (2001) also points out that cross-national rankings differ if one compares subgroups within the population, such as elderly people and children. On this point, also see Bradbury, Jenkins, and Micklewright (2001). Valletta (2006) also shows that the USA has substantially higher proportions of persons poor three years out of three (14.5 per cent).

All in all, differences in poverty persistence between polar types of welfare state—the social-democratic welfare states and the most 'liberal' state (the USA)—are apparent and robust to variations in definitions, but, otherwise, the association with welfare-state type or cross-sectional poverty rate is less clear. Britain is somewhere between the two extreme types of welfare state, but its performance depends on the definition used. The time period for the comparisons is also relevant since the analysis presented earlier shows a marked decline in the persistent poverty rate in Britain over time. Cross-European comparisons based on more up-to-date data must wait until sufficient longitudinal data from the EU Statistics and Living Conditions studies have accumulated.

Poverty over a Nine-Year Period

If one extends the window of observation substantially, from four years to nine, it is possible to differentiate additional types of poverty experience. Specifically, I now distinguish between short-term persistent, recurrent, and long-term persistent poverty. The first two types of poverty both refer to being observed poor between two and six times over a nine-year period, but the first case is when there is only a single spell within the window (all poverty years are consecutive), and the second case is where there are two or more separate spells. 'Long-term persistent poverty' is defined as being observed poor at least seven times over a nine-year period. The estimates are summarized in Figure 8.4 for all persons and dependent children, groups for which sample sizes are relatively large.

One striking result concerns the proportions of individuals who are never or ever observed poor over a nine-year window. Over the 1990s and early 2000s, the proportion never poor remains fairly constant at around 55 per cent (Figure 8.4(a)). That is, just under half (45 per cent) of all individuals could expect to be poor at least once in a nine-year period. So, approximately doubling the window length from four years to nine increases the chances of being observed poor at least once by a factor of about 50 per cent (from around 30 per cent). Over a nine-year period, nearly one-half of all individuals are touched by poverty at least once, which is more than double the proportion of people poor in any given year.

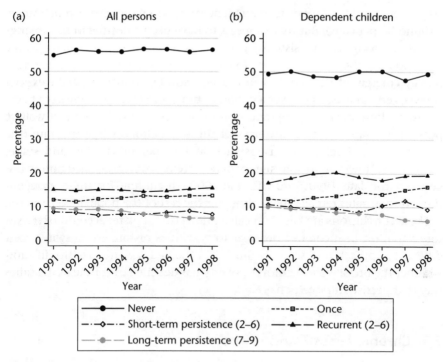

Figure 8.4. Number of times observed poor over a nine-year window, all persons and dependent children, by year

Notes: Estimates derived from weighted data for BHPS waves 1–16. Year refers to the first year of each nine-year period. The poverty line is 60% of contemporary median income. Individuals are classified into groups according to their characteristics in the first year of each nine-year period. See text for definitions of short-term persistence, recurrent, and long-term persistence.

For dependent children, the chances of being observed poor at least once are even higher: around one-half of all children can expect to be poor at least once over a nine-year period, and this fraction has remained relatively constant (Figure 8.4(a)). The good news, however, is that the prevalence of persistent poverty has declined over time for all persons and dependent children in particular. For both groups, the proportion observed poor at least seven times over a nine-year period has fallen from around one in ten to one in fifteen. The main difference between the population as a whole and dependent children is that the latter group experience greater recurrent poverty. Further examination of this finding using subgroup decompositions is constrained by the issues mentioned earlier, especially small sample sizes and changes in subgroup membership over time. It appears (from estimates not shown), however, that whereas the picture for couple-with-children families is similar to that shown for dependent children, the one for lone-parent families differs. The fraction of this group never observed poor is much smaller (nearer

20 per cent) and the proportion experiencing recurrent poverty is much larger (around 30 per cent). But there appears to have been a decline in the proportion that is long-term persistently poor.

Combining the results from the four- and nine-year window calculations, a picture emerges of a Britain in which a significant minority of people experience poverty at least once over a period of time, and recurrent poverty affects many of these people. The proportion of people who experience persistent poverty is relatively small in terms of the population as a whole, but is a relatively large fraction of groups such as lone-parent families and single pensioners. However, the prevalence of persistent poverty declined noticeably between the late 1990s and the mid-2000s, including for these groups—though their rates remain above those for the rest of the population.

These conclusions are based on calculations that took no account of transitory variation in incomes from year to year. It is of interest to switch to a different approach and see how much of observed poverty is 'chronic', and whether the prevalence of chronic poverty has declined over time in the same way that persistent poverty has.

8.2. Chronic versus Transitory Poverty

Chronic poverty in a population is defined as the poverty which would exist were each person's income spread evenly over time, that is, if each person were to receive every year a smoothed income equal to the longitudinal average of their income over a window of fixed length. As in Chapter 6, I take a window length of seven years and the longitudinal average income for each person is what I referred to earlier as his or her 'permanent' income. At the individual level, a person is chronically poor in a given year if their permanent income is less than the poverty-line income. Depending on how income varies over time, in a given year, someone may be chronically poor and currently poor, one or the other, or neither. If we discount transitory income variations on the grounds that people can take account of them by saving or borrowing and drawing down on assets (cf. Chapter 2), or treat such variations as representing measurement error, then we wish to minimize chronic poverty above current poverty, and the extent to which current and chronic poverty status overlap in any given year tells us something about the extent to which policies targeted using information about current income will be effective in reducing chronic poverty.

Total poverty in a population over a number of years is the longitudinal average of the poverty within each of those years. Thus, with a seven-year window, total poverty is the seven-year average of the proportions poor in each of the seven years. This can be interpreted as the amount of poverty in an 'average' year. (One can show that total poverty defined in this way is exactly the same as the average across the population of each person's poverty longitudinally averaged over the period.) Transitory poverty is the poverty remaining when chronic poverty is subtracted from total poverty. This approach was developed by Chaudhuri and Ravallion (1994), Jalan and Ravallion (1998), and Rodgers and Rodgers (1993, 2009). Hill and Jenkins (2001) used the approach to examine the dynamics of child poverty in Britain. OECD (2001) and Valletta (2006) present estimates of chronic poverty rates for selected European countries, Canada, and the USA. Kuchler and Göbel (2003) also compare rates across European countries.

The decomposition of total poverty into its chronic and transitory components is shown in Figure 8.5 for all persons and for selected family types, by year (the middle year of each seven-year period). For all persons, total poverty (poverty in an average year) declines between the beginning of the 1990s and the 2000s from 19.3 per cent to 16.5 per cent. Transitory poverty remains

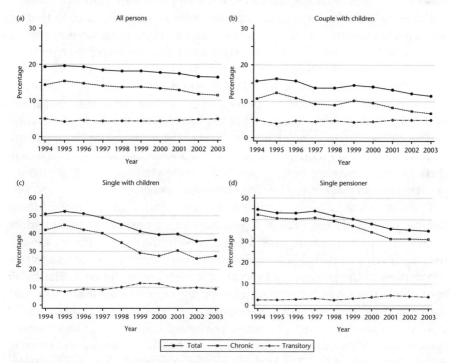

Figure 8.5. Decomposition of total poverty over a seven-year period into chronic and transitory poverty, by family type and year

Notes: Estimates derived from weighted data for BHPS waves 1–16. Year refers to the middle year of each seven-year period. The poverty line is 60% of contemporary median income. Individuals are classified into groups according to their characteristics in the first year of each seven-year period. The decomposition of total poverty into its chronic and transitory components is explained in the text.

constant at around 5 per cent of the total, while chronic poverty declined in tandem with total poverty. Clearly, for the population as a whole, most poverty is chronic rather than transitory. About three-quarters of total poverty is chronic at the start of the 1990s, and around 70 per cent by the 2000s. This result is consistent with the results concerning income mobility that were discussed in Chapters 5 and 6. That is, the finding that chronic poverty accounts for most of total poverty is consistent with there being lots of short-distance mobility but not much long-distance mobility.

The relative importance of chronic poverty does differ by family type, however. For example, for single pensioners (for whom total poverty rates are almost twice those for the population as a whole), almost all poverty is chronic rather than transitory. (Recall from Chapter 6 that elderly people had the lowest transitory variances of all groups.) Nonetheless there is also a distinct downward trend in chronic (and total) poverty among single pensioners between the 1990s and 2000s, with the drop most noticeable from the mid to late 1990s—echoing the earlier results for persistent poverty.

The experience for lone-parent families bears some similarities to that of single pensioners, in that chronic poverty rates are high relative to those of the population as a whole, chronic poverty forms by far the larger share of total poverty, and there is a sharp decline in chronic (and total) poverty rates in the late 1990s. The difference is more one of absolute levels. For individuals in lone-parent families, the chronic poverty rate was more than 40 per cent at the beginning of the 1990s (80 per cent of total poverty), but around 30 per cent in the 2000s (24 per cent of total poverty). The patterns for couple-with-children families are more similar to the population as a whole, except that their chronic and total poverty levels are somewhat lower and transitory poverty (and its share of the total) is somewhat higher.

To what extent is people's current poverty status a good signal of their chronic poverty status? Table 8.2 provides specific answers to the question of overlap between current and chronic poverty status for different groups over the seven-year period 2000–6. For each group, the first two rows show the percentages of the group who are currently and chronically poor. The third row shows the chances of being chronically poor among those who are currently poor: the higher the percentage, the more likely it is that current poverty is a good indicator of chronic poverty. For all of the groups shown, this overlap rate increased over time, and it reached 57 per cent by 2006 for the populations as a whole. The highest overlap rates are for persons living in lone-parent families, and especially single pensioners, for whom the rates reached two-thirds and three-quarters, respectively by 2006. (This is as expected since for these groups, especially the single pensioners, chronic poverty accounts for a large proportion of total poverty.) For individuals in couple-with-children families, the overlap remained well below 50 per cent

Table 8.2. Overlap between chronic and current poverty, by family type, 2000–2006 (percentages)

Group	Poverty rate	Year						
		2000	2001	2002	2003	2004	2005	2006
All persons	Current	17	16	16	17	15	17	18
	Chronic	9	10	11	12	12	13	14
	Chronic|current	42	48	54	56	58	55	57
Dependent children	Current	19	18	17	17	16	17	18
	Chronic	9	10	11	12	12	13	14
	Chronic|current	37	40	47	47	52	52	51
Couple with children	Current	12	11	12	12	11	12	12
	Chronic	9	10	11	12	12	13	14
	Chronic|current	33	37	35	37	46	43	42
Single with children	Current	45	42	35	37	33	29	33
	Chronic	9	10	11	12	12	13	14
	Chronic|current	43	43	64	59	60	62	65
Single pensioner	Current	39	34	37	37	33	32	33
	Chronic	9	10	11	12	12	13	14
	Chronic|current	55	65	73	74	75	80	76

Notes: Estimates derived from weighted data for BHPS waves 1–16. The poverty line is 60% of contemporary median income. Individuals are classified into groups according to their characteristics at their interview in survey year 2000. The 'Current' rows show percentages of persons currently poor, by year. The 'Chronic' rows show percentages of persons chronically poor, by year, where chronic poverty is defined using longitudinally average incomes (see text). The 'Chronic|current' rows show percentages of currently poor persons who are chronically poor, by year.

throughout the seven-year period. Because transitory variations in income are relatively large for this group, current and chronic poverty statuses are more likely to differ from each other in any particular year. If the primary aim of policy is to reduce chronic poverty, then there is a problem for anti-poverty programme designers since it is current poverty that is observed. See Hill and Jenkins (2001) for further discussion and a numerical illustration of the costs of targeting.

The patterns of chronic poverty across subgroups and trends over time are broadly similar to the patterns revealed by analysis of poverty persistence, defined as being poor three or four years out of four. This general congruence has also been shown in the cross-national context by OECD (2001) and Valletta (2006). Just as the UK was a middle-ranking European country in terms of the proportion poor three years out of three for the period 1993–5, it was also a middle-ranking country in terms of the proportion of persons that were chronically poor (defined as having a three-year-averaged income below the three-year-averaged half-median poverty line). The UK rate for all persons was 6.5 per cent, compared to the lowest rate of 1.8 per cent (for Denmark) and the highest rate of 13.4 per cent (for Greece), and the 12-country average of 7.9 per cent. For Germany, the corresponding rate was 8.1 per cent, and for the USA, 14.5 per cent (OECD 2001: table 2.1). If the accounting period is extended from three to six years (covering 1991–6), then the chronic poverty rate for Britain among people with a household head aged 16–64 years is 2.9 per cent, compared to the rates for Germany (4.4 per cent) and the USA (18.7 per cent): see Valletta (2006: table 2).

8.3. Poverty Entry and Exit Rates

I now document how annual poverty exit and entry rates have changed in Britain since the start of the 1990s, and contrast the experience of different groups within the population. A fall in the number of people who are poor can arise because the number of people entering poverty has fallen, or because the number of people leaving poverty has risen, or both. Moreover, the processes of exit and entry differ—different types of people are 'at risk' of a poverty transition in each case and, even among people with similar characteristics, those characteristics may have different impacts on the chances of exit and entry. These aspects are explored in greater detail in Chapters 9–11. In this chapter, the main aim is to set out 'the facts' about trends in poverty transition rates and how they differ across groups. Throughout, the focus is on the annual rate of poverty exit or poverty entry. That is, the poverty exit rate for some year t is defined as the fraction of people poor at t who are no longer poor in the following year $t+1$. Similarly, the poverty entry rate for some year t is defined as the fraction of people non-poor at t who become poor in the following year $t+1$. (Remember too that poverty status is measured at the time of the interview; intervening entries or exits are not observed.) Poverty entry rates tend to be smaller than poverty exit rates, because the number of people who are non-poor (at risk of poverty entry) is larger than the number of people who are poor (at risk of poverty exit). (Exceptions to this rule arise for groups with high poverty rates such as lone-parent families and single pensioners). Because the number of poor people is relatively small, poverty exit rates typically exhibit greater sampling variability than poverty entry rates.

Figure 8.6 shows annual poverty rates and poverty exit and entry rates for the period 1991–2006 for all persons, families with children, and single pensioners. I focus on the latter two groups as they are the ones experiencing the greatest changes in poverty rates over the period (see earlier). Information about entry and exit rates for other family types is presented shortly. The figure shows for the population as a whole that, in the mid-2000s, approximately half of those poor in one year were no longer observed poor a year

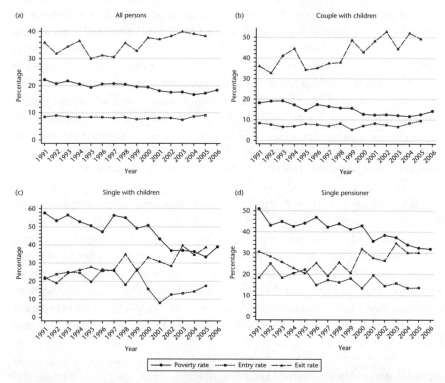

Figure 8.6. Rates of poverty, poverty entry, and poverty exit (%), by group and year

Notes: Estimates derived from weighted data for BHPS waves 1–16. The poverty line is 60% of contemporary median income. Entry and exit rates refer to transitions between year t and year $t+1$ (see text). Individuals are classified into groups according to their characteristics in year t.

later. And, among those who were not poor in one year, almost one in ten would be observed poor a year later. There is therefore substantial turnover in the low-income population from one year to the next. This tallies with the relatively low proportions estimated to be persistently poor (see above). The findings are also consistent with the estimates of proportions of people changing income group between one year and the next reported in Chapter 5.

Regarding trends over time, the headline finding is that decline in the poverty rate over the period is largely accounted for by the rise in the poverty exit rate rather than a decline in the poverty entry rate. Between the start of the 1990s and the mid-2000s, the exit rate rose from between 30 per cent and 35 per cent to around 40 per cent, whereas the entry rate was relatively constant at around 8 per cent or 9 per cent. This broad-brush conclusion does not describe the pattern in every subperiod. In particular, at the end of the 16-year period, it is a combination of a rise in the entry rate and a fall in the exit rate that accounts for the small rise in the poverty rate. (Recall that unemployment rates rose again slightly at this time after a long period of decline: see Figure 1.1 in Chapter 1.)

More pronounced trends over time are apparent when we look at subgroups. For individuals in couple-with-children families, there is a more distinct secular rise in poverty exit rate over the period (year-to-year fluctuations aside) and this appears to be behind the fall in the poverty rate until the early 2000s—the poverty exit rate changed relatively little. For lone-parent families, the fall in the poverty rate over the period is a combination of a secular rise in the exit rate, combined with, from 1999 onwards, a distinctly lower entry rate. The pattern for single pensioners is different again. The decline in the poverty rate is attributable to a drift downwards in the poverty entry throughout the period, reinforced by an increase in exit rate from the late 1990s onwards.

One issue concerning poverty transition rate estimates derived separately for each year, especially of exit rates, is their relatively large sampling variability due to relatively small sample sizes. To address this issue, and also to provide some additional numerical summaries of poverty transition rates, I also calculate 'average' rates for two six-year periods: 1992–7, and 1999–2007. (Within each period, annual transitions are pooled.) The estimates are reported in Table 8.3, for all individuals and by family type. The estimates are supplemented by estimates for samples of individuals differentiated according to poverty status in the year prior to being at risk of making a transition. These numbers are relevant to questions about poverty persistence, such as: are people who were recently poor more likely to re-enter poverty and do poverty exit rates depend on previous poverty status?

Table 8.3 shows that the annual poverty entry rate is the same for both periods for the population as a whole, 8 per cent, while the poverty exit rate rose from 32 per cent to 37 per cent. To put these figures in perspective, note

Table 8.3. Poverty entry and exit rates (%), by previous poverty status, family type, and year

Family type	Period	Entry rate (t to t+1)			Exit rate (t to t+1)		
		Rate	Rate given status at t-1		Rate	Rate given status at t-1	
			Non-poor	Poor		Non-poor	Poor
All persons	1992–7	8	6	35	32	48	24
	1999–2005	8	6	32	37	54	27
Dependent child	1992–7	10	7	37	31	44	25
	1999–2005	9	7	31	41	57	31
Pensioner couple	1992–7	10	8	36	31	50	20
	1999–2005	8	6	32	28	45	20
Single pensioner	1992–7	20	14	44	24	45	17
	1999–2005	16	10	40	28	48	21
Couple with children	1992–7	7	5	32	37	49	31
	1999–2005	7	6	29	49	61	38
Single with children	1992–7	24	16	48	25	39	20
	1999–2005	15	10	35	33	49	27
Couple, no children	1992–7	3	3	18	49	62	35
	1999–2005	4	4	26	46	58	32
Single, no children	1992–7	7	6	29	43	51	37
	1999–2005	7	6	28	44	55	34

Notes: Estimates derived from weighted data for BHPS waves 1–16. The poverty line is 60% of contemporary median income. Entry and exit rates refer to transitions between year t and year t+1 (see text). Transitions pooled within each six-year period. Individuals are classified into groups according to their characteristics in year t.

that the degree of poverty turnover in Britain's low-income population is slightly higher than the European average at the start of the 1990s. OECD (2001: table 2.2) reports annual transition rates for 11 European countries, Canada, and the USA (pooled data for 1993–5). With a half-median poverty line, the poverty rate for Britain is 12.1 per cent, compared to the 11-country average rate of 11.7 per cent, the entry rate is 6.0 per cent compared to 7.2 per cent, and the exit rate is 58.8 per cent compared to 46.1 per cent. The corresponding rates for the USA are 16.0 per cent, 4.5 per cent, and 29.5 per cent. Cross-national heterogeneity in cross-sectional poverty rates appears to arise more from heterogeneity in poverty exit rates than poverty entry rates.

The finding that, for the British population as a whole, the poverty entry rate remained relatively constant and the poverty exit rate increased between the start of the 1990s and the mid-2000s also describes the experience of most but not all family types. The decline in the poverty entry rate is relatively large for single pensioners and lone-parent families and, for childless couples, the entry rate actually increases slightly. Poverty exit rates increase for most family types, notably those with dependent children, but also for single pensioners. However, for pensioner couples and childless couples, the exit rate falls slightly between the two periods, and for childless single people, it hardly changes. These three groups are ones whose poverty rates change little between 1991 and 2006 (year-to-year fluctuations aside): see Figure 8.1. (They are also groups that were not targeted by the Labour government's redistributive policies summarized in Chapter 1.)

Table 8.3 also reveals clearly that, for both periods, your chances of making a poverty transition between one year and the next depend on whether you were poor in the previous year. For the population as a whole, and for each family type taken separately, the chances of entering poverty are slightly lower than average if you were also not poor the previous year. However, being poor in the previous year is associated with a substantial rise in the chances of poverty entry. For example, for the population as a whole, the entry rate for those previously poor is at least four times greater than the average rate. This repeated-poverty penalty is smaller for pensioners (single and couple), and larger for childless couples, but, in this latter case, the numbers concerned are small (poverty rates are relatively low for this group).

There is also a repeated-poverty penalty associated with poverty exit rates: the chances of exiting poverty are lower than average if you were poor the previous year. For the population as a whole, the penalty is about 50 per cent, with the exit rate being around 25 per cent compared to the average rate of about two-thirds. For those who were previously not poor, there is a corresponding bonus—an exit rate that is about 50 per cent larger than the average. There are broadly similar penalties and bonuses across the various family types, with the exception of childless couples and singles for whom they are somewhat smaller.

These patterns demonstrate that one's poverty history is associated with the chances of being poor or non-poor now. Past poverty appears to have a scarring effect, and being non-poor appears to have a protective effect. The associations shown in Table 8.3 do not prove that these associations are genuinely causal, however. Although the calculations control for family type, there is a lot of variation in personal or family characteristics within each family type that can lead to differences in the chances of being poor or non-poor and this heterogeneity is not controlled for. The poverty penalty may simply reflect these other factors. The multivariate analysis of poverty dynamics reported in Chapters 10 and 11 aims to address this issue, looking at the impact of past poverty, while also taking account of observed and unobserved differences between individuals.

The next set of estimates provides evidence about the length of poverty spells and how long it is before people who finish a poverty spell fall back into poverty. This is also an extension of the analysis of poverty exits and entries, because information about spell lengths is derived from evidence about how poverty exit rates vary with how long a person has been poor, and re-entry times are derived from evidence about how poverty entry rates vary with how long it is since a person left poverty.

8.4. How Long are Poverty Spells and How Long Until Poverty Re-entry?

Lengths of time spent poor and time to re-entry are derived using 'life-table' estimates of how poverty transition rates vary with the length of time someone has been at risk of making a transition. Spell lengths are summarized in terms of the probability of remaining poor for a particular number of years since first starting a poverty spell, and the probability of remaining non-poor for a particular number of years since ending a poverty spell. For example, if the probability of leaving poverty for the first year of a spell is one-half and the probability of leaving poverty after two years poor having remained poor for one year is one-quarter, then the probability of having a poverty spell that is at least two years long is the probability of not leaving in the first year $(1 - 0.5 = 0.5)$ times the probability of not leaving in the second year having remained poor for a year $(1 - 0.25 = 0.75)$, that is, a probability of 37.5 per cent (0.5×0.75). The term 'hazard rate' is used to describe transition rates that vary with spell length.

Life-table methods take into account the fact that many of the spells of poverty and non-poverty observed in the BHPS panel were still in progress when the person was last observed in the panel (before they dropped out, or the panel itself ended). This is the issue of right-censoring of spell-length data: see Chapter 2. In common with virtually all other analysis of this kind, spells that are in progress when people are first observed in the panel (left-censored spells) are omitted from the analysis. This means that analysis is of poverty re-entry rather than of poverty entry.

Figure 8.7 shows, for the population as a whole, how the chances of leaving poverty vary with the time spent poor, counting from entry into poverty, and how the chances of re-entering poverty vary with the time spent out of poverty, counting from exit from poverty. In my earlier work, based on nine waves of BHPS data (Jenkins and Rigg 2001), I was only able to show how poverty exit and re-entry hazard rates varied for spell lengths of up to seven years' work. With 16 waves of data, hazard rates for relatively long spells can be estimated for the first time for Britain.

The exit hazard after one year is 45 per cent (which is somewhat higher than the exit rate discussed in the previous section because left-censored spells are now excluded), but falls rapidly to half that figure after a further three years and then continues to decline. For someone remaining poor for a decade, the chances of leaving poverty over the next year are only around one in ten.

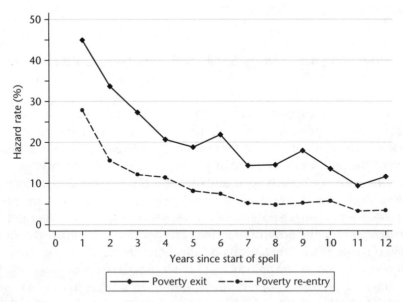

Figure 8.7. Conditional probabilities of leaving poverty and of re-entering poverty, by spell length (%)

Notes: Life-table estimates of the poverty exit and poverty re-entry hazards from BHPS data for waves 1–16 for all individuals. Years since start of spell refers to number of years since start of poverty spell for the exit hazard and to number of years since end of previous poverty spell for the re-entry hazard.

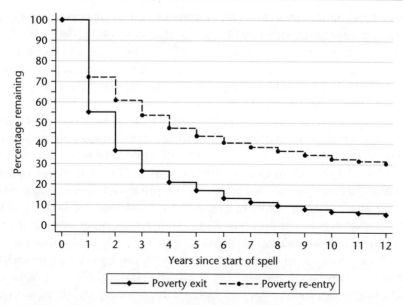

Figure 8.8. Probabilities of remaining poor and remaining non-poor, by spell length (%)
Note: As for Figure 8.7.

Similar observations describe the hazard rate of re-entry to poverty. The chances of re-entry decline with the number of years since last observed to be poor, falling relatively sharply at first and then more slowly. The probability of re-entry one year after leaving poverty is just 30 per cent, but more than halves after a further two years out of poverty. The rate then declines to around 5 per cent for spells of seven years or longer.

Figure 8.8 shows what these exit and re-entry rates imply in terms of spell lengths. Among a large group of people starting a poverty spell, 45 per cent leave after one year, with 55 per cent remaining poor. After two years, only around 35 per cent remain poor. The median spell length—the length of time after which half of the entry cohort has left poverty and half remain—is between one and two years. So, most of those who begin a poverty spell leave poverty relatively quickly. But there is a small minority with long spells. For example, around one in ten of those entering poverty are estimated to remain poor for at least eight years.

Cross-National Differences in Spell Lengths

These estimates are similar to those reported for US poverty spells, derived from a long run of PSID data by Bane and Ellwood (1986) and Stevens (1994, 1999). Comparability is compromised, however, because they used rather different definitions of income and of the poverty line.

More cross-nationally comparable estimates of annual poverty entry and exit hazard rates are reported by Oxley, Dang, and Antolín (2000: table 2) for Canada, Germany, the Netherlands, the USA, and the UK, and using a half-median poverty line. The data cover a six-year period from the beginning of the 1990s for all the countries except for the USA, for which the period used is 1989–93. The situation in the UK is shown to be more like that of the USA than the other European countries: the poverty exit hazard is relatively low, and the poverty re-entry hazard relatively high. For example, the proportion of persons exiting poverty after one year is estimated to be around 45 per cent for the UK and USA, compared with between 50 per cent and 60 per cent for Germany, Sweden, and the Netherlands. The proportion re-entering poverty one year after finishing a poverty spell is around one-third for the UK and the USA, but between 16 per cent and 25 per cent for the other three countries. These cross-national rankings in hazard rates persist at longer durations as well (except for Germany, which has poverty re-entry rates greater than the UK's after three years).

Even more comparable estimates, but only for poverty exit hazard rates, are reported by Fouarge and Layte (2005: table 4). They provide ECHP-based estimates of poverty exit hazard rates for up to three years for 11 European countries, using a poverty line equal to 60 per cent of median net income. Fouarge and Layte's results indicate that there is substantial cross-national heterogeneity in how poverty exit rates vary with time since the beginning of the poverty spell. Consistent with Oxley, Dang, and Antolín's (2000) estimates, the UK has the lowest exit rate after one year, 0.45—the same as for Portugal, and substantially less than the largest rate, 0.56, for Denmark. However, the proportion of persons who have left poverty after three years in the UK, 76 per cent, places the UK midway in the 11-country ranking. (The rates range from 79 per cent for Denmark to 72 per cent for France and Ireland.) Although the one-year exit hazard rate is relatively low for the UK, hazard rates at longer durations are relatively high.

Spell Lengths are Longer for Currently Poor People than for Ever-Poor People

It is important to distinguish between the poverty-spell lengths of all the people who start a poverty spell and the length of time that currently poor people will eventually spend in poverty. As stressed by Bane and Ellwood's (1986) pioneering study of poverty spells in the USA, a sample of the people who are currently poor contains more people who will have long poverty spells than does a sample of people entering poverty. The people prone to having long poverty spells accumulate among the currently poor, whereas those with relatively short spells leave. As Bane and Ellwood put it, '[o]nly a small fraction of those who enter poverty in any given year will be chronically poor. But people who will have long spells of poverty represent a sizable portion of the group we label "the poor" at any one time' (1986: 7).

This result has policy relevance. Emphasis on the average poverty-spell lengths of people who are currently poor provides an impression that poverty is something that is concentrated among an unfortunate minority of the population who experience long spells and leads to warnings about potential problems of dependence on welfare benefits. A recent British example of this emphasis is Cabinet Office (2010: chapter 3). This is not the full story, because most people starting a poverty spell also end it relatively quickly. As documented earlier in this chapter, poverty 'touches' many more people over a period of time than the numbers who are poor in any given year, and the tax-benefit system needs to account for this more universal experience of poverty.

Of course, the total amount of time that people in poverty remain poor also depends on the chances of poverty re-entry—poverty recurrence. One perspective on this was provided earlier using estimates of persistent poverty rates, and a spell-based approach provides another perspective, to which I now turn.

Poverty Re-entries and the Total Time Spent Poor over a Period of Time

Figure 8.8 shows that, among those who finish a poverty spell, around 70 per cent remain out of poverty after one year, 60 per cent after two years, and around one-third do not start another poverty spell for a decade. In short, if people manage to stay out of poverty for a couple of years, then they are unlikely to return to poverty for a very long time. But there is a non-trivial proportion of people who experience a repeat spell relatively soon, nonetheless.

This suggests that using only poverty exit rates, and the associated probabilities of remaining poor, as a guide to the total amount of time spent poor over a period may be misleading. This can be demonstrated by using the poverty exit and poverty re-entry rate estimates in combination to estimate the total number of years that someone beginning a poverty spell will experience over the following years. See, for example, Stevens (1999) for the USA, and Jarvis and Jenkins (1997), Devicienti (2001), and Jenkins and Rigg (2001) for Britain.

Table 8.4 reports estimates from Jenkins and Rigg (2001), based on nine waves of BHPS data, of the number of additional years observed poor over the following seven years for people entering poverty in wave 2. The reference point is the distribution of years that actually occurred, labelled 'actual'. The first column is the number of years predicted using life-table estimates of poverty exit rates and supposing there is only a single poverty spell. The second column derives the predicted numbers of years using both poverty

Table 8.4. Distribution of the number of years poor over an eight-year period

Number of years poor out of eight for a cohort entering poverty	Predicted percentage using:		Actual percentage
	Exit rates (single spell)	Exit and re-entry rates	
1	54	19	25
2	16	18	17
3	9	15	12
4	6	14	14
5	4	11	7
6	3	9	11
7	2	7	10
8	8	8	5
Total	100	100	100
Mean number of years in poverty	2.4	3.7	3.6

Notes: Predictions derived using all-persons life-table estimates of duration-specific poverty entry and exit rates from data for BHPS waves 1–9. 'Actual' estimates derived from the observed patterns for the cohort of individuals that entered poverty at wave 2. Column % do not add to exactly 100% due to rounding.

Source: Jenkins and Rigg (2001: table 4.7, with corrected single-spell estimates).

exit and re-entry rates, and hence allows for poverty recurrence and multiple spells.

It is immediately apparent that the repeated-spell estimates provide much better predictions of actual experience than the single-spell estimates, and throughout the distribution. The repeated-spell approach under-estimates the proportion of individuals poor for just one year—the predicted fraction was 19 per cent rather than 25 per cent—but the bias is much smaller in magnitude than the over-estimation from the single-spell approach (for which the corresponding fraction was 54 per cent). The proportions poor for two to seven years poor are substantially under-estimated by the single-spell approach, whereas the repeated-spell approach provides a remarkably good fit. This result is also found for other countries: see the studies cited in the previous paragraph.

Better predictions of the total time spent poor for poverty-spell entrants can be derived by allowing poverty exit hazard and re-entry hazards to vary with individual characteristics. See Chapters 11 and 12 for discussion of two multivariate approaches to modelling poverty exit and re-entry probabilities jointly.

Changes in Poverty Entry and Exit Hazard Rates over Time

The long run of panel data can be used not only to look at the prevalence of long poverty spells but also to examine, as I do now, whether poverty exit and re-entry hazards have changed over time and have done so differently for different groups within the population. It is of interest to know, for instance, whether poverty-spell lengths have fallen over time, especially for vulnerable groups such as children whom the Labour government specially targeted in their anti-poverty strategy.

My analysis is limited by the fact that breakdowns by period and subgroup lead to less reliable estimates. There are smaller sample sizes, especially at long durations: relatively few people in any group are observed to leave poverty at long-spell lengths. In recognition of this issue, my breakdowns are for three groups only: dependent children, adults aged less than 60 years, and adults aged 60+. Also, I compare only two periods, distinguishing between spells that begin between 1992 and 1997 and those than begin between 1998 and 2006, and I report estimates for the first five years of a spell only. Table 8.5 reports poverty exit hazard rates and poverty re-entry hazard rates, and the corresponding probabilities of remaining poor and remaining non-poor ('survival' probabilities). For reference, the first rows of the table show the estimates for all individuals for the period as a whole, as shown graphically in Figures 8.7 and 8.8.

Table 8.5 shows that, regardless of period, poverty exit hazard rates are higher and poverty re-entry lower, for adults aged less than 60 years than for the other two groups, that is, they have shorter poverty spells and more years between poverty spells than do dependent children or adults aged 60+, for whom experiences are relatively similar.

There are, however, some clear changes in hazard rates and survival probabilities between periods. This is most apparent for dependent children, for whom poverty exit hazard rates are larger for each poverty spell year, and poverty re-entry rates are smaller for each poverty spell year, for spells starting in the period 1998–2006 rather than in the period 1992–7. Hence poverty spell lengths are shorter and the time between poverty spells is longer. For example, of children beginning a spell in the earlier period, 38 per cent remain poor two years later, whereas for children beginning a spell in the later period, 32 per cent remain poor two years later. More than two-thirds of children leaving poverty in the earlier period remain out of poverty for a year, compared to nearly three-quarters of children in the later period.

For adults aged less than 60 years, it is hard to detect such clear-cut changes—any that exist are within the bounds of sampling variability. (If anything, poverty spell lengths may have increased slightly for this group.) For adults aged 60 or over, there is little change between periods in poverty spell lengths, but there appears to have been a distinct fall in the poverty re-entry hazard rates at each spell year. Hence, just under a half of those finishing a poverty spell in the earlier period stay out of poverty for at least two years, whereas for the later period, nearly 60 per cent do so.

One obvious explanation for the reduction in poverty spell lengths and increase in times to poverty re-entry is the Labour government's anti-poverty

Table 8.5. Cumulative proportions remaining poor and non-poor, and hazard rates, by elapsed duration, age, and period

Group and year spell started	Years since start of spell	Poverty exit		Poverty re-entry	
		Survival probability (%)	Hazard rate (%)	Survival probability (%)	Hazard rate (%)
All persons					
1992–2006	1	55	45	72	28
	2	37	34	61	16
	3	27	27	54	12
	4	21	21	47	11
	5	17	19	44	8
Dependent child					
1992–7	1	58	42	68	32
	2	38	34	54	20
	3	27	30	48	11
	4	22	17	41	14
	5	17	23	38	9
1998–2006	1	53	47	74	26
	2	33	39	64	13
	3	21	36	56	14
	4	13	39	49	12
	5	11	13	45	8
Adult aged less than 60 years					
1992–7	1	52	48	75	25
	2	32	39	64	15
	3	21	33	58	9
	4	16	27	53	9
	5	12	25	49	6
1998–2006	1	53	47	77	23
	2	34	36	68	11
	3	24	30	61	10
	4	18	24	55	11
	5	16	11	50	8
Adult aged 60+ years					
1992–7	1	58	42	63	37
	2	44	23	48	23
	3	37	17	38	21
	4	31	15	31	19
	5	26	16	26	14
1998–2006	1	60	40	70	30
	2	43	28	59	17
	3	34	21	51	13
	4	30	13	48	5
	5	26	13	45	7

Note: Life-table estimates from BHPS waves 1–16.

strategy, which had a particular focus on children. Though plausible, there may be other factors at work, including the continuing strength of the British economy over the 1990s, represented by declining and then low-level unemployment rates (at least until the mid-2000s): see Chapter 1. If it were the tax-benefit policy changes that played the predominant role, one might expect to see relatively sharp changes around key policy implementation dates in poverty exit hazard rates (upwards) and in poverty re-entry hazard rates (downwards). (Cf. the changes in annual poverty exit and entry rates summarized in Figure 8.8.)

To examine whether such sharp changes existed, I estimate poverty exit hazard rates and poverty re-entry hazard rates for groups of dependent children, classified according to the year in which the spell started, plotting the hazard rates for each cohort against survey year (not number of years since the start of the spell). The idea is that, if Labour's policies were important, one would see their impact reflected in changes in the hazard rates around key years (whether this is the initial spell year for one cohort, or a later spell year for another cohort). Start years are not pooled for this analysis, because the fine detail is necessary for the hypothesis in question, but the cost is that sample sizes are small, especially at longer spell durations. I therefore discarded hazard-rate estimates for spells longer than five years, but estimates for earlier spell years should also be treated with caution. The results are plotted in Figure 8.9: there is one line for each cohort of dependent children starting a spell.

The charts do not provide conclusive evidence in support of the hypothesis about the impact of Labour's policies. The cohort plots of poverty exit rates appear to have been shifting upwards and to the right throughout the 1990s (suggesting a role for the buoyant economy), though there does appear to be a large shift upwards and to the right relative to trend for the exit hazard plots for the cohorts of children starting poverty spells in 1997 and 1998. But observe also the levelling off thereafter over the period when the decline in unemployment rates had levelled off. There are some upward kinks in the exit hazard plots round about 1997 and 1998, and again round about 2003 and 2004, which might be attributable to the introduction of Working Families Tax Credit (WFTC) in the first case, and its transformation into Working Tax Credit and Child Tax Credit in the second case. But such conclusions are hard to draw because such kinks could also arise from the greater sampling variability associated with longer spell lengths.

The plots of poverty re-entry hazard rates do not provide conclusive evidence about the impact of Labour's policies either. The plots generally shift downwards to the right throughout the 1990s, consistent again with a macroeconomic explanation. Moreover, for cohorts of children ending a poverty spell in 2000 and over the next few years, the plots become less steep and actually shift upwards, that is, cohort re-entry rates rose, though clearly not to the levels of the early 1990s. Also, around 2000, the plots for spells that had been in progress for several years flattened more or even increased—though this may reflect sampling variability.

(a)

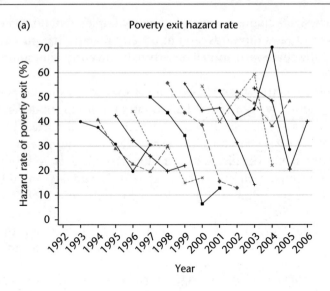

Poverty exit hazard rate

(b)

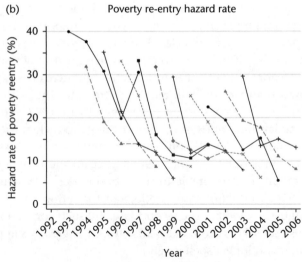

Poverty re-entry hazard rate

Figure 8.9. Poverty exit hazard rates and poverty re-entry hazard rates for dependent children (%), by year-of-spell-entry cohort of dependent children

Notes: Life-table estimates based on data from BHPS waves 1–16. In chart (a), there is one line for each cohort of dependent children starting a poverty spell in a given survey year (the year corresponding to the beginning of each line). In chart (b), there is one line for each cohort of dependent children ending a poverty spell in a given survey year (the year corresponding to the beginning of each line).

In sum, it appears that if Labour's anti-poverty policies did have an impact on the length of time that children are poor (and there is not definitive evidence from my analysis that they did), they mainly worked by increasing poverty exit rates rather than reducing poverty re-entry rates. The analysis also draws attention to the importance of the health of the macro-economy in general and the state of the labour market in particular in reducing the number of years that children spend in poverty.

8.5. Summary and Conclusions

This chapter has demonstrated that there is much that is dynamic about poverty when it is looked at from a longitudinal perspective. Whether one considers people's experience of poverty over time in terms of the number of times poor over a period, poverty transition rates and spell lengths, or whether one looks at their chronic and transitory poverty, it is clear that there is no fixed and unchanging group who constitute 'the poor'. Over a nine-year period, fewer than one in ten are poor for seven or more years out of nine.

Put differently, there is a substantial degree of turnover in the low-income population between one year and the next—which is of course consistent with the findings of income mobility throughout the income distribution that were revealed in the previous two chapters. Moreover, a significant fraction of low-income turnover reflects churning. Turnover arises partly because a significant number of people experience poverty once (but not more than once) and partly because poverty recurs for many people. The chapter has illustrated how people's accumulation of poverty experienced over time reflects the combination not only of their chances of entering poverty and of leaving poverty (once a spell has begun), but also of re-entering poverty.

The corollary of low-income turnover is that, over a period of time, many more people experience poverty at least once than are poor in any given year. During the 2000s, around a third of Britons experienced poverty at least one year in four, whereas the annual poverty rate is around half as large. It is also striking that around one-half of all children can expect to be poor at least once over a nine-year period and this proportion has not changed much over the time.

These results have implications for the design of tax-benefit and labour market policies. Reiterating earlier findings based on BHPS waves 1–4,

> The large amount of low income turnover means that the welfare benefit system has an important rôle providing short term support: over a year many more people are helped by the benefit system than would be revealed by focusing on the benefit caseload at a point in time (which disproportionately comprises long-term stayers). Longer term help from the benefit system is also important of course, particularly for poor people beyond retirement age. (Jarvis and Jenkins 1997: 141)

Poverty turnover and churning are not peculiarly British phenomena, but are also found in other European countries and in North America. The degree of turnover in Britain places it towards the top of the ranking relative to western European nations. In short, the high rates of low-income turnover and, correspondingly, low rates of long-term persistence, appear to be relatively universal phenomena and their implications are also widely applicable.

Underneath the overall picture for Britain's population as a whole, this chapter has also drawn attention to substantial heterogeneity in the experience of poverty for individuals from different groups and has revealed some large changes over time in patterns of poverty dynamics. These findings are illustrated especially by the results for lone-parent families and single pensioners. These are groups with relatively high poverty rates and poverty persistence rates, but they are also groups for whom these rates have declined substantially between the 1990s and the mid-2000s.

The next three chapters look in more detail at who is most at risk of exiting and entering poverty in Britain and the factors associated with this and how they have changed over time.

9

Routes Into and Out of Poverty and the Role of Trigger Events

This chapter analyses the routes by which individuals move into and out of poverty. The analysis is based on the idea that changes in income between one year and the next in general, and poverty transitions in particular, are triggered by the occurrence of significant life-course events such as changes in household members' labour market attachment and earnings, changes in non-labour income, or changes in household demography, and these events have different impacts on the risk of a poverty transition. I label these changes 'trigger events', borrowing the label from DiPrete and McManus (2006). Experience of a trigger event constitutes a potential route into or out of poverty, and the aim of this chapter is to assess for Britain which of the various events (routes) are the most important and whether their importance has changed over time.

Analysing poverty transitions in terms of trigger events follows precedents established by Bane and Ellwood's (1986) pioneering analysis for the USA. As they argued,

> [i]f dynamics are being considered, the changes themselves really are the driving force. Presumably those interested in understanding poverty are interested in knowing what sort of adverse events lead people into poverty, whether the duration of a stay varies depending on how it began, and how (if ever) families escape poverty. (Bane and Ellwood 1986: 4)

Bane and Ellwood's method and a closely related one have been used to study poverty transitions in Britain by Jenkins (2000), Jenkins and Schluter (2003), and Jenkins and Rigg (2001). Using the formats established by the latter, the Department for Work and Pension's annual *Low Income Dynamics* publication now also includes tables linking trigger events and poverty exits and entries.

Bane and Ellwood (1986) developed their method because of their dissatisfaction with the then existing approaches for studying poverty dynamics, notably variance components models of the type reviewed in Chapter 6, and tabulations of the number of times poor over a fixed time period (as presented in Chapter 8). In variance components models, 'income' is the dependent variable and dynamics are introduced through the residual error structure, with assumptions about permanent and transitory components. Lillard and Willis (1978) were the first to show how model estimates can be used to summarize the probabilities of making a poverty transition for persons with different characteristics when it is assumed that the error components are normally distributed. (Ulrick 2008 shows that the normality assumption is not essential for this exercise.)

To Bane and Ellwood (1986), the main problem with using variance components models to study poverty dynamics is that the models are better suited to modelling the dynamics of an individual's labour earnings than the dynamics of family income and it is income that determines poverty status. Indeed, although Lillard and Willis (1978) referred to 'poverty' in their analysis, they actually considered 'low pay' transitions for prime-aged men, defined as changes in their employment earnings relative to a cut-off equal to half median earnings. As Bane and Ellwood emphasized,

> [a]lthough the Lillard and Willis approach has great appeal for ascertaining the income dynamics of prime-age males, it has shortcomings as a method for understanding the nature and dynamics of poverty for the entire population. It is exceptionally difficult to cope with the fact that 'poverty' is a concept that applies to families—and that family membership changes.... In principle the income of each family member could be modeled individually, allowing for simultaneous influences from and to family structure, and allowing for life cycle changes. In fact such models are difficult to develop. (Bane and Ellwood 1986: 3)

Bane and Ellwood acknowledge that one could apply variance component modelling methods with needs-adjusted family income as the dependent variable, and there has been subsequent research that has done just that: see, for example, Biewen (2005), Devicienti (2001), Duncan (1983), and Stevens (1999). Chapter 7 also employs a variant of these models. However, as Bane and Ellwood point out, this approach also has problems.

First and most fundamentally, 'deviations from permanent income tend to be treated as random and behaviorally equivalent in those models. Typically all "disturbances" in income lead to the same temporal path of income in the future. But all changes in family income are not likely to lead to the same sort of long-run dynamics' (Bane and Ellwood 1986: 3.) Income consists of potentially many different income sources, aggregated across multiple household members, and so can change because any one of the income sources changes (not only the labour earnings of a male household head), or because household size and composition change. These demographic changes have a dual effect, changing the number of people contributing to the household total, while also changing the household equivalence-scale rate.

A second problem with focusing on the dynamics of men's earnings when the aim is to understand poverty dynamics concerns the under-coverage of the poverty population. Prime-aged men comprise a relatively small fraction of the population who are poor, as Bane and Ellwood point out. In their US example referring to 1981, men aged 22–64 comprised only 15.5 per cent of those classified as poor according to the US official definition. In the UK in 2008/9, only around one-third of individuals with a household income less than 60 per cent of median income are adult men (Department for Work and Pensions 2010: table 3.3). Thus, to study poverty and poverty transitions, one needs methods that enable one to examine the circumstances of everyone who is poor.

Tabulations of the number of times poor over a period (as in Chapter 8) also have weaknesses for understanding the dynamics of poverty. Bane and Ellwood acknowledge the simplicity and transparency of such tabulations, but point out that 'no attention is focused on the events which lead people into and out of poverty. It is very difficult to trace processes whereby persons may gradually or suddenly escape from poverty' (1986: 4). In addition, they emphasize what they believe to be a more important problem: the method takes no account of whether the poverty spells observed with the fixed-width time window are censored or not. They argue that this can lead to misleading conclusions about the total length of time that people spend poor and also about the prevalence of relatively short spells versus relatively long spells.

Bane and Ellwood propose instead that one should study spells of poverty and they describe 'the key innovation of [their] study as being [their] characterisation of the events which lead to the beginnings and endings of spells of poverty' (1986: 6). They claim that their 'straightforward methods ... offer the appeal of simplicity and still provide powerful insights into the dynamics of poverty' (1986: 22).

These reasons justify the use of Bane and Ellwood's methods to study poverty dynamics in Britain. Their methods are explained in Section 9.1, together with a closely related modification. Bane and Ellwood's approach distinguishes trigger events using a mutually exclusive and exhaustive hierarchy and, following Jenkins and Rigg (2001), I label this Method 1. The modified approach, labelled Method 2, uses a non-exhaustive classification of trigger events and poverty transitions. Section 9.2 presents results derived using Method 1, and Section 9.3 presents results based on Method 2. The trigger events include gaining and losing employment, changes in earnings

241

(without a job change), changes in non-labour income (for example, benefits and tax credits, investment income, transfers), and several different sorts of change in household composition (encompassing new partnerships and separations, births of children, death of a partner, etc.). The categorization of events refers to changes in the circumstances of the BHPS respondent's partner and other household members, in addition to those changes directly experienced by the respondent.

The principal innovation of the research presented in this chapter is that 14 waves of BHPS data are used compared with only nine waves used by Jenkins and Rigg (2001). The longer run of panel data allows examination of changes over time in the patterns of association between trigger events and poverty transitions. I compare two seven-year periods 1991–7 and 1998–2004 (transitions within the period are pooled in order to maintain sample sizes). This is the first study that I know of that uses these methods to examine changes in poverty transition rates over time. Similar methods to Bane and Ellwood's have been used to examine cross-national differences in poverty transitions: see Oxley et al.(2000), OECD (2001), and Valletta (2006). These studies, which include data for Britain, are discussed in Section 9.4 below. For an examination of differences between Britain and Germany in child poverty rates using Method 2, see Jenkins and Schluter (2003). Cantó (2003) studies poverty entries and exits in Spain using Methods 1 and 2.

This chapter employs the same definitions of poverty as in Chapter 8, that is, individuals are considered to be poor in a given year if the income of the household to which they belong is less than 60 per cent of median income for that year. Income is total net household income from all sources, as discussed in Chapter 4, except that the equivalence scale used is the McClements 'before housing costs' scale rather than the modified-OECD scale employed in the chapters to date. (Because the scales are broadly similar, I do not expect results to be sensitive to this choice.) And, also as before, the analysis considers poverty transitions over an interval of one year—more precisely, between two consecutive annual interviews. By construction, some short spells of poverty will be missed altogether and, hence, so too are some poverty exits and entries. The association between trigger events and poverty transitions that is documented in this chapter may differ from the association that would be found were all poverty transitions to be observed, but it is difficult to state how.

The analysis assumes that any income movement across the poverty line, however small, is a poverty transition. Some previous research distinguishes between 'genuine' transitions (where movements into and out of poverty represent a significant difference in terms of access to resources), and smaller income variations which may arise from income volatility and mis-reporting and which are arguably less significant. For example Jenkins (2000) focuses on poverty transitions that move individuals to an income at least 10 per cent above the poverty line (for poverty exits) or at least 10 per cent below the poverty line (for poverty entries). Jenkins and Rigg (2001) also utilized this approach in preliminary research, but they report that making this distinction made little difference to the conclusions drawn. I find this to be the case as well in the current research: censoring transitions involving small income transitions reduces the number of transitions significantly, but does not change the patterns of associations with trigger events. Unweighted calculations are presented in this chapter. Most statistics were also calculated using longitudinal weights and then again using cross-sectional weights. The results are very similar in each case. (See Chapter 4 for further discussion of the use of longitudinal weights when there are panel joiners and of why weighted and unweighted estimates are often similar.)

Although trigger-event analysis of poverty transitions is undoubtedly informative, it is only one of several possible approaches. Bane and Ellwood (1986) acknowledge that 'using hazard functions and other multivariate techniques, we will be able to glean still further information about those factors that influence dynamics' (1986: 21). Analysis based on multivariate methods is employed in Chapters 10 and 11 to follow.

Associations between trigger events and poverty transitions provide a potentially incomplete explanation of the underlying causes of poverty transitions. First, the direction of causation might run in the other direction, from transition to event. For example, a fall into poverty might lead to a rise in stress that, in turn, results in divorce. Second, there is the issue of attributing effects when events coincide. For example, a poverty exit may be associated with an increase in household earnings, but this may reflect the fact that an earner recently became the partner of a non-working lone parent. To some extent, mutually coinciding events will be picked up by the Method 2 analysis that follows, but a more fundamental issue is that 'changes in both income and household size are, themselves, driven by a number of inter-related decisions about household labour supply, household formation and fertility, as well as government tax and transfer decisions' (Oxley, Dang, and Antolín 2000: 23).

Assessment of the causes of poverty transitions is made harder by the panel data framework used here—more detailed information about the relative timings of trigger events and poverty transitions is likely to be informative. However, such information is not widely available and is also difficult to interpret: see, for example, Paull's (2007) BHPS-based study of the links between marital separations and work and their timing, using detailed monthly histories. There are a few studies evaluating the causal effect of divorce on income (see, for example, Aassve et al. 2007 and Ananat and Michaels 2007) and, as it happens, the findings are consistent with descriptive analysis of the type that follows in this chapter. A more fundamental problem, however, is that evaluation methods are focused on particular events or sub-samples of the population, whereas the intended scope of this chapter is much wider. It is to relate trigger events and poverty transitions, while considering a wide spectrum of events and accounting for poverty transitions among the population as a whole.

9.1. Assessing the Importance of Different Routes Into and Out of Poverty

In this section, I explain the importance of how I assess which routes into and out of poverty are the most important. I begin by explaining what is meant by 'important', and discussing the two methods that are used to assess importance (Methods 1 and 2). In order to do this, the routes themselves are also defined, that is, the trigger events that are associated with poverty transitions. A differently defined set of events is used for each of Method 1 and Method 2, for reasons explained shortly.

Consider two different questions about the association between a set of trigger events and poverty transitions:

1. Of all the poverty exits (or entries) that we observe, what fraction of them is attributable to event A, and what fraction is attributable to event B, to event C, or ... ?

2. Is an individual's chance of exiting (or entering) poverty higher if he or she experiences event A or if he or she experiences event B, or event C, or ... ?

Answers to Question 1 refer to the share of all poverty exits (or entries) that is accounted for by each of various events. An event is important in this context if it accounts for a relatively large share of all poverty transitions. This provides an aggregate perspective on importance.

Answers to Question 2 refer to the probabilities of making a poverty exit (or entry) associated with experiencing a particular type of event. An event is important in this context if the associated (conditional) probability of making a poverty transition is relatively large. This individual-level conditional tran-sition probability provides a perspective on importance from the point of view of the individual 'at risk' of making a poverty transition.

Answers to both types of question provide useful—and complementary—information about the relative importance of different trigger events. The aggregate and individual perspectives are analogous to two perspectives com-monly used when examining how poverty in a given year varies with indivi-duals' characteristics. One type of calculation is of the 'subgroup composition of poverty' for each of a number of subgroups, that is, the number of persons poor in the subgroup expressed as a fraction of the total number poor. This is analogous to an aggregate share statistic for poverty transitions. Or, second, one may calculate the 'risk' of poverty for each subgroup, which is the number of persons poor in the subgroup expressed as a fraction of the total number of persons in the subgroup (whether poor or non-poor). This point-in-time risk statistic is analogous to an individual-level conditional transition probability statistic.

The statistics underpinning answers to Questions 1 and 2 are related. The share of all poverty transitions that a given event accounts for depends on three components: the prevalence of the event, the probability of the event conditional on experience of the event (that is, Question 2 statistics), and the overall poverty transition rate. Put another way, an event accounts for a relatively large share of all poverty exits (or entries) if the event is relatively frequent or if the chances of leaving (entering) poverty are relatively large among those who experience the event, or both. Accordingly, changes in share statistics over time can arise from each of the component statistics.

To fix ideas, suppose that there is a set of mutually exclusive events $j = 1, \ldots,$ J, which trigger exits from poverty. (Simultaneously occurring events can be redefined as separate events.) Then, among those individuals at risk of exit from poverty between one year and the next, the probability of exiting is given by the sum of the probabilities of exit by experiencing each of the different events:

$$\text{Pr(exit poverty)} = \sum_{j=1}^{J} \text{Pr(exit poverty via event } j). \qquad (9.1)$$

In the empirical analysis, and assuming sufficiently large sample sizes, each probability is estimated by the corresponding sample proportion. So 'Pr(.)' can be read as 'proportion' as well as 'probability'.

Each term on the right hand side of (9.1) can be written as the product of the probability of each event and the probability of exit conditional on event occurrence:

$$\text{Pr(exit poverty)} = \sum_{j=1}^{J} \text{Pr(exit poverty} \mid \text{event } j) \times \text{Pr(event } j). \qquad (9.2)$$

By similar arguments, one can relate the probability that an at-risk individual will enter poverty due to a set of mutually exclusive trigger events $k = 1, \ldots, K$, to the probabilities of each event and the probability of poverty entry conditional on event occurrence:

$$\text{Pr(enter poverty)} = \sum_{k=1}^{k} \text{Pr(enter poverty} \mid \text{event } k) \times \text{Pr(event } k). \qquad (9.3)$$

In terms of the earlier discussion, the statistic that corresponds to the 'individual' perspective on importance is the conditional transition probability. In terms of the equations, an event j is important for poverty exits if Pr(exit poverty | event j) is large, and event k is important for poverty entries if Pr(enter poverty | event k) is large. I rate an event as important from this perspective only if the event-conditioned transition probability is larger than the overall (unconditional) transition probability because, if they are much the same, then the chances of a poverty transition are largely independent of experiencing the event. In effect, I am taking up the point made by Walker (1994) that

> The recognition that poverty inducing events are widespread but relatively rarely result in poverty, mean that any full explanation of the incidence of poverty has to take account not only of the probability that any particular event occurs, but also of the probability that the event triggers a spell of poverty. (Walker 1994: 47)

From the aggregate perspective, an event is important for poverty exits if it accounts for a relatively large share of all poverty exits that occurred (and analogously for poverty entries). More precisely the share of all poverty exits that is accounted for by some event j is given by

$$\text{Share of all exits accounted for by event } j = \frac{\text{Pr(event } j) \times \text{Pr(exit poverty} \mid \text{event } j)}{\text{Pr(exit poverty)}}$$

$$= \frac{\text{Pr(exit poverty via event } j)}{\text{Pr(exit poverty)}} \qquad (9.4)$$

with an analogous expression for poverty entries and entry events.

These various expressions also provide insights into the sources of change over time in poverty transition rates, and hence trends in the overall poverty rate. Changes in tax-benefit policies and in the labour market, and other factors, can have impacts on both the incidence of different types of event, or on the chances of making a transition if someone experiences a particular sort of event. These, in turn, will affect aggregate 'share' statistics associated with events. The fraction of all poverty exits accounted for by a particular event will be large if the event is common or if the event-conditional exit probability is large, or both. Similarly, an event's share of poverty entries will be large if the event is common or if the event-conditional entry probability is large, or both.

Earlier chapters of this book emphasize two main factors relevant to trends over time in Britain in poverty rates and poverty transition rates, namely the introduction of a series of anti-poverty measures by the Labour government from the end of the 1990s onwards, and also the improvement in labour market conditions from the early 1990s to the late 2000s. For adults of working age and their household members, one would expect the combination of the changes in policy and the state of the economy to be reflected in both changes in event-incidence rates and in event-conditioned poverty transition rates. In my analysis, I compare poverty dynamics patterns between two seven-year periods, 1991–7 and 1998–2004.

Looking at poverty exits, one would expect improvements in the state of the economy, contextual changes, and greater rewards to working relative to not working to lead to an increase in the proportion of poor adults who take up jobs between one year and the next—reflected in increases in the incidence of job-related and earnings-related events. (Potentially offsetting this is a change in the composition of the at-risk population: as poverty rates fall over time, the sorts of people who are poor are less likely to be able or available to work.) In addition, one would expect, there to be greater 'propulsion' effects on poverty exits associated with taking a job. A useful way to think about this is in terms of the poverty line and the incomes of working-age households, distinguishing between those with earners (with an income typically above the poverty line) and those without earners (with an income closer to or below the poverty line). Changing from the former group to the latter group is associated with an increase in the chances of being poor, and a change in the other direction is associated with a decrease in the chances of being poor. See Chapter 1 and Waldfogel (2010) for further information about incomes before and after the reforms.

Working Families Tax Credit (WFTC) and its successors were specifically intended to 'make work pay' to a greater extent than previously. The policies were directed specifically at families with children—the extension of tax credits to childless people did not occur until 2003 (and so any effects are unlikely to be revealed in my BHPS data for the 1998–2004 period). At the same time, there were also improvements in the generosity of benefits available to non-working families with children over this period—increases in child benefit (payable per child regardless of work status) and in the child allowances paid as part of Income Support. Thus, the income distribution for families with children shifted up relative to the distribution for other groups and also relative to the poverty line. Consequently, if the number of workers in a household with children increases, the chances of escaping poverty are expected to be higher in the second period than the first. This process should also be revealed by an increase between the two periods in the incidence of increases in income from benefits and tax credits and an increase in the chances of exiting poverty among those who do have such increases. The veracity of this story can be checked by comparing job and benefit income event-conditioned poverty exit rates for poor households with and without children—the effects described are expected to be confined to families with children. Finally, the combination of increases over time in incidence rate and event-conditioned exit rates are expected to lead to a corresponding increase between periods in the aggregate share of job-related and benefit income-related events as a proportion of the total number of poverty exits.

For poverty entries among working-age households, one would expect the fall over time in unemployment rates and improvement in incentives to work to be associated with fewer transitions out of work: the incidence of job loss between one year and the next should be lower in the second period relative to the first. One would also expect a decline between the two periods in the chances of entering poverty among households containing job losers. If the minimum income for the average family with dependent children increases relative to the poverty line, the chances of falling into poverty are smaller if someone loses his job or, indeed, loses non-labour income. (Again, one would expect to see a contrast between households with and without children.) What the expected differences are between periods in poverty entry rates among those who experience a non-negligible fall in benefit and tax credit income is less clear. The average income decrease for those non-poor households with children who do experience such income falls may be smaller in the second period (since falls in income from tax credits are more likely to be replaced by income from other types of benefit—see the previous paragraph), and so there may also be a reduction between periods in the chances of entering poverty for this group.

For pensioner households, one expects changes over time in the labour market to be of little relevance. Much more important are changes in income from benefits and from non-labour income in the form of private and occupational pensions and income from savings and investments. There were important changes to pensioner benefits between 1991 and 2004, notably the introduction of the means-tested Minimum Income Guarantee from April 1999, an increase in its generosity in 2001, and conversion to the Pensioner Credit in 2003 (see Chapter 1). Hence one would expect the incidence of increases in benefit income among poor pensioners to be larger from the late 1990s onwards (i.e. larger in the second period compared to the first), though this is also conditional on rates of take-up of the means-tested income supplements. Among pensioners with such an increase, one would expect the poverty exit rate to rise: increased assistance would be expected to propel more people out of poverty. And since the additional means-tested assistance raises the floor under pensioners' incomes, income falls are likely to be smaller if they do occur. With more cushioning, event-conditioned poverty entry rates are expected to fall. On the other hand, there is a substantial concentration of pensioners with incomes close to the poverty line (more so than for most other family types), and so results may be more affected by the variations in where the poverty line falls from one year to the next, even though these changes are relatively small.

Methods 1 and 2, in Detail

The exposition above supposes that there is a set of mutually exclusive trigger events that exhaustively accounts for all poverty transitions. However, derivation of such a classification of events is problematic because it requires prioritizing of some events over others if they occur over the same period. This issue led to the employment of two complementary methods.

Method 1 is based on specification of an exhaustive set of mutually exclusive trigger events, with the events defined using a hierarchy of event 'importance' following Bane and Ellwood (1986). In addition to allowing comparisons with their findings for the USA, a major advantage of Method 1 is that one can associate every poverty transition with one event or another and so, by construction, the sum of the share statistics is 100 per cent. It is therefore straightforward to assess the importance of different trigger events from the aggregate point of view.

With Method 2, attempts to define a mutually exclusive set of events are eschewed. Instead, following Jenkins and Rigg (2001) and Jenkins and Schluter (2003), I focus on a subset of major events and examine the three key statistics associated with each of these events, one event at a time. This has the major advantage of providing an individual perspective on trigger event importance. A disadvantage of Method 2 is that the poverty transition share statistics do not add up to 100 per cent, and so assessment of event importance from an aggregate perspective is harder. But, on the other hand, one gets the individual-level perspective and in addition there is greater flexibility in the number and type of events that can be analysed, and one can handle simultaneously occurring events more easily.

For Method 1, all the events are specified in advance, and the hierarchical nature of the specification leads to computer program code that is inflexible and much more complicated because of the detailed characterization of demographic events that is used: see below. In any case, if the events expected to be the most important ones do not in fact account for most of the transitions, then this is useful information. It points to there being a wide diversity of routes into and out of poverty, none of which predominates, or it may signal that some transitions are spurious and arise because of measurement error in income, or that changes in the poverty line over time have an effect.

Whereas both types of analysis refer to changes in the poverty status of individuals between one year and the next (individuals are the unit of analysis), trigger events are defined at the level of each individual's household. Poverty status depends on household income, and a person's household income is affected by changes in the incomes of any household member, and also by changes in the composition of the household itself. For example, if an unemployed husband finds a job, then all members of the household may be taken out of poverty. (For each individual in this household, the trigger event would be defined as an increase in the number of workers in the household.) If a non-dependent child leaves home (and nothing else changes), then the household income of the remaining household members changes, for two reasons. First, regardless of whether the child was earning, household needs have changed (captured by the change in the household's equivalence-scale rate). Second, there may also be an effect via a fall in household money income if the child had been employed or had some other income. The event in question (for each individual remaining in the household) would be a change in household size in the first case and, in the second case, a change in household size plus a change in the number of household earners.

Before proceeding to the results, I define the trigger events that are employed in the analysis, and hence the routes into and out of poverty.

The Mutually Exclusive Events Underpinning Method 1

The mutually exclusive and exhaustive categorization of event types for each person experiencing a poverty transition follows the approach pioneered by Bane and Ellwood (1986) and applied to US data for the 1970s and 1980s. The categorization is summarized in Figure 9.1.

Bane and Ellwood (1986: 9) argue that a change in household headship is particularly important, both in its own right and because 'many behavioral changes which might account for a higher or lower level of family income may be the direct result of the headship change, as in the case where a family breakup forces a woman to quit working'. So, the first step in the categorization is to classify individuals according to whether they experience a change in household head between two successive annual interviews. The BHPS definition of 'household head' is used. This person, also known as the 'household reference person', is the owner or renter of the property and, where ownership or tenancy is jointly held, the eldest owner or renter. In the vast majority of households containing couples, the household head is a man because husbands are typically older than their wives. Marriage refers to both legal marriages and cohabiting unions.

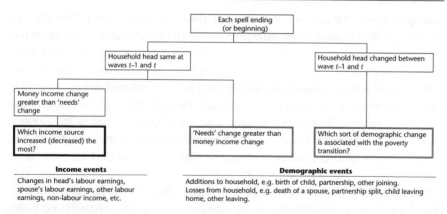

Figure 9.1. Classification of income events and demographic events associated with a poverty spell ending (or beginning) between waves t–1 and t
Source: Jenkins (2000: figure 1).

Second, among individuals with a change in household head, more detailed types of demographic event are identified using headings similar to Bane and Ellwood's. Examples include a child leaving the family home and becoming a household head, and partnership dissolution where a married woman and her children became a lone-parent family. Third, among individuals with no change in household head, I check whether the between-interview change in household 'needs'—as summarized by the proportional change in the individual's household equivalence-scale rate—was greater than the concurrent proportional change in household net money income. Examples of this type of demographic event include the birth of a child or death of a spouse. All the events identified so far are labelled demographic events.

All remaining poverty transitions are classified as arising from income events, and further subdivided by event type. Among persons with an unchanged household head and for whom household income changed by more than 'needs', I determine for poverty exits which income component increased the most and, similarly, for poverty entries, determine which income component decreased the most. Nine types of income event are distinguished, corresponding to nine components of household income.

The classification leads to the following sets of trigger events. For poverty exits, the income events are a rise in: head's labour earnings; spouse's labour earnings; other labour earnings; income from investments and savings; personal or occupational pension income; benefit income (including tax credits, and the state retirement pension); private transfer income; a fall in income taxes and national insurance contributions; and a fall in local taxes. An increase in earnings may reflect either a transition from unemployment to employment, or an increase in earnings while staying in the same job (for example, reflecting an increase in work hours or promotion). The income events potentially associated with poverty entries are the same as those listed, with the exception that the income changes are in the opposite direction from those for considered for poverty exits (that is, a fall rather than a rise, or vice versa). Some poverty transitions were found to be associated with implausibly large changes in benefit income, and so I exclude these from the analysis (following Jenkins 2000, and Jenkins and Rigg 2001). Specifically, I censor transitions where, for those for whom a benefit income change was the largest income source change, the benefit income change accounted for more than three-quarters of the total income change.

There are 11 types of demographic event: a fall in needs (same household head), or a rise in needs for poverty entries; child became household head; other relative became household head; spouse became female head; female head became spouse; child of male head became child of female head; child of female head became child of male head; or some other change (involving other relatives or unrelated persons). Also, following Bane and Ellwood (1986), some of the tabulations for poverty entries between the previous and current year also include individuals who are first observed in the panel in the current year: for example, a new-born baby, or a new partner of a panel member.

The Trigger Events Underpinning Method 2

Three types of major event are considered, labelled for convenience as labour market events, non-labour income events, and demographic events, though the distinction is not clear cut for the reasons explained below. These labels deliberately imitate the Bane-Ellwood-like event classification used for Method 1. The key difference, however, is that the events are defined separately rather than in sequence. (This also means that computer coding is substantially less complicated.) The mutually exclusive and exhaustive set of events that Bane and Ellwood (1986) define is reliant on their privileging of demographic change (in the form of change of household head) to define a hierarchy. This may be appropriate for 1980s USA, but is more debatable for 1990s Britain. Method 2 avoids this issue by not having an exhaustive and mutually exclusive classification of poverty transitions by event type (a transition may be associated with more than one event). As a result, share statistics summarizing event importance in the aggregate sense are harder to interpret with Method 2 than with Method 1. But Method 2 also straightforwardly provides the other individual-level statistics of event importance.

Among the various types of income change, I distinguish between 'pure' income changes—those occurring without concurrent household demographic change—and income changes that also coincide with a demographic event. For example, an increase in the number of workers may arise because a working adult moves in with a non-working adult; household size has also increased. To identify pure income changes, I restrict attention to cases in which household size remains the same for the two years defining the poverty transition. For example, when looking at changes in the numbers of workers, I derive estimates separately for the subgroup of individuals for whom household size did not change, as well as for individuals. This also provides me with a straightforward way of assessing how frequently labour market events occur along with or separately from demographic events. The labour market earnings event variables refer to earnings changes occurring without concurrent changes in the number of workers or in household size. Non-labour income changes are calculated for households without changes in household size.

For poverty exits, the labour market events include a rise in number of workers, a rise in the number of full-time workers, and a rise in household labour earnings. Non-labour income events are a rise in benefit income, and a rise in non-benefit non-labour income (personal or occupational pensions, investment income, or private transfers). Demographic events are a change in household head, household size, and household type and also, more specifically, a change in household type to married-couple household. For poverty entries, I consider the same types of event, though the income events refer to falls rather than rises in income. Also, among demographic events, I specifically consider changes from a couple household to a lone-parent household.

My definitions of each income event require that the relevant income source changes by at least 20 per cent and by more than £10 (in monetary terms, that is, unequivalized). These thresholds are chosen to ensure that transitory or 'modest' income variations are not counted.

A rise (or fall) in the number of full-time workers can occur as people move between full-time and part-time work, or between full-time work and no work. Because most transitions into and out of full-time work do not involve transitions to or from part-time work, I do not treat such moves as separate events. They are reflected in changes in household labour earnings.

Health events were also incorporated in preliminary analysis. One might expect the incidence of serious illness or injury to affect people's ability to work with consequent effects on the chances of falling into poverty, for example. Conversely, health improvements may allow a person to take up a job and increase their income. It is straightforward in principle to add health events to the portfolio considered in a Method 2 type analysis (but not in Method 1). Practical implementation was less successful, however, probably because the health measures available in the BHPS are not very specific. Specifically, there is a measure of poor mental well-being based on the General Health Questionnaire (GHQ), with a battery of questions asking respondents whether recently they had felt 'better', 'the same', 'worse', or 'much worse' than usual in terms of loss of sleep, loss of concentration, feelings of unhappiness or depression, etc.

Respondents are also asked whether their daily activities or their ability to work are limited by health. I found that changes in health accounted for a non-negligible share of poverty transitions. However, among households in which they occur, poverty transition rates are much the same as for households that did not experience them. In this sense, health events (as measured in the BHPS) are unimportant for poverty transitions. So, for brevity, I do not discuss them further in this chapter. For some analysis of health events based on the measures mentioned, see Jenkins and Rigg (2001).

For both Methods 1 and 2, poverty transitions are classified by trigger event type for the population as a whole, and also tabulated separately by household type. I distinguish seven household types: single non-pensioner; one adult plus dependent children (referred to as a 'lone-parent' household); childless couple; couple with children; couples with dependent children and other adults (mostly non-dependent children); single pensioner; couple pensioner; and other (mainly unrelated adults, but including a few lone-parent families in multi-family households). For poverty transitions between one year and the next, household type refers to status in the first year, that is, when the individual is at risk of making a transition into or out of poverty. This is the final year of a poverty spell for poverty exits and the final year of a non-poverty spell for poverty entries. (Exceptionally, in the Method 1 analysis of poverty entries, household type refers to status in the first year of the new poverty spell—this follows Bane and Ellwood (1986).) Household status may of course be different in the second year, in which case there is a demographic event.

Poverty Rates and Poverty Transition Rates, 1991–7 and 1998–2004

To set the scene for the analysis that follows, I summarize poverty rates and poverty transition rates for the two periods 1991–7 and 1998–2004, for the population as a whole and separately by household type. The rates for each period, here and in the next sections, are estimated by pooling data for the years within each period. Estimates of these poverty rates and poverty transition rates were presented in the previous chapter, but I provide them again because the definition of income is slightly different in this chapter, and the focus is on two specific periods between 1991 and 2004.

Poverty rates are shown in Figure 9.2. The poverty rate for the population as a whole is 21 per cent for 1991–7 and falls slightly in the second period, to 19 per cent. These overall average rates disguise substantial variations by household type. Poverty rates well above the average are experienced by lone-parent households and single pensioners, though, for both groups, there is also a marked fall in rates between the two periods. For the former group, the rate goes from 60 per cent to 48 per cent and, for the latter group, from 46 per cent

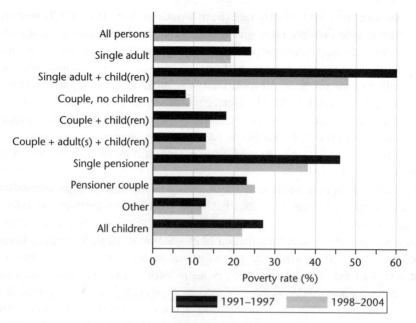

Figure 9.2. Poverty rates (%), by household type and period
Note: Author's calculations from BHPS waves 1–14.

to 38 per cent. The lowest poverty rates are experienced by childless couples, around 8 per cent in both periods. Individuals living in couple-with-children households have below average poverty rates, and the rate falls between periods, from 18 per cent to 14 per cent. The final bar of the chart shows the situation for children. Poverty rates are above average (reflecting the position of children in lone-parent households), but fall between periods from 27 per cent to 22 per cent.

Although couples with children have below average poverty rates, many individuals belong to this household type (around one-third of the population), and so this group forms a large fraction of all the individuals who are poor (and hence at risk of poverty exit). Couples with dependent children form 27 per cent of all individuals who are poor in the first period and 23 per cent in the second period. In contrast, relatively few individuals live in lone-parent households, and so form a much lower fraction of the population who is poor (around 17 per cent in both periods). About 27 per cent of the poor were children in the 1991–7 period, and 26 per cent in the 1998–2004 period. In both periods, about one-fifth of poor people were single pensioners.

Poverty exit rates are shown in Figure 9.3 and poverty entry rates in Figure 9.4. They show that the fall in the poverty rate represents a combination of an increase in the poverty exit rate (from 34 per cent to 40 per cent) and a decrease in the poverty entry rate (from 9 per cent to 6 per cent). The groups with the largest poverty rates—lone parents and single pensioners—are the groups with distinctively low poverty exit rates and high poverty entry rates. Nonetheless there are similar patterns of change in the transition rates between periods for most household types. Most exit rates rise, and most poverty entry rates fall. For lone-parent households, the poverty exit rate rose from 22 per cent to 34 per cent, and the poverty entry rate fell from 27 per cent to 16 per cent. For single pensioners, the exit rates for the two periods are 24 per cent and 31 per cent, and the corresponding entry rates are 22 per cent and 15 per cent.

In sum, the figures show that there are some marked changes in poverty rates and poverty transition rates between 1991–7 and 1998–2004. House-holds with children (including lone-parent households) and single pensioners stand out, either because they form a large fraction of all individuals who are poor or because the group's trends are distinctive. So, in what follows, there is a special focus on these household types in addition to examination of the population as a whole.

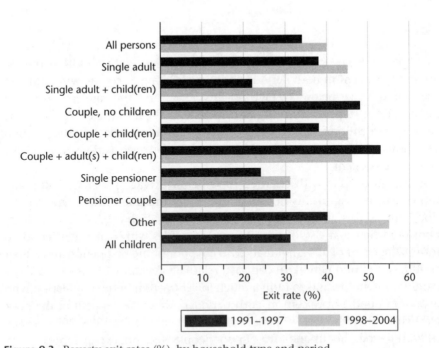

Figure 9.3. Poverty exit rates (%), by household type and period

Notes: Poverty exit rate is the number of poverty exits between years t–1 and t, expressed as a percentage of the total number of poor people at t–1. Household type refers to status in year t–1 for poverty transitions between years t–1 and t.

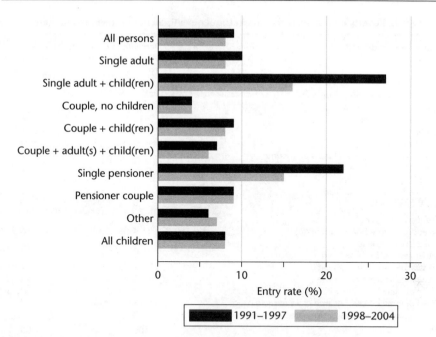

Figure 9.4. Poverty entry rates (%), by household type and period

Notes: Poverty entry rate refers to the number of poverty entries between years *t*–1 and *t*, expressed as a percentage of the total number of non-poor people at *t*–1. Household type refers to status in year *t*–1 for poverty transitions between years *t*–1 and *t*.

9.2. Routes Into and Out of Poverty: Method 1 Analysis

Using Method 1, I now analyse the events associated with making a poverty transition. Exits from poverty are discussed first, and then poverty entries.

Poverty Exits

The tabulation of poverty exits by event type is shown in Table 9.1 for all poor individuals. The percentages shown are Bane-Ellwood 'share' statistics as defined earlier, with the first column showing the estimates for the first period and the second column showing estimates for the second period. Income events are shown in the upper half of the table; demographic events in the lower half. It is immediately apparent that there is virtually no change in the incidence of the different types of poverty exit events between 1991–7 and 1998–2004 (especially once sampling variability is taken into account). This may be surprising given the changes in the tax-benefit system and in the labour market, but may also be a consequence of the construction of the mutually exclusive event hierarchy: by giving priority to demographic events,

Table 9.1. Poverty exits classified by main trigger event, all poor individuals (column %)

Main event associated with poverty exit	Percentage of all spell endings	
	1991–7	1998–2004
Increase in money income from:		
Head's labour earnings	31	30
Spouse's labour earnings	17	16
Other labour earnings	11	13
Investment income	6	4
Private and occupational pension income	6	7
Benefit and tax credit income	6	6
Private transfer income	3	3
Income taxes and NIC (fall)	0	0
Local taxes (fall)	0	0
Demographic event:		
Needs fall (same household head)	4	6
Child became head	1	1
Other relative became head	0	0
Spouse became female head	2	1
Female head became spouse	2	2
Child of male head became child of female head	2	2
Child of female head became child of male head	3	2
Other change (relatives or unrelated persons)	7	7
All	100	100
(Demographic events as % of total)	(21)	(21)

Notes: Some poverty exits associated with potentially unreliable increases in benefit income have been excluded (see text). NIC: employee National Insurance Contributions. Author's calculations from BHPS waves 1–14. Number of poverty exits is 2,922 (1991–7), 2,661 (1998–2004).

the role of some income events may be suppressed. Method 2 analysis, below, allows us to examine this. First, however, consider the patterns that are revealed from this breakdown.

Four-fifths (79 per cent) of poverty exits are associated with favourable income events, and one-fifth (21 per cent) with demographic events. Changes in household labour earnings account for three-quarters of all the income events (59 per cent of all poverty exits). The importance of labour earnings stands out, even though demographic events are prioritized in the construction of the event classification.

Although an increase in the earnings of the household head is the event that accounts for the largest share of exits (around 30 per cent), a change in the labour earnings of others in the household accounts for almost as many. The majority of the latter changes are associated with increases in the labour earnings of the household head's spouse, but a significant minority are associated with earnings increases for other adults in the household (who may include non-dependent children). Among the demographic events, no type dominates, but two appear to be more important than others. First, there are various changes in household composition that do not involve a change in household head. An example of such a fall in 'needs' is when a child leaves the parental home to live elsewhere. Second, there are various changes in household headship involving relatives or unrelated persons becoming the household head. A child moving in with grandparents is an example.

These statistics disguise substantial variations in the experience of individuals from different household types. Table 9.2 breaks down the exit events according to each person's household type at the interview prior to the poverty transition (that is, the last year of the poverty spell). Decompositions are constrained by sample numbers, but there are some patterns that are much the same for both periods. Among pensioner households, increases in non-labour income dominate, whereas, among non-pensioner households, increases in labour income are the most important. This is expected since employment earnings are relatively unimportant for the former group and the opposite for the latter group. The incidence of demographic events is most distinctively above the all-persons average for persons living in the 'other' household type (mostly unrelated adults), and is most likely associated with persons leaving the household.

Again, there appears to be no significant change between periods in the patterns for each group, with the possible exceptions being single non-pensioner householders and those living in 'other' types of household. For single householders, there is a rise in share of exits associated with increases in earnings and a corresponding decline in the share associated with non-labour income. The sample size for this group is relatively small, and the change may simply reflect sampling variability. For the 'other' group, sample sizes are even smaller, and the estimates of change over time may also not be reliable.

The breakdowns underline the fact that, although increases in the labour earnings of the household head are important for poverty exits, so too are increases from other household members. Among couple households, the main poverty exit event is a change in the earnings of the household head, associated with almost 40 per cent of poverty exits for couples with children and around one-quarter of exits for childless couples. However, the importance of changes in the labour income of other adults besides the household head is striking: among childless-couple households, the share of exits associated with changes in non-head earnings is larger than the share associated with head's earnings changes and, among couples with children, about the same. For individuals in lone-parent households, the non-head earnings increases are typically those of other adults joining the household (for example, a new partner moving in who did not become the household head). The results suggest that increases in a lone parent's earnings are more important than repartnering for getting out of poverty—at least in the short term. I return to the issue later when using Method 2.

Table 9.2. Poverty exits and trigger events, by individual's household type in last year of poverty spell (column %)

Main event associated with poverty exit	All		Single pensioner		Pensioner couple		Single		Couple, no children		Couple and children		Lone parent		Other	
	1991–7	1998–2004	1991–7	1998–2004	1991–7	1998–2004	1991–7	1998–2004	1991–7	1998–2004	1991–7	1998–2004	1991–7	1998–2004	1991–7	1998–2004
Household head's labour earnings rose	31	30	5	3	3	1	50	60	28	23	39	36	40	38	11	8
Spouse's or other labour earnings rose	28	29	1	2	12	16	4	2	33	33	36	37	16	16	37	56
Non-labour income rose	20	20	81	77	62	59	22	12	18	17	6	8	23	22	19	12
Demographic event	21	21	13	19	23	23	25	26	22	27	19	18	22	25	33	24
All	100	100	100	100	100	100	100	100	100	100	100	100	100	100	100	100
Proportion of persons (as % of all persons)	100	100	5	7	8	8	7	8	11	13	50	45	13	16	6	4

Notes: Some poverty exits associated with potentially unreliable increases in benefit income have been excluded (see text). Author's calculations from BHPS waves 1–14. Total number of poverty exits is 2,922 (1991–7), 2,661 (1998–2004).

So far, I have referred to increases in labour earnings per se, but these increases may have arisen for a variety of reasons: for example, an unemployed person taking a job, or someone already with a job working more hours or being promoted, etc. Among the persons for whom a rise in household head's labour earnings is the most important event associated with a poverty exit, the household head changed from 'not working' to 'working' in 45 per cent of the cases in the first period, but in only 36 per cent of cases in the second period. Since the labour market was in better shape in the second period, more people already had a job. Earnings changes and job changes are examined in more detail in the Method 2 analysis that follows in the next section.

Poverty Entries

Consider now the main events associated with poverty entries. Table 9.3 displays the breakdown for all individuals at risk of poverty entry. The first two columns provide the event breakdown for the case in which poor new entrants are included in the counts, and the second two columns are for the case when they are excluded. Looking at the first two columns initially, there are similarities and differences with the findings for poverty exits. First, as with exits, there appears to be no significant difference between the patterns for 1991–8 and 1999–2004. Second, in contrast, demographic events play a more important role for poverty entries than for poverty exits. In both periods, demographic events account for a greater proportion of the poverty-spell beginnings than of poverty-spell endings (about 38 per cent compared with 21 per cent). Income events account for 62 per cent of poverty entries, but 79 per cent of poverty exits.

Although demographic events are relatively more important for poverty entries, the result is driven by the events associated with 'new entrants' to the household, accounting for around 15 per cent of all poverty entries. These events refer to persons who were not present in the household in the year prior to the poverty transition, but were present in the subsequent year (and who were not the household head). Many of these individuals are children born into poverty. Others are new partners of the household head or other adults joining a household which is poor when they are present. The share statistic estimated for the latter group is an over-estimate because, when constructing the table, I assume that these persons were not poor prior to joining their current household. Some such assumption has to be made because, by definition, the income of their previous household is not observed in the panel. However, even if one takes the opposite view, and assumes that all these new entrants to the household were previously poor (and thus excluded from the table because they are not at risk of poverty entry), the

Table 9.3. Poverty entries classified by main trigger event, all non-poor individuals (column %)

Main event associated with poverty entry	Percentage of all spell beginnings			
	Including new entrants		Excluding new entrants	
	1991–7	1998–2004	1991–7	1998–2004
Decrease in money income from:				
Head's labour earnings	28	27	34	31
Spouse's labour earnings	11	13	13	15
Other labour earnings	6	7	7	8
Investment income	6	5	7	6
Private and occupational pension income	5	5	6	6
Benefit and tax credit income	4	3	5	4
Private transfer income	2	2	2	3
Income taxes and NIC (rise)	0	0	0	0
Local taxes (rise)	0	0	0	0
Demographic event:				
Needs rise (same household head)	6	6	7	7
Child became head	4	4	5	4
Other relative became head	0	1	0	1
Spouse became female head	3	3	3	3
Female head became spouse	1	1	1	2
Child of male head became child of female head	1	2	1	3
Child of female head became child of male head	4	3	4	3
Other change (relatives or unrelated persons)	3	5	4	5
New entrant to household: baby	6	4		
New entrant to household: partner	3	3		
New entrant to household: other	7	6		
All	100	100	100	100
(Demographic events as % of total)	(38)	(37)	(26)	(28)

Notes: Some poverty entries associated with potentially unreliable decreases in benefit income were excluded (see text). 'New entrant' refers to an individual who was not a member of a household surveyed by the BHPS in the previous year. NIC: employee National Insurance Contributions. Author's calculations from BHPS waves 1–14. Number of poverty entries is 2,395 or 3,668 including new entrants (1991–7), 2,788 or 3,218 including new entrants (1998–2004).

general conclusion about the greater importance of demographic events for poverty entries than for poverty exits does not change.

If I exclude new entrants from the calculations and focus on the individuals present at two consecutive waves (the sample selection rule used by Method 2), the effect is, unsurprisingly, to increase the fraction of all poverty entries that is accounted for by income events in general, and by labour earnings changes in particular. The share of poverty entries associated with demographic events falls from around 38 per cent to around 27 per cent, and the share associated with changes in total household labour earnings rises from just below one-half (46 per cent) to above one-half (54 per cent).

Poverty entries are broken down in Table 9.4 by event and household type in the first year of the new poverty spell. Broadly speaking, the diversity of patterns by household type is similar to that in Table 9.3, but with a shift within each household type towards a higher incidence of demographic

Table 9.4. Poverty entries and trigger events, by individual's household type in first year of poverty spell (column %)

Main event associated with poverty exit	All		Single pensioner		Pensioner couple		Single		Couple, no children		Couple and children		Lone parent		Other	
	1991–7	1998–2004	1991–7	1998–2004	1991–7	1998–2004	1991–7	1998–2004	1991–7	1998–2004	1991–7	1998–2004	1991–7	1998–2004	1991–7	1998–2004
Household head's labour earnings fell	28	27	9	8	17	10	32	36	38	29	40	36	17	24	7	8
Spouse's or other labour earnings fell	17	19	4	3	16	19	8	7	19	27	22	22	14	17	14	22
Non-labour income fell	18	16	75	73	53	47	13	8	14	12	5	5	15	13	10	9
Demographic event	21	24	11	16	14	20	47	49	16	20	16	24	36	30	18	16
New entrant	16	13	1	0	0	4	1	0	13	13	17	13	17	16	51	46
All	100	100	100	100	100	100	100	100	100	100	100	100	100	100	100	100
Proportion of persons (as % of all persons)	100	100	7	7	8	10	8	7	10	14	42	42	15	11	10	8

Notes: Some poverty entries associated with potentially unreliable decreases in benefit income have been excluded (see text). Author's calculations from BHPS waves 1–14. Demographic events row excludes new entrants. 'New entrant' refers to an individual who was not a member of a household surveyed by the BHPS in the previous year. Number of poverty entries is 2,395 or 3,668 including new entrants (1991–7), 2,788 or 3,218 including new entrants (1998–2004).

events. Moreover, as with the breakdown for poverty exits, there are few changes in patterns between the two periods, except for childless couples and perhaps lone-parent households. I discuss these cases shortly.

If the definition of a demographic event is taken to include poor new entrants, this combined category accounts for around half or more of all spell beginnings for non-pensioner single persons, and individuals in lone-parent and 'other' households (mostly unrelated adults sharing). For single householders, most of the changes refer to children who left their parents' household to become heads of their own households. For many of the lone parents, the poverty transition is associated with becoming a lone parent (household type is measured in the first year of the poverty spell). There is some suggestion from the estimates that the importance of demographic events is smaller in the second period than the first, with changes in labour earnings becoming more important. Among 'other' households, the arrival in the household of new unrelated adults is the most important event associated with poverty entries.

For pensioners, especially single pensioners, demographic events and labour earnings events account for a relatively small fraction of poverty entries, which is unsurprising. Most important are decreases in non-labour income, whether from benefits and credits, or from private and occupational pensions, or investments and savings.

Among non-pensioner couple households with and without children, both of which are households with an above-average incidence of labour earnings events—earnings decreases for secondary earners are less important for poverty entries than earnings rises are for poverty exits. However, it remains the case that losing a job is almost as important as pure earnings losses for those already with a job. For example, among the individuals for whom a fall in household head's labour earnings is the most important event associated with a poverty entry, the household head changed from 'not working' to 'working' in 47 per cent of the cases in the first period, compared with 40 per cent of cases in the second period. Since the labour market was in better shape in the second period, job loss was less likely. Earnings changes and job changes are examined in more detail in the next section.

The group for which there is the clearest suggestion of a change in patterns between periods is childless couples, and the change concerns the relative importance of falls in labour earnings of the household head relative to the fall for the spouse. The fraction of poverty entries accounted for by a decrease in household head's labour earnings is 38 per cent for 1991–7, but 29 per cent for 1998–2004. The fraction accounted for by a decrease in spouse's labour earnings was of about the same magnitude, but in the opposite direction. The share goes from 19 per cent to 27 per cent. My explanation for this refers to the secular increase in the prevalence of dual-earner couples in Britain (Gregg and

Wadsworth 2008). Over time, it has become increasingly important to have two or more earners in a household to stay above the poverty line and so, increasingly, if a secondary earner's earnings do decrease, the chances of her household being poor have risen. The impact on childless couples is greater than for families with children because of increasing support for the latter through the tax-benefit system. The extension of tax credits to childless families did not occur until 2003.

9.3. Routes Into and Out of Poverty: Method 2 Analysis

I now consider the importance of the various routes into and out of poverty using Method 2. By contrast with the Method 1 analysis, the emphasis differs in the sense that event 'importance' is examined from the individual perspective, rather than in terms of aggregate 'share' statistics. Poverty exits are discussed first and then poverty entries. In each case, results are presented first for all persons and then separately for households with children and single pensioners.

Poverty Exits: All Individuals

The evidence about poverty exits is shown in Table 9.5 for all poor individuals (those at risk of a poverty exit). This and subsequent tables all have the same format. The first row of each table shows the overall poverty transition rate: in this case, the table shows that the poverty exit rate for all poor individuals increases from 34 per cent to 40 per cent between 1991–7 and 1998–2004. The first two columns of the table show event-incidence rates for each period. The middle two columns show the poverty transition rates among those who experience each of the events, by period. The final two columns show the period-specific proportions of all exits that are accounted for by each of the events. (Recall that each of these statistics is proportional to the product of the event-incidence rate times the event-conditioned transition rate.) Because events are not defined in a hierarchical manner as with Method 1, the same underlying event can have effects that appear in several places in each table. In particular, an increase in the number of workers is likely to be reflected in a non-trivial increase in household labour earnings. As a result, eligibility for in-work benefits such as tax credits may increase also, and be reflected in a rise in benefit and tax credit income. (The latter effect is, of course, more likely in the second period than the first.) An increase in the number of workers in a household can occur either with or without an accompanying change in household size: note the difference between the first and second rows of the table.

Method 2 share statistics imply conclusions that are similar to those derived using Method 1. First, differences in corresponding share statistics for the two periods are not large, though there appear to be more than suggested earlier for Method 1. The most apparent differences are a small decrease in share of exits associated with increases in the number of workers in the household and a small increase in the share associated with a rise in labour earnings and benefit and tax credit income. The introduction of WFTC to 'make work pay' can explain this. Second, labour market events account for more poverty exits than do demographic events, but demographic events play a non-negligible role nonetheless. There is a diversity of routes out of poverty.

To illustrate this, I focus on the second period. A rise in the number of workers in the household is associated with the largest share of exits (32 per cent). Some of these events arise because a working adult joins the household (a concurrent demographic event) and some arise because existing members

Table 9.5. Poverty exits and trigger events: all individuals in poor households, by period (cell %)

Household event type	Event prevalence rate		Exit rate conditional on event		Share of all exits associated with event	
	1991–7	1998–2004	1991–7	1998–2004	1991–7	1998–2004
Poverty exit rate			34	40		
Labour market events						
Rise in number of workers	19	19	64	68	37	32
Rise in number of workers[a]	15	15	62	66	28	24
Rise in number of full-time workers	13	14	70	75	28	26
Rise in number of full-time workers[a]	10	10	68	71	20	18
Rise in labour earnings[b]	11	13	59	67	20	23
Non-labour income events						
Rise in benefit and tax credit income[a, b]	20	23	48	57	29	33
Rise in other non-labour income[a]	11	12	63	60	21	18
Demographic events						
Change in household head	7	8	62	57	13	11
Change in household type	12	13	48	53	16	17
Change to married-couple household	2	2	61	68	3	3
Increase in household size	8	7	42	56	10	10
Decrease in household size	5	6	44	51	6	7

Notes: Author's calculations from BHPS waves 1–14. Events are not mutually exclusive. [a] And also household size constant in both years. [b] And also number of workers in household constant in both years. Number of exits is 3,759 (1991–7), 4,197 (1998–2004).

take up jobs. The latter appears to be more important (in the aggregate sense) since, when household size is held constant, an increase in the number of workers still accounts for 24 per cent of all poverty exits. A number of other events also account for a significant proportion of exits: a rise in household labour earnings (23 per cent) and a rise in income from benefits and tax credits (33 per cent). In contrast, changes in the household head account for 11 per cent of poverty exits and changes in household type for 17 per cent. Changes in household headship are attributed a smaller share of poverty exits by Method 2 in comparison with Method 1, because they are not given precedence in the definition of event types.

The relatively large share statistics for increases in the number of workers, labour earnings, and benefit and credit incomes partly reflect the fact that these events occur more frequently than other types of events. (Observe too that the various incidence rates change little over time.) For example, among individuals in households at risk of finishing a poverty spell, the number of workers increases in about one-fifth of them, and about the same proportion experiences an increase in income from benefits and tax credits. In contrast, the fraction experiencing a change in household head is less than half that proportion, 7 to 8 per cent. Just over one in ten individuals change their household type between one year and the next.

Although event-incidence rates differ a lot, poverty exit rates for those who experience the various events are broadly similar. Put another way, from the individual rather than the aggregate perspective, favourable demographic events are associated with poverty exits to a degree almost as high as for some income events. In the second period, for example, the poverty exit rate for those who change household head is just under 60 per cent, which is about the same as the exit rate for those with a non-negligible increase in income from benefits and tax credits or other non-labour income. These exit rates are smaller than the rates for those with an increase in the number of workers in the household (around two-thirds) and smaller still than the rate for those with an increase in the number of full-time workers, around two-thirds. Of comparable magnitude is the poverty exit rate for individuals who move into a (non-pensioner) couple household: it is 68 per cent—but note that only 2 per cent of poor people experienced this event. (Of course, not all individuals can make this transition, as many are already living with a partner; an aspect that is addressed in the subgroup breakdowns to follow.) In sum, if there is more work and more work-related income, the chances of escaping poverty are high, but the chances are high too if there is a favourable demographic event.

There are noticeable changes between periods in the extent to which the various events propel people out of poverty, and these are consistent with the changes to the tax-benefit system from the late 1990s on. (Since event-incidence rates do not change much, it is the changes in event-conditioned poverty exit rates that underpin the rise in the overall poverty exit rate.) The poverty exit rate among individuals in households with more workers increased by a relatively small amount (around four percentage points, depending on which specific event is considered), whereas the increase in the rate for those with more labour earnings or more income from benefits and credits is larger. For the former group, the exit rate increases from 59 per cent to 67 per cent; for the latter, it increases from 48 per cent to 57 per cent. If it were largely improvements in the labour market per se that are responsible for the changes between period, then one might expect to see a greater propulsion effect for labour earnings than for benefit and tax credit income. Tax credits supplement labour earnings, so one sees a rise in both types of conditional poverty exit rates. This process is examined in further detail in the breakdowns by household type, using a contrast between couples with children and childless couples, in particular.

Although the evidence in Table 9.5 is informative about the importance of different routes out of poverty among the population as a whole, it masks considerable variation between individuals from different types of household, as I now demonstrate with separate analyses by type. Household type refers to an individual's household type at the interview prior to the potential poverty transition.

Poverty Exits: Couples with Children and Childless Couples

Poverty exits for poor individuals in households comprising non-pensioner couples and children are considered first: see Table 9.6. The estimates draw attention to the important poverty-reducing role of positive labour market events for this group. From the aggregate perspective, the share statistics for labour market events are much higher than for all other events, and higher than the corresponding statistics for the population as a whole. (This pattern is, of course, consistent with the results derived using Method 1 and reported earlier in Table 9.1.) Increases in the number of workers account for around 40 per cent of all exits for this group (46 per cent in the first period; 38 per cent in the second period). The corresponding estimate for increases in the number of full-time workers is around 30 per cent (35 per cent in the first period; 30 per cent in the second). Comparisons of the estimates in the first and second rows of the table show that about a quarter of the poverty exits associated with an increase in the number of workers are also accompanied by an increase in the number of household members. About a third of poverty exits are associated with an increase in labour earnings.

The differences from the all-persons pattern (Table 9.5) do not arise because these increases in numbers of workers have a stronger association with poverty exit rates at the individual level. Indeed, event-conditioned exit rates for

Table 9.6. Poverty exits and trigger events: individuals from poor couple-with-children households, by period (cell %)

Household event type	Event prevalence rate (%)		Exit rate conditional on event (%)		Share of all exits associated with event (%)	
	1991–7	1998–2004	1991–7	1998–2004	1991–7	1998–2004
Poverty exit rate			40	45		
Labour market events						
Rise in number of workers	28	27	65	64	46	38
Rise in number of workers[a]	24	23	63	64	39	33
Rise in number of full-time workers	21	19	66	66	35	28
Rise in number of full-time workers[a]	18	16	65	63	29	22
Rise in labour earnings[b]	20	23	58	67	29	34
Non-labour income events						
Rise in benefit and tax credit income[a, b]	18	23	36	52	16	27
Rise in other non-labour income[a]	7	8	71	57	12	10
Demographic events						
Change in household head	11	12	55	51	15	14
Change in household type	11	14	47	45	13	14
Increase in household size	9	6	32	50	8	7
Decrease in household size	6	9	53	49	8	9

Notes: Author's calculations from BHPS waves 1–14. Events are not mutually exclusive. [a] And also household size constant in both years. [b] And also number of workers in household constant in both years. Number of exits is 1,642 (1991–7), 1,640 (1998–2004).

these events are slightly smaller than for their all-persons counterparts, and they do change between the two periods. Instead, job-related share statistics are relatively high for this group because the events are more prevalent. More than one-quarter of individuals in poor couple-with-children households experience an increase in the number of workers, and around one-fifth experience an increase in the number of full-time workers and in labour earnings. These fractions change little between periods, which is perhaps surprising given the improvement in the labour market over time.

What stands out from Table 9.6 is some increases in event-conditioned poverty exit rates between the periods. Specifically, the exit rate associated with a rise in household labour earnings increases from 58 per cent to 67 per cent, and the exit rate associated with income from benefits and tax credits increases by an even larger amount, from 36 per cent to 52 per cent. The incidence of the two events also increases slightly. These results suggest that one of the main drivers behind the rise in the overall poverty exit rate for this group, from 40 per cent in the first period to 45 per cent in the second period, is the introduction of WFTC from 1999 onwards. It is not a rise in the rate of taking up jobs, as that appears to have stayed much the same, and one would expect a WFTC effect to show up through increases in both labour earnings and in benefit and tax credit income rather than in only one of them.

Further corroborative evidence is provided by the estimates for poor childless couples shown in Table 9.7. This group was not eligible for tax credits in either period (except in the final year of the second period) and so the WFTC argument is less plausible if we also find increases for this group in the event-conditioned exit rates associated with labour earnings and benefit and tax credit income. However, as the table shows, the two rates actually fell between the two periods for childless couples.

Table 9.7. Poverty exits and trigger events: individuals from poor childless-couple households, by period (cell %)

Household event type	Event prevalence rate (%)		Exit rate conditional on event (%)		Share of all exits associated with event (%)	
	1991–7	1998–2004	1991–7	1998–2004	1991–7	1998–2004
Poverty exit rate			48	45		
Labour market events						
Rise in number of workers	19	17	85	79	33	29
Rise in number of workers[a]	14	14	82	83	25	25
Rise in number of full-time workers	12	15	89	76	21	25
Rise in number of full-time workers[a]	8	13	88	76	15	21
Rise in labour earning[b]	13	17	80	61	21	23
Non-labour income events						
Rise in benefit and tax credit income[a, b]	23	24	66	59	31	31
Rise in other non-labour income[a]	20	20	74	72	30	32
Demographic events						
Change in household head	7	7	72	63	11	10
Change in household type	22	21	65	52	30	24
Increase in household size	8	8	67	46	12	8
Decrease in household size	2	2	53	19	3	1

Notes: Author's calculations from BHPS waves 1–14. Events are not mutually exclusive. [a] And also household size constant in both years. [b] And also number of workers in household constant in both years. Number of exits is 304 (1991–7), 361 (1998–2004).

Interestingly, Table 9.7 also shows that for childless-couple households, event-conditioned poverty exit rates also fell for demographic events. Caution should be exercised because the incidence of these events is generally small, and so underlying sample sizes are also small. However, for those who change household type—about one-fifth of poor childless couples—the poverty exit rate decreases from around two-thirds in the first period to around one-half in the second period. It is unclear what explains this.

Poverty Exits: Lone-Parent Households

Poor individuals in lone-parent households have the lowest poverty exit rate among all household types, but the exit rate did increase substantially between the two periods, from 22 per cent to 34 per cent. Table 9.8 shows that there are distinctive patterns for this group compared to those for all persons. The estimates shown within square brackets are derived from the subgroup of individuals who belonged to a lone-parent household both before and after a poverty exit, and are discussed later.

Compared to the estimates for all persons, favourable demographic events are more important according to both the aggregate and individual perspectives. For example, changes in household type account for around 30 per cent of all poverty exits for individuals in poor lone-parent households (in both periods), compared with around half that figure for all poor individuals. What also stands out is the large increase between periods in the poverty exit rates for those who experience demographic events. For instance, those who change household type have a poverty exit rate of 62 per cent in the first period, but 80 per cent in the second period.

Evidence pooled from several rows of the table suggests that the event underlying many of the observed changes between periods is repartnering. The 'change to married-couple household' rows show that the incidence of repartnering did not change between periods, but its impact on the chances of poverty exit did. Repartnering is associated with an increase in the poverty exit rate from 57 per cent to 69 per cent. The exit rate is much higher if the number of workers also increases—over 80 per cent—but this rate hardly changes between periods.

Repartnering also explains the increases in event-conditional poverty exit rates associated with changes in household head and household type, and with increases in household size. It may also explain the combination of a large increase in poverty exit rate for those with an increase in labour earnings (from 43 per cent to 64 per cent) and also—perhaps surprisingly—no change between periods in the poverty exit rate for those with an increase in benefit and tax income. The increase in labour earnings may arise because the lone parent takes a job or because she repartners with someone who has a job. And,

271

Table 9.8. Poverty exits and trigger events: individuals from poor lone-parent households, by period (cell %)

Household event type	Event prevalence rate (%)		Exit rate conditional on event (%)		Share of all exits associated with event (%)	
	1991–7	1998–2004	1991–7	1998–2004	1991–7	1998–2004
Poverty exit rate (%)			22	34		
Poverty exit rate (%)[c]			[18]	[28]		
Labour market events						
Rise in number of workers	21	24	57	59	54	41
Rise in number of workers[a]	14	16	49	48	32	21
	[14]	[15]	[52]	[46]	[38]	[23]
Rise in number of full-time workers	10	14	76	79	35	33
Rise in number of full-time workers[a]	4	7	72	71	14	14
	[3]	[5]	[75]	[81]	[13]	[14]
Rise in labour earnings[b]	6	10	43	64	11	19
	[5]	[10]	[42]	[66]	[13]	[23]
Non-labour income events						
Rise in benefit and tax credit income[a, b]	22	22	31	31	31	31
	[24]	[28]	[32]	[52]	[41]	[50]
Rise in other non-labour income[a]	9	10	42	57	17	17
	[9]	[10]	[45]	[56]	[22]	[20]
Demographic events						
Change in household head	3	3	62	80	7	7
Change in household type	16	19	41	55	31	30
Increase in household size	13	15	40	56	23	25
	[4]	[5]	[6]	[32]	[1]	[5]
Decrease in household size	2	2	39	60	3	3
Decrease in number of children	1	2	27	67	1	3
Change to married-couple household	9	9	57	69	23	18
Change to married-couple household and more workers	5	7	86	83	23	18

Notes: Author's calculations from BHPS waves 1–14. Events are not mutually exclusive. [a] And also household size constant in both years. [b] And also number of workers in household constant in both years. Number of exits is 426 (1991–7), 555 (1998–2004). [c] estimates in brackets are for individuals who belong to lone-parent households at both *t* and *t*–1, in which case, the number of exits is 295 (1991–7), 385 (1998–2004).

arguably, the poverty exit rate associated with an increase in benefit and tax credit income does not increase between periods because the larger household income of the newly formed couple household is more likely to take them out of the range of eligibility for WFTC.

Put another way, WFTC may be particularly important for poor lone parents who remain lone parents and increase their own labour earnings, but play less of a role for poor lone parents who repartner. This can be seen directly by focusing on the subgroup of individuals who remain in a lone-parent house-hold. Table 9.8 shows that the effect of this selection, and almost the only change of substance, is to reveal an increase between periods in the event-conditioned poverty exit rate associated with increases in benefit and tax credit income. In the first period, one-third of those experiencing this event leave poverty; in the second period, the fraction rises to just over one-half.

These results about repartnering, and about WFTC effects for those who remain in lone-parent households, should not be interpreted as saying that increases in labour force participation by poor lone parents have no impact on their chances of exiting poverty. Table 9.8 shows that the proportion of poor lone-parent households with an increase in the number of workers and in the number of full-time workers is slightly higher in the second period compared with the first (holding household size constant). For example, the fraction with an increase in the number of full-time workers goes from 4 per cent to 7 per cent. Gaining more full-time workers has a strong association with the chances of poverty exit too: almost three-quarters of this subgroup escape poverty. If attention is restricted to those who remain in a lone-parent house-hold, the event-conditioned rate is even larger (though the incidence is slightly less).

The increase between periods in the event-conditioned exit rates for non-negligible increases in non-benefit non-labour income, from 42 per cent to 57 per cent, could arise from two sources. First, it may reflect an increase over time in the amounts of maintenance income received from a former partner. These increases have a greater net effect on income and hence the chances of being poor in the second period relative to the first because all income from maintenance is fully disregarded under WFTC. The proportion of separating mothers receiving maintenance also increased between the two periods: see Jenkins (2009a: table 13.3). Second, among those who repartner, it may reflect the impact of other income brought by the new partner.

Poverty Exits: Single Pensioners

Estimates for single pensioners are presented in Table 9.9. The table suggests that increases in non-labour income are the most common route out of poverty for this group. Increases in income from benefits and tax credit account for two-thirds of all poverty exits (in both periods), and increases in other non-labour income account for about one-third of exits. The greater share statistic for benefit and tax credit income increases comes about because this event is more prevalent and the chances of escaping poverty among those who experience the event are slightly larger.

Unsurprisingly, labour market and demographic events account for almost no poverty exits. Pensioners have a low attachment to the labour market on

Table 9.9. Poverty exits and trigger events: individuals from poor single-pensioner households, by period (cell %)

Household event type	Event prevalence rate		Exit rate conditional on event		Share of all exits associated with event	
	1991–7	1998–2004	1991–7	1998–2004	1991–7	1998–2004
Poverty exit rate			24	31		
Labour market events						
Rise in number of workers	1	1	60	80	1	2
Rise in labour earnings[b]	1	1	77	67	2	2
Non-labour income events						
Rise in benefit and tax credit income[a, b]	23	31	68	66	66	65
Rise in other non-labour income[b]	12	16	63	61	32	31
Demographic events						
Change in household type	1	1	50	64	1	2
Increase in household size	1	1	50	64	1	2

Notes: Author's calculations from BHPS waves 1–14. Events are not mutually exclusive. [a] And also household size constant in both years. [b] And also number of workers in household constant in both years. Number of exits is 415 (1991–7), 442 (1998–2004).

average, and changes in household type are relatively rare by comparison with non-elderly households, and this is reflected in the low incidence of labour market and demographic events for this group. It is these low incidence rates that explain the small share statistics for these events since, among the select few that did experience positive labour market events, the chances of leaving poverty were relatively high. For example, at least two-thirds of poor single pensioners with a non-negligible increase in labour earnings escaped poverty.

From these results, it is not clear what best explains the increase in the poverty exit rate for single pensioners between 1991–7 and 1998–2004. One obvious contributory factor is the rise in the incidence of increases in benefit and tax credit income, from 23 per cent to 31 per cent. This is consistent with greater take-up of means-tested assistance for pensioners, notably the Minimum Income Guarantee (MIG) from 1999. (Pensioner Credit is less relevant because it was introduced in October 2003, that is, at the end of the second period.) I refer to an increase in take-up rates rather than in the level of assistance provided to recipients because the event-conditioned poverty exit rate is the much the same for both periods (around two-thirds), suggesting that the increase in MIG generosity in 2001 did not have a large impact on poverty-exit propulsion. There are increases between periods in various other event-conditioned poverty exit rates, but they are unlikely to have much effect on the overall exit rate because their incidence is so low.

Poverty Entries: All Individuals

I now turn to consider the association between trigger events and poverty entries. The evidence for all non-poor individuals is reported in Table 9.10. Observe first that the aggregate entry rate changed little between the two periods, falling one percentage point from 9 per cent to 8 per cent. One would therefore not expect to see substantial between-period changes in the various statistics, and this is the case whether one looks at event-incidence rates, event-conditioned poverty exit rates, or share statistics. One exception is the substantial fall in the poverty entry rate for the small fraction of individuals who move to a lone-parent household, from 54 per cent to 36 per cent. A second exception is the decrease in the poverty exit rate for individuals experiencing a non-negligible fall in benefit and tax credit income, from 28 per cent to 21 per cent. I return to examine these in more detail in the analysis restricted to couple-with-children households. Third, there is a small fall

Table 9.10. Poverty entries and trigger events: all individuals in non-poor households, by period (cell %)

Household event type	Event prevalence rate (%)		Entry rate conditional on event (%)		Share of all entries associated with event (%)	
	1991–7	1998–2004	1991–7	1998–2004	1991–7	1998–2004
Poverty entry rate			9	8		
Labour market events						
Fall in number of workers	14	13	21	20	35	34
Fall in number of workers[a]	8	7	22	21	21	20
Fall in number of full-time workers	13	12	20	18	30	30
Fall in number of full-time workers[a]	8	7	19	18	17	18
Fall in labour earnings[b]	8	8	21	21	19	23
Non-labour income events						
Fall in benefit and tax credit income[a, b]	7	7	28	21	22	20
Fall in other non-labour income[a]	13	12	13	12	21	19
Demographic events						
Change in household head	9	11	13	12	14	17
Change in household type	14	13	12	11	20	19
Change to lone-parent household	1	1	54	36	5	3
Increase in household size	6	6	9	9	7	7
Decrease in household size	7	7	17	15	15	13

Notes: Author's calculations from BHPS waves 1–14. Events are not mutually exclusive. [a] And also household size constant in both years. [b] And also number of workers in household constant in both years. Number of entries is 3,914 (1991–7), 3,939 (1998–2004).

275

between periods in the incidence of decreases in the number of workers, as expected.

The largest share of poverty entries is accounted for by decreases in the number of workers in the household, at just over one-third in both periods. Falls in the number of full-time workers account for around three in ten poverty entries. Between one-third and one-half of these job events are accompanied by changes in household size. For example, if calculations are restricted to individuals for whom household size remains constant, the percentages of all poverty entries associated with fewer workers or fewer full-time workers are quite a bit smaller, around 20 per cent and 18 per cent in both periods (a 14 percentage point difference). Non-negligible decreases in household labour earnings account for roughly the same fraction of poverty entries: fewer workers means less income. And so too do decreases in income from benefits and tax credits, and in other non-labour income, and changes in household type. The share associated with a change in household head is slightly smaller, at around 15 per cent. The similarity of these various estimates suggests that there is diversity in the routes into poverty.

Although the various events have similar-sized share statistics, they arise from different combinations of event-incidence and event-conditioned poverty entry rates. For example, 8 per cent of non-poor individuals experience a fall in the number of workers in the household (holding household size constant), and the poverty entry rate for this subgroup is just above 20 per cent, implying an entry share of around 20 per cent. For a change in household type, the same-sized share arises from an incidence rate that is almost twice as large, and an event-conditioned poverty entry rate that is almost half as large. The statistics for falls in labour earnings are similar to those for the former case; those for non-benefit non-labour income are similar to those for the latter case.

One of the conclusions from the Method 1 analysis is that the demographic events have a larger share of poverty entries than they have of poverty exits. This is also so according to Method 2 analysis, but it is less directly apparent from the tables. For example, a comparison of the share statistics from the analysis of poverty exits and entries (Tables 9.5 and 9.10) suggests that corresponding estimates are of broadly similar magnitude for most types of events, including labour market, income, and demographic events. Changes in household type and in household headship account for slightly more poverty entries (20 per cent and 19 per cent in the second period) than they do poverty exits (11 per cent and 17 per cent in the second period), and these differences are not as large as those revealed by comparisons based on Tables 9.1 and 9.3. However this comparison can be misleading. Changes in the number of workers can also occur in conjunction with changes in household size, as emphasized in the earlier discussion. If these are discounted, the shares of poverty entries and exits associated with 'pure' changes in the number of workers are significantly smaller, and more similar to the shares associated with 'pure' demographic events. In addition, the evidence presented earlier in this section suggests that demographic events and labour market events are more likely to coincide in the case of poverty entries than in the case of poverty exits.

Having seen that the association of different events in accounting for poverty exits from poverty varies widely across different types of households, I now consider the extent to which this is also the case for poverty entries.

Poverty Entries: Couples with Children

There is little change between periods in the poverty entry rate for this group—the rate falls from 8 per cent to 7 per cent. Table 9.11 shows that this is due to quite small decreases in both event-conditioned entry rates and in incidence rates. I discuss some exceptions shortly.

Both labour market events and demographic events are important for poverty entries among individuals in couple households with children: see Table 9.11. Decreases in the number of workers in the household account for around 40 per cent of poverty entries (42 per cent in the first period and 37 per cent in the second period) or, if household size is held constant as well, for around 22 per cent of entries (24 per cent and 22 per cent). The corresponding statistics for decreases in the number of full-time workers in the household are not much smaller, which suggests that almost all of the job losses associated with poverty entries were full-time rather than part-time positions. Decreases in labour earnings account for 30 per cent of entries (in both periods). Demographic events such as a change in household head or in household size are also important, accounting for just over one in five poverty entries in both periods.

Demographic events are more frequent than labour market events for this group. During the second period, for example, 12 per cent of non-poor individuals in this group experience a change in household head, and 13 per cent a change in household type. About the same fraction experiences a fall in the number of workers or in the number of full-time workers. Some of these events coincide with demographic change and, when the calculations are restricted to those with constant household size, the incidence falls to around 7 per cent. The proportion with a fall in labour earnings (household size and number of workers constant) is 9 per cent, and the same fraction experiences a non-negligible decrease in benefit and tax credit income or in other non-labour income.

The chances of entering poverty are greater for those who experience labour market events than for those who experience demographic events, however.

Table 9.11. Poverty entries and trigger events: individuals from non-poor couple-with-children households, by period (cell %)

Household event type	Event prevalence rate		Entry rate conditional on event		Share of all entries associated with event	
	1991–7	1998–2004	1991–7	1998–2004	1991–7	1998–2004
Poverty entry rate			8	7		
Labour market events						
Fall in number of workers	14	13	25	22	42	37
Fall in number of workers[a]	8	7	24	21	24	21
Fall in number of full-time workers	13	12	25	20	38	33
Fall in number of full-time workers[a]	8	7	21	19	21	19
Fall in labour earnings[b]	9	9	27	25	29	30
Non-labour income events						
Fall in benefit and tax credit income[a, b]	7	9	15	15	12	18
Fall in other non-labour income[a]	11	10	8	7	11	9
Demographic events						
Change in household head	9	12	18	14	19	24
Change in household type	15	13	14	11	24	21
Change to lone-parent household	2	2	54	36	11	8
Change to lone-parent household and fewer workers	1	1	55	36	9	6
Increase in household size	6	7	11	9	9	8
Increase in number of children	5	6	13	9	8	6

Notes: Author's calculations from BHPS waves 1–14. Events are not mutually exclusive. [a] And also household size constant in both years. [b] And also number of workers in household constant in both years. Number of entries is 1,729 (1991–7), 1,721 (1998–2004).

Focusing on the second period, among individuals experiencing a change in household head or household type, the poverty entry rate is between 10 per cent and 15 per cent. In contrast, individuals in households with a fall in the number of workers (household size constant) have a poverty entry rate of around 20 per cent, and those with a decrease in labour earnings a poverty entry rate of 25 per cent.

There is a small decrease between the two periods in event-conditioned poverty entry rates associated with labour market events, which is consistent with the hypotheses set out in Section 9.2, concerning the greater cushioning provided by the more generous benefits for families with children. (The incidence of such events hardly changes, however.) I also argued earlier that this explanation also required that there be no corresponding trend for childless couples. And this turns out to be the case: see Table 9.12 which contains corresponding estimates for this group.

For one particular demographic event experienced by non-poor couples with children, the association with entering poverty is particularly strong. Specifically, moves to a lone-parent household are infrequent, but, among those who do make the move, the poverty entry rate is more than one-half in the first period (54 per cent) and more than one-third in the second period (36 per cent). So, with a marital split, the chances of falling into poverty are high, but have fallen over time.

I study this phenomenon and its sources in greater detail elsewhere (Jenkins 2009a), and draw attention to related changes in the labour market and the tax-benefit system between the two periods. I conclude that

> [t]he most plausible explanations for these trends are the secular rise in women's labour force participation rates and, related, the changes in the social security system, especially to in-work benefits, introduced by the Labour government in the late 1990s which stimulated lone mothers' employment rates and made work pay. (Jenkins 2009a: 229)

One feature of this is a decline in the association between entry to lone parenthood and exit from work. If the marital partnership of a working

Table 9.12. Poverty entries and trigger events: individuals from non-poor childless-couple households, by period (cell %)

Household event type	Event prevalence rate		Entry rate conditional on event		Share of all entries associated with event	
	1991–7	1998–2004	1991–7	1998–2004	1991–7	1998–2004
Poverty entry rate			4	4		
Labour market events						
Fall in number of workers	12	10	15	18	45	45
Fall in number of workers[a]	9	8	16	20	34	37
Fall in number of full-time workers	13	13	11	13	37	39
Fall in number of full-time workers[a]	9	9	12	15	27	32
Fall in labour earnings[b]	9	9	11	14	25	30
Non-labour income events						
Fall in benefit and tax credit income[a, b]	3	3	28	21	19	13
Fall in other non-labour income[a]	14	11	7	9	23	23
Demographic events						
Change in household head	10	12	4	4	10	11
Change in household type	14	14	7	6	23	21
Increase in household size	9	8	5	3	11	5
Increase in number of children	7	6	6	3	9	5

Notes: Author's calculations from BHPS waves 1–14. Events are not mutually exclusive. [a] And also household size constant in both years. [b] And also number of workers in household constant in both years. Number of entries is 313 (1991–7), 365 (1998–2004).

mother dissolves, the average mother is now more likely to stay in work than she was 15 to 20 years ago. On this, also see Harkness, Gregg, and Smith (2009) and Paull (2007).

Poverty Entries: Lone-Parent Households

Among individuals in non-poor lone-parent households, the poverty entry rate almost halved between the two periods, falling from 27 per cent to 16 per cent: see Table 9.13. Both demographic and income events account for a significant share of poverty entries, as for other household types. There are two main contrasts with couple households with children. The first concerns the share of all entries accounted for by non-negligible falls in income from benefit and tax credits, which is substantially above the fraction for the other group in the first period (46 per cent compared to 12 per cent) and which also falls substantially between periods (to 26 per cent compared with 18 per cent). Second, there is the contrast in shares associated with falls in other non-labour income. For lone-parent households, the share is 24 per cent in the first period and 20 per cent in the second, which is at least twice the corresponding share for couple-with-children households (around 10 per cent in both periods).

Both of these contrasts relate to cross-group differences in event-incidence rates and in event-conditioned poverty entry rates. Non-poor lone-parent households are more likely than non-poor couple-with-children households to experience decreases in either of these two income sources. The chances of entering poverty for those with such a decrease are also larger (in both periods), and it is only for lone-parent households that these entry rates fall substantially between the two periods. Among those with non-negligible falls in income from benefits and tax credits, the poverty entry rate more than halves (from 66 per cent to 30 per cent), whereas, among those with non-negligible falls in other non-labour income (including maintenance from a former partner), the poverty entry rate nearly halves (from 49 per cent to 26 per cent).

Observe too that the chances of becoming poor if the number of workers or the number of full-time workers falls are much larger for lone parents than for couple-with-children households (in both periods), which is unsurprising. However, also distinctively, these probabilities fall between the two periods for lone-parent households. For instance, if a lone parent stops working, the chances of being poor are nearly 80 per cent in the first period, but fall to 53 per cent in the second period. Those with a non-negligible fall in labour earnings have a poverty entry rate of 46 per cent in the first period, but 30 per cent in the second.

Together, these various results can be summarized as a substantial improvement in the cushioning of adverse income and demographic events between the two periods. There is also a small but noticeable decline in the incidence of

Table 9.13. Poverty entries and trigger events: individuals from non-poor lone-parent households, by period (cell %)

Household event type	Event prevalence rate		Entry rate conditional on event		Share of all entries associated with event	
	1991–7	1998–2004	1991–7	1998–2004	1991–7	1998–2004
Poverty entry rate			27	16		
Labour market events						
Fall in number of workers	9	6	77	59	26	23
Fall in number of workers[a]	8	5	78	53	22	17
Fall in number of full-time workers	7	6	59	47	14	16
Fall in number of full-time workers[a]	6	5	59	44	13	14
Fall in labour earnings[b]	8	11	44	29	13	19
Non-labour income events						
Fall in benefit and tax credit income[a, b]	17	14	66	30	43	26
Fall in other non-labour income[a]	13	14	48	23	24	20
Demographic events						
Change in household head	4	3	23	34	4	6
Change in household type	24	17	15	15	13	16
Increase in household size	14	9	18	22	10	12
Increase in number of children	2	1	58	63	5	4

Notes: Author's calculations from BHPS waves 1–14. Events are not mutually exclusive. [a] And also household size constant in both years. [b] And also number of workers in household constant in both years. Number of entries is 368 (1991–7), 303 (1998–2004).

falls in the number of workers (and full-time workers) and falls in benefit and tax credit income. Together, these underlying trends contribute to the substantial fall in the poverty entry rate for the group as a whole. The most plausible explanations for both these sets of changes are the improvement in labour market conditions and the more generous support made available to families with children (regardless of parental work status). Compared to 1991–7, in the period 1998–2004, working lone parents are more likely to retain their jobs but, if they do lose their jobs, the higher rates of Child Benefit and child allowances incorporated in Income Support reduce the likelihood of becoming poor. Of course, it also needs to be emphasized that, although cushioning has improved, the entry rate remains relatively high.

Some of the individuals included in the calculations move from lone-parent households to other types; for example, some may repartner over the two-year period. When I repeated the calculations using data only for the subgroup who remain in a lone-parent household, I found the conclusions to be the same (with the exception that demographic events are less relevant of course,

281

by construction). This is reassuring, though unsurprising, because this group forms the majority.

Poverty Entries—Single Pensioners

Single pensioners are the household type besides lone parents with a marked fall in poverty entry rate between 1991–7 and 1998–2004, a decrease from 21 per cent to 15 per cent. See Table 9.14. The largest share of poverty entries is associated with non-negligible falls in non-labour income. Decreases in benefit and tax credit income account for half of all exits in the first period and 39 per cent in the second. Decreases in non-benefit non-labour income (including income from private and occupational pensions and from savings and investments) account for around a third of poverty entries in the first period and 44 per cent in the second period. All other events account for hardly any exits. Put another way, for this group in particular, there appears to be a large number of poverty entries that are unaccounted for by the set of trigger events that is used. It may simply be that income variation attributable to measurement error is greater for this group, combined with the fact that many have incomes located close to the poverty line.

However, there does appear to be a decline between the two periods in the poverty entry rate among single pensioners who experience a fall in benefit and credit income, even if one makes allowance for the relatively small number of cases involved. Benefit and credit income is a combination of a number of sources, including the state retirement pension, Income Support, Housing Benefit, and Council Tax benefits, together with other means-tested support. A plausible explanation for the trend is the more generous income floor provided by the means-tested Minimum Income Guarantee (and its successor at the end of the second period, Pensioner Credit). That is, even if one of the various income types making up total benefit and credit income decreases, the overall total income was larger in the second period for less well-off pensioners. Evidence supporting the latter is provided by HBAI statistics (Department for Work and Pensions 2008: table 2.3ts), which show that the bottom quintile income for single female pensioners (the majority) expressed as a fraction of overall mean income increased between the mid-1990s and the mid-2000s from less than 30 per cent to about 35 per cent of overall mean income (the corresponding statistic for single male pensioners was 40 per cent in both periods). Hence, an income fall is less likely to lead to a fall into poverty in the second period compared to the first.

Table 9.14. Poverty entries and trigger events: individuals from non-poor single-pensioner households, by period (cell %)

Household event type	Event prevalence rate		Entry rate conditional on event		Share of all entries associated with event	
	1991–7	1998–2004	1991–7	1998–2004	1991–7	1998–2004
Poverty entry rate			21	15		
Labour market events						
Fall in number of workers	2	1	33	39	3	4
Fall in labour earnings[a]	2	2	29	24	2	3
Non-labour income events						
Fall in benefit and tax credit income[a, b]	15	11	73	53	50	39
Fall in other non-labour income[b]	19	18	39	37	35	44
Demographic events						
Change in household type	1	1	4	17	0	0
Increase in household size	1	1	4	17	0	0

Notes: Author's calculations from BHPS waves 1–14. Events are not mutually exclusive. [a] And also household size constant in both years. [b] And also number of workers in household constant in both years. Number of exits is 467 (1991–7), 382 (1998–2004).

9.4. Routes Into and Out of Poverty: Britain from a Cross-National Perspective

There are few cross-national comparative studies of routes into and out of poverty that use data that are truly comparable in terms of definitions and time period studied. Most have used a version of Method 1.

The problems of comparability are illustrated by Bane and Ellwood's (1986) US study that inspires the Method 1 analysis of this chapter. These findings for Britain echo those of Bane and Ellwood (1986) for the USA, in the sense of emphasizing the role played by demographic change. Bane and Ellwood report that

> less than 40 percent of poverty spells begin because of a drop of head's earnings, while 60 percent of the spells end when the heads' earnings increase. Thus, researchers must focus on household formation decisions and on the behavior of secondary family members. (Bane and Ellwood 1986: 1)

My findings in Section 9.3 attribute a greater role to secondary earners and a lesser role to demographic events than Bane and Ellwood do. However, more substantive comparisons of findings are necessarily constrained by important differences. For example, Bane and Ellwood use a different income definition, equivalence scale, and poverty line, and focus on non-elderly households only. Also, Britain in the 1990s and 2000s is different from the USA in the

1970s and 1980s: dual-earner households are more prevalent now than then, in the USA as well as Britain (Gregg and Wadsworth 1996). I use the household as the income unit—reflecting British conventions—rather than the narrower concept of the family as do Bane and Ellwood, thereby allowing greater scope for household members other than the head and spouse to play a role.

A more recent six-country study by Oxley, Dang, and Antolín (2000) also illustrates comparability issues. The data for three countries comes from tax administration records (Canada, Sweden, and the Netherlands) and for the remaining three from household panel survey data (Britain, western Germany, and the USA). The income variables differ (for example, only pre-tax incomes are used for Britain) and, more importantly, so too do the definitions of the 'household' and who is followed over time, reflecting the different types of data source. Oxley, Dang, and Antolín report event share statistics for the early 1990s, distinguishing between 'employment/earnings-related' events such as job change or earnings change, 'family-structure-related' events, and 'other events' (which mostly relate to changes in social security benefit income). These are defined in such a way that, with a fourth category labelled 'unidentified' events, the sum of the four share statistics is 100 per cent. The general pattern for most countries is that employment/earnings-related events have the largest shares of both poverty exits and poverty entries, but 'family-structure-related' events are relatively more important for poverty entries—findings which echo those of Bane and Ellwood (1986) and my Method 1 analysis. However, it is difficult to assess the results for Canada, in particular, since the share of poverty entries and poverty exits for 'unidentified' events is around twice the shares for the other countries (Oxley, Dang, and Antolín 2000: table 5). For Sweden, the share of 'family-structure-related' events is distinctively small and the share of employment/earnings-related events distinctively high, which might be related to the definition of the household in the Swedish data—all persons aged 18 or more are treated as separate households.

The best cross-national studies of trigger events and poverty transitions analysis are by OECD (2001) and Valletta (2006) because they have the most comparable data. The two papers use similar methods, but I focus on the first one because it considers a larger number of countries. In both papers, income is equivalized household net income (as in this book), and the poverty line is half the contemporary national median (lower than the line used in this book). OECD (2001) uses comparable household panel survey data from 12 European countries from three waves of the European Community Household Panel (ECHP; income years 1993–5), supplemented by comparable panel data for Canada and the USA (SLID and PSID data, as provided through the CNEF). Valletta (2006) considers Britain, Canada, Germany, and the United States. In Bane and Ellwood (1986) and Method 1 hierarchical and sequential fashion,

Valletta first identifies the poverty transitions associated with a change in household structure, second identifies transitions associated with changes in the number of full-time workers, and then three income events—whether the largest income change associated with the transition was a change in labour earnings, in government-provided cash benefits ('transfers'), or in capital and other income.

The estimates of the relative frequency of each type of event expressed as a proportion of all poverty exits and all poverty shares that are reported by OECD (2001: table 2.6) are summarized in Figure 9.5 for the four major events. Share statistics for changes in 'capital and other income' and in 'other' income are small and so omitted for brevity. Figure 9.5 contains a chart for each of the four main events, with each chart plotting poverty exit shares against poverty entry shares for the event in question, by country. Data about the change in the number of workers are not available for the Netherlands. Results for the UK are highlighted using dotted lines. The graphs suggest several regularities.

First, changes in household structure are more important in share terms for poverty entries than for poverty exits. All the country-specific data points in Figure 9.5(a) lie below a 45° ray from the origin. This finding is familiar from Bane and Ellwood (1986) for the USA and the research about Britain presented earlier in this chapter. Valletta (2006) and Oxley et al. (2000) also report the same finding. Second, and less frequently remarked on, for each of the other three events there is a close association between poverty exit shares and poverty entry shares. The country data points in each of Figures 9.5(a), (b), and (c) line up around a 45° ray from the origin, with the correlation being greatest for changes in household income from transfers.

Third, there is no clear-cut grouping of countries into clusters. A welfare-state typology of the sort proposed by Esping-Andersen (1990) is the most commonly used device for exploring patterns in cross-national data on income distribution, but its application does not work well in the current context. Following Fouarge and Layte (2005), one might classify these European countries into four groups: social democrat (Denmark, the Netherlands), corporatist (Belgium, France, Germany, Luxembourg), liberal (Ireland, the UK), and a residual 'mediterranean' category (Greece, Italy, Portugal, and Spain). I place Canada and the USA in a separate 'North American liberal' group, while acknowledging that the Canadian welfare state is more similar to European arrangements than to those in the USA. These five groups do not fall into obvious clusters defined by combinations of poverty exit and entry event shares.

Taking all four charts together, the USA is the most distinctive country. A very small share of poverty exits and entries are accounted for by changes in household income from transfers, reflecting the US's relatively low provision of cash benefits. In contrast, the USA has relatively large shares of poverty

285

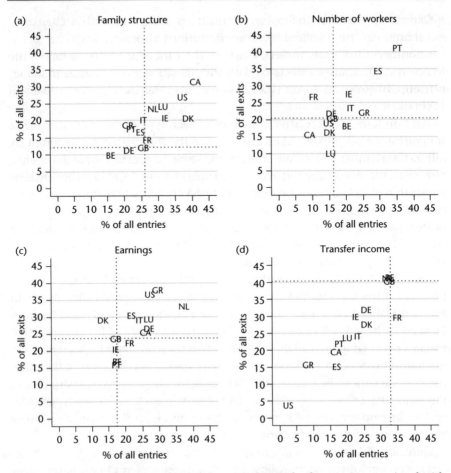

Figure 9.5. Relative frequency (%) of demographic and other events associated with poverty entries and exits in 12 European countries, Canada, and the USA, by type of event

Notes: Graphs derived by author from estimates reported by OECD (2001: table 2.6). Data refer to pooled transitions for 1995–8 for 12 European countries (source: ECHP) and Canada (SLID), and 1987–9 for the USA (PSID): see text. OECD (2001) distinguishes six event types using a hierarchical classification method (see text); share statistics for changes in capital and other income, and 'other' events, are omitted here. Dotted lines highlight estimates for the United Kingdom ('GB'). Reading note: in the United Kingdom, 25.9% of all poverty entries and 12.1% of all poverty exits are associated with a change in family structure.

entries and exits associated with changes in family structure. These features of US poverty dynamics are also remarked on by Oxley, Dang, and Antolín (2000) and Valletta (2006). Canada is similar to the USA in terms of the importance of changes in family structure and changes in the number of workers, but otherwise is more European. Arguably, the four Mediterranean countries form a cluster: compared to the other European countries, changes in transfer income are less important (their welfare states are less extensive) and changes in the numbers of workers are more important.

In contrast, the UK and the other European countries are heterogeneous and do not systematically cluster according to welfare-state type. Similarities and differences depend on which type of event is considered. Britain, the focus of this book, is a country similar to the other country with a 'liberal' welfare state (Ireland) in terms of the share of poverty transitions associated with changes in family earnings, but the share associated with changes in family structure and in the number of workers is smaller in the UK, and the share associated with changes in transfer income is markedly smaller in Ireland. The UK is similar to the USA in terms of the share of poverty transitions associated with changes in the number of workers, but, for the other three events, Britain is located well away from the USA. In fact, the countries that Britain appears closest to are Germany, France, and Belgium—each of which has a 'corporatist' welfare state.

One of the reasons for an indistinct clustering of countries relates to the method of analysis. As explained earlier, aggregate share statistics of the type summarized in Figure 9.5 depend on several components. For example, the share of all poverty exits that is accounted for by a particular trigger event depends on how frequently the event occurs among the poor, the poverty exit rate among the people who experience the event, and the overall poverty exit rate. Each of these components can differ across countries and, on each dimension, there may be clustering that is more or less aligned with expectations derived from welfare-state or other typologies. (In this connection, also recall the discussion of cross-national differences in persistent poverty rates in Chapter 8.) Put another way, analysis based on Method 2, in which the various components are looked at separately, may lead to patterns more consistent with expectations. This is illustrated by Jenkins and Schluter's (2003) study of child poverty in Britain and Germany.

Jenkins and Schluter (2003) address the question of why, in the 1990s, Britain had lower child poverty exit rates and higher child poverty entry rates than western Germany. Their data, covering 1991–8, are drawn from the BHPS and SOEP, using variables available in the Cross-National Equivalent File (see Chapter 3 about the CNEF). The principal findings are that

> it is primarily cross-national differences in the chances of making a poverty transition conditional on experiencing a trigger event, rather than differences in the prevalence of trigger events per se, that explain why child poverty exit rates in Britain are lower and poverty entry rates are higher than in Western Germany. The results point to the importance of the welfare-state-related differences as the principal source of Anglo-German differences in child poverty rates. In particular, relative to British children, German children are better protected against the

consequences of adverse labor market events, and positive labor market events are reinforced to a greater extent. (Jenkins and Schluter 2003: 444)

In this sense, systematic differences in poverty transition rates can be linked to systematic differences in tax-benefit systems across countries and not only to systematic changes over time in the tax-benefit system of a single country (as demonstrated in the preceding section).

9.5. Summary and Conclusions

Studying poverty dynamics in relation to trigger events is a useful method of assessing the factors associated with poverty transitions. Although not fully informative regarding the underlying causes of poverty entries and exits, the framework accords with common-sense views about there being important connections between the occurrence of life-course events and changes in income. The approach is relatively comprehensive in the sense of being able to encompass a wide range of types of event, and poverty transitions for all individuals in society, as well as subgroups within it.

This chapter makes a distinction between assessing the importance of a life-course event for poverty exits and entries at the aggregate level and at the individual level. Aggregate-level importance refers to answers to the question of what share of all poverty transitions is associated with that event compared to the shares of other events. Individual-level importance refers to the answers to the question: if a person experiences a particular event, what are the chances that the person will escape (or enter) poverty?

From the aggregate perspective, this chapter shows that changes in household labour earnings are the events that account for the largest shares of poverty exits and entries for almost all groups (pensioners being the most obvious exception). Almost as importantly, the chapter emphasizes that, for most households of working age, changes in earnings for household members other than the household head play a substantial role, especially for exits from poverty. In one sense, this finding is a restatement of the well-known fact that dual-earner households are relatively affluent on average, with relatively small chances of being poor. However, the focus on dynamics in this chapter also reminds us of the adverse consequences in terms of greater chances of becoming poor for households that lose dual-earner status. An important lesson for analysis is that the conclusions about the poverty dynamics of the population as a whole that can be drawn from analysis of the dynamics of the labour earnings of continuously married male household heads (commonly undertaken) is substantially limited, even if the interest is only in households of working age.

The chapter has also drawn attention to the diversity of routes into and out of poverty. Even though changes in labour market attachment in earnings play a major role, demographic events are important, accounting for at least a fifth of all poverty exits and a larger fraction of all poverty entries. No one type of event appears to dominate: there are those associated with changes in household headship, such as when marital partnerships form or split, or other demographic change, such as the birth of children or their change from dependent to non-dependent status. The greater importance of demographic events for poverty entries than for poverty exits is a finding that is relatively universal, and found in all related cross-national studies to date. The analysis has also highlighted that a significant fraction of changes in household labour market attachment arises via demographic change—the number of workers increases or decreases through people joining or leaving the household rather than through existing non-workers taking a job or vice versa.

These findings are the same as those reported by Jenkins and Rigg (2001) for Britain between 1991 and 1999. An innovation of the current research is the use of BHPS data from 14 waves and examination of changes in patterns between a first period (1991–7) and a second period (1998–2004), which coincided with a more buoyant labour market and the introduction of more generous support for low-income working families with children.

In this chapter, I have shown that there are differences between the two periods that are consistent with the changes in tax-benefit policies having effects that increase the chances of poverty exit and reduce the chances of poverty entry for this group. Specifically, there appears to be greater propulsion out of poverty among people who experience favourable labour market, income, and demographic events, and greater cushioning for those who experience unfavourable events. This 'test' of the impact of policy change is not a powerful one. As discussed in the introduction to this chapter, trigger-event analysis does not provide definitive evidence about causation. But the findings do join the accumulated evidence of other kinds that points to Labour's policies having a positive effect on poverty reduction. (See Waldfogel's (2010) review of the evidence from mostly cross-sectional perspectives.)

A distinguishing feature of trigger analysis is its reliance on straightforward cross-tabulations rather than using multivariate analysis. I have argued that this is one of its strengths. With Method 2, for instance, one has an encompassing framework for examining the impact of both changes in the incidence of events favourable or unfavourable to poverty transitions and also changes in the chances of making a poverty transition among those who experience a particular event. This is harder to do within a multiple regression framework.

However, there are some advantages to a multivariate approach. One can economize on sample size by characterizing differences in poverty transition rates between individuals from different household types using explanatory variables. One can look at the impact of one factor while controlling for the impact of others, and one can explore the impacts of factors that are unobserved. Modelling poverty entries and exits jointly can provide better descriptions of how long individuals who begin a poverty spell are likely to be poor over the next several years. The next two chapters illustrate these points, using two alternative but complementary multivariate approaches to modelling poverty transitions.

10

The Length of Time Spent Poor: Estimates from Hazard Regression Models

This chapter analyses the length of poverty spells for individuals who become poor and the lengths of time between finishing one poverty spell and starting another for those individuals who leave poverty. The estimates are used to predict how long in total a poverty entrant will spend poor, taking into account not only the initial poverty spell but also possible later spells.

There is a close connection between this chapter and the previous two: all three are about poverty transition rates. Chapter 9 relates poverty entry and exit rates to trigger events, considering all poverty exits and entries regardless of how long individuals have been at risk of making the poverty transition. By contrast, in this chapter, the length of time at risk is a fundamental part of the analysis. Duration dependence was discussed in Chapter 8, but differences in transition rates for different types of individuals were not considered in detail in the life-table analysis. In this chapter, duration dependence and individual heterogeneity in poverty exit and re-entry hazard rates are both considered, using multivariate regression modelling approaches. With model estimates, and for different types of individual, one can predict poverty spell lengths, poverty recurrence times, and the total time spent poor over a period for poverty entrants.

The analysis is based on waves 1 to 9 of the BHPS, covering survey years 1991–9. Changes over time in the determinants of poverty transition rates are not considered. However, changes over time are addressed using BHPS data by Damioli (2011b), who also compares Britain's experience with that of other European countries, using ECHP data in other work (Damioli 2011a). I summarize his research at the end of this chapter. Note too that the estimates presented in this chapter refer to poverty spells for individuals who entered poverty after wave 1, and to poverty recurrence times for individuals who finished a poverty spell after wave 1. It is not possible to model individuals' first entry into poverty or first exit from poverty because pre-1991 income histories are not available in the BHPS—an illustration of the left-censoring problem mentioned in Chapter 2.

Section 10.1 provides a brief overview of the models used and explains how they may be used to predict spell lengths. The definitions of the variables and the subsamples used in the analysis are explained in Section 10.2. Results are presented in Sections 10.3–10.5. First, poverty exits and poverty recurrence are modelled separately, following common practice in the literature. Section 10.3 reports analysis of models of poverty exit rates and predictions of poverty spell lengths for individuals with different characteristics. Section 10.4 provides evidence about poverty re-entry rates and predictions of poverty recurrence times.

In order to get predictions about how long in total people are likely to be poor over a period of time, information about poverty exit and recurrence chances has to be combined (see Chapter 5). This takes account of the possibility that people who are more at risk of having longer poverty spells are also more likely to re-enter poverty relatively quickly. Section 10.6 is devoted to this topic. First, predictions of the total time poor are derived using the estimates presented in Sections 10.3 and 10.4. Second, a more sophisticated model is employed in which poverty entry and exit hazards are modelled jointly and also some allowance is made for the effects of unobserved differences between individuals in their transition rates. I use a multi-state multi-transition hazard regression model of the kind first applied to poverty dynamics by Stevens (1995, 1999). Section 10.6 provides a summary and conclusions.

10.1. Hazard Regression Methods for Analysing Spell Lengths

Life-table methods such as employed in Chapter 8 provide estimates, for the population as a whole (or specific subgroups), of how poverty transition rates vary with the length of time that a person has been at risk of making a transition. From these can also be derived estimates of the distribution of spell lengths for that population. Multivariate hazard regression models are a generalization of life-table methods, since they allow transition rates to vary not only with time at risk but also with personal characteristics. Hence predictions of spell lengths can also be derived for different types of person. Both methods take account of right-censoring in the spell data—the fact that spells for some individuals have not finished when the people are last observed in the data set (see Chapter 2). A distinctive feature of the spell data in the current context is that spell lengths are observed only in units of a year—the data are grouped ('interval censored')—rather than having exact dates for poverty-spell beginnings and endings. So, methods for discrete-time survival data are used rather than those for continuous time. For an introduction to these, see inter alia Allison (1984) or Jenkins (2005). A more advanced treatment is provided by Lancaster (1990).

The fundamental building block of event-history analysis is the hazard rate. The poverty exit hazard rate for a given year of an individual's poverty spell is the probability of exiting poverty in that year, conditional on having remained poor until then and on the person's characteristics. Similarly, an individual's poverty re-entry hazard rate is the probability of re-entering poverty, conditional on having remained non-poor until then and on the person's characteristics.

To understand the structure of the models, and how they can be used to generate predictions of spell-length distributions, consider the example of poverty exits. (Analogous arguments apply to poverty re-entries.) In this case, one has, for a sample of spells, information of three types: the length of each poverty spell in years; whether each poverty spell has finished or whether it was still in progress (that is, censored) when last observed; and information about the characteristics of the individual experiencing the spell.

The data about spell lengths and censoring status summarize, for each spell, an 'event history'—a sequence of years during which the individual was at risk of leaving poverty (poverty exit is the event in question). Thus for someone with a completed spell length of three years (that is, he or she is not poor in the fourth year), there is a data sequence of three years, with no exit event recorded for each of the first two years and one recorded for the final year. If, instead, the individual's spell is censored, the individual has been at risk of poverty exit for three years, but there is no exit event recorded for any of the years. Thus a data set about spells can be re-organized into a data set in which the unit of observation is the spell year, with one observation for each year that each individual was at risk of experiencing the relevant event. (A data set comprising two spells, five and ten years long, becomes a data set comprising 15 person-year observations.) Instead of having a person-specific censoring indicator as in the original data set, the re-organized data set has the equivalent information encapsulated in a person-year indicator of whether of a transition occurred between that year and the next for the relevant person.

With spell data organized in person-year event-history form, the multivariate models that are used in Sections 10.3 and 10.4 can be written in the following form:

$$\text{cloglog}(h_{id}) = f(d) + \beta' X_{id}. \tag{10.1}$$

The equation says that, for each person $i = 1, \ldots, N$, and for each year during the spell $d = 1, \ldots, D$, a non-linear ('cloglog') transformation of the annual hazard rate, h_{id}, is the sum of a spell-year-specific constant and a linear index function of the person's characteristics as summarized in the vector X_{id}. The specification is implied by the grouping of the spell-length data into year-long intervals, combined with the assumption that the hazard rate of poverty exit at any point in time within a year takes the so-called proportional hazards form (explained shortly). The model is known as the discrete-time proportional hazard model, in which the dependent variable is the complementary log-log (cloglog) transformation of the hazard rate.

The function $f(d)$ summarizes how the hazard rate in a given year varies with how long the person has been poor. This function, known as the baseline hazard function, has the same shape for all persons, regardless of their characteristics. In this chapter, I report results based on a non-parametric specification that does not impose any restrictions on the shape of $f(d)$: the baseline hazard rate takes on different values for each spell year. In practice, the function is fitted by using a set of spell-year-specific dummy variables δ_d, $d = 1, \ldots, D$, set equal to 1 for the dth year of the spell and 0 otherwise. (Since nine waves of BHPS data are used, the maximum spell length observed is seven years.) The interpretation is that, if the estimates of δ_d are smaller for larger d, then hazard rates fall as the spell lengthens.

The vector X_{id} incorporates the characteristics of each person i during the relevant spell year d. If the regression coefficient associated with a given explanatory variable has a positive sign, then increases in the value of the variable are associated with a larger hazard rate, other things being equal, and thence shorter spells. If instead the coefficient had a negative sign, then increases in the explanatory variable would be associated with a smaller hazard rate (and longer spells). In fact, we can say rather more about the relationship between hazard rates and characteristics, as follows.

In this model, absolute differences in a characteristic shift the baseline hazard function up (or down) by an equiproportionate amount, where the amount of scaling depends on the magnitude of the associated regression coefficient—this is the 'proportional hazards' assumption. If a characteristic, say the kth one, increases by one unit, with everything else held constant, then the difference in hazard rates is given by the hazard ratio, calculated as $\exp(\beta_k)$, where $\exp(.)$ is the exponential function. More concretely, suppose that the kth explanatory variable is a binary (dummy) variable, summarizing whether or not the head of household is in employment in the relevant spell year, and the estimate of β_k is 1.25. For two individuals whose characteristics were identical except that the head of household was in employment in the first case but not in the second, the first individual has a hazard rate that is 3.49 times larger than the second individual and for each year within a spell ($3.49 = e^{1.25}$). If the explanatory variable were instead a continuous variable such as the person's age at the start of the spell, then the hazard ratio refers to a one-year difference in ages. For example, if β_k equals -0.02, a one-year increase in age, other things being equal, is associated with a hazard rate that is 2 per cent smaller ($e^{-0.02} = 0.98$).

The hazard regression model can be used to derive predictions of spell lengths for persons with different characteristics. The probability of having a poverty spell lasting at least three years, say, is given by the probability of not leaving poverty in the first year times the probability of not leaving poverty in the second year times the probability of not leaving poverty in the third year. More generally, the probability of having a spell lasting at least d years is given by the probability of not experiencing the relevant event in every year up to and including the dth year. Algebraically, the probability for an individual i is given by the survivor function:

$$S_{id} = (1 - h_{i1})(1 - h_{i2})(1 - h_{i3})(...)(1 - h_{id}). \qquad (10.2)$$

The probability of experiencing the event by the dth year—leaving poverty in this case—is given by $1-S_{id}$. If there is a large cohort of individuals with the same characteristics who begin a spell, the survivor function summarizes the proportion of persons from that entry cohort that remain poor after different intervals of time. A useful measure of the average spell length is the median duration. This is the number of years after which one-half of the entry cohort has experienced the event (and also, by construction, one-half has not), that is, the number of years such that $S_{id} = 0.5$.

The survivor function refers to the distribution of spell lengths for all persons who start a spell. This distribution is not the same as the distribution of spell lengths for those individuals who are in the midst of a poverty spell in a given year. Among those who are poor at a particular point in time, there is an over-representation of persons prone to have longer poverty spells relative to the population as a whole. See Chapter 8 for further discussion.

Because poverty status is defined at the household level, there are replicated observations in the event-history data in the cases where there are multi-person households. This clustering of individuals introduces correlations across observations in the data, whereas the statistical theory underlying calculations of the statistical significance of the parameter estimates of the multivariate model assumes independence across observations. If these correlations are ignored, then estimates appear more precise than they really are (standard errors are too small). This issue is controlled for by using so-called 'cluster-robust' estimators of the standard errors of model parameters, where each group of individuals from the same household forms a cluster.

Consistent with common practice, attrition from the sample is treated as conditionally independent of the process determining individual histories of poverty and non-poverty. This means that spells that end because of attrition from the BHPS can be treated as right-censored and hence straightforwardly incorporated in the analysis without further adjustments. (See Chapter 11 for a model allowing correlated attrition.)

Variations on the single-spell model described by (10.1) were also estimated. In particular, some specifications also allow unobserved differences between individuals to affect hazard rates, in addition to observed differences summarized by the vector X_{id}. (These are discrete-time proportional hazard models with gamma distributed unobserved heterogeneity and with normally distributed unobserved heterogeneity.) In all the models for poverty exits and for poverty re-entries, there was never any statistically significant evidence of unobserved heterogeneity, and so these models are not discussed further here. One explanation for this finding is that the effects of unobserved differences are hard to identify when using single-spell data. However, unobserved heterogeneity is considered in the context of the multiple-state multiple-transition models in which poverty and non-poverty spells are modelled jointly, as follows.

The more sophisticated model is a version of the one applied to US poverty and non-poverty spells by Stevens (1995, 1999). Subsequent applications include those by Biewen (2006), using German data and Hansen and Wahlberg (2009), using Swedish data. Devicienti (2001) fits a version of the model to data from BHPS waves 1–7. In the single-spell hazard model described by (10.1), a non-linear function of the poverty exit rate is related to a baseline hazard function common to all individuals and a set of individual-specific explanatory variables, and there is an analogous relationship for the poverty re-entry rate. The multiple-state multiple-transition models of poverty and non-poverty spells assume in addition that there are unobserved differences in individuals' propensities to exit and to re-enter poverty and, crucially, that these may be correlated. For example, it is plausible to suggest that more able individuals are not only more likely to exit poverty than less able individuals (other things being equal), but also less likely to re-enter poverty. If these unobservable factors affecting poverty exits and entries are correlated, then the simple combination of estimates from single-spell models (as above) provides biased estimates of the number of times individuals are poor over an interval of several years.

The joint model with correlated unobserved heterogeneity is specified as follows, noting that an explicit distinction is now made between the poverty exit hazard, denoted e_{id}, and the poverty entry hazard, denoted r_{id}. In particular, suppose that, controlling for observed differences, individuals differ according to whether they have a relatively high propensity to exit poverty or a relatively low propensity to exit poverty. (These propensities are unobserved.) That is, there are two classes of person, with the hazard rate of poverty exit represented for each class by:

$$\text{cloglog}(e_{id}) = f(d) + \gamma X_{id} + \lambda_{\text{low}} \tag{10.3}$$

$$\text{cloglog}(e_{id}) = f(d) + \gamma X_{id} + \lambda_{high}. \tag{10.4}$$

The unobserved exit propensities are summarized by the parameters λ_{low} and λ_{high}, which were absent from equation (10.1). People belonging to the class characterized by λ_{high} have poverty exit rates that are greater than the poverty rates for people belonging to the class characterized by λ_{low}, all else equal. The former group has shorter poverty spells.

Analogously, suppose that individuals fall into one of two groups according to whether they have a relatively high propensity to re-enter poverty or a relatively low propensity to re-enter poverty. There are two classes of person, with the hazard rate of poverty re-entry represented for each class by:

$$\text{cloglog}(r_{id}) = g(d) + \delta X_{id} + \theta_{low} \tag{10.5}$$

$$\text{cloglog}(r_{id}) = g(d) + \delta X_{id} + \theta_{high}. \tag{10.6}$$

The unobserved exit propensities are summarized by the parameters θ_{low} and θ_{high}. Duration dependence is characterized by the baseline hazard function g (d), and δ is a vector of parameters to be estimated. The model has a proportional hazards interpretation, as defined earlier.

There are four groups into which individuals can be classified corresponding to the four possible combinations of poverty transition propensities: $(\lambda_{\text{low}}, \theta_{\text{low}})$, $(\lambda_{\text{low}}, \theta_{\text{high}})$, $(\lambda_{\text{high}}, \theta_{\text{low}})$, $(\lambda_{\text{high}}, \theta_{\text{high}})$. The proportions of the population that fall into each group are estimable parameters along with the propensities. Preliminary analysis indicated that there are no individuals with the combination of high propensities for poverty exit and poverty re-entry and also no individuals with low propensities for both poverty exit and poverty re-entry. The later discussion therefore focuses on the model in which the proportions in these two groups are constrained to equal zero. With this restriction there are four unobserved heterogeneity parameters in the exit and re-entry hazard model: the proportion in the group with a high exit propensity and a low entry propensity; the proportion in the group with a high exit propensity and a low entry propensity; and the transition propensity parameters λ_{low} and θ_{low}. The λ_{high} and θ_{high} are normalized to equal zero: only differences in hazards between the classes can be identified.

Deriving predictions about spell lengths using this model is more complicated than for the separate single-spell models because of the presence of the unobserved heterogeneity terms. These are individual-specific but unobserved. The population average of the predictions is calculated using simulation methods of the type employed by Stevens (1999). That is, one takes a cohort of 10,000 individuals, each of whom is allocated the same observed characteristics. These individuals are randomly allocated a high or low unobserved propensity in such a way that the overall proportions in the groups match those estimated from the data (and reported later). The predicted distributions of 'number of years poor out of the next eight' for individuals with different combinations of observed characteristics are derived by averaging the simulated estimates across each of several cohorts of individuals.

In principle, one can allow for a greater number of transition propensity parameters—distinguishing more than two latent propensities for each of the exits and re-entries. Devicienti (2001) and Stevens (1999) estimate such models, but report that they are hard to fit, often do not converge, or provide statistically insignificant results for key parameters. Like them, the focus here is on the simpler model. Devicienti (2001) also addressed the 'initial conditions' problem that arises when one allows for unobservable differences in hazard rates. The issue is that, if the model is true, then an individual's poverty status when first observed is no longer random. For example, individuals with a relative high propensity to enter poverty have higher chances of being found to be poor when they are first observed. Preliminary analysis for this chapter followed Devicienti (2001) by modelling the probability that the first non-left-censored spell in the data is a poverty spell, estimating this probability jointly together with the poverty exit and re-entry model specified in equations (10.3) to (10.6). The models did not fit well and the initial conditions parameters were statistically insignificant, as Devicienti (2001) also found. For brevity, the estimates are not presented here.

10.2. Variables and Estimation Samples

The Measure of Poverty Status, and the Explanatory Variables

Poverty status is measured in the same way as in previous chapters of the book: an individual is counted as poor if the income of his or her household is less than 60 per cent of the contemporary median income. Income is 'current' income, referring to income round about the time of the annual BHPS interview. A poverty spell begins if an individual is non-poor at one interview in one survey year and poor at the next annual interview. Similarly, a poverty spell ends if an individual is poor at one annual interview and non-poor at the next interview. No adjustments are made for potential measurement error such as recording a poverty transition only if the underlying income change is of some minimum size (cf. Devicienti 2001).

For simplicity, the length of a poverty and a non-poverty spell is referred to as a number of 'years' rather than the number of annual interviews at which individuals were observed to be poor (or non-poor). In effect, the assumption is made that current income provides a suitable measure of living standards (and thence poverty status) for the whole of the year between interviews. The assumption is inevitable given the nature of the data available, and use of an annual measure of income is also problematic. Chapters 2 and 4 discuss these issues in detail, pointing out that short episodes of poverty are not observed at all when a current income measure is used in combination with annual interviews. But short spells of non-poverty within longer poverty spells are also not observed. As a result, it is unclear whether predictions of total time in poverty over a period are upwardly or downwardly biased and by how much.

The differences between individuals that are incorporated in the hazard regression models primarily refer to differences in the composition of an individual's household and differences in measures of household labour market attachment (defined below). For poverty transitions between some year $t-1$ and t, the value of each explanatory variable used is the value in the base year $t-1$. (This is more satisfactory than using year t values because, in that case, there is a greater chance that the values are a consequence of the transition itself. See the discussion of endogeneity below.) Characteristics such as labour market attachment are allowed to vary year by year within a spell. The exceptions to this are age variables (defined below), which were set equal to their values at the start of the spell. This is done in order to avoid collinearities between age and duration dependence: spell length and age each increase by one year as time progresses.

Household composition is summarized in terms of: the number of dependent children in the household; whether there are children aged 0–5 years in the household; the number of adults; whether the household has a female head or not; and the age of the household head at the start of the spell (whether aged less than 30 years, 30–39 years, 40–49 years, 50–59 years, or 60+ years). This specification allows me to contrast the experience of lone parents with married couples, large families with small families, and elderly people with younger individuals. The discussion of poverty persistence in Chapter 8 suggests that individuals from lone-parent households and pensioners (especially single pensioners) have relatively long poverty spells and shorter recurrence times.

Household labour market attachment is summarized by whether the household head was in paid work, and whether any adults other than the household head are in paid work. These variables allow me to contrast workless, single-earner, and multi-earner households. One expects that the greater the work attachment, the greater the chances of leaving poverty and the smaller the chances of re-entering poverty. The impacts on poverty exit and re-entry rates of differences in local labour market tightness were also considered. The specific measures used include the unemployment rate; and the unemployment-to-vacancy ratio in each individual's travel-to-work area (measures of local labour market tightness). As shown below, these variables were never found to have a statistically significant association with poverty transition rates. An additional possibility would be to allow poverty transition rates to vary by survey year. (For example, Chapter 8 shows that poverty exit rates rose in the 1990s when the economy moved out of recession.) Such effects are hard to estimate reliably, however. With only a relatively short panel of nine waves, the passage of calendar time is closely associated with spell duration.

All the explanatory variables cited so far (except the local labour market unemployment rate) are defined at the level of an individual's household. Poverty status is measured at the household level, so it is household-level demographic and labour market factors that are important. Arguably, however, individual-specific characteristics also play a role in addition to and separately from the household-level characteristics. For example, it is well-known that divorced and separated women have lower living standards than divorced and separated men after a household split (Jarvis and Jenkins 1997; Jenkins 2009a), so, other things being equal, one might expect the poverty (re-)entry risks for a husband and a wife from the same household to differ, and risks might also vary by age. For this reason, models were also fitted which included as explanatory variables each individual's age (at the start of the relevant spell); and sex. They turned out not to have statistically significant associations with hazard rates and so are dropped from the specifications reported in this chapter.

The explanatory variables mentioned so far refer to characteristics measured at a particular point in time (the relevant survey interview), but there is no mention of 'trigger events' (changes in characteristics) as explanatory variables. This may appear surprising after the focus on these in the previous chapter. I am aware of only two studies using hazard regression models of poverty transitions that do include them: Hill, Hill, and Walker (1998) and Cantó-Sanchez (1998). A third study, by DiPrete and McManus (2006), includes trigger events in a model of income change more generally. Why are trigger events not generally included as explanatory variables?

There are several reasons. First, some previous research suggests that it is difficult to identify statistically significant associations between poverty transition rates and trigger-event variables if one also controls for characteristics at a point in time. Characteristics specify who is at risk of experiencing the various events, and actual experience of the event appears in practice not to add further leverage in terms of explanation. For example, Stevens (1995) states that:

> I find relatively insignificant effects of these event types on the transition probabilities . . . Overall, the length of spells in or out of poverty does not vary substantially by the nature of the associated transitions across the poverty line. In

particular, conditional on [other covariates], transitions out of poverty related to household structure changes are not systematically more or less permanent than those involving changes with a static household composition. (Stevens 1995: 21.)

The published version of her article (Stevens 1999) makes no reference to the issue.

A second reason is that experience of such events is synonymous with a poverty transition and therefore does not add to the explanation—an argument that has been put to me by an experienced income distribution researcher. I dismiss this reasoning: Chapter 9 shows that trigger events are not perfectly associated with poverty transitions.

A third reason for not using trigger events as explanatory variables is that, by definition, they are a special type of time-varying covariate. That is, their value may change over the course of a spell—in the same way that other explanatory variables such as household composition and household work attachment may also do. Time-varying covariates of all types complicate predictions of spell-length distributions because assumptions have to be made about how these measures vary with spell duration. The most common assumption used when making predictions, also employed in this chapter, is that these variables remain constant. The only exception to this practice that I am aware of is the research by Hill, Hill, and Walker (1998). They specify temporal sequences of covariate patterns, including assumptions about marriage and birth events and their timing, and predict sequences of poverty risks using their model estimates. Thus, the argument for not using trigger events as explanatory variables under this heading is really an argument that projections of them are more complicated than for other time-varying covariates. Differently said, predictions about spell lengths may be used to help target policy measures at those most at risk of long poverty spells and, in most cases, research users will only have at their disposal information about the current characteristics of the relevant population at risk and projections are made on the basis of these. So, the models on which the predictions are based should also use this information—but not trigger-event variables.

A fourth reason is that, arguably, trigger-event variables cannot be treated as exogenous. A poverty transition and a trigger event may be jointly determined by some common unobservable factor and so inclusion of a trigger-event variable may lead to biased parameter estimates. I have not found any published statement of this argument, but informal discussions with other researchers suggest that endogeneity issues are a concern. However, one might as easily argue that many of the point-in-time variables used as explanatory variables are also potentially endogenous. That is, there are unobserved factors that determine, for example, whether someone is living with a partner or labour market participation at a point in time, and which also affect the chances of a poverty transition. See Biewen (2009) for discussion of endogeneity issues in the context of a discrete Markov model of poverty transitions of the kind considered in Chapter 12. I conclude that endogeneity issues are important and need further attention in future research. This is a complex and difficult task because one has to model a number of processes simultaneously. I return to this issue in Chapter 12. The findings presented in this chapter are descriptive in the sense of identifying the types of individuals who have long poverty spells and short recurrence times; the research does not claim to identify causal effects in the formal sense.

Estimation Samples

The implicit assumption so far is that the same model describes the pattern of poverty transition rates for all individuals: although individuals differ in their characteristics, model parameters are common. However, some researchers fit poverty transition models using data about adults only (as in Chapter 11): children are excluded from their estimation samples. The argument is that children are economically dependent on their parents, and that it is adults not children that make the behavioural choices (about work and demography) that affect income and thence poverty. However, since these models are descriptive rather than causal behavioural models, this argument loses its force. (These issues are reviewed by Jenkins 2000, 2007.) As it happens, when most of the models were re-estimated using samples of adults rather than samples of all individuals, corresponding estimates changed little. Results from the adults-only models are therefore not reported.

The research does, however, fit different models for elderly and non-elderly households: separate models are fitted for individuals living in households with a head aged 60+ years and those with a household head aged less than 60 years. The labour market for older people differs from that for younger people, and most elderly people are retired. Thus one might expect, for example, that the association between labour market attachment and hazard rates differ for elderly and non-elderly households. Models fitted to data in which both samples are pooled are not reported here: see Jenkins and Rigg (2001: chapter 4).

I now turn to discuss the model estimates and their implications for spell lengths. Separate models for poverty exits and poverty re-entries are discussed first, followed by the specifications modelling them jointly.

10.3. Poverty Exit Rates and the Length of Poverty Spells

The estimation strategy involves initially fitting a general model incorporating all the explanatory variables referred to earlier, followed by fitting of more parsimonious models—models that explain the data virtually as well as the general model, but use fewer explanatory variables. (Standard statistical criteria were used to select the explanatory variables that were dropped.) A large number of models were fitted, but only those from the final parsimonious specifications are reported here.

The explanatory variables without a statistically significant association with poverty exit rates in the general model are: having a female household head; the unemployment-vacancy ratio in the local travel-to-work-area; the individual's age; and the individual's sex. The lack of association may be surprising to some readers. For example, with lone mothers in mind, one might expect female headship to be associated with lower poverty exit rates. But that is not so, once the presence of children and household work attachment is controlled for. One

Table 10.1. Multivariate models of the hazard rate of poverty exit: individuals with non-elderly household heads and individuals with elderly household heads

Explanatory variable	Household head aged < 60 years		Household head aged 60+ years	
	Coeff.	(s.e.)	Coeff.	(s.e.)
Number of dependent children in household	−0.214	(0.05)***	0.883	(0.39)**
Children aged 1–5 in household	−0.349	(0.11)***	−1.711	(0.89)**
Number of adults in household	0.222	(0.08)***		
Household head aged 30–39	−0.056	(0.12)		
Household head aged 40–49	−0.164	(0.14)		
Household head aged 50–59	−0.447	(0.14)***		
Household head aged 65–69			−0.411	(0.17)**
Household head aged 70–74			−0.464	(0.17)***
Household head aged 75–79			−0.468	(0.18)***
Household head aged 80+			−0.466	(0.17)***
Household head has A-levels or higher educational qualifications	0.201	(0.09)**		
Household head in paid work	0.318	(0.09)**	0.554	(0.23)**
Other paid workers in household	0.475	(0.11)***		
Spell year 1	−0.489	(0.14)***	0.079	(0.13)
Spell year 2	−0.889	(0.16)***	−0.692	(0.18)***
Spell year 3	−1.002	(0.19)***	−1.013	(0.24)***
Spell year 4	−1.175	(0.25)***	−0.958	(0.28)***
Spell year 5	−1.387	(0.34)***	−1.165	(0.41)***
Spell year 6	−1.528	(0.48)**	−1.483	(0.62)**
Spell year 7	−1.804	(0.80)**	−1.663	(1.05)
Log-likelihood	−2325		−867	
Number of observations (person-years)	3782		1417	

Notes: *** $p < 0.01$; ** $0.01 \leq p < 0.05$; * $0.05 \leq p \leq 0.10$. Reference categories for dummy variables are: no children in household aged 1–5, household head aged less than 30 or household head aged 60–64, household head with educational qualifications less than A-level, household head not working, no other adult in the household. Estimates derived using discrete-time proportional hazards regression with standard errors adjusted for clustering within households. Age refers to age at the start of the spell.

Source: Jenkins and Rigg (2001: table 4.2), using BHPS waves 1–9.

might expect higher unemployment-vacancy ratios to be associated with lower poverty exit rates, on the grounds that they are a measure of the slackness of the local labour market. It may be that all such effects were already mediated by the household labour market attachment variables, though exploratory modelling did not confirm this conjecture. (For example, the unemployment-vacancy ratio did not have a statistically significant association with exit rates even when the labour market variables were excluded from the model.) Alternative measures such as the local unemployment rate did not have statistically significant associations either. The lack of association between exit hazard rates and the individual-level variables (age and sex) may arise because of relatively high correlations with the household composition variables already included in the model. (For single-person households, of course, the age and sex of the individual and of the household head coincide. And among married-couple households, the age of the head and spouse are likely to be similar.)

The estimates for the parsimonious models for poverty exits are reported in Table 10.1. The first two columns of numbers refer to the estimates for the sample of individuals with a household head aged less than 60; the second two columns refer to estimates for the sample of individuals with a household head aged 60+. For brevity, the two samples are referred to as non-elderly and elderly households, respectively, and their estimates are discussed in turn. Virtually all explanatory variables have statistically significant associations with poverty exit hazards and the coefficient estimates are of the expected sign. The quantitative implications of the estimates are examined in more detail using graphs. First, I consider the estimated shape of the baseline hazard function and second, how the exit hazard varies with differences in characteristics.

Poverty Exits among Non-Elderly Households

Figure 10.1 shows predicted poverty exit hazard rates for two types of individual: a non-elderly DINK (double-income-no-kids; Person 1), and a non-working lone mother with two children (Person 2). See the notes to the figure for more details. Also shown is the life-table estimator of the exit hazard rate—the sample-average baseline hazard function, which does not control for differences between individuals.

The relationship between hazard rates and duration is one that is assumed to be common to all individuals, with differences in characteristics shifting the common baseline hazard function up or down proportionally (see the earlier discussion). Figure 10.1 suggests that, when characteristics are controlled for, the hazard rate function declines slightly faster with the length of the poverty spell than the life-table estimates indicate. Despite the common shape of the multivariate model hazard function, the magnitude of the exit rates differs substantially between individuals. Those for non-elderly DINKs

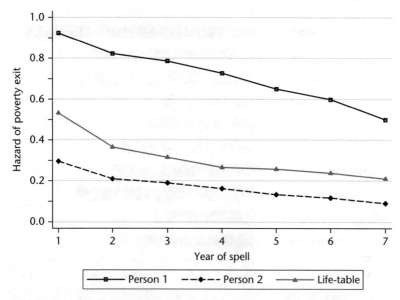

Figure 10.1. Poverty exit rates for individuals with a household head aged less than 60 years, by length of poverty spell

Notes: Person 1: Household head aged less than 30 years, has A-levels or higher educational qualifications, household with no children, two adults, both working. Person 2: one-adult household, two children, one aged 0–5 years, household head has no A-levels and is not working.

Source: Jenkins and Rigg (2001, figure 4.1), using BHPS waves 1–9.

are more than twice as large as the rates for lone parents. This indicates that hazard rates vary a lot across different types of individual and, hence, there is also substantial heterogeneity in the lengths of time spent poor.

The impact of differences in characteristics is assessed with reference to the hazard ratios associated with each explanatory variable. They are summarized for non-elderly households in Figure 10.2. The length of each bar shows the hazard ratio for each of the explanatory variables in turn. There is a clear decline in hazard ratio the older the household head is. Other things equal, the hazard rate for someone with a household head aged 50–59 is almost 40 per cent lower than the rate for someone with a household head aged less than 30. This may reflect some early retirement (or disguised unemployment) effect for the 50–59 group that is not picked up by the other explanatory variables.

Exit hazards are at least 20 per cent higher for those with a head who had A-levels or higher rather than lower educational qualifications. An even larger positive effect is associated with higher labour market attachment. Interestingly, having someone other than the household head in paid work raises the poverty exit hazard by more than it is raised by having a working head (1.6 times higher rather than 1.4 times higher). This effect is present having controlled for the numbers of adults in the household. An extra adult raises

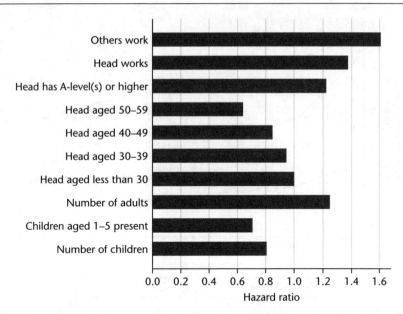

Figure 10.2. Hazard ratios from model of exit rates for individuals with a household head aged less than 60 years

Notes: The hazard ratio shows the proportionate change in the hazard rate associated with a one-unit change in the explanatory variable, other things equal. A hazard ratio of one indicates no change in the hazard rate; a value less than one, a decrease in the hazard rate; and a value greater than one, an increase in the hazard rate. Calculated from the estimates reported in Table 10.1.
Source: Jenkins and Rigg (2001, figure 4.2), using BHPS waves 1–9.

the poverty exit hazard rate by 25 per cent, other things equal. By contrast, an extra dependent child reduces the chances of poverty exit by almost 20 per cent. The presence of young children has an additional separate effect on the hazard, reducing it by almost 30 per cent.

The model estimates for elderly households are assessed using the same methods. Hazard functions and hazard ratios are displayed in Figures 10.3 and 10.4. There are differences in the set of explanatory variables, with statistically significant associations compared to estimates for non-elderly households. In the parsimonious model for elderly households, fewer explanatory variables are statistically significant. Specifically, the number of adults in the household, whether the household head has A-level(s) or higher educational qualifications, and the presence of workers other than the household head, are all variables included in the model for non-elderly households but not the one for elderly households.

The poverty exit hazard functions shown in Figure 10.3 suggest that there is a relatively high exit rate in the first year of a poverty spell, but a sharp decline in rates over the next two years of the poverty spell, with a more gradual decline thereafter. (This was also seen in the life-table estimates for all

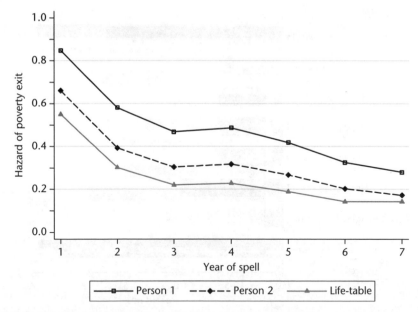

Figure 10.3. Poverty exit rates for individuals with a household head aged 60+ years, by length of poverty spell

Notes: Person 1: household head aged 60–64 years, in paid work, no children in household. Person 2: household head aged 60–64, not in paid work, no children in household.
Source: Jenkins and Rigg (2001: Figure 4.3), using BHPS waves 1–9.

individuals shown in Chapter 8.) This pattern contrasts with that for non-elderly households, for whom the decline in hazard rates over the spell is at much the same rate over the spell: the graphs shown in Figure 10.3 are more curved than those in Figure 10.1.

The hazard ratios shown in Figure 10.4 draw attention to a very large positive impact on poverty exit rates of having dependent children in the household: the estimates imply that each additional child raised the exit rate by over 400 per cent, other things equal. This finding is difficult to explain. It cannot be argued that the effect arises because elderly persons benefit from living with their (adult) children because the explanatory variable refers to the number of dependent children: non-dependent adult children are not included in the count. However, the effect should be kept in perspective: few households headed by someone aged 60+ contain dependent children (the number is about 0.04 on average). For the same reason, the relatively large association between the presence of young children and lower poverty exit rates should not be given much emphasis either—it is relevant for only about 1 per cent of the subsample.

More relevant for policy is the impact on poverty exit chances of having a working household head. Other things equal, individuals with a household

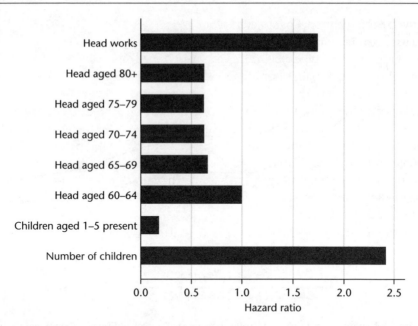

Figure 10.4. Hazard ratios from model of poverty exit rates for individuals with a household head aged 60+ years

Notes: The hazard ratio shows the proportionate change in the hazard rate associated with a one-unit change in the explanatory variable, other things equal. A hazard ratio of one indicates no change in the hazard rate; a value less than one, a decrease in the hazard rate; and a value greater than one, an increase in the hazard rate. Calculated from the estimates reported in Table 10.1.

Source: Jenkins and Rigg (2001: figure 4.4), using BHPS waves 1–9.

head in paid work have poverty exit rates about 70 per cent higher than individuals in households with non-working heads. There are also statistically significant associations between hazard rates and the age of the household head. Figure 10.4 shows that the main distinction is between individuals with a head aged 60–64 and individuals with a head aged 65+ (the hazard ratios for all the older age groups are very similar). The latter group has poverty exit rates about 40 per cent lower than the former group. The explanation is that men become eligible for the state retirement pension at age 65: retired persons can no longer rely on the labour market to increase their incomes in the same way that working-age individuals could. This effect is in addition to the effect arising from having a household head in paid work.

Predicted Poverty-Spell Lengths

Predicted poverty-spell lengths are shown in Table 10.2. Each row in the table provides predictions for a different type of individual, the characteristics of whom are described in detail in the note to the table. The predictions were derived from the model parameters reported in Table 10.1 using the methods discussed earlier in the chapter. The table shows, for a large number of persons of a given person type beginning a poverty spell, the proportion of persons who would remain poor for at least one year, for at least two years, and so on, up to seven years. The proportion of the entry cohort who would have left poverty after a given number of years is simply one minus the proportion shown. The predictions assume that the characteristics of the relevant individual do not change over time. This is potentially inappropriate because people do move in and out of work, etc., but, for the reasons discussed earlier, it is much more straightforward to assume that characteristics are constant. The predicted spell lengths shown here, and in similar tables later, are projections of a particular kind.

For non-elderly households, there are two base-level person types. The first (case 1) refers to persons belonging to the young DINK household discussed earlier. For this group, poverty exit rates are rapid: 92 per cent leave poverty after one year, 99 per cent after two years, and everyone after three years. If the age of the household head is 30–39 or 40–49 years (rather than less than 30), then the proportions remaining poor are larger for each year of a spell, but only slightly so (cases 2 and 3). Having a household head aged 50–59 years has a more substantial impact (case 4). Almost one-fifth of this group remains poor at least one year, and 6 per cent for at least two years. The presence of children, especially young children, has a large impact on poverty-spell lengths. For example, if the reference person has two children rather than one, one of whom is aged 0–5 years, then the chance of remaining poor after one year increases to 23 per cent rather than 8 per cent (cf. cases 7 and 1). After three years, the probability is still 7 per cent. The impact of having two children is, however, less than the effect of living in a workless household: compare cases 10 and 7. In case 10, almost one-third remained poor after one year. Having one child aged 6+ has much the same effect on spell lengths as the household head not having A-levels or higher qualifications (cf. cases 8 and 5).

The second reference person type for non-elderly households describes someone in a lone-parent household. Case 11 refers to a one-adult household headed by an individual with A-levels or higher qualifications, not in paid work, and with one child aged 0–5 years. Individuals such as these experience relatively long poverty spells (as the evidence about persistent poverty in Chapter 5 suggested). One year after starting a spell, fewer than half (41 per cent) of this type have left poverty, and after two years, only 59 per cent have finished their spell. After four years, 18 per cent of the entry cohort remain poor, and after seven years, there is still more than one-tenth (13 per cent) that stay poor. Being in paid work reduces poverty-spell durations, but spell lengths are still much longer than those for the two-adult household considered earlier. After seven years, some 6 per cent remain poor (case 12). Having

Table 10.2. Predicted poverty spell lengths for individuals beginning a poverty spell

Type of individual	Proportion remaining poor after number of years is:						
	1	2	3	4	5	6	7
Household head aged less than 60 years							
1. Head aged < 30, has A-levels, no children, two adults, both working	0.08	0.01	0.00	0.00	0.00	0.00	0.00
2. As (1), except head aged 30–39	0.09	0.02	0.00	0.00	0.00	0.00	0.00
3. As (1), except head aged 40–49	0.11	0.03	0.01	0.00	0.00	0.00	0.00
4. As (1), except head aged 50–59	0.19	0.06	0.02	0.01	0.01	0.00	0.00
5. As (1), except one child	0.12	0.03	0.01	0.00	0.00	0.00	0.00
6. As (1), except two children	0.19	0.06	0.02	0.01	0.00	0.00	0.00
7. As (1), except two children, one aged < 6	0.23	0.09	0.04	0.02	0.01	0.01	0.00
8. As (1), except head has no A-levels	0.12	0.03	0.01	0.00	0.00	0.00	0.00
9. As (1), except other(s) not working	0.20	0.07	0.03	0.01	0.01	0.00	0.00
10. As (1), except none in paid work	0.31	0.14	0.07	0.04	0.02	0.02	0.01
11. One adult household, head has A-levels, not in paid work, one child aged < 6	0.59	0.41	0.30	0.23	0.18	0.15	0.13
12. As (11), except head in paid work	0.48	0.29	0.19	0.13	0.10	0.08	0.06
13. As (11), except two children	0.65	0.49	0.38	0.30	0.25	0.22	0.19
14. As (11), except two children, no A-levels	0.70	0.56	0.45	0.38	0.33	0.29	0.26
Household head aged 60+ years							
15. Head aged 60–64, in paid work, no children in household	0.15	0.06	0.03	0.02	0.01	0.01	0.00
16. As (15), except head aged 65–69	0.29	0.16	0.11	0.07	0.05	0.04	0.03
17. As (15), except head aged 70–74	0.31	0.18	0.12	0.08	0.06	0.04	0.04
18. As (15), except head aged 75–79	0.31	0.18	0.12	0.08	0.06	0.04	0.04
19. As (15), except head aged 80+	0.31	0.18	0.12	0.08	0.06	0.04	0.04
20. As (15), except head not in paid work	0.34	0.21	0.14	0.10	0.07	0.06	0.05
21. As (15), except head aged 70–74 and not in paid work	0.51	0.37	0.29	0.23	0.19	0.16	0.15
22. As (15), except one child in household	0.01	0.00	0.00	0.00	0.00	0.00	0.00

Notes: Predictions derived from the parameter estimates shown in Table 10.1. Age refers to age at the start of the spell.
Source: Jenkins and Rigg (2001: table 4.3), using BHPS waves 1–9.

additional children makes the situation substantially worse. If the household head has two children and educational qualifications lower than A-level standard (case 14), then the probability of being poor after one year is almost 70 per cent. After a second year, 56 per cent remain poor. After five years, one-third are still poor and, after seven years, just over one-quarter.

Consider now elderly households. The reference person (case 15) has a household head aged 60–64 who is in paid work, and there are no dependent children in the household. One year after starting a spell, only 15 per cent of people like this are predicted to remain poor and, after a further year, the fraction more than halves to 6 per cent, and falls to 1 per cent after three years. Spell lengths are much longer—approximately doubled—if the household head is instead aged 65 or more (cases 16 to 19). About 30 per cent of this older group starting a poverty spell remain poor at least one year, and 8 per cent are poor for at least four years. After seven years, the proportion remaining poor is still non-negligible, about 4 per cent. If each individual's household head is aged 60–64 but not in paid work rather than working, then spells are also much longer (case 20). Just over one-third (34 per cent) of those entering poverty remain poor at least one year, and just over one-fifth (21 per cent) remain poor at least two years. After seven years, one-twentieth are predicted still to be poor. Spells are even longer for individuals with the relatively common combination of old age and lack of paid work (case 21). One-half of this group leave poverty within one year of beginning a spell, but the rate of exit then slows down. Almost one-fifth (19 per cent) have a poverty spell lasting at least five years and, for about 15 per cent, the spell lasts at least seven years. Finally, observe the huge impact on spell lengths of the presence of dependent children: even with one child present in the household (case 22), all individuals in this (relatively rare) group are predicted to leave poverty within one year of starting a spell.

10.4. Poverty Re-entry Rates and the Time Between Poverty Spells

The modelling of poverty re-entry hazards mimics the strategy applied to the analysis of poverty exit rates. Initial modelling began with a general specification and then fitted more parsimonious models. Again, only selected results are reported.

There are fewer statistically significant associations than for the poverty exit rate models. In a general model, the explanatory variables that did not have a statistically significant association with poverty re-entry rates are: having a child aged 1–5 in the household; having more adults in the household; having a female household head; having a younger rather than older household head;

Table 10.3. Multivariate models of the hazard rate of poverty re-entry, individuals with a non-elderly household head and individuals with an elderly household head

Explanatory variable	Household head aged < 60 years		Household head aged 60+ years	
	Coeff.	(s.e.)	Coeff.	(s.e.)
Number of dependent children in household	0.314	(0.05)***	0.508	(0.27)*
Household head has A-levels or higher educational qualifications	−0.255	(0.12)**	−0.293	(0.18)*
Household head in paid work	−0.639	(0.12)***	0.577	(0.19)***
Other paid workers in household	−0.627	(0.11)***	−0.570	(0.22)***
Spell year 1	−0.797	(0.12)***	−0.945	(0.09)***
Spell year 2	−1.198	(0.16)***	−1.472	(0.14)***
Spell year 3	−1.260	(0.19)***	−1.514	(0.17)***
Spell year 4	−1.749	(0.26)***	−1.494	(0.20)***
Spell year 5	−2.293	(0.41)***	−1.786	(0.30)***
Spell year 6	−1.576	(0.37)***	−1.704	(0.34)***
Spell year 7	−1.374	(0.51)***	−1.580	(0.53)***
Log-likelihood	−2314		−1027	
Number of observations (person-years)	5357		1947	

Notes: *** $p < 0.01$; ** $0.01 \leq p < 0.05$; * $0.05 \leq p \leq 0.10$. Reference categories for dummy variables are: household head with educational qualifications less than A-level, household head not working, no other adult in the household working. Estimates derived using discrete-time proportional hazards regression, with standard errors adjusted for clustering within households.

Source: Jenkins and Rigg (2001, table 4.5), using BHPS waves 1–9.

the unemployment-vacancy ratio in the local travel-to-work area; the individual's age; and the individual's sex.

The parameter estimates from the final parsimonious specifications are shown in Table 10.3. As for poverty exits, there are separate models for non-elderly and elderly households, and the parameter estimates are interpreted using graphs of baseline hazard functions and hazard ratios.

Figure 10.5 shows a baseline hazard function for non-elderly households that declines over the first five years since leaving poverty, but then increases again thereafter. This is a surprising result and differs from the shape of the poverty re-entry hazard function shown in Chapter 8. There is a simple explanation for the apparent U-shape: it arises because there is a sharp fall-off in the number of individuals at risk of experiencing poverty re-entry rather than a rise in the number of re-entries (terms forming the denominator and the numerator, respectively, of the life-table estimator of the hazard rate). The fall-off arises largely because the nine-year panel is relatively short; with the 16-year panel used in Chapter 8, the problem does not arise. (Note, however, that the poverty re-entry hazard is generally flatter than the poverty exit hazard, also reported in Chapter 8.) In the predictions summarized shortly, the model estimates are used 'as is', but predictions for non-poverty spell

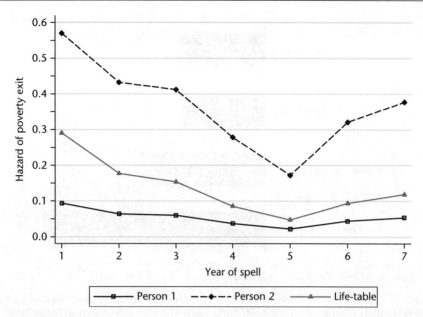

Figure 10.5. Poverty re-entry rates for individuals with a household head aged less than 60 years, by length of time since end of last poverty spell

Notes: Person 1: household head has A-levels or higher educational qualifications, is in paid work, other(s) in household in paid work, no children in household. Person 2: one-adult household, two children, one aged 0–5 years, household head not in paid work and has no A-levels.

Source: Jenkins and Rigg (2001: figure 4.5), using BHPS waves 1–9.

lengths longer than five years should be treated with caution. The differences between the hazard functions for the DINK and the lone parent indicate a large degree of heterogeneity in re-entry hazard rates across individuals and thence in differences in poverty recurrence times.

Hazard ratios implied by the multivariate model for the non-elderly group are displayed in Figure 10.6. Having household members in paid work reduces poverty re-entry risks substantially. Other things being equal, if the household head is in paid work rather than not working, the re-entry hazard rate is almost halved, or if one or more other persons in the household are in paid work, the hazard is also almost 50 per cent smaller. The impact of the household head having A-levels or higher educational qualifications is somewhat smaller: other things being equal, possession is associated with a re-entry hazard rate 23 per cent smaller. The presence of children has a big effect on the chances of becoming poor again. Each extra child is estimated to increase the risk of poverty re-entry by over one-third.

Consider now the estimates for elderly households and their implications. Figure 10.7 shows that re-entry hazard rates decline relatively gently with time since previously poor, at least by comparison with those for individuals in

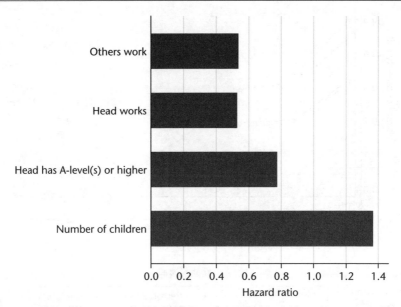

Figure 10.6. Hazard ratios from model of poverty re-entry rates for individuals with a household head aged less than 60 years

Notes: The hazard ratio shows the proportionate change in the hazard rate associated with a one-unit change in the explanatory variable, other things equal. A hazard ratio of one indicates no change in the hazard rate; a value less than one, a decrease in the hazard rate; and a value greater than one, an increase in the hazard rate. Calculated from the estimates reported in Table 10.3.
Source: Jenkins and Rigg (2001: figure 4.6), using BHPS waves 1–9.

non-elderly households. The hazard increases slightly after five years out of poverty, and the explanation is the same as provided for non-elderly households.

The hazard ratios summarized in Figure 10.8 point to some surprising findings about work attachment. As expected, if persons in the individual's household other than the household head are in paid work rather than not working, then the re-entry hazard rate is substantially lower, by about 45 per cent. But in addition if the household head works, the re-entry hazard rate is almost 80 per cent higher compared to if the head is not in paid work. An explanation for this puzzling finding is that there is a relatively high incidence of part-time work among elderly people and it is well-known that part-time work is not very well paid (at least relative to full-time work). So, it may be that this variable is picking out individuals whose incomes from other sources are low and they have to work to try and make ends meet. This plan may not be successful if labour market income is also not a reliable source. Further research about this conjecture and other potential explanations is required. To put the results into perspective, observe that about one-tenth of the individuals in our elderly household sample had household heads in paid

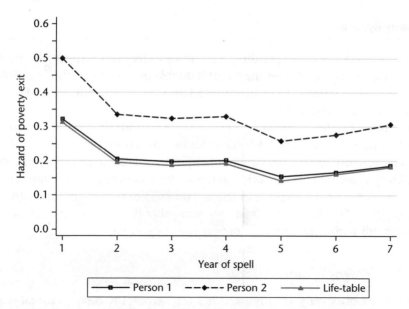

Figure 10.7. Poverty re-entry rates for individuals with household heads aged 60+, by length of time since last poverty spell

Notes: Person 1: household head has no A-levels, no one in paid work in household, no children present. Person 2: as Person 1, except that household head is in paid work.

Source: Jenkins and Rigg (2001: figure 4.7), using BHPS waves 1–9.

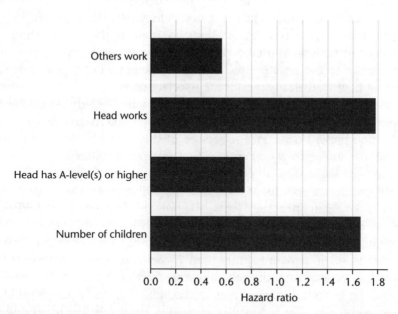

Figure 10.8. Hazard ratios from model of poverty re-entry rates for individuals with a household head aged 60+ years

Notes: The hazard ratio shows the proportionate change in the hazard rate associated with a one-unit change in the explanatory variable, other things equal. A hazard ratio of one indicates no change in the hazard rate; a value less than one, a decrease in the hazard rate; and a value greater than one, an increase in the hazard rate. Calculated from the estimates reported in Table 10.3.

Source: Jenkins and Rigg (2001: figure 4.8), using BHPS waves 1–9.

work, whereas the corresponding fraction of individuals with others in the household working (besides the head) is double that fraction. Thus the unexpected finding applies to a relatively small number of cases and so need not be given too much attention.

The other results are more in line with expectations. Individuals in households with a head who has A-level or higher educational qualifications have poverty re-entry hazard rates about one-quarter smaller than those with less-qualified household heads. Each additional dependent child in the household is associated with an increase in the hazard ratio of two-thirds, other things being equal. This is a large effect, but remember that the number of elderly households with dependent children is relatively small.

Predicted Poverty Recurrence Times

Predictions of poverty recurrence times implied by the model estimates are shown in Table 10.4. This has the same format as Table 10.2, except that the statistics shown now refer to the lengths of time between the end of one poverty spell and the start of another (rather than poverty spell lengths). Again the predictions are derived assuming that personal characteristics do not change over time. The notes to the table describe in detail the characteristics of each type of individual. For non-elderly households, there are two reference types of person with characteristics similar to those of the DINK and the one-adult household used earlier in the discussion of poverty exits. The modifications to the descriptions reflect the different set of explanatory variables that have statistically significant associations.

Consider first a person in a household with a non-elderly head who has A-levels or higher qualifications, with the head and other(s) in paid work, and no children present (case 1). For persons of this type who finish a poverty spell, almost one-tenth (9 per cent) fell back into poverty after one year (91 per cent stay out). Eighty-five per cent remain out of poverty for at least two years, and 80 per cent stay out for at least three years. Put another way, about one-fifth are poor again after three years. The presence of dependent children in the household increases the chances of returning to poverty markedly. With one child, the proportion staying out of poverty for at least five years is predicted to be 68 per cent rather than 75 per cent (case 2 versus case 1). And with a second child, the corresponding fraction is 58 per cent (case 3). The lack of A-levels has an effect of much the same size as having one child (cf. case 4 and case 2). The lack of labour market attachment shortens poverty recurrence times more markedly. For the group with no other persons in the household besides the head in paid work, just under one-fifth are predicted to re-enter poverty after one year and about 40 per cent after five years (case 5), whereas the corresponding proportions for the DINK are 9 per cent and 25 per

Table 10.4. Predicted time between poverty spells for individuals finishing a poverty spell

Type of individual	Proportion remaining non-poor after number of years is:						
	1	2	3	4	5	6	7
Household head aged less than 60 years							
1. Head has A-levels, no children, head and other(s) in paid work	0.91	0.85	0.80	0.77	0.75	0.72	0.68
2. As (1), except one child	0.87	0.80	0.73	0.70	0.68	0.64	0.59
3. As (1), except two children	0.83	0.74	0.65	0.61	0.58	0.54	0.48
4. As (1), except head has no A-levels	0.88	0.81	0.75	0.71	0.69	0.65	0.61
5. As (1), except no others working	0.83	0.74	0.65	0.61	0.59	0.54	0.48
6. As (1), except none in paid work	0.71	0.56	0.45	0.39	0.36	0.31	0.25
7. One adult household, head has A-levels, not in paid work, one child aged < 6	0.62	0.45	0.33	0.28	0.25	0.20	0.15
8. As (7), except head in paid work	0.78	0.66	0.56	0.51	0.48	0.43	0.37
9. As (7), except two children	0.52	0.34	0.22	0.17	0.15	0.11	0.08
10. As (7), except two children, no A-levels	0.43	0.24	0.14	0.10	0.09	0.06	0.04
Household head aged 60+ years							
11. Head not in paid work and has A-levels, other(s) in paid work, no children in household	0.85	0.77	0.70	0.64	0.60	0.55	0.51
12. As (11), except one child in household	0.76	0.65	0.56	0.47	0.42	0.37	0.32
13. As (11), except none in paid work, head without A-levels	0.75	0.63	0.54	0.45	0.40	0.35	0.30
14. As (11), except head working, no others in paid work	0.60	0.44	0.33	0.24	0.20	0.15	0.12

Notes: Predictions derived from parameter estimates shown in Table 10.3.
Source: Jenkins and Rigg (2001, table 4.6), using BHPS waves 1–9.

cent. Poverty recurrence times are shortened further by a notable amount if, in addition, the household head is not in paid work (case 6). Almost 30 per cent of this group are predicted to be poor again after one year, and 64 per cent after five years.

The second type of reference person for non-elderly households belongs to a one-adult household with a non-working head who has A-levels or higher educational qualifications and one child aged 1–5 years (case 7). She has markedly shorter poverty recurrence times than any of the two-adult household cases discussed in the previous paragraph. More than one-third (38 per cent) of persons in this group are predicted to be poor again within one year, and two-thirds within three years. The proportion staying out of poverty for at least five years is 25 per cent. If the household head is in paid work rather than not working, poverty recurrence times are much longer (case 8). For example, the proportion staying out of poverty for at least five years is just under one-half. By contrast, poverty recurrence times are much shorter when there are additional children present. For example, almost half (48 per cent) of the lone parents with two children fall back into poverty within one year (case 9). If the lone parent also does not have A-levels, then the corresponding figure is higher still, 57 per cent (case 10). Among this group, just 9 per cent are predicted to stay out of poverty for at least five years.

For elderly households, the base case is someone with a household head who is not in paid work, has A-levels or higher educational qualifications, and there are others in paid work but no children (case 11). For persons like this, poverty recurrence times are predicted to be quite similar (marginally lower) to those for individuals in non-elderly DINK households (case 1). For example 15 per cent are estimated to be poor again within one year. This figure increases to 24 per cent if there are dependent children in the household (case 12). Perhaps the most prototypical case is when there is no one in the household in paid work and the head does not have A-levels (case 13). For this group, almost one-quarter are predicted to fall back into poverty within one year. Only 40 per cent stay out of poverty for at least five years. The final case considered illustrates the (surprising and large) impact of having a household head in paid work rather than not working. Poverty recurrence times for this group are of a similar magnitude to those in one-adult non-elderly households (cf. cases 14 and 7).

10.5. Combining the Risks of Poverty Exit and Poverty Re-entry

So far the hazards of poverty exit and of poverty re-entry have been modelled separately and predictions have been of the distributions of the length of poverty spells for those beginning a spell, and of the length of time between poverty spells for those ending a poverty spell. That is, not only have exits and entries been modelled separately, but also predictions have been done separately. However, even if one has separately estimated models, one can combine their results in order to look at repeated poverty.

Common sense tells us that if we wish to get a handle on the total amount of poverty that individuals experience over a given number of years, then better estimates can be derived by looking at the risks of poverty exit and poverty re-entry in combination. Lone parents, for example, appear to have relatively low poverty exit rates and relatively high poverty re-entry rates, so they are likely to be poor more times over a given period than a focus on just poverty exits might suggest. One can go further and also model exits and entries in combination, while also taking account of correlations between unobserved characteristics that affect poverty transition rates. Before considering such a model and its predictions, I draw on the estimates from the separate models discussed in the previous two sections in order to show how taking multiple spells into account provides better estimates of poverty experience over some fixed time interval. This point was made in Chapter 8 using life-table estimates of poverty exit and re-entry hazards; the current exercise extends that discussion to provide estimates that vary with personal characteristics.

Poverty over a Period: Predictions from Separate Models of Poverty Exit and Re-entry

I take a cohort of entrants to poverty—a group of individuals beginning a spell of poverty—who are then followed for the next eight years (nine years in total, reflecting the number of waves of BHPS data used in this chapter). Table 10.5 shows the estimates of the distribution of number of times poor for persons with different sets of characteristics, generated using the parameter estimates reported in Tables 10.1 and 10.3. There are estimates for 14 different types of individual, seven belonging to non-elderly two-adult households, four belonging to lone-parent households, and three belonging to elderly households. Their characteristics are described in detail in the table notes. As before, the predictions assume that these characteristics remain constant over time.

For a person in a DINK household beginning a poverty spell (case 1), the experience of poverty over the subsequent eight years is limited. More than two-thirds (67 per cent) have just one further year of poverty, and one-quarter have two extra years. The mean number of waves in poverty out of eight is estimated to be 1.4 years. Poverty spells are longer if the working couple has children. With one young child, the mean number of years poor increases to 1.9 years; with two children, one aged under 6, the mean number is 2.4 years (cases 2 and 3). A single-earner couple with no children is predicted to have two years of poverty over the eight-year period (case 4), but, if they had two children, one aged under 6, the mean number is almost twice as high, 3.7 years (case 5). If neither husband nor wife works, and they have no children (case 6), the predicted average number of years poor out of eight is 2.9, increasing to five years if they have two children. Clearly, the presence of children and a lack of work both contribute to greater poverty persistence.

This is emphasized further by the results for individuals in lone-parent households. Compared to DINKs (case 1), only 8 per cent of non-working lone parents with one child (case 8) are predicted to be poor for just one extra

Table 10.5. Distribution of the number of years poor over an eight-year period (row percentages): predictions from separate models of poverty exit and re-entry

Type of individual	Number of years poor for a cohort of poverty entrants								Total	Mean number of waves in poverty
	1	2	3	4	5	6	7	8		
Two-adult household										
1. Both working, no children[a]	66.8	24.8	6.6	1.4	0.3	0.0	0.0	0.0	100	1.44
2. Both working, one child aged under 6[b]	48.6	27.6	13.3	6.1	2.6	1.0	0.4	0.4	100	1.93
3. Both working, two children, one aged under 6[c]	36.8	26.8	16.5	9.9	5.2	2.5	1.2	1.1	100	2.37
4. Head working but no others, no children[d]	42.7	29.8	15.9	7.3	2.8	0.4	0.3	0.2	100	2.03
5. Head working but no others, two children, one aged under 6[e]	16.2	18.1	16.6	15.7	12.8	8.8	5.6	6.0	100	3.70
6. No one working, no children[f]	21.1	24.8	21.7	16.1	9.1	4.2	1.8	1.2	100	2.93
7. No one working, two children, one aged under 6[g]	4.7	8.0	10.9	15.6	18.1	16.7	13.1	13.0	100	5.02
Lone-parent household										
8. Not working, one child aged under 6[h]	8.2	11.2	12.3	14.9	15.6	13.6	11.0	13.2	100	4.70
9. Not working, two children, one child aged under 6[i]	3.9	6.4	8.5	12.6	16.2	16.9	16.0	19.5	100	5.43
10. Not working, two children, one child aged under 6, no A-levels[j]	1.8	3.4	5.2	9.5	14.8	18.6	20.5	26.2	100	6.01
11. Working, two children, one aged under 6[k]	14.0	15.4	14.3	14.5	13.2	10.3	7.8	10.4	100	4.11
Elderly household										
12. Head aged 60–64, head working[l]	6.8	19.8	32.1	26.5	10.0	3.3	1.0	0.5	100	3.29
13. Head aged 60–64, no one working[m]	16.0	21.9	20.2	15.4	10.6	6.8	4.3	4.8	100	3.44
14. Head aged 80+ years, no one working[n]	11.9	14.6	14.1	13.6	12.1	10.0	8.9	15.0	100	4.39

Notes: [a] Household head aged less than 30 years, has A-levels or higher educational qualifications, household with no children, two adults, both working. [b] As (a), except one child aged under 6 years. [c] As (a), except two children, at least one aged under 6. [d] As (a), except others in household besides head not working. [e] As (d), except that two children, at least one aged under 6. [f] As (a), except no one in household working. [g] As (f), except two children, at least one aged under 6. [h] One-adult household, head aged less than 30 years, has A-levels or higher educational qualifications, not working, one child aged under 6. [i] As (h), except two children in household, at least one child aged under 6, household head does not have A-levels or higher educational qualifications, at least one child aged under 6. [j] As (h), except two children in household, at least one child aged under 6, no A-levels / As (i), except head working. [k] As (j), except head working. [l] Household head aged 60–64, household head only working, does not have A-levels or higher educational qualifications, no children in household. [m] As (l), except no one working. [n] As (g), except head aged 80+ years, and no one working.

Source: Jenkins and Rigg (2001: table 4.8), using BHPS waves 1–9.

year (rather than 67 per cent), and 24 per cent are poor for at least seven of the subsequent eight years (rather than zero). The mean number of years poor is 4.7 years, and more than six months longer (5.4 years) if the non-working lone parent has two children (case 9). If she also does not have A-levels, the predicted mean is even longer, six years (case 10). Being in paid work reduces the number of years poor substantially: for a working lone parent with two children (case 11), the mean number of years poor out of eight, four years, is about 15 months shorter than if she is not working. On the other hand, that number is still high compared to the predicted means for individuals in two-adult households, a greater proportion of whom do not belong to workless households.

The experience of individuals in elderly households falls between that of individuals in two-adult and lone-parent households. If the household head is aged 60–64 and still working (case 12), then the predicted mean number of years poor is 3.3 years, and virtually the same if the head is working. The average is almost a year longer, 4.4 years, among workless elderly households with the head aged 80+ years rather than 60–64 (case 14). In assessing these estimates, remember that they are derived assuming that the individual's characteristics remain constant over the period. This is more likely to hold true for pensioners than for lone parents—many of whom may (re)partner over an eight-year period. If they do so, then the experience of repeated poverty is likely to have been less than shown in Table 10.5.

Poverty over a Period: Predictions from a Joint Model of Poverty Exit and Re-entry

So far poverty entry and exit rates have been modelled separately rather than jointly. The case for joint estimation hinges on there being unobserved differences between individuals (such as in ability, effort, or tastes) which influence both poverty entry and poverty exit risks. A model incorporating these aspects was set out earlier in the chapter. Now I report the model estimates, together with the implied predictions of time spent poor over a period for cohorts of poverty entrants. The joint model is estimated using the same set of explanatory variables as are used in the separate poverty exit and re-entry models discussed earlier (Tables 10.1 and 10.3) and, again, fitted separately for elderly and non-elderly households. The definition of an elderly household is whether or not the household head was aged 60 or more at the beginning of the first spell of the sequence used in the analysis, rather than at the beginning of each separate spell as in the earlier analysis.

The parameter estimates of the joint model are reported in Table 10.6 (for coefficients on characteristics and duration-dependence variables) and Table 10.7 (unobserved heterogeneity propensities and associated proportions in

Table 10.6. Multivariate model of poverty exit and re-entry with correlated unobserved heterogeneity

Explanatory variable	Household head aged < 60 years		Household head aged 60+ years	
	Coeff.	(s.e.)	Coeff.	(s.e.)
Poverty exits				
Number of dependent children in household	−0.273	(0.03)***	0.376	(0.16)**
Children aged 1–5 in household	−0.263	(0.07)***	−1.157	(0.44)***
Number of adults in household	0.267	(0.05)***		
Household head aged 30–39	−0.109	(0.08)		
Household head aged 40–49	−0.139	(0.09)		
Household head aged 50–59	−0.473	(0.11)***		
Household head aged 65–69			−0.324	(0.14)**
Household head aged 70–74			−0.437	(0.14)***
Household head aged 75–79			−0.389	(0.14)***
Household head aged 80+			−0.347	(0.14)**
Household head has A-levels or higher educational qualifications	0.258	(0.06)***		
Household head in paid work	0.452	(0.06)***	0.406	(0.20)**
Other paid workers in household	0.520	(0.07)***		
Spell year 1	0.566	(0.20)***	0.747	(0.21)***
Spell year 2	0.459	(0.23)**	0.099	(0.25)
Spell year 3	0.445	(0.24)*	−0.095	(0.28)
Spell year 4	0.244	(0.25)	−0.154	(0.32)
Spell year 5	0.154	(0.27)*	−0.257	(0.39)
Spell year 6	0.007	(0.33)	−0.544	(0.56)
Spell year 7	−0.241	(0.54)	−0.709	(1.03)
Poverty re-entries				
Number of dependent children in household	0.323	(0.02)***	0.497	(0.19)***
Household head has A-levels or higher educational qualifications	−0.190	(0.06)***	−0.422	(0.17)**
Household head in paid work	−0.631	(0.06)***	0.580	(0.21)***
Other paid workers in household	−0.621	(0.06)***	−0.596	(0.20)***
Spell year 1	−0.619	(0.08)***	−0.291	(0.12)**
Spell year 2	−0.944	(0.10)***	−0.721	(0.18)***
Spell year 3	−1.026	(0.12)***	−0.540	(0.23)**
Spell year 4	−1.310	(0.16)***	−0.257	(0.30)
Spell year 5	−1.926	(0.24)***	0.024	(0.38)
Spell year 6	−1.291	(0.23)***	0.362	(0.46)
Spell year 7	−1.105	(0.31)***	0.759	(0.57)
Log-likelihood	−5684		−2249	
Number of observations (person-years)	10,969		3,915	

Notes: *** $p < 0.01$; ** $0.01 \leq p < 0.05$; * $0.05 \leq p \leq 0.10$. Reference categories for dummy variables are: household head with educational qualifications less than A-level, household head not working, no other adult in the household working. Estimates derived using discrete-time proportional hazards regression. Model also includes unobserved heterogeneity parameter estimates shown in Table 10.7. See text for model description.

Source: Jenkins and Rigg (2001, table C12), using BHPS waves 1–9.

Table 10.7. Estimates of unobserved heterogeneity parameters in joint model of poverty exit and re-entry

Parameter	Household head aged < 60 years		Household head aged 60+ years	
	Coeff.	(s.e.)	Coeff.	(s.e.)
Poverty exit propensity—low (λ_{low})	−1.652	−0.19***	−1.023	−0.2 ***
Poverty exit propensity—high (λ_{high})	0	—	0	—
Poverty re-entry propensity—low (θ_{low})	−0.775	−0.13***	−2.506	−0.37 ***
Poverty re-entry propensity—high (θ_{high})	0	—	0	—
Proportion with high exit propensity and low re-entry propensity	0.690	−0.05***	0.644	−0.06 ***
Proportion with low exit propensity and high re-entry propensity	0.310	−0.05***	0.356	−0.06 ***

Notes: *** $p < 0.01$. Estimates for the other parameters of the model are shown in Table 10.6. The proportion with a low exit propensity and a low re-entry propensity, and the proportion with a high exit propensity and a high re-entry propensity, are each assumed to equal zero. See text for model description.

Source: Jenkins and Rigg (2001: table C13), using BHPS waves 1–9.

the latent classes). Because of the complexity of the model, the parameter estimates are not discussed in detail. Instead, the discussion focuses on the contrasts between the predictions of total time poor from the joint-spell model and the predictions derived by combining estimates from the single-spell models.

The estimated impacts of the various explanatory variables are generally quite similar to those reported earlier, for both elderly and non-elderly households. (Compare Table 10.6 with Tables 10.1 and 10.3.) The most noticeable difference between the results is that the estimates of the duration-dependence parameters are generally no longer statistically significant (with the exception of those for poverty re-entries among individuals in non-elderly households). One explanation for this is that the duration-dependence estimates for the separate models (shown earlier) are confounded by not taking account of unobserved heterogeneity. If unobserved heterogeneity is important but ignored, then among the sample members with relatively long poverty spells will be a relatively large proportion of individuals with a low exit propensity—since those with a high exit propensity will already have left—and individuals with relatively long spell lengths will have a relatively low poverty exit hazard rate on average. Hence, the extent to which poverty exit rates decline with the length of a poverty spell will be over-estimated. (Similar arguments suggest biases in estimates of duration dependence in poverty re-entry rates.) The difficulty of distinguishing between duration-dependence effects and unobserved heterogeneity is an oft-cited issue in the literature, and so the results are not exceptional in that respect. The problem is exacerbated because the panel is relatively short. With a much longer panel—Stevens (1999) used US Panel Study of Income Dynamics data spanning two decades—there are more spells for each individual and so one can be more confident of identifying unobservable individual effects separately from duration dependence. Aside from this point, it is reassuring that all of the models provide similar estimates of the impacts of the explanatory variables.

Table 10.7 shows that there is statistically significant and correlated unobserved heterogeneity among both non-elderly and elderly households. Within each sample, there is a relatively advantaged group of individuals who have unobserved characteristics associated with greater chances of poverty exit and smaller chances of poverty (re-)entry. And within each sample there is a relatively disadvantaged group with smaller chances of poverty exit and larger chances of poverty (re-)entry. For each of the non-elderly and elderly samples, the relatively disadvantaged group forms about one-third of the total sample.

Does the jointly estimated model lead to different predictions of the length of time that individuals spent poor over a period of time? To answer this question, calculations of the type underlying Table 10.5 are repeated, but now use the estimates from the joint model rather than from the separate models. The new predictions are shown in Table 10.8. The predicted mean numbers of years poor over an eight-year period for individuals beginning a poverty spell are not too different from those that are reported in Table 10.6. The mean number of year is now somewhat smaller, typically by about six months.

Looking instead at the distribution of numbers of years poor out of eight rather than focusing on the mean numbers, there are more striking contrasts between the predictions. For all types of individual considered, the distribution of years poor is much more bimodal when unobserved heterogeneity is incorporated. There is a much greater proportion estimated to have either a small number of years poor or a large number of years poor—the middle of the distribution has been hollowed out. For example, for a cohort of DINKs starting a poverty spell, it is now predicted that 82 per cent spend just one year poor, and that 0.6 per cent spend six or more years out of eight poor (Table 10.8, case 1). The corresponding separate model estimates are 67 per cent and zero per cent. Similarly, for a cohort of non-working lone mothers with one child aged under 6 (case 8), the prediction from the joint model is that 39 per cent spend only one year poor and 27 per cent spend all eight years poor, whereas the predicted proportions from combining the separate models are 8 per cent and 13 per cent.

In explaining these differences in predicted distributions, the earlier discussion of the difficulties of distinguishing between duration dependence and unobserved heterogeneity is relevant again. For the separate models of poverty exits and re-entries, the intrinsic dynamics of poverty persistence (that is,

Table 10.8. Distribution of the number of years poor over an eight-year period (row percentages): predictions from joint model of poverty exit and re-entry

Type of individual	Number of years poor for a cohort of poverty entrants								Total	Mean number of waves in poverty
	1	2	3	4	5	6	7	8		
Two-adult household										
1. Both working, no children[a]	81.8	12.1	3.8	1.1	0.5	0.3	0.0	0.3	100	1.30
2. Both working, one child aged under 6[b]	72.3	14.8	5.9	2.4	1.2	0.9	0.4	2.2	100	1.61
3. Both working, two children, one aged under 6[c]	66.0	15.9	6.4	2.5	1.6	1.1	0.7	5.7	100	1.93
4. Head working but no others, no children[d]	72.4	14.7	5.8	2.3	1.3	0.9	0.5	2.1	100	1.60
5. Head working but no others, two children, one aged under 6[e]	51.9	16.8	6.7	2.8	1.7	1.2	1.5	17.5	100	2.83
6. No one working, no children[f]	60.2	16.1	6.4	2.9	1.9	1.7	1.7	9.1	100	2.27
7. No one working, two children, one aged under 6[g]	34.5	17.2	9.3	4.7	3.2	1.9	2.0	27.3	100	3.75
Lone-parent household										
8. Not working, one child aged under 6[h]	38.8	17.0	8.4	3.6	2.3	1.3	1.3	27.2	100	3.59
9. Not working, two children, one child aged under 6[i]	28.5	15.7	10.1	5.4	3.7	2.4	2.1	32.2	100	4.16
10. Not working, two children, one child aged under 6, no A-levels[j]	20.1	13.6	10.2	6.5	5.3	3.6	3.0	37.8	100	4.75
11. Working, two children, one aged under 6[k]	45.0	17.1	7.1	3.1	1.8	0.9	1.0	23.9	100	3.26
Elderly household										
12. Head aged 60–64, head working[l]	48.0	12.0	7.5	6.2	5.1	4.5	5.1	11.7	100	3.01
13. Head aged 60–64, no one working[m]	42.4	12.7	7.5	5.0	3.5	1.8	3.0	24.1	100	3.52
14. Head aged 80+ years, no one working[n]	34.1	10.4	6.1	4.2	3.4	1.5	2.3	38.0	100	4.36

Notes: [a] Household head aged less than 30 years, has A-levels or higher educational qualifications, household with no children, two adults, both working. [b] As (a), except one child aged under 6 years. [c] As (a), except two children, at least one aged under 6. [d] As (a), except others in household besides head not working. [e] As (d), except that two children, at least one aged under 6. [f] As (a), except no one in household working. [g] As (f), except two children, at least one aged under 6. [h] One-adult household, head aged less than 30 years, has A-levels or higher educational qualifications, not working, one child aged under 6. [i] As (h), except two children in household, at least one child aged under 6. [j] As (i), except two children in household, at least one child aged under 6, household head does not have A-levels or higher educational qualifications. [k] As (j), except head working. [l] Household head aged 60–64, household head only working, does not have A-levels or higher educational qualifications, no children in household. [m] As (l), except no one working. [n] As (g), except head aged 80+ years, and no one working.

Source: Jenkins and Rigg (2001: table 4.9), using BHPS waves 1–9.

controlling for differences in observed characteristics) are encapsulated in the estimates of how poverty transition rates decline through a spell (whether the spell is of poverty or non-poverty). The estimated distribution of numbers of years poor is therefore spread over the full range from one through to eight. By contrast, the estimates of the joint model with unobserved heterogeneity indicate significant unobserved differences in transition propensities combined with—for the most part—statistically insignificant negative duration dependence. By construction, this implies a much more discrete clustering of individuals with either relatively short or relatively long spell lengths.

In sum, the choice of modelling approach makes a substantial difference to estimates of the precise shape of the distribution of predicted numbers of years poor over a period. But, at the same time, the estimates of the average number of years poor are broadly robust to model specification. As mentioned earlier, using a longer panel is one route to getting more reliable estimates of duration dependence and the nature of unobserved heterogeneity, and I review some estimates based on 16 waves of BHPS data in the next section. At the same time, it should also be recognized that fitting models with these features is an intrinsically tricky business.

10.6. Summary and Conclusions

The focus of this chapter has been on spells—the lengths of time that individuals in Britain spend in poverty and the lengths of time between poverty spells. Combining the information provides information about the total number of years that someone starting a poverty spell will be poor over subsequent years. Multivariate hazard regression models provide a convenient way of characterizing differences between individuals. They are an extension of the life-table methods that are used in Chapter 8 to derive similar information for the population as a whole. Also the estimates of the total time spent poor over a period provide a contrast to the simple summaries of poverty persistence, such as counts of the number of times poor over a period, while also taking account of the censoring of poverty spells (one of the major criticisms of the simple method).

The chapter shows, like Chapter 8, that most people starting a poverty spell are poor for only a short time, but there is a significant minority with long spells. Also, of those people who have a poverty spell, most do not fall back into poverty again for a long time, but a non-negligible fraction do so quickly.

The characteristics associated with shorter spells of poverty are: having fewer dependent children in total; not having a young child (aged 1–5); having more adults; having a younger rather than older household head; having a household head with A-level or higher educational qualifications; having a household head in paid work; and having at least one other person in the household (apart from the head) in paid work.

The characteristics associated with longer intervals of time between poverty spells are similar: having fewer dependent children in the household; having a household head with A-level or higher educational qualifications; having a household head in paid work; and having at least one other in the household (apart from the head) in paid work.

The estimates imply that, of all the individuals who happen to fall into poverty, most of those who belong to working-age couple households have relatively short poverty spells. Relatively long spells are experienced by lone parents and their children, and by pensioners. Among those who finish a poverty spell, lone parents and their children stand out as a group that becomes poor again relatively quickly. These general findings are illustrated by the predictions of poverty persistence based on the estimates of the joint model of poverty entries and exits. The estimates imply that, if an individual from a double-income-no-kids (DINK) household starts a poverty spell, the number of years spent poor over the next eight years is 1.3 years on average. For someone aged 60–64 with no one working in the household, the average number of years poor over the next eight is predicted to be 3.5 years. For a lone parent with one young child, the average number is predicted to be 3.5 years on average and 4.2 years if she has two children.

It is an important question whether these patterns describe contemporary Britain. The data used in this chapter cover 1991–9, but, subsequently, between 1999 and the onset of the financial crisis in 2008, there were major changes in tax-benefit policy and unemployment rates remained low. Chapter 8 shows, using a variety of statistics, that patterns of poverty dynamics in the post-1999 period up to the mid-2000s differ from patterns in the 1991–9 period. For instance, poverty persistence declined (Figure 8.1), primarily reflecting an increase in the annual rate of poverty exit rather than a decline in the annual rate of poverty entry (Figure 8.5). But these changes are concentrated among particular groups, notably those including dependent children and single pensioners. Table 8.4, which summarizes life-table estimates of poverty exit and re-entry hazard rates, shows how, for dependent children, the chances of exiting poverty increased and the chances of re-entry decreased, regardless of spell durations. For adults aged 60+, the poverty re-entry hazard is higher in the second period than the first. For adults aged less than 60, no clear-cut changes are apparent.

Damioli (2011*b*) investigates Britain's poverty dynamics over the full 1991–2006 period, using data from BHPS waves 1–16. He fits a model of poverty exit and re-entry with correlated unobserved heterogeneity—the same as that discussed in this chapter—but extends the model to allow parameters to change over time. (His sample is restricted to adults aged 20–60, rather than all individuals as in this chapter, but this is unlikely to affect the results substantially.) Damioli allows baseline hazard rates to vary by survey year and, in one variation of the model, the coefficient on each explanatory variable can have different values for the pre-1998 period and the post-1998 period. (To be precise, the second period refers to 1998–2006 for poverty exits and refers to 1997–2006 for poverty re-entries.) Damioli's principal findings are consistent with the life-table estimates summarized in the previous paragraph. In particular, calendar time effects are more apparent for the poverty exit hazard than the re-entry hazard (Damioli 2011*b*: table 4, model 2). In the later period, poverty exit rates are larger for several types of individuals, but, particularly interestingly, there are statistically significant increases for lone parents and couples with children for prime-aged adults but not childless singles or couples (Damioli 2011*b*: table 5). This is circumstantial evidence that the introduction of tax credits and other policies to make work pay were responsible for the changes in the chances of escaping poverty. Nonetheless, as Damioli (2011*b*) points out, there is an unexplained puzzle concerning the timing of the most distinct changes in hazard rates—they are one year before Working Families Tax Credit was introduced.

It is worth emphasizing, however, that the findings of Damioli (2011*b*) concerning who is most likely to leave poverty or to fall back in are broadly the same as the findings reported in this chapter. That is, the individuals with larger poverty exit hazards and small re-entry hazards are those in households with a head (and spouse) in paid work, in couple rather than lone-parent households, with fewer dependent children, and a household head with more educational qualifications. Damioli (2011*b*) also finds that the unemployment rate in the local area has no statistically significant association with poverty exit or re-entry hazards, which may reflect a lack of variation independent of that captured by the survey year and duration-dependence variables.

It is also of interest to compare patterns of poverty persistence dynamics in Britain with patterns in other countries. Damioli (2011*a*) provides model-based estimates of the total time poor over a period for 11 European countries including Britain, derived from eight waves of ECHP data for survey years 1994–2001. For each country, he fits a model of poverty exit and re-entry with correlated unobserved heterogeneity and, from the estimates, generates, for poverty entrants in 1995, predictions of the total number of years poor over the next six years, using the same methods as utilized in this chapter. The predictions for each type of individual are averaged to produce a country-level figure, with the data for each type weighted by the (weighted) number in the group. The headline result is that Britain, along with Ireland, has much the largest estimates of the number of years poor out of five following poverty entry. The British average number is 3.46 years and the Irish average is 3.71

years. The third highest average is for Italy (3.19 years). The smallest average is for Denmark (2.23 years) and the second smallest average for Denmark (2.65 years). Given the limited range of possible values for the estimates, the British average is relatively large.

Damioli (2011*b*) carefully relates differences in the country-level averages to cross-national differences in population composition (for example, whether some countries have a relatively large proportion of elderly people or families with children among the poor) and to cross-national differences in the relationship between characteristics and poverty exit and re-entry hazard rates (that is, cross-national differences in model parameters). As is often the case in these sorts of decompositions, the differences in country averages are explained by a mixture of both factors. However, Damioli's overall assessment is that 'the cross-country variation in poverty persistence is driven more by differences in the poverty-generating process than by the heterogeneity in population composition' (2011*a*: 21).

In sum, this chapter has shown that hazard regression models are a useful way of describing people's chances of falling into poverty and climbing back out, and thence the total amount of time that people spend in poverty and the time between spells. Differences between individuals are straightforwardly described. The underlying event history for each individual is a binary sequence, with a string of ones representing a poverty spell and a string of zeros representing time out of poverty. But event-history analysis of spells is not the only way in which such data can be analysed. The next chapter considers an alternative method, a first-order Markov modelling approach.

11

Modelling Low Income Transitions: Estimates from a Markov Model

There are two types of multivariate model that are usually employed to study poverty dynamics. Most commonly used are hazard regression models of poverty exit rates and re-entry rates using data on spells, as in the previous chapter. The second approach fits a stochastic time-series structure to income itself, from which the implications for poverty are derived—these are the variance components models discussed earlier in the book (Chapters 6 and 7). There have been 'beauty contests' between the two approaches in which both types of model are fitted to the same data set and their goodness of fit to observed patterns of poverty dynamics compared. Stevens, using PSID data for the USA, reports 'that the hazard model reproduces observed patterns of poverty persistence somewhat better than the variance components model' (1999: 582), and Devicienti (2001: 31), using BHPS data for Britain, comes to a similar conclusion. In this chapter, a third type of model is proposed—a first-order Markov model of poverty transitions. This is fitted to BHPS data for working-age adults, covering survey years 1991–9, and used to summarize who is most likely to stay poor or to re-enter poverty, and poverty-spell lengths.

The Markovian model has strengths and weaknesses compared to its principal competitor, the hazard regression approach that jointly models poverty exits and entries and accounts for unobserved heterogeneity. The Markovian model is therefore proposed as a complement to the hazard regression approach rather than a substitute. As it happens, the two approaches yield broadly similar conclusions about patterns of poverty dynamics in Britain, as shown later in the chapter. The rest of this introduction summarizes the advantages and disadvantages of the Markovian approach relative to its competitors, with details of the model elaborated in Section 11.1.

The first strength of the Markovian model is that it is relatively straightforward to take account of 'initial conditions' problems (Heckman 1981*a*) and non-random attrition. These are both examples of so-called endogenous sample selection which, if ignored, can lead to biased estimates of the relationship between individual characteristics and the chances of poverty exit and entry. Although these endogenous selections could in principle be incorporated in hazard regression models, this is typically not done because of the difficulties of doing so.

The underlying problem is that if there are unobserved factors which determine the chances of poverty exit and entry, then this heterogeneity affects the poverty spell patterns that are observed in one's data set. At the start of the period covered by one's data set, there will be an over-representation of people who are prone to be poor. To get unbiased estimates of how poverty exit and entry chances differ for different types of individual, one needs to model initial poverty status jointly with poverty transition chances. Similar arguments apply to attrition. All applications of hazard regression models to poverty dynamics that I am aware of, including that of the previous chapter, assume that unobserved factors associated with poverty transition chances are unrelated to attrition, whether attrition arises because of refusal to participate further in the study or continuing to participate but not providing sufficient information to ascertain poverty status. (Models of labour market participation that allow for correlated attrition include those of Van den Berg, Lindeboom, and Ridder 1994 and Van den Berg and Lindeboom 1998.) But it may be that people who are less likely to exit poverty or more likely to re-enter are also more likely to attrit. In short, one needs to model the processes of poverty transition jointly with attrition, allowing for correlated unobservables. This can be done relatively straightforwardly in the Markovian model, as shown below.

The second strength of Markovian models is that left-censored spells are straightforwardly incorporated in the analysis. In the previous chapter, and in virtually all studies of poverty dynamics based on hazard regression models, left-censored observations are dropped from the analysis. Again, this is a practical matter: in principle, models can be developed incorporating left-censored spells, but it is complicated to do so in general either for computational reasons or because the data required to 'backcast' explanatory variables over time periods before the panel are simply unavailable (see Chapter 2). The left-censored spells that are dropped include the data for individuals who are observed to be poor every year that they are in the panel and for individuals who are never observed to be poor during the panel. The number of individuals dropped is substantial, increasing the chances that the data used to fit a hazard regression model are unrepresentative—long spells are more likely to be excluded. For a discussion of these issues with illustrations based on US poverty dynamics, see Iceland (1997) and Stevens (1999).

As illustrated in detail below, Markovian models can use all observed data for individuals because they are models of transitions between one year and the next—both transitions into and transitions out of poverty. Poverty status this year depends on poverty status last year, but not poverty status further back in time. This constrasts with hazard regression models in which poverty transition hazards are duration dependent—transition chances vary with the number of years a person has been poor (or non-poor). This contrast between the models also highlights a major disadvantage of Markovian models. The intrinsic dynamics of such models are not as sophisticated as those incorporated in hazard regression models or indeed in variance components models. Markovian models assume the accumulated impact of a person's history of poverty (and non-poverty) is expressed entirely by last year's poverty status. The effects of the past arise through 'state dependence' rather than depending on a longer history, as summarized by a pattern of duration dependence that arises as a spell unfolds.

A third advantage of first-order Markov models, and again a consequence of the way in which their dynamics are specified, is that simple closed-form expressions are available to summarize the distribution of poverty and non-poverty spell lengths (as I show below). This is not the case for discrete-time hazard regression models in general: the expressions relating differences in median poverty lengths to differences in characteristics are complicated non-linear expressions, and have to be derived numerically.

Markovian models for analysing dynamics are not new in general. What is new about this chapter's model is that it includes extensions to account for both initial conditions and attrition. The paper on which the chapter is based (Cappellari and Jenkins 2004) is the first such application to poverty dynamics, apart from the brief summary of preliminary estimates provided by Cappellari and Jenkins (2002a). Also a special case of the model has been applied to Australian data on poverty dynamics by Buddelmeyer and Verick (2008).

Most previous applications of Markovian models have been to the dynamics of benefit receipt or to the dynamics of low pay. Boskin and Nold's (1975) pioneering paper set out a Markovian model of US welfare benefit receipt dynamics which was applied to the UK by Böheim, Ermisch, and Jenkins (1999). See also Noble, Cheung, and Smith (1998). None of the papers cited account for unobserved heterogeneity, correlated attrition, or initial conditions. Chay and Hyslop (2000) and Chay, Hoynes, and Hyslop (2004) fit a number of Markovian models to data on US welfare benefit receipt, taking account of initial conditions issues and demonstrating their importance. The two models closest to the one set out in this chapter are those by Ribar (2005) of US welfare dynamics and by Cappellari and Jenkins (2008c, 2009) of social assistance dynamics in Britain, both of which jointly model entries and exits and take account of initial conditions. Among the models applied to transitions into and out of low earnings (rather than low income) in Britain, Stewart and Swaffield (1999) control for the endogeneity of initial conditions.

Cappellari and Jenkins (2008*a*, 2008*b*) extend their model to also incorporate correlated attrition and other endogenous selections. Bingley, Bjørn, and Westergård-Nielsen (1995) and Cappellari (2007) control for endogeneity in attrition as well as initial conditions in studies of earnings mobility in Denmark and Italy. Dutta, Sefton, and Weale (2001) propose a Markovian model of the dynamics of the market income (not poverty status) of working-age household heads, and fit it to data from BHPS waves 1–5. They take no account of attrition or initial conditions issues.

In Section 11.1, the extended Markovian model for poverty transitions is set out in detail, together with discussion of how estimates can be used to predict spell lengths for individuals with different sets of characteristics. Poverty status is measured using the 60 per cent of median line employed elsewhere in the book. Section 11.2 describes the BHPS data that are employed. Model estimates and their implications for poverty transition rates and spell lengths are set out in Section 11.3. An extension of the model that generalizes the specification of state dependence is considered in Section 11.4. Section 11.5 provides a brief summary and conclusions.

Before proceeding to the model, however, the relevance of issues such as state dependence, initial conditions, and selective attrition is illustrated by an examination of the raw poverty transition matrix from the data set (definitions are explained in detail later): see Table 11.1. Panel (a) shows the transition matrix constructed using data for all adults with two consecutive observations on income. This suggests that a substantial proportion, about four in ten, of those who were poor one year are no longer poor the following year. But clearly the chances of being poor in a given year differ substantially depending on poverty status in the previous year. (Also recall the similar

Table 11.1. Annual poverty inflow and outflow rates (row %), with and without missing income data

Poverty status, year t–1	Poverty status, year t		
	Not poor	Poor	Missing
(a) Sample with non-missing income at t			
Not poor	94.2	5.8	
Poor	41.5	58.5	
All	*87.9*	*12.1*	
(b) All individuals			
Not poor	84.3	5.2	10.6
Poor	36.3	50.8	13.3
All	*78.3*	*10.8*	*10.9*

Notes: Pooled transitions from BHPS waves 1–9. Sample size (panel b) = 44,772 adults aged 20–59, excluding full-time students. The poverty line is 60% of median contemporary equivalized real net household income. Missing income data at t arise from either sample attrition or incomplete response within a respondent's household. See text for further details.

findings reported in Table 8.3.) The poverty rate among those poor in the previous year is some 54 percentage points higher than the poverty rate among those non-poor in the previous year. This measure of 'aggregate' state dependence does not control for individual heterogeneity, observed or unobserved—a measure of 'genuine' state dependence that is developed later.

The high rates of persistence in the same state also raise questions about how it arises. Is it because people with relatively disadvantageous unobserved characteristics are over-represented among those who start out poor (in year t–1 here)? And, similarly, are people with relatively advantageous observed characteristics over-represented among those who are not poor? This 'endogenous selection' process is addressed by controlling for the observed and unobserved determinants of initial poverty status and allowing them to be correlated with the determinants of current poverty status. Another possible reason for the high rates of persistence in the same state—with potential knock-on effects for the estimates of state dependence—might be that that they are an artefact of using only two income categories, poor and non-poor. This issue is addressed in two ways, by investigating the effect on the results of varying the value of the poverty line, and considering a model in which there are five income classes at t–1.

The 'Missing' column in Table 11.1 panel (b) draws attention to the issue of non-random attrition because of sample dropout or item non-response on household income. (The attrition rate of 10.9 per cent arises in roughly equal measure from non-response by the individual concerned (5.6 per cent) and non-response by someone else in the individual's household.) The problem is not so much that a non-trivial proportion of the sample is not retained from one year to the next (reducing sample size), but that the retention rates differ by poverty status at t–1: 13.3 per cent for the poor and 10.6 per cent for the non-poor (raising questions about representativeness). The specification of the Markovian model allows for non-random retention and for its joint determination along with the initial conditions and poverty transition processes.

11.1. An Econometric Model of Poverty Transitions

The extended Markov approach models poverty transitions between two consecutive years, the base year and current year, labelled t–1 and t. There are four parts to the model: the determination of poverty status in period t–1 (to account for initial conditions), the determination of whether incomes are observed at both t–1 and t (income retention), the determination of poverty status in period t, and the correlations between the unobservables affecting

each of these processes. The combination of these four components characterizes the determinants of poverty persistence and poverty entry rates.

Assume that in the base year, period $t–1$, individuals have a latent propensity to be poor, p^*_{it-1}, of the following form:

$$p^*_{it-1} = \beta'x_{it-1} + \mu_i + \delta_{it-1}, \tag{11.1}$$

where $i = 1, \ldots N$ indexes individuals, x_{it-1} is a vector of explanatory variables
describing individual i and her household, β is a vector of parameters, and
error term u_{it-1} is the sum of an individual-specific effect plus an orthogonal
white noise error: $u_{it-1} = \mu_i + \delta_{it-1}$. The μ_i and δ_{it-1} are assumed to be normally
distributed; in particular u_{it-1} follows the standard normal distribution: $u_{it-1} \sim$
$N(0,1)$. The specification is equivalent to assuming a model of income in
which an arbitrary monotonic transformation of income is a linear function
of personal characteristics plus an error term that has the standard normal
distribution (Stewart and Swaffield 1999). If individual i's poverty propensity
exceeds some unobserved value (which can be set equal to zero without loss
of generality), then she is observed to be poor. Define a variable $P_{it-1} = 1$ if
$p^*_{it-1} > 0$ and zero otherwise.

Now consider the chances that those individuals with incomes observed in
the base year, period $t–1$, also have incomes observed at period t. Let r^*_{it}, i's
latent propensity of retention between $t–1$ and t, be summarized by the
relationship:

$$r^*_{it} = \psi'w_{it-1} + \eta_i + \xi_{it}, \tag{11.2}$$

where the error term v_{it} is the sum of a normal individual-specific effect (η_i)
plus a normal orthogonal white noise error (ξ_{it}) with $v_{it} \sim N(0,1)$, and ψ and
w_{it-1} are column vectors. If i's latent retention propensity is lower than some
critical threshold (again normalized to 0), then her income is not observed in
period t, and hence her poverty transition status is also not observed. Let R_{it} be
a binary indicator of the income retention outcome for each individual, where
$R_{it} = 1$ if $r^*_{it} > 0$ and zero otherwise.

The third component of the model is the specification for poverty status in
the current year, t. Let the latent propensity of poverty be characterized by

$$p^*_{it} = [(P_{it-1})\gamma_1' + (1 - P_{it-1})\gamma_2']z_{it-1} + \tau_i + \zeta_{it}, \tag{11.3}$$

where γ_1, γ_2, and z_{it-1} are column vectors, and the error term ε_{it} is the sum of a
normal individual-specific effect (τ_i) plus a normal orthogonal white noise
error (ζ_{it}), with $\varepsilon_{it} \sim N(0,1)$. Observed attributes are measured using base-year
values in order to better ensure that changes in poverty status reflect changes
in attributes rather than vice versa. Since equation (11.3) refers to poverty
status conditional on lagged poverty and attrition, the error term differs from
the error term in the expression for unconditional poverty status in the base

year, that is, equation (11.1). Define a variable $P_{it} = 1$ if $p_{it}^* > 0$ and zero otherwise. P_{it} is only observed if $R_{it} = 1$.

The specification in equation (11.3) states that the impact of explanatory variables on poverty in the current year differs depending on whether an individual is poor or not in the base year. The equation is an equation for conditional current poverty status but it is convenient to also refer to it as an equation for poverty transitions because, as shown below, the model also implies that a characteristic can have different impacts on poverty exit chances and poverty entry chances.

The error terms u_{it-1}, v_{it}, and ε_{it} are assumed to have a trivariate standard normal distribution which is characterized by three correlations to be estimated. The three variances are each normalized to be equal to one as they cannot be identified. Given the model assumptions, the correlations can be written as:

$$
\begin{aligned}
\rho_1 &\equiv \mathrm{corr}(u_{it-1}, v_{it}) = \mathrm{cov}(\mu_i, \eta_i) \\
\rho_2 &\equiv \mathrm{corr}(u_{it-1}, \varepsilon_{it}) = \mathrm{cov}(\mu_i, \tau_i) \\
\rho_3 &\equiv \mathrm{corr}(v_{it-1}, \varepsilon_{it}) = \mathrm{cov}(\eta_i, \tau_i).
\end{aligned}
\tag{11.4}
$$

Thus, the distribution of unobserved heterogeneity is parameterized (apart from the normalizations) in terms of the cross-equation correlations. The correlation ρ_1 summarizes the association between unobservable individual-specific factors determining base-year poverty status and income retention. A positive (respectively negative) sign indicates that individuals who are more likely to be initially poor are more (respectively less) likely to remain in the income distribution of the subsequent year compared to the non-poor. The ρ_2 is the correlation between unobservable individual-specific factors determining base-year poverty status and poverty transitions (that is, conditional current poverty status, $P_{it}|P_{it-1}$). A positive (respectively negative) sign indicates that individuals who are more likely to be initially poor are more (respectively less) likely to remain poor compared to the non-poor. The correlation ρ_3 summarizes the association between unobservable individual-specific factors determining retention propensities and those determining conditional current poverty status. A positive (respectively negative) sign indicates that individuals with incomes observed in two successive periods are more (respectively less) likely to remain poor or to fall into poverty compared to individuals more likely to attrit.

A sufficient condition for statistical identification of the transition model, given unconstrained cross-equation correlations, is a set of exclusion restrictions. There need to be factors affecting initial poverty or retention that have no direct effect on poverty transitions, that is, variables entering the x_{it-1} or w_{it-1} vectors but not the z_{it-1} one (see Section 11.3 for details). An alternative way to identify the model would be to constrain the cross-equation correlations to zero from the outset. Instead, the approach used here is to fit the general model with unconstrained correlations and to test whether income retention and initial conditions are exogenous. After all, these processes are of particular interest here. If $\rho_1 = \rho_3 = 0$, the income retention process is ignorable and the model reduces to a bivariate probit model of the type used by Stewart and Swaffield (1999) in their study of low earnings. If $\rho_1 = \rho_2 = 0$, there is no initial conditions problem: poverty status at t–1 may be treated as exogenous. And if $\rho_1 = \rho_2 = \rho_3 = 0$, poverty entry and exit equations may be estimated separately using simple univariate probit models.

Poverty Transition Probabilities

Of particular interest are the transition probabilities implied by the model: the probability of being poor at t, conditional on being poor at t–1 (the poverty persistence rate, s_{it}), and the probability of being poor at t, conditional on being non-poor at t–1 (the poverty entry rate, e_{it}). These are given, respectively, by:

$$s_{it} \equiv \Pr(P_{it} = 1 | P_{it-1} = 1) = \frac{\Phi_2(\gamma_1' z_{it-1}, \beta' x_{it-1}; \rho_2)}{\Phi(\beta' x_{it-1})} \qquad (11.5)$$

and

$$e_{it} \equiv \Pr(P_{it} = 1 | P_{it-1} = 0) = \frac{\Phi_2(\gamma_2' z_{it-1}, -\beta' x_{it-1}; \rho_2)}{\Phi(-\beta' x_{it-1})} \qquad (11.6)$$

where $\Phi(\cdot)$ and $\Phi_2(.)$ are the cumulative density functions of the univariate and bivariate standard normal distributions.

In the empirical application to follow, expressions for transition probabilities are derived by replacing population parameters by their sample estimates. Since explanatory variables are measured at year t–1, transition probabilities can be predicted also for the attritor subsample (individuals with $R_{it} = 0$), using estimates that are robust to non-random retention. Thus, one can predict what poverty persistence and entry rates would be were the subsample with $R_{it} = 0$ to have been observed in the income distribution at year t. By contrast, the aggregate transition rates in Table 11.1(a) only refer to the subsample with $R_{it} = 1$.

Implications of the Model for Poverty-Spell Durations and Poverty Recurrence Times

A feature of a first-order Markov model is that simple closed-form expressions are available to describe the distributions of spells of poverty and non-poverty (Boskin and Nold 1975). If one assumes a stationary environment, that is, that the system is in a long-run steady state, spell lengths of poverty and of non-poverty have a geometric distribution. The mean duration of a poverty spell is $1/(1-s_i)$, and the median duration is $\log(0.5)/\log(s_i)$, where the poverty persistence rate s_i is defined in (11.5) and the time subscript t has been omitted because of the stationarity assumption. The mean duration of a spell of non-poverty is $1/(e_i)$, and the median duration is $\log(0.5)/\log(1-e_i)$, where the poverty entry rate e_i is defined in (11.6). The unconditional (state) probability of being poor is $e_i/(e_i + 1-s_i)$.

Estimates of these statistics for individuals of different types are presented in Section 11.4. Assuming a stationary environment may sound problematic. But the assumption is effectively the same as that which is used when predicting spell distributions using hazard regression models. Recall from Chapter 10 that predictions are almost invariably undertaken assuming that all explanatory variables, including potentially time-varying ones, are fixed at constant values.

Testing for and Measuring State Dependence

In both hazard regression and Markovian models, the relationship between current poverty status and past poverty status is of critical interest. In the former approach, this relationship is characterized by the duration-dependence function; in the latter approach, it is state dependence that is the focus—the issue of whether past poverty genuinely affects current poverty chances or whether observed associations simply reflect the outcomes of observed or unobserved differences between individuals. It is useful to distinguish between aggregate state dependence and genuine state dependence. Aggregate state dependence is the simple difference between the probability of being poor for those who were poor last period and the probability of being poor for those who were not poor, as discussed in the context of Table 11.1(a) in the introduction. This measure takes no account of individual heterogeneity. Using transition rates predicted from the model, a straightforward measure of aggregate state dependence (ASD) is:

$$\text{ASD} = \left(\frac{\displaystyle\sum_{i \in \{P_{it-1}=1\}} \Pr(P_{it} = 1 | P_{it-1} = 1)}{\displaystyle\sum_i P_{it-1}} \right) \left(\frac{\displaystyle\sum_{i \in \{P_{it-1}=0\}} \Pr(P_{it} = 1 | P_{it-1} = 0)}{\displaystyle\sum_i (1 - P_{it-1})} \right)$$

(11.7)

Genuine state dependence arises ∈\when the chances of being poor in the current year depend on poverty status in the previous year, controlling for individual heterogeneity (observed and unobserved). For example, the experience of poverty itself might induce a loss of motivation, lowering the chances that an individual with given attributes escapes poverty in the future. Or it may be that employers treat past poverty as being informative about low employability so that poor unemployed people are less likely to get job offers, other things being equal.

A test for the absence of genuine state dependence can be formulated, given the model set out earlier, as a test of whether the impacts of characteristics do not depend on base-year poverty status, that is, the null hypothesis is that $\gamma_1 = \gamma_2$. Tests for genuine state dependence have been formulated differently in the context of other types of Markovian model. For example, Arulampalam, Booth, and Taylor (2000) use a dynamic random effects probit model of unemployment in which a binary variable summarizing unemployment status last period is used as a regressor. Their test for genuine state dependence in unemployment is based on whether the coefficient on lagged unemployment status is equal to zero. The test proposed in this chapter generalizes the Arulampalam, Booth, and Taylor (2000) test because the whole parameter vector associated with personal characteristics is allowed to differ according to status in the previous period.

This chapter's measure of the magnitude of genuine state dependence (GSD) is derived by calculating, for each individual, the difference between the predicted probability of being poor conditional on being poor last period and the predicted probability of being poor conditional on being non-poor last period, and then taking the average across all N individuals:

$$\text{GSD} = (1/N) \sum_{i=1}^{N} \Pr(P_{it} = 1|P_{it-1} = 1) - \Pr(P_{it} = 1|P_{it-1} = 0). \qquad (11.8)$$

The calculation of individual-specific probability differences (which are then averaged) ensures that individual heterogeneity is controlled for. Measures of aggregate and genuine state dependence can be computed for the whole sample (including individuals that attrit between $t-1$ and t). In Section 11.4, these measures are generalized to the case where there are five income classes at $t-1$ rather than two.

The Sample Likelihood and the Partial Likelihood Estimator

In the observed data, each individual may fall into one of six regimes corresponding to the six cells of Table 11.1(b). If incomes are observed for two consecutive periods ($R_{it} = 1$), then there are four possible outcomes depending on poverty status at each of period $t-1$ and t. And if individuals are not retained in the panel, then all that is observed is whether they were poor or non-poor at $t-1$ (two outcomes). It follows that the contribution to the log-likelihood for each individual i with poverty status observed in period $t-1$ is:

Poverty dynamics

$$\log L_i = P_{it-1}R_{it}\log[\Phi_3(k_i\gamma_1'z_{it-1}, m_i\psi'w_{it-1}, q_i\beta'x_{it-1}; k_im_i\rho_3, k_iq_i\rho_2; m_iq_i\rho_i)]$$
$$+(1-P_{it-1})R_{it}\log[\Phi_3(k_i\gamma_2'z_{it-1}, m_i\psi'w_{it-1}, q_i\beta'x_{it-1}; k_im_i\rho_3, k_iq_i\rho_2; m_iq_i\rho_2)]$$
$$+(1-R_{it})\log[\Phi_2(m_i\psi'w_{it-1}, q_i\beta'x_{it-1}; m_iq_i\rho_i)]$$

(11.9)

where $k_i \equiv 2P_{it}-1$, $m_i \equiv 2R_{it-1}-1$, $q_i \equiv 2P_{it-1}-1$.

The sample data consist of repeated observations on individuals from the same household at each t, and repeated observations on the same individual across successive pairs of years, because transitions are pooled from waves 1–9 of the BHPS (see below). Both types of repeated observation mean that the standard assumption underlying the maximum likelihood principle that observations are independently and identically distributed is violated. One approach to handling this issue is to assume a multi-level model structure with an individual-specific random effect (level one) and a household-specific random effect (level two), and to integrate these effects out across the pooled transitions, generalizing the model of Ribar (2005) to take account of non-random attrition. Conditional on the specification of the correlation structure, this approach provides consistent and efficient estimates of parameters and their asymptotic standard errors. It is computationally difficult to implement, however, and so instead an approach is used here that provides consistent parameter estimates, and which adjusts the standard errors using a robust variance estimator in order to account for the repeated observations (see the next paragraph). Another virtue of estimating the model by pooling transitions rather than integrating out the unobservables over the full sequence of observations is that it helps sidestep problems of bias that arise if experience of poverty in the past affects current living arrangements or labour market participation. (At the same time, such feedback effects between P_{t-2} and x_{t-1} are not examined and the longitudinal character of the data is not fully exploited and so estimates are inefficient relative to a model that does exploit them.) On this issue, and for a model extended to include feedback effects, see Biewen (2009).

In the language of Wooldridge (2002b: chapter 13), the sum of the expression given in equation (11.9) across individuals within households and across transition-years defines a sample partial log-likelihood. (See also Gourieroux and Monfort 1996 who use the term pseudo-likelihood.) Wooldridge explains that this is an M-estimator problem for which the estimators maximizing the partial likelihood are consistent and asymptotically normal (assuming fixed T and $N \to \infty$), but for which the standard errors need to be adjusted for the correlations between observations. The method is analogous to that used in the survey statistics literature for adjusting the estimates of the parameter covariance matrix to account for clustering induced by survey design. The robust variance estimators allow for arbitrary correlations between

340

observations within the same sample cluster, while assuming independence across clusters. See inter alia Huber (1967) and Binder (1983). In this chapter, each cluster is defined to consist of all the observations for all the individuals that were ever members of the same household in wave 1 of the BHPS panel. Adult respondents living in the same household at wave 1, but in a different household in wave 2 or subsequently (for example because of divorce or separation), are allocated to the same cluster. Adults who join the panel after wave 1 (typically by marriage to a respondent) are allocated to the same cluster as that of their household head. Children turning 16 and being interviewed as adult respondents in their own right are allocated to the same cluster as their parents. This approach allows for arbitrary correlations between observations from different individuals belonging to the same household, and also between observations on the same individual from different panel transitions.

The model looks computationally complicated, especially because of the dependence of the sample log-likelihood function on the trivariate standard normal distribution function $\Phi_3(.)$, and this function is not available in most statistical software packages. However, the function can be straightforwardly evaluated using simulation methods based on the so-called GHK simulator (Gourieroux and Monfort 1996: 93–107) and code for this is now freely available: see, for example, Cappellari and Jenkins (2006). The model parameter estimates reported in this chapter are derived using the GHK simulator with 250 random draws.

11.2. Data and Variables

This chapter uses data from waves 1–9 (survey years 1991–9) of the BHPS. Pairs of consecutive waves are used to identify low-income transitions, and estimation was based on a sample that pooled these transitions, as described in the previous section. The estimation sample is restricted to individuals aged 20–59 years in year t–1 who were not in full-time education.

As in the rest of this book, poverty status is assessed in terms of each individual's household income. The estimates reported here are based on a poverty line of 60 per cent of median income. The calculations were repeated with a number of alternative poverty lines but led to the same conclusions: see Cappellari and Jenkins (2002b).

The choice of explanatory variables follows previous literature: they mostly summarize the demographic composition and labour market attachment of the household in which an individual lives. All explanatory variables in the poverty transition equation (11.3) are measured using the values pertaining at the interview in the base year (t–1) and, again in common with virtually all the poverty modelling literature, are assumed to be pre-determined. (These form the elements of z_{it-1}.) Because poverty status is measured using a household-level income variable, most of the explanatory variables are measured at the household level. Variables summarizing the occurrence of trigger events are not used for the same reasons as discussed in the previous chapter. More specifically, the explanatory variables refer to the individual (age, sex), to the household head (age, sex, employment status, ethnic group), and to the household itself (several variables summarizing household composition, housing tenure, and the number of workers). In other words, the explanatory variables are very similar to those used in the hazard regression models discussed in the previous chapter. One difference is that the model in this chapter allows all three outcomes to vary by survey year as well as with other characteristics.

As explained in the previous section, statistical identification of model parameters requires exclusion restrictions, specifically that there are explanatory variables ('instruments') that affect initial conditions and sample retention but not poverty transitions, that is, variables entering the x_{it-1} or w_{it-1} vectors but not the z_{it-1} one. Heckman (1981b) suggests that, when modelling labour market outcomes, information about the individual prior to labour market entry can be used as an instrument for initial conditions. The instruments used here for base-year poverty status are a set of variables summarizing a respondent's parental socio-economic status measured when the respondent was aged 14. A set of binary variables is used to summarize parents' occupation (also including variables to indicate missing information on the items of interest). Thus, the explanatory variables for initial conditions (x_{it-1}) include all the variables used to explain poverty transitions (z_{it-1}) plus the parental background indicators. The instrument for sample retention is a binary variable indicating whether the individual is a BHPS original sample member (OSM) or not. BHPS respondents can be classified as OSMs or joiners (see Chapter 4). The former group have been in the panel since the first wave (1991); the latter joined the survey later by moving into an OSM's household. The use of this variable as an instrument assumes that OSMs are more stable survey members than joiners and that sample membership status is unrelated to poverty transition propensity. Thus, the determinants of sample retention (w_{it-1}) include all the variables used to explain poverty transitions plus the OSM indicator. In principle, other variables could be used as instruments, but they do not work well in the sense of being rejected by the formal statistical test described in the next paragraph. The specific variables are the share of respondents in the household classified by the interviewer as 'very good co-operators' in the interview and a binary variable summarizing whether there has been a change of interviewer between $t-2$ and $t-1$. Reassuringly, the parameter estimates are robust to whichever set of instruments is used.

The validity of the exclusion restrictions is tested by supposing that identification is achieved by the combination of the exclusion restrictions and the non-linear functional form of the model. If functional form is treated as a sole identifying restriction, the exclusion restrictions about parental background and sample membership status can be treated as over-identifying restrictions and their statistical significance tested. Test statistics are reported in the next section.

11.3. Model Estimates and their Implications

The results are discussed in two stages. Presented first are the estimates of the correlations between unobservables, associated tests of the exogeneity of initial conditions and of sample retention, and tests of goodness of fit. Second, the estimated impact of each explanatory variable on the poverty status is discussed, and I draw out the implications of the model for poverty transition probabilities, state dependence, and differences in spell lengths between different types of individual.

Testing the Model Specification

The introduction to this chapter emphasized that one of the strengths of the Markovian approach is the ability to straightforwardly account for initial conditions and non-random attrition. But are these issues important in practice? Testing for the exogeneity of the two selection mechanisms corresponds to testing for the separate and joint significance of the correlation coefficients associated with each of the two selection equations. Consider first the estimates of the correlations per se: see the top panel of Table 11.2. The correlation between unobservables affecting initial poverty and income retention (ρ_1) is negative and statistically significant, indicating a lower retention propensity among the initially poor compared to the non-poor—as found in Table 11.1(b). The correlation between unobservables affecting initial poverty and conditional current poverty (ρ_2) is also negative and statistically significant. Since this measures the correlation between the unobservable factors affecting initial poverty status and conditional current poverty status (which characterizes the poverty transition propensity), the negative sign can be interpreted as an example of regression towards the mean (Stewart and Swaffield 1999). Finally, the correlation between unobservable factors affecting income retention and poverty transition (ρ_3) is not precisely estimated.

The exogeneity tests are reported in the bottom panel of Table 11.2. Exogeneity of initial conditions would imply that ρ_1 and ρ_2 are jointly zero, but this hypothesis is strongly rejected (Wald test $p < 0.000$). Exogeneity of

Table 11.2. Estimates of model correlations, and model test statistics

Correlations between unobservables affecting:	Estimate	|t-ratio|
Base-year poverty status and retention (ρ_1)	−0.061	(2.980)
Base-year poverty status and conditional current poverty status (ρ_2)	−0.265	(2.980)
Retention and conditional current poverty status (ρ_3)	−0.029	(0.250)
Null hypotheses for tests	**Test statistic**	**p-value**
Exogeneity of initial conditions, $\rho_1 = \rho_2 = 0$	17.55	0.0002
Exogeneity of sample retention, $\rho_1 = \rho_3 = 0$	8.98	0.0112
Joint exogeneity, $\rho_1 = \rho_2 = \rho_3 = 0$	17.66	0.0005
Exclusion of parental background from transition equation (d.f. = 28)	32.15	0.2686
Exclusion of sample membership status from transition equation (d.f. = 2)	0.96	0.6190
Exclusion of parental background and sample membership status from transition equation (d.f. = 30)	33.51	0.3007
Inclusion of parental background in initial conditions equation (d.f. = 14)	24.87	0.0359
Inclusion of sample membership status in retention equation (d.f. = 1)	466.68	0.0000
Normality of u_{it-1} (base-year poverty)	48.12	0.000
Normality of v_{it} (sample retention)	123.04	0.000
Normality of ε_{it} (current poverty)	1.77	0.413
No state dependence, $\gamma_1 = \gamma_2$ (d.f. = 36)	332.47	0.0000

Notes: See text for discussion of model estimation method and tests.

income retention, on the other hand, can be tested by testing the joint significance of ρ_1 and ρ_3. Again, a Wald test rejects the null hypothesis, although rejection is less evident than in the previous case—which is unsurprising given that ρ_3 was imprecisely estimated—but still with a level of joint significance of 1 per cent. The result indicates that retention is endogenous for poverty transitions, whereas the point estimates of the correlation coefficients indicate that endogeneity operates via a correlation with initial conditions rather than directly affecting transition probabilities. Finally, the test for the joint significance of the three correlation coefficients indicates that they are jointly significant with a p-value of less than 1 per cent. In sum, the tests on correlations of the unobservables indicate that initial conditions and income retention are endogenous—which justifies the general modelling approach.

Regarding the validity of the instruments, the estimates shown in the bottom panel of Table 11.2 indicate that parental background indicators and the sample membership variable can be excluded from the transition equation, both separately and jointly, with excludability more evident in the case of sample membership status. (The p-values for the separate Wald tests are 0.27 and 0.62, and 0.30 for the joint test.) Note too that these variables are found to be statistically significant in the two selection equations (p-values of 0.04 and 0.00). In sum, the validity of the proposed instruments is supported by the data.

The assumption of normality of the marginal distributions of random effects u_{it-1}, v_{it}, and ε_{it} is tested using standard conditional moment tests. Normality cannot be rejected for the current poverty equation, but is strongly rejected in the other equations (Table 11.2). Note, however, that the normality assumption is required for tractability of estimation and, in any case, despite the normality test statistics, the model fits the data remarkably well. For example, the average predicted probability of poverty persistence among respondents present at t and t–1 is 0.5846, which is almost identical to the sample transition proportion of 0.5850 (Table 11.1a). Similarly, the average predicted probability of poverty entry among respondents present at t and t–1 is 0.0576, which is identical to the sample transition proportion (Table 11.1a).

The Impacts of the Explanatory Variables on Transition Probabilities

The impacts of the explanatory variables on poverty transitions (equation 11.3) are summarized in Table 11.3. (The estimates for initial poverty status and retention are provided by Cappellari and Jenkins 2002b: table A1.) There are two sets of estimates, depending on poverty status at t–1. The first column of each set shows the marginal effect of a change in each explanatory variable in z_{it-1} on the probability of poverty persistence and on the probability of poverty entry, that is, s_{it} and e_{it} in equations (11.5) and (11.6). The probability of the conditioning event—being poor or non-poor in the base year, respectively—is held constant in each case.

To define the marginal effects associated with the probability of remaining poor (s_{it}), one has to take account of the fact that a change in one of the determinants of poverty transitions (an element of z_{it-1}) also implies a change in the corresponding element of the x_{it-1} vector (as the determinants of initial conditions share many common elements), and this latter change alters the value of the denominator in (11.5), that is, the probability of being poor in the base year. In order to hold this constant, the marginal effect is calculated as follows (see also Stewart and Swaffield 1999). First, the predicted probability of poverty in the base year is computed for all respondents who are poor, and the average taken of these values. Label this average c. The value of the index corresponding to this probability, $d \equiv \Phi^{-1}(c)$, is then substituted into equation (11.5), leading to the expression $\Phi_2(\gamma_1' z_{it-1}, d; \rho_2)/d$. Marginal effects for binary explanatory variables are calculated as the changes in this expression that are implied by a unit change in each characteristic, other things being equal, relative to the characteristics of a reference person. (For age variables, the marginal effect is the change induced by an infinitesimal change in the covariate, with other covariates evaluated at sample mean values.) The reference person is defined by setting the continuous covariates (age and household head's age) equal to the sample median values (37 years and 41 years), and all the remaining binary variables to zero. The marginal effects associated with the poverty entry probability (e_{it}) are calculated similarly.

Table 11.3. Estimates of model of poverty status at t, conditional on poverty status at $t–1$

Covariate (measured at $t–1$)	Poor at $t–1$		Non-poor at $t–1$	
	Marginal effect	|t-ratio|	Marginal effect	|t-ratio|
Individual characteristics				
Age	0.003	(0.43)	–0.004	(2.00)
Age squared	–0.00002	(0.22)	0.00006	(3.00)
Female	–0.015	(1.50)	0.010	(3.33)
Household head's characteristics				
Age	0.008	(1.14)	–0.003	(3.00)
Age squared	–0.00004	(0.50)	0.00004	(4.00)
Female	0.041	(1.58)	–0.018	(2.57)
Has A-levels or higher educational qualification	–0.061	(1.97)	–0.031	(5.17)
Works full-time	0.011	(0.30)	–0.029	(3.22)
Works part–time	0.022	(0.55)	0.040	(2.50)
Ethnic group				
Black Caribbean	0.132	(1.59)	–0.069	(2.65)
Black African	–0.014	(0.10)	–0.011	(0.31)
Black Other	0.039	(0.40)	0.028	(0.42)
Indian	0.070	(0.58)	0.032	(0.80)
Pakistani or Bangladeshi	0.158	(2.26)	0.205	(1.69)
Chinese	–0.151	(0.91)	0.397	(3.20)
Other ethnic origin	0.150	(1.30)	–0.053	(2.30)
Household characteristics				
Lone-parent household	0.008	(0.25)	0.047	(2.94)
Other household type	0.064	(1.07)	–0.002	(0.13)
Presence in household of				
adult aged 60–75	–0.045	(0.69)	–0.034	(2.62)
adult aged 76+	–0.106	(0.79)	–0.080	(5.00)
children aged 0–2	0.043	(1.43)	0.032	(2.67)
children aged 3–4	0.077	(2.85)	0.052	(4.00)
children aged 5–11	0.092	(3.68)	0.052	(5.20)
children aged 12–15	0.021	(0.72)	0.049	(4.08)
children aged 16–18	0.053	(0.91)	0.015	(0.79)
Number of workers	–0.047	(1.38)	–0.043	(8.60)
Lives in social housing	0.033	(1.32)	0.112	(8.00)
Multi-family household	–0.185	(3.49)	0.043	(2.39)
Log-likelihood		–34,832		
Model chi-square (d.f. = 155)		5,830 ($p < 0.000$)		
Number of clusters (wave 1 households)		3,426		
Number of observations (persons)		9,279		
Number of observations (person-waves)		44,602		

Notes: See text for description of estimation method and definition of marginal effects. Regressions also include survey-year dummies. Reference categories for binary variables: male, male household head with no A-levels, not working and of European ethnic origin, married couple household with no elderly or children, not living in social housing and single family, base year is 1991.

Consider first the estimates of probability of being poor at t for people who are poor at $t–1$. There are few explanatory variables with statistically significant associations at the 5 per cent level or better. This may surprise some readers, but recall that the equation is for the probability of remaining poor for people who are poor. If the transition equation is fitted ignoring initial conditions, then some characteristics, such as educational qualifications and the number of household workers, are more strongly statistically significant. This suggests that the weaker effects observed in more general models arise because the effects of endogeneity are being accounted for.

Having a household head with A-levels is associated with a conditional poverty probability some six percentage points lower than someone with less education. Ethnic group effects are often hard to identify in the BHPS because of small cell sizes, but it is apparent nonetheless that individuals with household heads of Pakistani or Bangladeshi ethnic origin have much higher poverty probabilities than those of European origin: the marginal effect is 16 percentage points. Having more children aged 3–4 years or 5–11 years is associated with conditional poverty risks eight and nine percentage points higher. Finally, living in a multi-family household is associated with a decrease in conditional poverty risk: the probability is 19 percentage points lower than for those in single-family households. This is a large decrease relative to a sample average poverty persistence probability of between 50 and 60 per cent (Table 11.1).

Consider now the estimates of the probability of being poor at t for those who are not poor at $t-1$. In this part of the model, there are many statistically significant associations. For instance, higher risks of poverty are associated with being older, and having a household head who is older, is male, has educational qualifications below A-levels, and who does not work at all or who works part-time. Ethnic origin has large effects. Compared to individuals with a household head of European origin, having a household head of Pakistani/ Bangladeshi or Chinese ethnic origin means a poverty risk of about 21 and 40 percentage points higher respectively. (The sample average entry probability is around 6 per cent: see Table 11.1.) Poverty risks are also higher for individuals living in lone-parent families and multi-family households (for whom the marginal effects are four to five percentage points), for those living in social housing (11 percentage points), and for those having fewer workers in the household (four percentage points). In addition, the presence of individuals aged 60+ lowers poverty risks, whereas the presence of dependent children aged 0–15 raises them.

Predicted Poverty Transition Probabilities and Poverty Spell Lengths

An alternative and perhaps more intuitive way of exploring the implications of the estimates is to examine the predicted probabilities of poverty entry and exit that they imply for persons with different combinations of characteristics. With the additional assumption that all relevant processes are in a stationary equilibrium, then one can also derive what these poverty transition rates imply for the (cross-sectional) probability of being poor in any given year, for the average lengths of time spent poor for those beginning a spell, and the average poverty recurrence time for those ending a poverty spell, as shown in Section 11.2. By construction, the estimates control for the selection biases associated with initial poverty status and retention.

The predictions are summarized in Table 11.4, and are derived using the point estimates of the parameters shown in Table 11.3 and the formulae in equations (11.5) and (11.6). (Since a number of estimated coefficients were not statistically significant, the table refers only to changes in characteristics associated with coefficients that are significant.) The reference person, case 1, is a man aged 40, working full-time, whose household head has no A-levels and is of European origin, living in a single-family single-earner household comprising a married couple with one child aged 5–11, with no adults aged 60+ present, and who are not living in social housing. This man's predicted poverty persistence rate is just under one-half (0.48) and his predicted poverty entry rate is about one in 15 (0.07). With the stationarity assumption, these rates imply a probability of being poor of just over one in ten (0.12), a mean poverty spell length of 1.9 years, and mean time between poverty spells of 14.7 years. The estimates of median spell lengths are smaller than the corresponding means (0.9 years and 9.9 years respectively). This is what one expects because spell-length distributions are typically skewed, with a high prevalence of relatively short spells and a lower prevalence of long spells. However, the magnitude of the differences between the mean and the median indicates that there is much dispersion in spell lengths even among individuals sharing the same characteristics.

Having A-level or higher educational qualifications (case 2) lowers the poverty persistence rate and the poverty entry rate compared to the reference person, to 0.42 and 0.05 years respectively, implying shorter poverty spells (the median falls to 0.79 years from 0.94 years) and longer median poverty recurrence times (up to 14.2 years from 9.9 years). By contrast, having a household head of Pakistani or Bangladeshi ethnic origin (case 3) implies a much larger persistence rate (0.64) and a much larger entry rate (0.22). The predicted probability of being poor in any given year is 0.38, the median poverty spell length is 1.6 years, and the median recurrence time is only 2.7 years. Having an additional young child in the household has an even larger impact (case 5): the persistence rate becomes 0.56 and the entry rate 0.10, implying a median poverty spell length of 2.3 years and a median recurrence time of 1.9 years. The predicted probability of being poor in a given year is almost one-fifth (0.19). Living in social housing (case 4) provides estimates in between those for the reference man and these two cases. Having no children (case 6) or an additional worker in the household (case 7) has a clearly beneficial effect—predicted spell lengths are shorter and recurrence times are longer than for the reference person—and of much the same magnitude. For

Table 11.4. Predicted poverty transition probabilities, and steady-state probabilities and spell durations

Characteristics	Poverty persistence rate (s_{it})	Poverty entry rate (e_{it})	Pr(poor)	Poverty spell duration (years) mean	median	Non-poverty spell duration (years) mean	median
1. Man aged 40, working full-time; household head has no A-levels, of European origin, one worker in household, single-family household, married couple with one child aged 5–11, no adults aged 60+ present, not living in social housing	0.48	0.07	0.12	1.9	0.9	14.7	9.9
2. As (1), except household head has A-levels	0.42	0.05	0.08	1.7	0.8	21.0	14.2
3. As (1), except household head of Pakistani or Bangladeshi origin	0.64	0.22	0.38	2.8	1.6	4.5	2.8
4. As (1), except lives in social housing	0.51	0.15	0.23	2.1	1.0	6.7	4.3
5. As (1), except also has child aged 3–4	0.56	0.10	0.19	2.3	1.2	9.6	6.3
6. As (1), except no children present	0.38	0.04	0.06	1.6	0.7	23.7	16.1
7. As (1), except one additional worker	0.43	0.04	0.07	1.8	0.8	24.9	16.9
8. As (1), except woman, not working; no workers in household	0.55	0.18	0.29	2.2	1.2	5.4	3.4
9. As (8), except lives in social housing	0.58	0.33	0.44	2.4	1.3	3.1	1.8
10. As (8), except also has child aged 3–4	0.63	0.25	0.40	2.7	1.5	4.0	2.4
11. As (8), except head works full-time	0.51	0.09	0.16	2.1	1.0	10.8	7.2

Notes: Predicted persistence rates and entry rates derived from equations (11.5) and (11.6), together with the point estimates reported in Table 11.3. The estimates in the other columns are derived assuming a steady-state equilibrium and using the formulae presented in Section 11.2.

example, the state probabilities of poverty are roughly halved, to 0.06 and 0.07 respectively.

The non-working lone mother described in cases 8–10 has, as expected, a much higher poverty persistence rate and a higher poverty rate than the corresponding reference married man in full-time work. For example, the state probability of being poor for the reference lone mother (case 8) is more than double that of the reference man (case 1): 0.29 compared to 0.12. This adverse differential persists across the other types of lone mother. If the lone mother has an additional child aged 3–4 (case 9), the probability of being poor in a given year increases to 0.40 (compared to 0.19 for case 5), the predicted median poverty spell length is 1.5 years (compared to 1.2 years), and the median recurrence time 2.4 years (compared to 6.3 years). Even if the lone mother is in full-time work (case 11), the probability of being poor remains relatively high (0.16).

Table 11.4 also suggests that there is greater individual heterogeneity in poverty entry rates than in poverty persistence rates. To put things another way, the large differences in predicted state probabilities of being poor appear related more to differences in the lengths of time spent out of poverty rather than to differences in the lengths of time spent in poverty. (And this in turn arises from the fact that coefficients in the poverty persistence equation are smaller and less significant than those in the entry equation.) This finding is of policy relevance: anti-poverty policies need not only to facilitate exits from poverty but also to stop people falling back in or becoming poor for the first time.

Predicted transition rates also provide information about the consequences of ignoring the endogeneity of initial poverty status and of retention. This issue is examined with reference to estimates from three variants of the general model: (a) one treating initial poverty status as endogenous and retention as exogenous, (b) one treating retention as endogenous and initial poverty status as exogenous, and (c) one treating both processes as exogenous. Model (a) leads to under-estimates of both poverty persistence rates and poverty entry rates (relative to the corresponding estmates shown in Table 11.4), whereas models (b) and (c) each lead to over-estimates. For example, for the reference person, the preferred model implies a poverty persistence rate of 0.480 and a poverty entry rate of 0.068 (Table 11.4, row 1). By contrast, for model (a), the corresponding estimates are 0.47 and 0.07; for model (b), they are 0.57 and 0.08 and, for model (c), 0.53 and 0.07. The predicted probabilities of being poor in a given year are 0.11, 0.15, 0.14 for models (a)–(c) respectively, and the predicted mean poverty-spell durations are 1.87, 2.32, and 2.14 years. That is, they are substantially different from the corresponding estimates in Table 11.4, especially for model (b). Model (a) provides predicted rates that are the least biased, which suggests that neglecting to control for initial conditions is more problematic than neglecting to control for endogeneity of retention. Consistent with this observation, recall that the estimated correlation between base-year poverty status and conditional current poverty status (ρ_2) is much larger in magnitude than the other two correlations. The practical importance of initial conditions relative to non-random attrition is also reported by Cappellari and Jenkins (2008a, 2008b) in their analysis using Markovian models of low pay dynamics in Britain. The relative unimportance of controlling for attrition also echoes the conclusions earlier in this book that estimates of income mobility are little affected by whether the data are weighted or not.

State Dependence in Low Income

The results displayed in Table 11.3 suggest that observed characteristics have different impacts on the chances of being poor depending on whether an individual is already poor or not—a finding consistent with the existence of genuine state dependence in low income. A formal test for the absence of genuine state dependence, based on the null hypothesis that $\gamma_1 = \gamma_2$, has a Wald test statistic of 332.470 (d.f. = 36), with $p < 0.0000$ (Table 11.2). The null hypothesis is therefore overwhelmingly rejected.

Measures of aggregate state dependence and genuine state dependence can be calculated using the formulae shown in equations (11.7) and (11.8). Aggregate state dependence is estimated to be 0.526 when calculated using all sample respondents present at t–1. By contrast, the corresponding estimate of genuine state dependence is 0.310, indicating that a substantial proportion of state dependence is genuine (0.310 is 59 per cent of 0.526). This fraction is in line with the estimates of aggregate and genuine state dependence that Stewart and Swaffield (1999) report, albeit for low pay rather than for household income as in this chapter. Although the degree of aggregate state dependence in poverty found here is similar to that reported by Hill (1981) for the USA in the 1970s, the estimate of genuine state dependence is rather larger than hers, though she did not control for initial conditions or differential retention.

11.4. Is the Estimate of Genuine State Dependence Sensitive to Model Specification?

The estimates indicate that the magnitude of genuine state dependence is substantial, but it might be argued that this result arises simply because only two income bands are used to describe the base-year income distribution and this constrains the nature of its relationship to current poverty chances. The genuine state dependence measure characterized in (11.8) is based on the difference in the parameters indexing transition probabilities, γ_1 and γ_2. Since γ_2 is estimated using data for all individuals with a base-year income above the poverty line, then arguably the genuine state dependence finding might simply reflect substantial heterogeneity among all of the individuals who are initially not poor. This section assesses the robustness of the earlier result by using a greater number of categories of base-year income in order to differentiate among non-poor individuals.

Specifically, while continuing to use a 60-per-cent-of-median cut-off to differentiate between poor and non-poor individuals, the non-poor group is now broken down into four groups by introducing three additional income thresholds, namely 80 per cent, 100 per cent, and 150 per cent of the median. Examination of aggregate poverty transition rates based on this five income band classification reveals that, when moving from lower to higher incomes, the probability of entering poverty declines monotonically, with a considerable drop (14 percentage points) occurring between the poorest and second poorest of the non-poor income groups (Cappellari and Jenkins 2002b, table 7). Differences in retention rates across the four groups of non-poor individuals are negligible.

Heterogeneity among the initially non-poor is introduced by re-specifying the initial condition equation as an ordered probit regression for the five income classes defined in the previous paragraph. There are three additional thresholds in the support of p_{it-1}^*, and the discrete indicator of initial income becomes polychotomous: $p_{it-1}^* = 1$ if $p_{it-1}^* > 0$, 0 if $0 \geq p_{it-1}^* > \tau_1$, -1 if $\tau_1 \geq p_{it-1}^* > \tau_2$, -2 if $\tau_2 \geq p_{it-1}^* > \tau_3$, and -3 if $\tau_3 \geq p_{it-1}^*$, where $0 > \tau_1 > \tau_2 > \tau_3$. Accordingly, the period t poverty equation has five regimes:

$$\Pr(P_{it} = 1) = \Phi(\gamma_j' z_{it-1}) \text{ if } p_{it-1}^\circ = j \text{ and } R_{it} = 1, \qquad (11.10)$$

where $j = -3, -2, -1, 0$, and 1.

The other model components (the retention equation and distribution of the error terms) remain specified as in Section 11.2. The absence of genuine state dependence is tested by examining the difference between γ_1 and each of the other vectors of coefficients indexing transition probabilities. To measure aggregate and genuine state dependence in this context, the definition proposed earlier is extended to take account of multiple base-year income bands. Since the two measures of state dependence are computed by comparing conditional poverty probabilities between the initially poor and non-poor, one can now compute as many indicators of them as there are non-poverty states in the base year. For initial non-poor income class j, aggregate state dependence (ASD_j) is computed as the difference between the predicted probability of persistence (averaged over the initially poor) and the weighted average of predicted entry probabilities taken over the initially non-poor in all classes up to the jth, with the weights being the proportion of respondents falling into each of the non-poor income classes:

$$\mathrm{ASD}_j = \left[\sum_{i \in \{P^\circ_{it-1}=1\}} \Pr(P_{it-1}|P^\circ_{it-1}=1) \Big/ \sum_i (P^\circ_{it-1}=1) \right]$$
$$- \sum_{k=0}^{|j|} w^j_k \left[\sum_{i \in \{P^\circ_{it-1}=-k\}} \Pr(P_{it}=1|P^\circ_{it-1}=-k) \Big/ \sum_i (P^\circ_{it-1}=-k) \right] \tag{11.11}$$

for $j = -3, -2, -1$, and 0, where w^j_k are the weights and $I(.)$ is an indicator function taking value 1 when its argument holds and 0 otherwise. (Weights are normalized to sum to unity, that is, different sets of weights are used for the four indices of aggregate state dependence that can be computed.) Similarly, the measure of genuine state dependence (GSDj) for initial non-poor income class j is obtained by computing, for each individual in j, the difference between the conditional poverty probability for each individual i were she poor in the base year and the weighted average of the poverty probabilities conditional on membership of all non-poor income classes up to and including j:

$$\mathrm{GSD}_{ij} = \Pr(P_{it}=1|P^\circ_{it-1}=1) - \sum_{k=0}^{|j|} w^j_k \Pr(P_{it}=1|P_{it-1}=-k) \tag{11.12}$$

for $j = -3, -2, -1$, and 0. The summary measure of genuine state dependence for class j is obtained by averaging this expression over all individuals.

Estimates of the model with the five-class distribution in year t–1 are reported by Cappellari and Jenkins (2002b: tables 8 and A2). Tests for the absence of genuine state dependence confirm the previous findings, always rejecting this hypothesis with p-values < 0.0000. Thus, even for individuals with base-year incomes just above the poverty line, the impact of observed characteristics on poverty transition propensities differs from the impact for those who are initially poor. This finding indicates that the earlier results are robust to the categorization of the base-year income distribution. Estimates of state dependence based on the measures defined in equations (11.11) and (11.12) indicate that genuine state dependence is relevant even if one focuses only on the lower range of the year t–1 income distribution. Comparisons of the conditional poverty probabilities for the initially poor and those with an income between the poverty line (60 per cent of median income) and 80 per cent of the median show that 65 per cent of aggregate state dependence is accounted for by genuine state dependence. In other words, the earlier results about the importance of genuine state dependence are not driven by neglect of heterogeneous impacts of past income among the non-poor population.

The large proportion of aggregate state dependence accounted for by genuine state dependence indicates that a non-trivial part of poverty persistence may be ascribed to past poverty experiences. The labour market is the most obvious source of state dependence, since labour earnings form the largest fraction of household income packages and is the source most researched so far in Britain: see, for example, Stewart and Swaffield (1999), Arulampalam, Booth, and Taylor (2000), and the papers in the November 2001 *Economic Journal* (Arulampalam, Gregg, and Gregory 2001).

11.5. Summary and Conclusions

The aims of this chapter have been twofold: to set out the case for an approach to modelling poverty dynamics that complements existing multivariate methods, of which discrete-time hazard regression models are the most commonly employed, and to illustrate the proposed model in action. The chapter shows that there is a useful role for first-order Markov models as they can relatively straightforwardly account for the potential endogeneity of both initial poverty status and sample retention, and handle left-censored spell data, and yet also provide estimates of the probabilities of entering and remaining poor, poverty spell lengths, and poverty recurrence times, for individuals with different characteristics. The main disadvantages of the Markovian approach are that it does not fully exploit the longitudinal sequences of data for individuals nor, related, does it allow for more sophisticated dynamics. Development of second-order Markov models would be one route to addressing this deficit: see Chay, Hoynes, and Hyslop (2004) for an example.

Fitting of the Markovian model to BHPS data for the 1990s confirms that initial conditions and sample retention issues are endogenous in the estimation of poverty transition equations, with the former appearing to be of greater practical importance. The substantive results about the chances of poverty entry and exit are similar to those reported in the previous chapter and derived using hazard regression models. That is, there appears to be substantial heterogeneity in the rates of movement into and out of poverty. Married couples have both lower poverty entry rates and lower poverty persistence rates than lone mothers, which is another way of saying that the latter group have longer spells of poverty and shorter spells of non-poverty. These relativities are, of course, exactly what one would expect; the strength of multivariate models is that they also provide predictions about the specific magnitudes of differences for individuals from a range of household types.

Finally, the estimates from the Markovian model show that, notwithstanding the substantial differences in poverty propensities associated with individual heterogeneity, there is also non-trivial state dependence in low income in Britain. Experience of poverty in the past affects your chances of being poor—which is the same message as implied by the estimates of duration dependence in the hazard regression models. Precisely why there are these effects is an important topic for further research about the causes of poverty.

Envoi

12

Summary and Conclusions

This book is a study of Britain's income distribution that provides an avowedly longitudinal perspective to complement and supplement the (repeated) cross-section perspective that is more commonly available. In this concluding chapter, I review some of the main lessons of the book, referring in turn to concepts, research findings and policy implications, data and measures, and modelling. Under each heading, I also refer to a number of topics for future research.

Concepts

There are important ways in which information about longitudinal changes in people's incomes—income mobility and poverty dynamics—are relevant to social assessments of the income distribution (Chapter 1). Income mobility can be defined in terms of changes in relative position, longer-term inequality reduction, individual income growth, and income risk, each with different connections with social welfare. For example, greater independence of income destinations from income origins may be viewed as welfare-improving because it corresponds to greater equality of opportunity. Such turnover in positions may also reduce longer-term inequality. But for every income rise, there is typically an income fall. From a mobility-as-income-growth perspective, the income increases and decreases—or differential growth more generally—have different effects on social welfare and the overall gain or loss depends on whether it is rich people or poor people who gain more. And greater longitudinal flux in incomes can also correspond to greater income risk, depending on the extent to which people are able to cope with greater variability.

Poverty dynamics are a special case of income mobility, referring to longitudinal changes in income relative to a low income cut-off, but of special importance because of particular social interest in maintaining incomes above some minimum level. As with income mobility, there are multiple ways of summarizing poverty dynamics and poverty persistence, ranging from simple counts of the numbers of time poor over a period to spell-based approaches (Chapter 8). Whichever approach is taken, the longitudinal approach draws attention to differences between one-off experiences of poverty, repeated poverty, and persistent poverty, each of which has different implications for individuals' economic well-being. How long and how often people are poor are important dimensions of poverty that are missed by cross-sectional measures.

There is scope for future research clarifying what it is about income mobility and poverty dynamics that are of fundamental social concern. For example, regarding mobility, I have explained the different concepts but not seriously evaluated their relative merits—apart from raising some questions about the merits of the mobility-as-equality-of-opportunity idea in the context of short-run intragenerational income change rather than intergenerational income change. On poverty dynamics, more reflection is required about the trade-off in social assessments between different types of longitudinal poverty patterns, for example between a long but continuous spell and multiple repeated spells of the same total time spent poor. This analysis needs to be informed by detailed empirical evidence about people's lifestyles and living standards in the two situations—how they cope with 'shocks' and their abilities to borrow and save, draw down, or accumulate assets, or utilize private and social insurance mechanisms. This evidence is also relevant to judgements about the extent to which existing measures of transitory variation and vulnerability are genuinely informative about income 'risk'. Additional factors to take into account in the development of longitudinal measures are the depth of poverty throughout a spell (ignored in this book) and how to deal with censored spell data.

Patterns of Income Mobility and Poverty Dynamics: Longitudinal Flux is Pervasive

There is a substantial degree of income mobility between one year and the next in Britain, though most mobility is short distance rather than long distance. There is a lot of change in relative position and some reduction in longer-term inequality, but associations between income origins and destinations do not fall to zero even after a decade and a half. This pattern describes the situation for all income groups, from rich to poor (Chapter 5).

The research reported in this book also shows that there is no unchanging population of poor people (Chapter 7). The biblical statement that 'For ye have the poor always with you' (Matthew 26: 11) remains true today, especially when poverty is defined as a cut-off that is a fraction of contemporary average income, but it is also important to remember that it is not the same people who are poor always. There is substantial turnover and churning in the low-income population between one year and the next. It also means that over a period of several years, many more people experience poverty than are poor in any single year.

These longitudinal patterns are consistent with what I call a Rubber Band model of income (which is the canonical random effects model of Chapter 6 expressed in metaphorical terms):

> Each person's income fluctuates about a relatively fixed longer-term average—this value is a tether on the income scale to which people are attached by a rubber band. They may move away from the tether from one year to the next, but not too far because of the band holding them. And they tend to rebound back towards and around the tether over a period of several years. In the short-term some of the observed movement may simply be measurement error and, in the long term, the position of each person's tether will move with secular income growth or career developments. But, in addition, rubber bands will break if stretched too far by 'shocks', leading to significant changes in relative income position. (Jenkins 2008: 2)

Examples of these shocks are job gain and loss, household formation and dissolution, and so on—these are the trigger events whose associations with poverty entries and exits are considered in Chapter 9. (Not all trigger events lead to a poverty transition, as the chapter also shows.) For households headed by people of working age, changes in household labour earnings are the events that account for the largest shares of all poverty exits and entries. Changes in earnings for household members other than the household head play a substantial role, especially for exits from poverty. Changes in household headship such as when marital partnerships form or split, or other demographic change, account for a non-negligible proportion of poverty transitions with the share greater for poverty entries than for poverty exits.

To some extent, these results are the straightforward consequence of using equivalized household income as the measure of an individual's living standards. But they are also an important reminder that individuals' experiences of income mobility and poverty dynamics depend on their household context and changes in it—not only the changing combination of income sources from all the individuals in the household but also changes in household composition itself.

Underneath the broad-brush picture describing the situation for the population as a whole, there are major differences in the experiences of income mobility and poverty dynamics for different groups. To pick two examples, transitory variability in income is lower for older people (Chapter 6), and lone-parent families and pensioners have distinctly high rates of persistent poverty, whether this is summarized using simple descriptive statistics or more sophisticated multivariate econometric models of poverty exit and re-entry (Chapters 8, 10, and 11).

The accumulation of year-on-year changes, combined with secular growth in income and career income growth, characterize longer-term income mobility—the shapes of people's age-income trajectories. The main lesson of Chapter 7 is that, even among groups of individuals with similar character-istics, there is substantial heterogeneity in the shapes of income profiles. Just as when summarizing a cross-sectional distribution one must beware of the mean because the average income is unrepresentative of all incomes, so too must one beware of the mean trajectory when thinking longitudinally.

Trends over Time

A distinguishing feature of this book is its examination of trends over time in patterns of income mobility and poverty dynamics utilizing the long run of BHPS data that is now available (Chapters 5, 6, and 8). Mobility defined in terms of change in relative position, longer-term inequality reduction, transi-tory variability, or volatility has not changed much between the start of the 1990s and the mid-2000s for the population as a whole or groups within it. This is a striking finding because so much else occurred in the economy over this period, such as large falls in the unemployment rate and major changes to the tax-benefit system. It appears that the no-change result is the result of various offsetting factors, a finding to which I return to shortly.

Patterns of poverty dynamics have changed, however: there has been a reduction in the prevalence of persistent poverty and a rise in the proportion of people who never experience poverty over a four-year period. The trend is driven by the changes for families with children (couples and lone parents) and single pensioners, groups for whom poverty exit rates rose and poverty entry rates fell. (They are also the groups with the highest rates of poverty persistence at the beginning of the 1990s.) Although the trend is also striking, it is perhaps less surprising than the finding for mobility because these were groups targeted by the Labour government's anti-poverty measures.

Policy Implications and the Role of Tax-Benefit Policy

Although not a book specifically about income distribution policy design or programme evaluation, there are findings in the book that are relevant to the assessment and formulation of social policies. There are relatively univer-sal policy implications and some more specific remarks concerned with Britain between the 1990s and mid-2000s, which I consider in turn. Under the former heading, I do not count arguments for a longitudinal perspective per se: as intimated in Chapter 1, that case has largely been accepted (though I refer to a sceptic shortly). Rather, I mean relatively simple lessons. The lessons are well-known in Britain—see, for example, Walker (1994), Jarvis and Jenkins (1997), Gardiner and Hills (1999), and Jenkins and Rigg (2001)—but they bear repetition because of their continuing importance. I refer to two examples.

First, since more people are 'touched' by poverty over a period of time than are poor in any one year, the income maintenance system has an important role in providing temporary support for large numbers of people. More people are helped by the benefit system than would be revealed by focusing on the caseload at a point in time (which disproportionately comprises long-term stayers—see Chapter 8). The tax-benefit system for working-age households needs to accommodate and support the change that appears pervasive in many people's lives, not only to reflect the (rather small) number of people who remain stuck at the bottom.

Second, and related, another way of describing turnover and churning among the low-income population is to point to the prevalence of poverty recurrence and repeat spells. Changes in the numbers of poor people depend not only on the poverty exit rate but also on the poverty (re-)entry rate. So, getting people out of poverty should not be the only concern of policy; it should also aim to stopping them falling (back) in. Anti-poverty policies should not simply be about help for 'the poor'. For example, for people of working age, policy should be concerned with measures that promote job retention and wage growth, not only with those promoting employment of any kind for people currently without jobs. Cappellari and Jenkins (2008b) and Stewart (1999, 2007) draw attention to the 'low pay—no pay' cycle, in particular that 'low-wage jobs act as the main conduit for repeat unemployment' (Stewart 2007: 529). On the hand, getting a low-paid job with income topped up by tax credits may have positive benefits for some. For example, Lydon and Walker (2005) find that wage growth was at least as high among WFTC recipients and non-recipients and they also investigate differences in the chances of being trained. More research is required to document the longer-term outcomes for people who move out of poverty into low-paid jobs, and to identify the policies that successfully move people into jobs with secure long-term prospects rather than a low-paid dead end.

There are some researchers who are sceptical about the value added by taking a longitudinal perspective. For example, Daly refers to

> the latest fashion in poverty research, which searches after duration and movement ... However none of the recent work on the dynamics of poverty gives cause to assume that the structures of poverty uncovered here [by cross-sectional analysis] would be any different to those found by dynamic analyses. For what is often

under-emphasized by the duration-oriented analyses is that those moving out of poverty are replaced almost immediately by somebody else. As a result, the overall structural pattern tends to be reproduced although poverty as an individual experience would be different. (Daly 2000: 183)

To be sure, the groups with relatively high poverty rates in Britain such as lone-parent families and single pensioners are also those with relatively high persistence poverty rates (Chapter 8): family type and gender breakdowns by poverty risk reveal similar 'structures' according to both cross-sectional and longitudinal perspectives. But there is much more to policy analysis than simply identifying high risk groups. First and foremost, the longitudinal approach involves a total reorientation in policy thinking, as the quotation from David Ellwood in Chapter 1 illustrates. Second, and at a practical level, longitudinal analysis shows that factors associated with higher poverty exit rates differ from the factors associated with lower poverty (re-)entry rates (Chapters 10 and 11). And there are differences in the compositions of the groups at risk of making a transition. Policies should not simply be about helping 'the poor'; rather they should be orientated towards helping poor people climb out of poverty and preventing the non-poor from falling or falling back into poverty.

Are cross-national comparative studies useful for the understanding of the relationship between policy regimes and distributional outcomes? I concur with Daly's arguments (2000) that we should move away from reliance on typologies of welfare states towards more detailed studies of micro-level outcomes and I sympathize with her preference for two-country rather than many-country comparisons for developing a deeper understanding (Jenkins 2001b). Cross-national comparisons of income mobility and poverty dynamics of the kind referred to in many of the chapters of this book are valuable for providing yardsticks that help us to assess a country's performance. Such comparisons reveal that some aspects of dynamics are universal. For example, longitudinal flux in incomes is ubiquitous, and demographic events account for a greater share of poverty entries that they do of poverty exits. (The growing availability over the last decade of comparable household panel data, such as in the Cross-National Equivalent File or the European Community Household Panel, represents a substantial advance.) However, cross-national comparisons are less useful for assessing the merits of one specific policy measure or another. Indeed, throughout this book there are examples of where classifications of countries according to patterns of income dynamics either do not correspond particularly closely to the commonly used typologies of the Esping-Andersen (1990) type or the findings are relatively superficial and unsurprising, showing, for example, that Britain's performance lies somewhere between the polar extremes of the USA and Germany.

Changes in Britain's tax-benefit system, especially those introduced by the Labour government from the end of the 1990s, have inevitably loomed large in my discussion of trends over time in patterns of income mobility and poverty dynamics. I have stressed that descriptive analysis of the type presented in this book cannot identify the causal effects of specific programmes and reforms. In part, this is because of the intentionally broad scope of the analysis and in part it is also because it is hard to separate the effects of the tax-benefit reforms from other favourable macroeconomic changes over the period—I refer to the decline in unemployment rates and return to steady economic growth in particular (see Chapter 1).

That said, it is clear that many of the developments over time charted in this book are consistent with the intentions of Labour's reforms, in particular their goals to reduce poverty rates among children and pensioners. For example, there have been significant falls in persistent poverty rates among dependent children; their poverty spell lengths have shortened and poverty recurrence times have become longer (Chapter 8). The pattern of individual income growth has become more pro-poor (Chapter 5). The analysis of the association between trigger events and poverty transitions (Chapter 9) reveals evidence of Britain's welfare state in the post-1999 period providing families with children with greater propulsion effects for those at risk of moving out of poverty and greater cushioning effects for those at risk of moving in. All in all, the findings represent a longitudinal version of the success story documented from a comprehensive cross-sectional perspective by Waldfogel (2010).

At the same time, the analysis also raises a number of questions for further analysis. The discussion in Chapter 6 provides preliminary evidence that the introduction of WFTC was associated with an increase in transitory variation and income volatility—though this was offset by other factors, so that there was no trend overall. This needs to be investigated further. Chapter 6 also discussed, with reference to US research, how volatility appears to be closely associated with the business cycle: in the USA, higher unemployment rates have been associated with a large transitory variance and greater volatility. Why this association is not so apparent for Britain needs further research, considering for example whether the relationship is weaker because of the nature of Britain's more generous welfare state or a matter of differences in measurement. Prominent US studies, such as by Gottschalk and Moffitt (2009), use a measure of income that does not include income from the Earned Income Tax Credit or food stamps.

One of the biggest questions for further research is how all the patterns and relationships changed after the onset of the major recession in 2008. All the analysis in this book is of pre-crisis Britain: my data run to 2006 at the latest. There are not only the direct effects of higher unemployment rates on incomes to consider, but also the interaction between the macro-economy and the workings of the tax-benefit system—for example, whether a system increasingly based on in-work benefits remains as successful when the economy is much less buoyant. The effects of the major changes to the benefit system and cuts to public expenditure that were announced by the UK government in 2010 also need to be assessed.

Examination of these issues from a longitudinal perspective is complicated by changes in data availability. The last interview wave of the BHPS was completed in the autumn of 2008. The BHPS has been superseded by a much larger household panel survey, Understanding Society, which will incorporate the BHPS sample as well as a large new nationally representative general population sample and an ethnic minority over-sample. Interviewing for the new samples began in January 2009 and so longitudinal data will not be available for a while and, of course, will only be short run in coverage initially. Samples will be much larger, which will enable more fine-grained analysis, but consideration of issues such as transitory income variability or persistent poverty will be not be possible for several years. For the BHPS sample, interviewing as part of Understanding Society began in January 2010, so the gap between successive interview sweeps is longer than previously.

Data and Measurement

Besides providing substantive findings, this book has also been concerned to emphasize the importance of knowing one's data in detail. The reliability of the conclusions drawn depends on the quality of the data used. I agree with Atkinson and Brandolini, who state that

> In our view, we need a constructive approach to the very real problems of data deficiencies. We should not ignore them nor should we paint a picture of total disaster. But to make further progress, issues of data quality should be higher in the priorities of the economics profession. (Atkinson and Brandolini 2009: 399)

Although their case study refers to the evolution of income inequality across time and across countries, the points also apply to longitudinal analysis.

This book's findings are based almost entirely on the BHPS, a leading example of a household panel survey. It is important to appreciate the strengths and weakness of this source of longitudinal data, both in absolute terms and relative to other sources such as linked administrative registers (Chapter 3). I have explained the advantages and disadvantages of measuring individuals' economic well-being in terms of income (Chapter 2), and I have taken pains to explain the construction of the BHPS net household income measure in detail and to show that there is a reassuringly close correspondence between the cross-sectional income distributions derived from BHPS and the distributions derived from the data used to compile

Britain's official income statistics and derived from a much larger specialist survey (Chapter 4).

It is clear that substantial progress on the longitudinal data front has been made in Britain—and elsewhere—since the early 1990s. Walker's (1994) monograph arguing the merits of the longitudinal approach to poverty analysis and anti-poverty policy could only acknowledge the potential of the then-infant BHPS. I hope that this book is an example of potential realized. Nonetheless, there are many ways in which longitudinal data on income can be improved.

Measurement error in household survey measures of income is a topic that requires much more consideration (Chapter 2). A number of studies show that error leads to systematic biases in many longitudinal (and cross-sectional) measures of income distribution. And several analyses of poverty dynamics using latent class models suggest that the bias in, for example, poverty transition rates can be large. But most of these studies assume that measurement errors in income have 'classical' properties, and yet recent research finds this is an inaccurate description. In particular, measurement error appears to be mean-reverting, and this provides an offsetting impetus to bias in measures.

Determining the character of measurement error more conclusively, especially for household income, and not only for men's labour earnings, is an important priority. To do this, more validation studies are required, data sets in which survey responses are linked with administrative data for the same set of people—assuming that the latter provide a better approximation to an error-free measure, and assuming that consent to linkage can be secured for a representative sample of respondents. There has been only one validation study of the BHPS (Lynn et al. 2004), focusing on measures of a number of income sources. The study was limited by the representativeness of the sample and small numbers of recipients of many benefits. Also it was not possible to compute a measure of total household income in the validation (administrative) data.

This discussion suggests a greater role can be played in the future by administrative record data of various kinds. As Chapter 2 elaborates, administrative data have some advantages relative to household panel survey data as a source of longitudinal data, including smaller measurement error and larger sample sizes. It is only using administrative data that one can derive reliable information about mobility at the very top of the income distribution, since sample surveys do not cover this group well (Chapter 4). See Kopczuk, Saez, and Song (2010) for a study of top earnings mobility using US administrative data. However, the specialist nature of administrative data means that information is typically available only for particular income sources (such as earnings or benefits) and it is difficult or impossible to construct measures of family or household income—this requires linkages across individuals as well as across income sources. There is also the issue of researchers securing access to the data, with various confidentiality and privacy issues to be overcome in Britain at the time of writing (Chapter 2). If this issue can be resolved, administrative data have an important complementary role to play in the analysis of income dynamics, both in their own right or linked to survey data (as is planned for Understanding Society), though they are unlikely to substitute for survey measures of total household income.

Two related aspects of the BHPS and its income measure are also highlighted in this book, namely that household income is a current rather than an annual measure, and that very short spells of poverty are missed altogether by the survey. I argue in favour of current income measures, citing issues such as the need for consistency in the match between income receivers and the reference period for income (Chapter 2), and demonstrate that BHPS measures of current and annual income provide similar pictures of the income distribution in any case (Chapter 4). Current income measures are also used in all Britain's major household surveys, including the official HBAI statistics. In any case, annual income measures also miss short poverty spells (Chapter 2). The real issue is the frequency of observation rather than the accounting period per se. To examine the prevalence of short poverty spells, Britain needs a counterpart to the US Survey of Income and Program Participation (SIPP)—this has quarterly interviews and derives monthly income histories (albeit relatively short ones). Substantial sub-annual income variability for a small sample of British low-income working families is revealed by the important study by Hills, McKnight, and Smithies (2006), and it would be valuable to undertake similar work using a larger and more representative sample.

Approaches to Modelling the Dynamics of Income and Poverty

The approaches taken to modelling the dynamics of income and poverty in this book are empirically grounded rather than derived from a well-developed theoretical model that implies specifications, the parameters of which are estimated from the data. In economists' jargon, the approach is 'reduced form' rather than 'structural'. The advantage of a structural approach is that there is a close relationship between parameter estimates and behavioural model parameters and so interpretation is improved and one may be able to say more about underlying causes. The problem with a structural approach is that clear-cut implications for model specification and proofs of relationships can often only be derived by massive simplification—simplification that compromises claims that the model describes empirical reality.

The tension between reduced-form and structural approaches has existed for a long time and is likely to remain (Jenkins 2000). The reason for the tension is obvious—approaches combining structure, practicality, and feasibility are very difficult to develop, as also observed long ago by Bane and Ellwood (1986). The problem is that a model is needed not only for the dynamics of labour earnings for an individual but also for the earnings and possibly other income sources of other individuals in a multi-person household, and the dynamics of household structure itself also needs to be modelled.

Some progress is being made, however, and I give two illustrations of empirical models with structural features. Blundell, Pistaferri, and Preston (2008) develop sophisticated statistical models of the dynamics of household income on the one hand and consumption dynamics on the other which are strongly characterized by economic theoretic considerations. In particular, model estimates are informative about how 'shocks' to earnings are transmitted to consumption and hence the extent to which individuals and households insure themselves against these shocks. The model is fitted to US PSID data for households headed by working-age men who are continuously married over the sample period and who experience no significant family compositional change. Blundell, Pistaferri, and Preston blithely remark that their sample selections are made to 'avoid problems related to changes in family composition and education . . . and retirement' (2008: 1915). See also Casado (2011), who uses the same approach and similar demographic selections. In the light of the substantial household demographic change that occurs in reality (as demonstrated for Britain in Chapter 1), it is clear that many important problems are being avoided and need to be addressed in future research.

A second approach is that proposed by Burgess and Propper and their co-authors. Burgess and Propper (1998) model poverty dynamics amongst US women aged 20–35 years using data from the National Longitudinal Survey of Youth (NLSY) and Aassve et al. (2006) model poverty dynamics among British adults using BHPS data—the retrospective histories of employment, partnership, and fertility are combined with panel data for waves 1–6. Rather than relating poverty transitions directly to explanatory variables as in reduced-form approaches (such as used in Chapters 10 and 11), both papers model the underlying dynamic processes which determine income, using methods more commonly used in dynamic microsimulation modelling (see, for example, Harding 1996). See also Burgess, Propper, and Dickson (2006) for further arguments in favour of their structural approach. In Aassve et al.'s (2006) British application, for instance, five dynamic processes are modelled simultaneously: having a child, partnership formation and dissolution, employment, and unemployment. Income, and hence poverty status, is not modelled directly, but imputed to individuals depending on the 'state' in which they are found at a point in time (the chances of being poor depend on partnership status, employment status, and so on). The models are structural though in a rather different way from those of Blundell, Pistaferri, and Preston (2008). Burgess and Propper and colleagues focus on fundamental socio-economic processes rather than reduced-form outcomes, and they include not only labour market behaviours but also demographic behaviours. For an extended review of the Burgess-Propper modelling approach, see Jenkins (2000).

The two modelling approaches just discussed are important complements to the reduced-form methods more commonly used. I say complement rather than substitute because their application requires not only suitable longitudinal data but also substantial resources of time and technical expertise. There are demands for empirical models that produce results relatively quickly and, for many purposes, the statistical descriptions provided by reduced-form approaches may be sufficient. They will continue to be useful.

I have previously expressed a hope that researchers 'will take up the many interesting theoretical and empirical challenges which the study of income and poverty dynamics offers and exploit the new longitudinal data sources now becoming available' (Jenkins 2000: 562–3). Although definite progress has been made, there remains much to be done and new and richer data sets are emerging. My invitation remains open.

References

Aaberge, R., Björklund, A., Jäntti, M., Palme, M., Pedersen, P., Smith, N., and Wennemo, T. (2002). 'Income Inequality and Income Mobility in the Scandinavian Countries Compared to the United States', *Review of Income and Wealth*, 48: 443–69.

Abowd, J. and Card, D. (1989). 'On the Covariance Structure of Earnings and Hours Changes', *Econometrica*, 57: 411–45.

Aassve, A., Betti, G., Mazzuco, S., and Mencarini, L. (2007). 'Marital Disruption and Economic Well-Being: A Comparative Analysis', *Journal of the Royal Statistical Society, Series A*, 170: 781–99.

—— Burgess, S., Dickson, M., and Propper, C. (2006). 'Modelling Poverty by Not Modelling Poverty: An Application of a Simultaneous Hazards Approach to the UK'. CASEpaper 106. London: Centre for the Analysis of Social Exclusion, London School of Economics. <http://sticerd.lse.ac.uk/dps/case/cp/CASEpaper106.pdf>.

AIM-AP (2009). *Accurate Income Measurement for the Assessment of Public Policies*, Reports to the European Commission Sixth Framework Programme, Project Number 028412. Colchester: Institute for Social and Economic Research, University of Essex. <http://www.iser.essex.ac.uk/research/euromod/research-and-policy-analysis-using-euromod/aim-ap>.

Alkire, S., Bastagli, F., Burchardt, T., Clark, D., Holder, H., Ibrahim, S., Munoz, M., Terrazas, P., Tsang, T., and Vizard, P. (2009). *Developing the Equality Measurement Framework: Selecting the Indicators*. Equality and Human Rights Research Report 31. Manchester: Equality and Human Rights Commission. <http://www.equalityhumanrights.com/fairer-britain/equality-measurement-framework/>.

Allison, P. (1984). *Event History Analysis*. Thousand Oaks, Calif.: Sage.

Ananat, E. O. and Michaels, M. (2007). 'The Effect of Marital Breakup on the Income Distribution of Women with Children', *Journal of Human Resources*, 43: 611–29.

Arulampalam, W., Booth, A. L., and Taylor, M. P. (2000). 'Unemployment Persistence', *Oxford Economic Papers*, 52: 24–50.

—— Gregg, P., and Gregory, M. (2001). 'Introduction: Unemployment Scarring', *Economic Journal*, 111: F577–84.

Ashworth, K., Hill, M., and Walker, R. (1994). 'Patterns of Childhood Poverty: New Challenges for Policy', *Journal of Policy Analysis and Management*, 13: 658–80.

Atkinson, A. B. (1991). 'Comparing Poverty Rates Internationally: Lessons from Recent Studies in Developed Countries', *World Bank Economic Review*, 5: 3–21.

—— (2003). 'Multidimensional Deprivation: Contrasting Social Welfare and Counting Approaches', *Journal of Economic Inequality*, 1: 51–65.

References

Atkinson, A. B. (2005). 'Top Incomes in the UK over the 20th Century', *Journal of the Royal Statistical Society, Series A*, 168: 325–43.

—— Bourguignon, F., and Morrisson, C. (1992). *Empirical Studies of Earnings Mobility*. Chur, Switzerland: Harwood Academic Publishers.

—— and Brandolini, A. (2009). 'On Data: A Case Study of the Evolution of Income Inequality Across Time and Across Countries', *Cambridge Journal of Economics*, 33: 381–404.

—— Cantillon, B., Marlier, E., and Nolan, B. (2002). *Social Indicators: The EU and Social Inclusion*. Oxford: Oxford University Press.

—— Piketty, T., and Saez, E. (2011). 'Top Incomes in the Long Run of History', *Journal of Economic Literature*, 49: 3–71.

—— Rainwater, L., and Smeeding, T. M. (1995). *Income Distribution in OECD Countries: Evidence from the Luxembourg Income Study (LIS)*. Social Policy Studies 18. Paris: Organisation for Economic Cooperation and Development.

Ayala, L. and Sastre, M. (2008). 'The Structure of Income Mobility: Empirical Evidence from Five UE Countries', *Empirical Economics*, 35: 451–73.

Baker, M. (1997). 'Growth-Rate Heterogeneity and the Covariance Structure of Life-Cycle Earnings', *Journal of Labor Economics*, 15: 338–75.

—— and Solon, G. (2003). 'Earnings Dynamics and Inequality among Canadian Men, 1976–1992: Evidence from Longitudinal Income Tax Records', *Journal of Labor Economics*, 21: 289–321.

Bane, M. and Ellwood, D. (1986). 'Slipping Into and Out of Poverty: The Dynamics of Spells', *Journal of Human Resources*, 21: 1–23.

Bardasi, E., Jenkins, S. P., and Rigg, J. (2002). 'Retirement and the Economic Well-Being of the Elderly: A British Perspective', *Ageing and Society*, 22: 131–59.

Bartels, C. and Bönke, T. (2010). 'German Male Income Volatility 1984 to 2008: Trends in Permanent and Transitory Income Components and the Role of the Welfare State'. Unpublished Paper. Berlin: Department of Economics, Free University.

Beach, C. M., Finnie, R., and Gray, D. (2010). 'Long-Run Inequality and Short-Run Instability of Men's and Women's Earnings in Canada', *Review of Income and Wealth*, 56: 572–96.

Becker, G. S. (1993). *Human Capital: A Theoretical and Empirical Analysis, with Special Reference to Education*, third edition. Chicago: University of Chicago Press.

Behr, A., Bellgardt, E., and Rendtel, U. (2005). 'Extent and Determinants of Panel Attrition in the European Community Household Panel', *European Sociological Review*, 21: 489–512.

BHPS Documentation Team (2009). BHPS Documentation (On-Line Materials). Colchester: Institute for Social and Economic Research, University of Essex. <http://www.iser.essex.ac.uk/survey/bhps/documentation>.

Biemer, P. P., Groves, R. M., Lyberg, L. E., Mathiowetz, N. A., and Sudman, S. (eds) (1991). *Measurement Error in Surveys*. New York: John Wiley and Sons.

Biewen, M. (2005). 'The Covariance Structure of East and West German Incomes and its Implications for the Persistence of Poverty and Inequality', *German Economic Review*, 6: 445–69.

—— (2006). 'Who are the Chronic Poor? An Econometric Analysis of Chronic Poverty in Germany', *Research on Economic Inequality*, 13: 31–62.

—— (2009). 'Measuring State Dependence in Individual Poverty Histories when There is Feedback to Employment Status and Household Composition', *Journal of Applied Econometrics*, 24: 1095–116.

Binder, D. A. (1983). 'On the Variances of Asymptotically Normal Estimators from Complex Surveys', *International Statistical Review*, 51: 279–92.

Bingley, P., Bjørn, N. H., Westergård-Nielsen, N. (1995). 'Wage Mobility in Denmark'. CLS Working Paper 95–10. Aarhus: Aarhus University.

Björklund, A. (1993). 'A Comparison between Actual Distributions of Annual and Lifetime Income: Sweden 1951–89', *Review of Income and Wealth*, 39: 377–86.

Blair, A. (2001). Transcript of interview on BBC Newsnight, 5 June 2001, <http://news.bbc.co.uk/1/hi/events/newsnight/1372220.stm>.

Blundell, R. (2001). 'Welfare Reform for Low Income Workers', *Oxford Economic Papers*, 53: 189–214.

—— and Etheridge, B. (2010). 'Consumption, Income and Earnings Inequality in Britain', *Review of Economic Dynamics*, 13: 76–102.

—— and Hoynes, H. (2004). 'Has In-Work Benefit Reform Helped the Labour Market?', in R. Blundell, D. Card, and R. B. Freeman (eds), *Seeking a Premier Economy: The Economic Effects of British Economic Reforms, 1980–2000*. Chicago: University of Chicago Press, 411–60.

—— Pistaferri, L., and Preston, I. (2008). 'Consumption Inequality and Partial Insurance', *American Economic Review*, 98: 1887–921.

—— Reed, H., and Stoker, T. M. (2003). 'Interpreting Aggregate Wage Growth: The Role of Labor Force Participation', *American Economic Review*, 93: 1114–31.

Böheim, R., Ermisch, J. F., and Jenkins, S. P. (1999). 'The Dynamics of Lone Mothers' Incomes: Public and Private Income Sources Compared'. Working Paper 99–5. Colchester: Institute for Social and Economic Research, University of Essex. <http://www.iser.essex.ac.uk/pubs/workpaps/wp99-05.php>.

—— and Jenkins, S. P. (2006). 'A Comparison of Current and Annual Measures of Income in the British Household Panel Survey', *Journal of Official Statistics*, 22: 733–58.

Boskin, M. J. and Nold, F. C. (1975). 'A Markov Model of Turnover in Aid to Families with Dependent Children', *Journal of Human Resources*, 10: 476–81.

Bossert, W., Chakravarty, S., and D'Ambrosio, C. (2008). 'Poverty and Time'. Working Paper 2008–87. Milan: Society for the Study of Economic Inequality. <http://www.ecineq.org/milano/WP/ECINEQ2008-87.pdf>.

Bound, J., Brown, C., and Mathiowetz, N. (2001). 'Measurement Error in Survey Data', in J. J. Heckman and E. Leamer (eds), *Handbook of Econometrics, Volume 5*. Amsterdam: Elsevier Science, 3707–45.

Bourguignon, F. and Chakravarty, S. R. (2003). 'The Measurement of Multidimensional Poverty', *Journal of Economic Inequality*, 1: 25–49.

—— and Chiappori, P.-A. (1992). 'Collective Models of Household Behaviour: An Introduction', *European Economic Review*, 36: 355–65.

References

Box, G. E. P. (1979). 'Robustness in the Strategy of Scientific Model Building', in R. L. Launer and G. N. Wilkinson (eds), *Robustness in Statistics*. New York: Academic Press, 201–35.

Bradbury, B., Jenkins, S. P., and Micklewright, J. (2001). 'The Dynamics of Child Poverty: Conceptual and Measurement Issues', in B. Bradbury, S. P. Jenkins, and J. Micklewright (eds), *The Dynamics of Child Poverty in Industrialised Countries*. Cambridge: Cambridge University Press, 27–61.

Breen, R. and Moisio, P. (2004). 'Poverty Dynamics Corrected for Measurement Error', *Journal of Economic Inequality*, 2: 171–91.

Brewer, M., Muriel, A., Phillips, D., and Sibieta, L. (2009*a*). 'Inequality and Poverty Spreadsheet', accompanying *Poverty and Inequality in the UK: 2009*. Commentary 109. London: Institute for Fiscal Studies. <http://www.ifs.org.uk/bns/bn19figs.zip>.

—— O'Dea, C., Paull, G., and Sibieta, L. (2009*b*). *The Living Standards of Families with Children Reporting Low Incomes*. Research Report 577. London: Department for Work and Pensions. <http://research.dwp.gov.uk/asd/asd5/rports2009-2010/rrep577.pdf>.

—— and Shephard, A. (2004). *Has Labour Made Work Pay?* York: York Publishing Services for the Joseph Rowntree Foundation. <http://www.jrf.org.uk/bookshop/eBooks/1859352626.pdf>.

—— Duncan, A., Shephard, A., and Suarez, M. J. (2006). 'Did Working Families' Tax Credit Work? The Impact of In-Work Support on Labour Supply in Britain', *Labour Economics*, 13: 699–720.

Browning, M., Crossley, T. F., and Weber, G. (2003). 'Asking Consumption Questions in General Purpose Surveys', *Economic Journal*, 113: F540–67.

Browning, M., Ejrnæs, M., and Alvarez, J. (2010). 'Modelling Income Processes with Lots of Heterogeneity', *Review of Economic Studies*, 77: 1353–81.

Buck, N., Ermisch, J. F., and Jenkins, S. P. (1996). *Choosing a Longitudinal Survey Design: the Issues*. Occasional Paper No. 96–1. Colchester: Institute for Social and Economic Research, University of Essex. <http://www.iser.essex.ac.uk/pubs/occpaps/pdf/op96-1.pdf>.

Buddelmeyer, H. and Verick, S. (2008). 'The Dynamics and Persistence of Income Poverty in Australia', *Economic Record*, 84: 310–21.

Buhmann, B., Rainwater, L., Schmauss, G., and Smeeding, T. (1988). 'Equivalence Scales, Well-Being, Inequality and Poverty: Sensitivity Estimates across Ten Countries using the Luxembourg Income Study (LIS) Database', *Review of Income and Wealth*, 34: 115–42.

Burgess, S., Jenkins, S. P., Propper, C., and Gardiner, K. (2000). 'Measurement of Income Risk'. Working Paper 2000–15. Colchester: Institute for Social and Economic Research, University of Essex. <http://www.iser.essex.ac.uk/pubs/workpaps/pdf/2000-15.pdf>.

—— and Propper, C. (1998). 'An Economic Model of Household Income Dynamics, with an Application to Poverty Dynamics among American Women'. CASEpaper 9. London: Centre for the Analysis of Social Exclusion, London School of Economics. <http://sticerd.lse.ac.uk/dps/case/cp/CASEpaper9.pdf>.

—— —— and Dickson, M. (2006). 'The Analysis of Poverty Data with Endogenous Transitions', *Fiscal Studies*, 27: 75–98.

Burkhauser, R. V., and Poupore, J. (1997). 'A Cross-National Comparison of Permanent Income Inequality', *Review of Economics and Statistics*, 79: 10–17.

Cabinet Office (2008). *Getting On, Getting Ahead, A Discussion Paper: Analysing the Trends and Drivers of Social Mobility*. London: Cabinet Office.

—— (2009). *New Opportunities: Fair Chances for the Future*. London: Cabinet Office.

—— (2010). *State of the Nation Report: Poverty, Worklessness and Welfare Dependency in the UK*. London: Cabinet Office. <http://www.cabinetoffice.gov.uk/media/410872/web -poverty-report.pdf>.

Cantó, O. (2003). 'Finding out the Reasons to Escape Poverty: The Relevance of Demographic vs. Labour Market Events in Spain', *Review of Income and Wealth*, 49: 569–89.

Cantó-Sanchez, O. (1998). 'The Dynamics of Poverty in Spain: The Permanent and the Transitory Poor'. Unpublished Paper. Florence: European University Institute.

Cappellari, L. (2007). 'Earnings Mobility among Italian Low-Paid Workers', *Journal of Population Economics*, 20: 465–82.

—— and Jenkins, S. P. (2002a). 'Who Stays Poor? Who Becomes Poor? Evidence from the British Household Panel Survey', *Economic Journal*, 112: C60–7.

—— —— (2002b). 'Modelling Low Income Transitions'. Working Paper 2002–8. Colchester: Institute for Social and Economic Research, University of Essex. <http:// www.iser.essex.ac.uk/pubs/workpaps/pdf/2002-08.pdf>.

—— —— (2004). 'Modelling Low Income Transitions', *Journal of Applied Econometrics*, 19: 593–610.

—— —— (2006). 'Calculation of Multivariate Normal Probabilities by Simulation, with Applications to Maximum Simulated Likelihood Estimation', *Stata Journal*, 6: 156–89.

—— —— (2007). 'Summarising Multiple Deprivation Indicators', in S. P. Jenkins and J. Micklewright (eds), *Inequality and Poverty Re-Examined*. Oxford: Oxford University Press, 166–84.

—— —— (2008a). 'Estimating Low Pay Transition Probabilities Accounting for Endogenous Selection Mechanisms', *Journal of the Royal Statistical Society, Series C (Applied Statistics)*, 57: 165–86.

—— —— (2008b). 'Transitions Between Low Pay and Unemployment', in S. Polachek and K. Tatsiramos (eds), *Research in Labor Economics, Volume 28*. Amsterdam: Elsevier, 57–79.

—— —— (2008c). 'The Dynamics of Social Assistance Receipt: Measurement and Modelling Issues, with an Application to Britain'. OECD Social, Employment and Migration Working Paper 67. Paris: OECD. <http://www.oecd.org/dataoecd/30/42/ 41414013.pdf>.

—— —— (2009). 'The Dynamics of Social Assistance Benefit Receipt in Britain'. ISER Working Paper 2009-29. Colchester: Institute for Social and Economic Research, University of Essex. <http://www.iser.essex.ac.uk/publications/working-papers/iser/ 2009-29>.

Casado, J. M. (2011). 'From Income to Consumption: Measuring Households Partial Insurance', *Empirical Economics*, 40(2): 471–95.

CESifo (2005). *DICE Report 1/2005*. Munich: CESifo, University of Munich. <http:// www.cesifo-group.de/portal/page/portal/ifoHome/b-publ/b2journal/40publdice/ _ZS-DICE-LISTE05>.

References

Chamberlain, G. and Hirano, K. (1999). 'Predictive Distributions Based on Longitudinal Earnings Data', *Annales d'Économie et de Statistique*, 55/56: 211–42.

Chaudhuri, S. and Ravallion, M. (1994). 'How Well Do Static Indicators Identify the Chronically Poor?' *Journal of Public Economics*, 53: 367–94.

Chay, K. Y. and Hyslop, D. (2000). 'Identification and Estimation of Dynamic Binary Response Panel Data Models: Empirical Evidence Using Alternative Approaches'. Unpublished Paper. Berkeley, Calif.: University of California Berkeley. <http://www.econ.berkeley.edu/~kenchay/ftp/binresp/working_paper/hyslop.pdf>.

—— Hoynes, H., and Hyslop, D. (2004). 'True State Dependence in Monthly Welfare Participation: a Nonexperimental Analysis'. Working Paper 05–33. Davis, Calif.: Department of Economics, University of California Davis. <http://www.econ.ucdavis.edu/working_papers/05-33.pdf>.

Chen, W.-H. (2009). 'Cross-National Differences in Income Mobility: Evidence from Canada, the United States, Great Britain and Germany', *Review of Income and Wealth*, 55: 75–100.

Chesher, A. and Schluter, C. (2002). 'Welfare Measurement and Measurement Error', *Review of Economic Studies*, 69, 357–78.

Chiappori, P.-A. and Donni, O. (2009). 'Non-Unitary Models of Household Behavior: A Survey of the Literature', IZA Discussion Paper 4603. Bonn: IZA. <http://ftp.iza.org/dp4603.pdf>.

Citro, C. F., and Kalton, G. (1993). *The Future of the Survey of Income and Program Participation*. Washington: National Academy Press.

—— and Michael, R. T. (eds) (1995). *Measuring Poverty: A New Approach*. Washington: National Academy Press.

Clark, A. E., Frijters, P., and Shields, M.A. (2008). 'Relative Income, Happiness, and Utility: An Explanation for the Easterlin Paradox and Other Puzzles', *Journal of Economic Literature*, 46: 95–144.

Conti, G. and Pudney, S. E. (2011). 'Survey Design and the Analysis of Satisfaction', *Review of Economics and Statistics*, forthcoming.

Coulter, F. A. C., Cowell, F. A., and Jenkins, S. P. (1992*a*). 'Differences in Needs and Assessment of Income Distributions', *Bulletin of Economic Research*, 44: 77–124.

—— —— —— (1992*b*). 'Equivalence Scale Relativities and the Extent of Inequality and Poverty', *Economic Journal*, 102: 1067–82.

Cowell, F. A., and Schluter, C. (1998). 'Income Mobility: A Robust Approach'. DARP Working Paper 37. London: Distributional Analysis Research Programme, London School of Economics. <http://eprints.lse.ac.uk/2210/1/Income_Mobility_A_Robust_Approach.pdf>.

Crawford, I. and Smith, Z. (2002). *Distributional Aspects of Inflation*. Commentary 90. London: Institute for Fiscal Studies. <http://www.ifs.org.uk/comms/comm90.pdf>.

Creedy, J. (1985). *Dynamics of Income Distribution*. Oxford: Basil Blackwell.

—— (1992). *Income, Inequality, and the Lifecycle*. Cheltenham: Edward Elgar.

—— (1998). *The Dynamics of Inequality and Poverty: Comparing Income Distributions*. Cheltenham: Edward Elgar.

Cunha, F., Heckman, J., and Navarro, S. (2005). 'Separating Uncertainty from Heterogeneity in Life Cycle Earnings', *Oxford Economic Papers*, 57: 191–261.

Dahl, M., DeLeire, T., and Schwabish, J. (2007). 'Trends in Earnings Variability over the Past 20 Years'. Washington: Congressional Budget Office, US Congress. <http://www.cbo.gov/ftpdocs/80xx/doc8007/04-17-EarningsVariability.pdf>.

Daly, M. C. and Valletta, R. G. (2008). 'Cross-National Trends in Earnings Inequality and Instability', *Economics Letters*, 99: 215–19.

Damioli, G. (2011a). 'How and Why the Dynamics of Poverty Differ across European Countries'. Unpublished Paper. Colchester: Institute for Social and Economic Research, University of Essex.

—— (2011b). 'The Dynamics of Poverty in Pre-Crisis Britain'. Unpublished Paper. Colchester: Institute for Social and Economic Research, University of Essex.

Daly, M. (2000). *The Gender Division of Welfare: The Impact of the British and German Welfare States*. Cambridge: Cambridge University Press.

Deaton, A. (1997). *The Analysis of Household Surveys*. Baltimore, Md.: The Johns Hopkins University Press for the World Bank.

—— and Paxson, C. (1994). 'Saving, Growth and Aging in Taiwan', in D. A. Wise (ed.), *Studies in the Economics of Aging*. Chicago: University of Chicago Press, 331–57.

Debels, A. and Vandecasteele, L. (2008). 'The Time Lag in Annual Household-Based Income Measures: Assessing and Correcting the Bias', *Review of Income and Wealth*, 54: 71–88.

Department of Health and Social Security (1988). *Low Income Statistics: Report of a Technical Review*. London: Department of Health and Social Security.

Department of Social Security (1994). *Social Security Statistics*. London: HMSO.

—— (1999), *Opportunity for All: Tackling Poverty and Social Exclusion*. First Annual Report, Cm 4445. London: The Stationery Office.

Department for Work and Pensions (2008). *Households below Average Income: An Analysis of the Income Distribution 1994/95–2006/07*. London: Department for Work and Pensions. <http://statistics.dwp.gov.uk/asd/index.php?page=hbai_arc#hbai>.

—— (2009a). *Low Income Dynamics, 1991–2007 (Great Britain)*. London: Department for Work and Pensions. <http://statistics.dwp.gov.uk/asd/index.php?page=hbai_arc#low_income>.

—— (2009b). *Households Below Average Income: An Analysis of the Income Distribution 1994/95–2007/08*. London: Department for Work and Pensions. <http://statistics.dwp.gov.uk/asd/index.php?page=hbai_arc#hbai>.

—— (2010). *Households below Average Income: An Analysis of the Income Distribution 1994/5–2008/09*. London: Department for Work and Pensions. <http://statistics.dwp.gov.uk/asd/index.php?page=hbai_arc#hbai>.

Devicienti, F. (2001). 'Estimating Poverty Persistence in Britain'. Working Paper No. 1, Turin: LABORatorio Riccardo Revelli, Collegio 'Carlo Alberto'. <http://repec.org/res2002/Devicienti.pdf>.

Dickens, R. (2000). 'The Evolution of Individual Male Earnings in Great Britain: 1975–95', *Economic Journal*, 110: 27–49.

—— and McKnight, A. (2008). 'Changes in Earnings Inequality and Mobility in Great Britain 1978/9–2005/6'. CASEpaper 132. London: Centre for the Analysis of Social Exclusion, London School of Economics. <http://sticerd.lse.ac.uk/dps/case/cp/CASEpaper132.pdf>.

References

DiPrete, T. A. and McManus, P. A. (2006). 'Family Change, Employment Transitions, and the Welfare State: Household Income Dynamics in the United States and Germany', *American Sociological Review*, 65: 343–70.

Dragoset, L. M. and Fields, G. S. (2006). 'U.S. Earnings Mobility: Comparing Survey-Based and Administrative-Based Estimates'. ECINEQ Working Paper 2006–55. Milan: Society for the Study of Economic Inequality. <http://www.ecineq.org/milano/WP/ECINEQ2006-55.pdf>.

Duclos, J. -Y., Araar, A., and Giles, J. (2010). 'Chronic and Transient Poverty: Measurement and Estimation, with Evidence from China', *Journal of Development Economics*, 91: 266–77.

Duncan, G. J. (1983). 'The Implications of Changing Family Composition for the Dynamic Analysis of Family Economic Well-Being', in A. B. Atkinson and F. A. Cowell (eds), *Panel Data on Incomes*. Occasional Paper No. 2. London: ICERD, London School of Economics, 203–39.

—— Coe, R. D., and Hill, M. S. (1984). 'The Dynamics of Poverty', in G. J. Duncan, R. D. Coe, M. E. Corcoran, M. S. Hill, S. D. Hoffman, and J. N. Morgan (eds), *Years of Poverty, Years of Plenty: The Changing Economic Fortunes of American Workers and Families*. Ann Arbor: Institute for Social Research, University of Michigan, 33–70.

—— Gustafsson, B., Hauser, R., Schmauss, G., Messinger, H., Muffels, R., Nolan, B., Ray, J.-C. (1993). 'Poverty Dynamics in Eight Countries', *Journal of Population Economics*, 6: 295–334.

—— and Hill, M. S. (1985). 'Conceptions of Longitudinal Households: Fertile or Futile?', *Journal of Economic and Social Measurement*, 13: 361–75.

Dutta, J., Sefton, J. A., and Weale, M. R. (2001). 'Income Distribution and Income Dynamics in the United Kingdom', *Journal of Applied Econometrics*, 16: 599–617.

Dynan, K. E., Elmendorf, D. W., and Sichel, D. E. (2008). 'The Evolution of Household Income Volatility'. Unpublished Paper. Washington: Federal Reserve Board and Brookings Institution. <http://www.brookings.edu/~/media/Files/rc/papers/2008/02_useconomics_elmendorf/02_useconomics_elmendorf.pdf>.

Dynarski, S. and Gruber, J. (1997). 'Can Families Smooth Variable Earnings?' *Brookings Papers on Economic Activity*, 1997–1: 229–303.

Ebert, U. (1997). 'Social Welfare when Needs Differ: An Axiomatic Approach', *Economica* 64: 233–44.

Ellwood, D. (1998). 'Dynamic Policy Making: An Insider's Account of Reforming US Welfare', in L. Leisering and R. Walker (eds), *The Dynamics of Modern Society: Policy, Poverty and Welfare*. Bristol: The Policy Press, 49–59.

Epland, J. and Kirkeberg, M.I. (2002). 'Comparing Norwegian Income Data in Administrative Registers with Income Data in the Survey of Living Conditions'. Paper presented at the International Conference on Improving Surveys (ICIS), Copenhagen, Denmark, 25–8 August 2002.

Esping-Andersen, G. (1990). *The Three Worlds of Welfare Capitalism*. Princeton: Princeton University Press.

European Commission (2009). 'Portfolio of Indicators for the Monitoring of the European Strategy for Social Protection and Social Inclusion—2009 Update'. Brussels:

378

Employment, Social Affairs and Equal Opportunities DG, European Commission. <http://ec.europa.eu/social/main.jsp?catId=756&langId=en>.

Eurostat (2000). 'Imputation of Income in the ECHP', DocPan 164/00. Luxembourg: Statistical Office of the European Communities.

—— (2007). *Comparative EU Statistics on Income and Living Conditions: Issues and Challenges*. Proceedings of the EUSILC Conference (Helsinki, 6–8 November 2006). Luxembourg: Eurostat. <http://epp.eurostat.ec.europa.eu/cache/ITY_OFFPUB/KS-RA-07 -007/EN/KS-RA-07-007-EN.PDF>.

Expert Group on Household Income Statistics (The Canberra Group) (2001). *Final Report and Recommendations*. Ottawa: Statistics Canada. <http://www.lisproject.org/ links/canberra/finalreport.pdf>.

Fabig, H. (1999). 'Income Mobility and the Welfare State: An International Comparison with Panel Data', *Journal of European Social Policy*, 9: 331–49.

Fields, G. S. (2006). 'The Many Facets of Economic Mobility', in M. McGillivray (ed.), *Inequality, Poverty, and Well-Being*. Houndsmills: Palgrave Macmillan, 123–42.

—— (2010). 'Does Income Mobility Equalize Longer-Term Incomes? New Measures of an Old Concept', *Journal of Economic Inequality*, 8: 409–27.

—— and Ok, E. A. (1996). 'The Meaning and Measurement of Income Mobility', *Journal of Economic Theory*, 71: 349–77.

—— —— (1999a). 'The Measurement of Income Mobility: An Introduction to the Literature', in J. Silber (ed.), *Handbook of Income Inequality Measurement*. Deventer: Kluwer, 557–96.

—— —— (1999b). 'Measuring Movement of Incomes', *Economica*, 66: 455–71.

Fitzgerald, J., Gottschalk, P., and Moffitt, R. (1998). 'An Analysis of Attrition in Panel Data: The Michigan Panel Study of Income Dynamics', *Journal of Human Resources*, 33: 251–99.

Foster, J. E. (2007). 'A Class of Chronic Poverty Measures'. Working Paper No. 07-W01. Nashville, Tenn.: Department of Economics, Vanderbilt University. <http://www .vanderbilt.edu/Econ/wparchive/workpaper/vu07-w01.pdf>.

Fouarge, D. and Layte, R. (2005). 'Welfare Regimes and Poverty Dynamics: The Duration and Recurrence of Poverty Spells in Europe', *Journal of Social Policy*, 34: 407–26.

Francesconi, M. and van der Klaauw, W. (2007). 'The Socioeconomic Consequences of In-Work Benefit Reform for British Lone Mothers', *Journal of Human Resources*, 42: 1–31.

Frey, B. S. and Stutzer, A. (2002). 'What can Economists Learn from Happiness Research?', *Journal of Economic Literature*, 40: 402–35.

Frick, J. R. and Grabka, M. M. (2005). 'Item Nonresponse on Income Questions in Panel Surveys: Incidence, Imputation and the Impact on Inequality and Mobility', *Allgemeines Statistisches Archiv*, 89: 49–61.

—— —— and Groh-Samberg, O. (2009). 'Dealing with Incomplete Household Panel Data in Inequality Research'. Unpublished Paper. Berlin: DIW Berlin.

—— Jenkins, S. P., Lillard, D. R., Lipps, O., and Wooden, M. (2007).'The Cross-National Equivalent File (CNEF) and its Member Country Household Panel Studies', *Schmollers Jahrbuch—Journal of Applied Social Sciences Studies*, 127: 627–54.

References

Gangl, M. (2005). 'Income Inequality, Permanent Incomes, and Income Dynamics. Comparing Europe to the United States', *Work and Occupations*, 37: 140–62.

Gardiner, K. and Hills, J. (1999). 'Policy Implications of New Data on Income Mobility', *Economic Journal*, 109: F91–111.

Geweke, J. and Keane, M. (2000). 'An Empirical Analysis of Income Dynamics among Men in the PSID: 1968–1989', *Journal of Econometrics*, 96: 293–356.

Gittleman, M. and Joyce, M. (1999). 'Have Family Income Mobility Patterns Changed?' *Demography*, 36: 299–314.

Goodman, A., Johnson, P., and Webb, S. (1997). *Inequality in the UK*. Oxford: Oxford University Press.

Gordon, D. and Pantazis, C. (1997). *Breadline Britain in the 1990s*. Aldershot: Ashgate.

—— Levitas, R., Pantazis, C., Patsios, D., Payne, S., Townsend, P., Adelman, L., Ashworth, K., Middleton, S., Bradshaw, J., and Williams, J. (2000). *Poverty and Social Exclusion in Britain*. York: Joseph Rowntree Foundation.

Gosselin, P. (2008). *High Wire: The Precarious Financial Lives of American Families*. New York: Basic Books.

—— and Zimmerman, S. D. (2008). 'Trends in Income Volatility and Risk, 1970–2004'. Working Paper. Washington: Urban Institute. <http://www.urban.org/publications/411672.html>.

Gottschalk, P. and Danziger, S. (2005). 'Inequality of Wage Rates, Earnings and Family Income in the United States, 1975–2002', *Review of Income and Wealth*, 51: 231–54.

—— and Huynh, M. (2010). 'Are Earnings Inequality and Mobility Overstated? The Impact of Non-Classical Measurement Error', *Review of Economics and Statistics*, 92: 302–15.

—— and Moffitt, R. (1994a). 'Welfare Dependence: Concepts, Measures, and Trends', *American Economic Review (Papers and Proceedings)*, 84: 38–42.

—— —— (1994b). 'The Growth of Earnings Instability in the U.S. Labor Market', *Brookings Papers on Economic Activity*, 2–1994: 217–72.

—— —— (2007). 'Trends in Earnings Volatility in the U.S: 1970–2002'. Paper presented to the Annual Meetings of the American Economic Association, Chicago, January 2007.

—— —— (2009). 'The Rising Instability of U.S. Earnings', *Journal of Economic Perspectives*, 23: 3–24.

—— and Smeeding, T. M. (2000). 'Empirical Evidence on Income Inequality in Industrialized Countries', in A. B. Atkinson and F. Bourguignon (eds), *Handbook of Income Distribution*. Amsterdam: North-Holland, 261–307.

—— and Spolaore, E. (2002). 'On the Evaluation of Economic Mobility', *Review of Economic Studies*, 69: 191–208.

Gourieroux, C. and Monfort, A. (1996). *Simulation Based Econometric Methods*. Oxford: Oxford University Press.

Grawe, N. D. (2004). 'The 3-Day Week of 1974 and Earnings Data Reliability in the Family Expenditure Survey and the National Child Development Survey', *Oxford Bulletin of Economics and Statistics*, 66: 567–79.

Gregg, P. and Vittori, C. (2009). 'Earnings Mobility in Europe: Global and Disaggregate Measures'. Unpublished Paper. Bristol: Centre for Market and Public Organisation, University of Bristol.

—— and Wadsworth, J. (1996). 'It Takes Two: Employment Polarisation in the OECD'. Discussion Paper 304. London: Centre for Economic Performance, London School of Economics, London.

—— —— (2008). 'Two Sides to Every Story: Measuring Polarization and Inequality in the Distribution of Work', *Journal of the Royal Statistical Society, Series A*, 171: 857–75.

Gustafsson, B. (1994). 'The Degree and Pattern of Income Immobility in Sweden'. *Review of Income and Wealth*, 40: 67–86.

Guvenen, F. (2009). 'An Empirical Investigation of Labor Income Processes', *Review of Economic Dynamics*, 12: 58–79.

Hacker, J. S. (2004). 'Privatizing Risk without Privatizing the Welfare State: The Hidden Politics of Social Policy Retrenchment in the United States', *American Political Science Review*, 98: 243–60.

—— (2008). *The Great Risk Shift* (revised and expanded edition). Oxford: Oxford University Press.

—— and Jacobs, E. (2008). 'The Rising Instability of American Family Incomes, 1969–2004: Evidence from the Panel Study of Income Dynamics'. Briefing Paper No. 213. Washington DC: Economic Policy Institute. <http://www.epi.org/content.cfm/bp213>.

—— and Rehm, P. (2009). 'Risk, Insurance, and Redistribution: Income Instability and the Welfare State in Rich Democracies'. Paper presented at Workshop on 'Making Welfare States Work: Citizens, Workers and Welfare States in Comparative Perspective', Cornell University, Ithaca, NY, 25–6 September 2009.

Haider, S. J. (2001). 'Earnings Instability and Earnings Inequality of Males in the United States: 1967–1991', *Journal of Labor Economics*, 19: 799–836.

Hansen, J. and Wahlberg, R. (2009). 'Poverty and its Persistence: A Comparison of Natives and Immigrants in Sweden', *Review of Economics of the Household*, 7: 105–32.

Harding, A. (ed.) (1996). *Microsimulation and Public Policy*. Amsterdam: North-Holland.

Harkness, S., Gregg, P., and Smith, S. (2009). 'Welfare Reform and Lone Parents in the UK', *Economic Journal*, 119: F38–65.

Hause, J. C. (1980). 'The Fine Structure of Earnings and the On-The-Job Training Hypothesis', *Econometrica*, 48: 1013–29.

Hausman, J. A., Abrevaya, J., and Scott-Morton, F. M. (1998). 'Misclassification of the Dependent Variable in a Discrete-Response Setting', *Journal of Econometrics*, 87: 239–69.

Heckman, J. J. (1981a). 'The Incidental Parameters Problem and the Problem of Initial Conditions in Estimating a Discrete Time-Discrete Data Stochastic Process', in C. F. Manski and D. McFadden (eds), *Structural Analysis of Discrete Data with Econometric Applications*. Cambridge, Mass.: MIT Press, 179–95.

—— (1981b). 'Statistical Models for Discrete Panel Data', in C. F. Manski and D. McFadden (eds), *Structural Analysis of Discrete Data with Econometric Applications*. Cambridge, Mass.: MIT Press, 114–78.

References

Heuberger, R. (2003). 'What Household Gets What Income?' Paper presented to EPU-Net-2003 Conference, University of Essex, Colchester UK, 3–5 July 2003. <http://www.iser.essex.ac.uk/files/conferences/epunet/2003/docs/pdf/papers/heuberger.pdf>.

Hill, M. S. (1981). 'Some Dynamic Aspects of Poverty', in M. S. Hill, D. Hill, and J. Morgan (eds), *Five Thousand American Families—Patterns of Economic Progress, Volume 9*. Ann Arbor: Institute for Social Research, University of Michigan, 93–120.

—— (1992). *The Panel Study of Income Dynamics: a User's Guide*. Newbury Park, Calif.: Sage Publications.

—— Hill, D., and Walker, R. (1998). 'Intergenerational Dynamics in the USA: Poverty Processes in Young Adulthood', in L. Leisering and R. Walker (eds), *The Dynamics of Modern Society: Policy, Poverty and Welfare*. Bristol: The Policy Press, 85–107.

—— and Jenkins, S. P. (2001). 'Poverty Amongst British Children: Chronic or Transitory?', in B. Bradbury, S. P. Jenkins, and J. Micklewright (eds), *The Dynamics of Child Poverty in Industrialised Countries*. Cambridge: Cambridge University Press, 174–95.

Hills, J. (1995). *Inquiry into Income and Wealth, Volume 2: A Summary of the Evidence*. York: Joseph Rowntree Foundation.

—— (1998). *Income and Wealth: The Latest Evidence*. York: Joseph Rowntree Foundation.

—— (2004). *Inequality and the State*. Oxford: Oxford University Press.

—— McKnight, A., and Smithies, R. (2006). 'Tracking Income: How Working Families' Incomes Vary through the Year'. CASEreport 32. London: Centre for the Analysis of Social Exclusion, London School of Economics. <http://sticerd.lse.ac.uk/dps/case/cr/CASEreport32.pdf>.

House of Commons Treasury Committee (2006). *The Administration of Tax Credits*. Sixth Report of Session 2005–06, Volume 1 (Report, together with formal minutes), HC 811–1. London: The Stationery Office.

Huber, P. J. (1967). 'The Behaviour of Maximum Likelihood Estimators under Non-Standard Conditions', in *Proceedings of the Fifth Berkeley Symposium in Mathematical Statistics and Probability, 1*. Berkeley, Calif.: University of California Press, 221–33.

Hungerford, T. L. (1993). 'U.S. Income Mobility in the Seventies and Eighties', *Review of Income and Wealth*, 39: 403–17.

—— (2008). 'U.S. Income Inequality and Income Mobility in the 1980s and 1990s'. Unpublished Paper. Washington: Congressional Research Service.

Iceland, J. (1997). 'The Dynamics of Poverty Spells and Issues of Left-Censoring'. Population Studies Center Research Report 97-378. Ann Arbor: Institute for Social Research, University of Michigan. <http://www.psc.isr.umich.edu/pubs/pdf/rr97-378.pdf>.

Jäckle, A. (2008a). 'Measurement Error and Data Collection Methods: Effects on Estimates from Event History Data'. Working Paper 2008–13. Colchester: Institute for Social and Economic Research, University of Essex. <http://www.iser.essex.ac.uk/publications/working-papers/iser/2008-13.pdf>.

—— (2008b). 'Causes of Seam Effects in Panel Surveys'. ISER Working Paper 2008–14. Colchester: Institute for Social and Economic Research, University of Essex. <http://www.iser.essex.ac.uk/publications/working-papers/iser/2008-14.pdf>.

—— and Lynn, P. (2007). 'Dependent Interviewing and Seam Effects in Work History Data', *Journal of Official Statistics*, 23: 529–52.

—— Sala, E., Jenkins, S. P., and Lynn, P. (2004). 'Validation of Survey Data on Income and Employment: The ISMIE Experience'. Working Paper 2004–14. Colchester: Institute for Social and Economic Research, University of Essex. <http://www.iser.essex.ac.uk/pubs/workpaps/pdf/2004-14.pdf>.

Jalan, J. and Ravallion, M. (1998). 'Transient Poverty in Postreform Rural China', *Journal of Comparative Economics*, 26: 338–57.

Jarvis, S. and Jenkins, S. P. (1995). *Do The Poor Stay Poor? New Evidence about Income Dynamics from the British Household Panel Survey*. Occasional Paper No. 95–2. Colchester: Institute for Social and Economic Research, University of Essex. <http://www.iser.essex.ac.uk/files/occasional_papers/pdf/op95-2_text.pdf>, <http://www.iser.essex.ac.uk/files/occasional_papers/pdf/op95-2_appen.pdf>.

Jarvis, S. and Jenkins, S. P. (1997). 'Low Income Dynamics in 1990s Britain', *Fiscal Studies*, 18: 1–20.

—— —— (1998). 'How Much Income Mobility is There in Britain?', *Economic Journal*, 108: 428–43.

—— —— (1999). 'Marital Splits and Income Changes: Evidence from the British Household Panel Survey', *Population Studies*, 53: 237–54.

Jenkins, S. P. (1991). 'Poverty Measurement and the Within-Household Distribution: Agenda for Action', *Journal of Social Policy*, 20(4), October: 457–83.

—— (2000). 'Modelling Household Income Dynamics'. *Journal of Population Economics*, 13: 529–67.

—— (2001a). 'Getting a Job = Getting a Life? British Evidence on the Relationship between Getting a Job and Changes in Income, Well-Being, and Social Participation'. New Zealand Treasury General Lecture, Wellington, New Zealand, 3 April 2001. <https://filestore.iser.essex.ac.uk/d/nzt-gl2001-jenkins/>.

—— (2001b). 'Review of *The Gender Division of Welfare. The Impact of the British and German Welfare States*, by Mary Daly', *British Journal of Sociology*, 52: 354–5.

—— (2005). 'Survival Analysis'. Unpublished Book Manuscript. Colchester: Institute for Social and Economic Research, University of Essex. <http://www.iser.essex.ac.uk/survival-analysis>.

—— (2007). 'Approaches to Modelling Poverty Dynamics'. Paper presented at Workshop on 'Dynamic Analysis Using Panel Data—Applications to Poverty and Social Exclusion', Laboratorio Riccardo Revelli, Collegio Carlo Alberto, Moncalieri (Torino), 25 June 2007. <http://www.laboratoriorevelli.it/pagine/25_June_2007.html>.

—— (2008). 'Income and Poverty: The Rubber Band Theory', in R. Berthoud and J. Burton (eds), *In Praise of Panel Surveys*. Colchester: Institute for Social and Economic Research, University of Essex, 2–3. <http://research.understandingsociety.org.uk/files/research/IPOPS.pdf>.

—— (2009a). 'Marital Splits and Income Changes over the Longer Term', in M. Brynin and J. F. Ermisch (eds), *Changing Relationships*. London: Routledge, 217–36.

—— (2009b), 'Spaghetti Unravelled: A Model-Based Description of Differences in Income-Age Trajectories'. Report to the National Equality Panel and ISER Working Paper 2009–30. <http://www.iser.essex.ac.uk/pubs/workpaps/pdf/2009-30.pdf>.

References

Jenkins, S. P. (2010*a*). 'Comparisons of BHPS and HBAI Distributions of Net Household Income'. Unpublished Paper. Colchester: Institute for Social and Economic Research, University of Essex. <https://filestore.iser.essex.ac.uk/d/3a16c2>.

—— (2010*b*). 'How Can We Improve our Knowledge of Poverty Dynamics in Europe?' Paper presented at the EU Presidency 'Science Against Poverty' Conference, Segovia, 8–9 April 2010. <http://www.iser.essex.ac.uk/assets/327>.

—— Cappellari, L., Lynn, P., Jäckle, A. and Sala, E. (2006). 'Patterns of Consent: Evidence from a General Household Survey', *Journal of the Royal Statistical Society, Series A*, 169: 701–22.

—— Lynn, P., Jäckle, A., and Sala, E. (2008). 'The Feasibility of Linking Household Survey and Administrative Record Data: New Evidence for Britain', *International Journal of Social Research Methodology*, 11: 29–43.

—— and Cowell, F. A. (1994). 'Parametric Equivalence Scales and Scale Relativities', *Economic Journal*, 104: 891–900.

—— and Micklewright, J. (2007). 'New Directions in the Analysis of Inequality and Poverty', in S. P. Jenkins and J. Micklewright (eds), *Inequality and Poverty Re-examined*. Oxford: Oxford University Press, 3–33.

—— and Rigg, J.A., with the assistance of Devicienti, F. (2001). *The Dynamics of Poverty in Britain*. Department for Work and Pensions Research Report No. 157. Leeds: Corporate Document Services. <http://research.dwp.gov.uk/asd/asd5/rrep157.pdf>.

—— —— (2004). 'Disability and Disadvantage: Selection, Onset, and Duration Effects', *Journal of Social Policy*, 33: 479–501.

—— and Schluter, C. (2003). 'Why are Child Poverty Rates Higher in Britain than in Germany? A Longitudinal Perspective', *Journal of Human Resources*, 38: 441–65.

—— and Van Kerm, P. (2006). 'Trends in Income Inequality, Pro-Poor Income Growth, and Income Mobility', *Oxford Economic Papers*, 58: 531–48.

—— —— (2009). 'The Measurement of Economic Inequality', in W. Salverda, B. Nolan, and T. M. Smeeding (eds), *The Oxford Handbook on Economic Inequality*. Oxford: Oxford University Press, 40–67.

—— —— (2011). 'Trends in Individual Income Growth: Measurement Methods and British Evidence', ISER Working Paper 2011-06. Colchester: Institute for Social and Economic Research, University of Essex. <http://www.iser.essex.ac.uk/pubs/workpaps/pdf/2011-06.pdf>.

Johnson, P. and Webb, S. (1989). 'Counting People with Low Incomes: The Impact of Recent Changes in Official Statistics', *Fiscal Studies*, 10: 66–82.

Jones, A. M., Koolman, X., and Rice, N. (2006). 'Health-Related Non-Response in the British Household Panel Survey and European Community Household Panel: Using Inverse-Probability Weighted Estimators in Non-Linear Models', *Journal of the Royal Statistical Society, Series A*, 169: 543–69.

Joyce, R., Muriel, A., Phillips, D., and Sibieta, L. (2010). *Poverty and Inequality in the UK. 2010*. Commentary C116. London: Institute for Fiscal Studies. <http://www.ifs.org.uk/comms/comm116.pdf>.

Kahneman, D. and Krueger, A. B. (2006). 'Developments in the Measurement of Subjective Well-Being', *Journal of Economic Perspectives*, 20: 3–24.

Kasprzyk, D., Duncan, G., Kalton, G., and Singh, M. P. (eds) (1989). *Panel Surveys*. New York: Wiley.

Kempson, E. (1996). *Life on a Low Income*. York: Joseph Rowntree Foundation.

Keys, B. J. (2008). 'Trends in Income And Consumption Volatility, 1970–2000', in D. Jolliffe and J. Ziliak (eds), *Income Volatility and Food Assistance in the United States*. Kalamazoo, Mich.: Upjohn Institute for Employment Research, 11–34.

Kopczuk, W., Saez, E., and Song, J. (2010). 'Earnings Inequality and Mobility in the United States: Evidence from Social Security Data since 1937', *Quarterly Journal of Economics*, 125: 91–128.

Kristensen, N. and Westergaard-Nielsen, N. (2007). 'A Large-Scale Validation Study of Measurement Errors in Longitudinal Survey Data', *Journal of Economic and Social Measurement*, 32: 65–92.

Kroh, M. (2009). 'Documentation of Sample Sizes and Panel Attrition in the German Socio Economic Panel (SOEP) (1984 until 2008)'. SOEP Data Documentation Paper 47. Berlin: SOEP Group, DIW Berlin. <http://www.diw.de/documents/publikationen/73/diw_01.c.341747.de/diw_datadoc_2009-047.pdf>.

Kuchler, B. and Göbel, J. (2003). 'Incidence and Intensity of Smoothed Income Poverty in European Countries', *Journal of European Social Policy*, 13: 357–69.

Lancaster, T. (1990). *The Econometric Analysis of Transition Data*. Cambridge: Cambridge University Press.

Laurie, H. (2003). 'From PAPI to CAPI: Consequences for Data Quality on the British Household Panel Survey'. Working Paper 2003–14. Colchester: Institute for Social and Economic Research, University of Essex. <http://www.iser.essex.ac.uk/publications/working-papers/iser/2003-14>.

Lazear, E. (1995). *Personnel Economics*. Cambridge, Mass.: The MIT Press.

—— and Michael, R. T. (1986). 'Estimating the Personal Distribution of Income with Adjustment for Within-Family Variation', *Journal of Labor Economics*, 4: S216–44.

—— —— (1988). *Allocation of Income within the Household*. Chicago: University of Chicago Press.

Leigh, A. (2009). 'Permanent Income Inequality: Australia, Britain, Germany, and the United States Compared'. Discussion Paper 628. Canberra, ACT: Centre for Economic Policy Research, Australian National University. <http://econrsss.anu.edu.au/pdf/DP628.pdf>.

Leisering, L. and Leibfried, S. (1999). *Time and Poverty in Western Welfare States: United Germany in Perspective*. Cambridge: Cambridge University Press.

Lepkowski, J. M., Tucker, C., Brick, J. M., de Leeuw, E. D., Japec, L., Lavrakas, P. J., Link, M. W., and Sangster, R. L. (eds) (2008). *Advances in Telephone Survey Methodology*. Hoboken, NJ: John Wiley and Sons.

Levy, H. and Jenkins, S. P. (2008). 'Documentation for Derived Current and Annual Net Household Income Variables, BHPS Waves 1–16'. Unpublished Paper. Colchester: Institute for Social and Economic Research, University of Essex. <http://www.data-archive.ac.uk/doc/3909/mrdoc/pdf/3909userguide.pdf>.

Lillard, L. and Weiss, Y. (1979). 'Components of Variation in Panel Earnings Data: American Scientists, 1960–1970', *Econometrica*, 47: 437–54.

References

Lillard, L. and Willis, R. (1978). 'Dynamic Aspects of Earnings Mobility', *Econometrica*, 46: 985–1012.

Little, R. J. A. and Su, H. -L. (1989). 'Item Nonresponse in Panel Surveys', in D. Kasprzyk, G. Duncan, G. Kalton, and M. P. Singh (eds) *Panel Surveys*. New York: John Wiley and Sons, 400–25.

Lydon, R. and Walker, I. (2005). 'Welfare to Work, Wages and Wage Growth', *Fiscal Studies*, 26: 335–70.

Lynn, P. (ed.) (2006). 'Quality Profile: British Household Panel Survey Version 2.0: Waves 1 to 13: 1991–2003'. Unpublished Paper. Colchester: Institute for Social and Economic Research, University of Essex. <http://www.iser.essex.ac.uk/files/bhps/quality-profiles/BHPS-QP-01-03-06-v2.pdf>.

—— (ed.) (2009). *Methodology of Longitudinal Surveys*. New York and London: John Wiley and Sons.

—— and Sala, E. (2006). 'Measuring Change in Employment Characteristics: The Effects of Dependent Interviewing'. *International Journal of Public Opinion Research*, 18: 500–9.

—— Jäckle, A., Jenkins, S. P., and Sala, E. (2004). 'The Impact of Questioning Method on Measurement Error in Panel Survey Measures of Benefit Receipt: Evidence from a Validation Study'. Working Paper 2004–28. Colchester: Institute for Social and Economic Research, University of Essex. <http://www.iser.essex.ac.uk/pubs/workpaps/pdf/2004-28.pdf>. *Journal of the Royal Statistical Society, Series A*, forthcoming.

—— —— —— —— (2006). 'The Effects of Dependent Interviewing on Responses to Questions on Income Sources', *Journal of Official Statistics*, 22: 357–84.

Maasoumi, E. (1998). 'On Mobility', in D. Giles and A. Ullah (eds), *Handbook of Applied Economic Statistics*. New York: Marcel Dekker, 119–75.

Mack, J. and Lansley, S. (1985). *Poor Britain*. London: George Allen & Unwin.

MaCurdy, T. (1982). 'The Use of Time Series Processes to Model the Error Structure of Earnings in a Longitudinal Data Analysis', *Journal of Econometrics*, 18: 83–114.

Manning, A. (2009). You Can't Always Get What You Want: The Impact of the UK Jobseeker's Allowance', *Labour Economics*, 16: 239–50.

Markandya, A. (1984). 'The Welfare Measurement of Changes in Economic Mobility', *Economica*, 51: 457–71.

Meghir, C. and Pistaferri, L. (2004). 'Income Variance Dynamics and Heterogeneity', *Econometrica*, 72: 1–32.

—— —— (2010). 'Earnings, Consumption and Lifecycle Choices'. Working Paper 15914. Cambridge, Mass.: National Bureau of Economic Research. <http://www.nber.org/papers/w15914>.

Meyer, B. D. and Sullivan, J. X. (2003). 'Measuring the Well-Being of the Poor using Income and Consumption', *Journal of Human Resources*, 38 (Supplement): 1180–220.

Michaud, S. and Latouche, M. (1996). 'Some Data Quality Impacts when Merging Survey Data on Income with Tax Data'. SLID Research Paper 96–12. Ottawa: Statistics Canada. <http://dsp-psd.pwgsc.gc.ca/Collection/Statcan/75F0002MIE/75F0002MIE1996012.pdf>.

Micklewright, J. (1986). 'A Note on Household Income Data in NCDS3', NCDS User Support Group Discussion Paper 18. London: Social Statistics Research Unit, The City University. <http://www.cls.ioe.ac.uk/core/documents/download.asp?id=172&log_stat=1>.

Middleton, S., Ashworth, K., and Braithwaite, L. (1997). *Small Fortunes: Spending on Childhood Poverty and Parental Sacrifice*. York: Joseph Rowntree Foundation.

Mincer, J. (1974). *Schooling, Experience and Earnings*. New York: Columbia University Press.

Moffitt, R. A. and Gottschalk, P. (1995). 'Trends in the Covariance Structure of Earnings in the U.S.: 1969–1987'. Unpublished Paper. Baltimore, Md.: Economics Department, The Johns Hopkins University. <http://www.econ.jhu.edu/People/Moffitt/mg2_0795.pdf>.

—— —— (2002). 'Trends in the Transitory Variance of Earnings in the United States', *Economic Journal*, 112: C68–73.

—— —— (2008*a*). 'Trends in the Transitory Variance of Male Earnings in the U. S., 1991–2003: Preliminary Evidence from LEHD Data'. Working Paper 696. Boston: Economics Department, Boston College. <http://fmwww.bc.edu/ec-p/wp696.pdf>.

—— —— (2008*b*). 'Trends in the Transitory Variance of Male Earnings in the U. S., 1970–2004'. Working Paper 697. Boston: Economics Department, Boston College. <http://fmwww.bc.edu/EC-P/WP697.pdf>.

—— and Rendall, M. S. (1995). 'Cohort Trends in the Lifetime Distribution of Female Family Headship in the United States, 1968–1985', *Demography*, 32: 407–24.

National Equality Panel (J. Hills, Chair). (2010). *An Anatomy of Economic Inequality in the UK: Report of the National Equality Panel*. London: Government Inequalities Office. <http://www.equalities.gov.uk/pdf/NEP%20Report%20bookmarkedfinal.pdf>.

Nickell, S. (1979). 'Estimating the Probability of Leaving Unemployment', *Econometrica*, 47: 1249–66.

Nicoletti, C. and Peracchi, F. (2005). 'Survey Response and Survey Characteristics: Microlevel Evidence from the European Community Household Panel'. *Journal of the Royal Statistical Society, Series A*, 168: 763–81.

Noble, M., Cheung, S. Y., and Smith, G. (1998). 'Origins and Destinations—Social Security Claimant Dynamics' *Journal of Social Policy*, 27: 351–69.

Nolan, B. and Whelan, C. (1996). *Resources, Deprivation and Poverty*. Oxford: Clarendon Press.

OECD (2001). 'When Money is Tight: Poverty Dynamics in OECD Countries', *OECD Employment Outlook 2001*: 37–87.

—— (2004). *Benefits and Wages, OECD Indicators 2004*. Paris: OECD.

—— (2008). *Growing Unequal? Income Distribution and Poverty in OECD Countries*. Paris: OECD.

Oxley, H., Dang, T. -T., and Antolín, P. (2000). 'Poverty Dynamics in Six OECD Countries', *OECD Economic Studies*, 30: 7–52.

Pahl, J. (1983). 'The Allocation of Money and the Structuring of Inequality within Marriage'. *Sociological Review*, 31: 237–62.

Panel on Fair Access to the Professions (Rt. Hon. A. Milburn, Chair) (2009). *Unleashing Aspiration: The Final Report of the Panel on Fair Access to the Professions*. London: Cabinet Office. <http://www.cabinetoffice.gov.uk/media/227102/fair-access.pdf>.

References

Paull, G. (2007). *Partnership Transitions and Mothers' Employment*. Department for Work and Pensions Research Report No. 452. Leeds: Corporate Document Services. <http://research.dwp.gov.uk/asd/asd5/rports2007-2008/rrep452.pdf>.

Petrongolo, B. (2009). 'The Long-Term Effects of Job Search Requirements: Evidence from the UK JSA Reform', *Journal of Public Economics*, 93: 1234–53.

Platt, L. (2009). *Ethnicity and Child Poverty*. Department for Work and Pensions Research Report 576. Leeds: Corporate Document Services. <http://research.dwp.gov.uk/asd/asd5/rports2009-2010/rrep576.pdf>.

Pudney, S. (2008). 'Heaping and Leaping: Survey Response Behaviour and the Dynamics of Self-Reported Consumption Expenditure'. Working Paper 2008–09. Colchester: Institute for Social and Economic Research, University of Essex. <http://www.iser.essex.ac.uk/publications/working-papers/iser/2008-09>.

Ramos, X. (2003). 'The Covariance Structure of Earnings in Britain, 1991–1999', *Economica*, 70: 353–74.

Redmond, G. (1997). 'Imputing Council Tax Bands for Households in the British Household Panel Study'. Working Paper 97–10. Colchester: Institute for Social and Economic Research, University of Essex.

Rendtel, U., Langeheine, R., and Berndtsen, R. (1998). 'The Estimation of Poverty Dynamics using Different Measurements of Household Income', *Review of Income and Wealth*, 44: 81–98.

—— Nordberg, L., Jäntti, M., Hanisch, J., and Basic, E. (2004). 'Report on Quality of Income Data'. CHINTEX Working Paper 21. <http://www.destatis.de/jetspeed/portal/cms/Sites/destatis/Internet/DE/Content/Wissenschaftsforum/Chintex/Research Results/Einfuehrung,templateId=renderPrint.psml>.

Ribar, D. C. (2005). 'Transitions from Welfare and the Employment Prospects of Low-Skill Workers', *Southern Economic Journal*, 71: 514–33.

Rigg, J. and Sefton, T. (2006). 'Income Dynamics and the Life Cycle', *Journal of Social Policy*, 35: 411–35.

Rodgers, J. R. and Rodgers, J. L. (1993). 'Chronic Poverty in the United States', *Journal of Human Resources*, 28: 25–54.

—— —— (2009), 'Contributions of Longitudinal Data to Poverty Measurement in Australia', *Economic Record*, 85: S35–47.

Rose, D. (ed.) (2000). *Researching Social and Economic Change: The Uses of Household Panel Studies*. London: Routledge.

Rosenzweig, M. R. (2003). 'Payoffs from Panels in Low-Income Countries: Economic Development and Economic Mobility', *American Economic Review (Papers and Proceedings)*, 93: 112–17.

Rowntree, B. S. (2000, originally 1901). *Poverty: A Study of Town Life*, centennial edition. Bristol: The Policy Press. (Originally: Macmillan, London.)

Rubin, D. B. (1987). *Multiple Imputation for Non-Response in Surveys*. New York: John Wiley and Sons.

Ruggles, P. (1990). *Drawing the Line: Alternative Poverty Measures and their Implications for Public Policy*. Washington: The Urban Institute Press.

Schluter, C. and Trede, M. (2003). 'Local versus Global Assessments of Mobility', *International Economic Review*, 44: 1313–35.

Sefton, T. (2009). 'Moving in the Right Direction? Public Attitudes to Poverty, Inequality and Redistribution', in J. Hills, T. Sefton, and K. Stewart (eds), *Towards a More Equal Society? Poverty, Inequality and Policy since 1997*. Bristol: The Policy Press, 223–44.

Sen, A. K. (1979). 'Equality of What?' Tanner Lecture, Stanford University, 22 May 1979. <http://www.tannerlectures.utah.edu/lectures/documents/sen80.pdf>.

—— (1985). *Commodities and Capabilities*. Oxford: Oxford University Press.

Shin, D. and Solon, G. (2009). 'Trends in Men's Earnings Volatility: What does the Panel Study of Income Dynamics Show?' Unpublished Paper. East Lancing, Mich.: Economics Department, Michigan State University. <http://www.hks.harvard.edu/inequality/Seminar/Papers/Solon09.pdf>.

Shorrocks, A. F. (1978). 'Income Inequality and Income Mobility', *Journal of Economic Theory*, 19: 376–93.

—— (1981). 'Income Stability in the United States', in N. A. Klevmarken and J. A. Lybeck (eds), *The Statics and Dynamics of Income*. Clevedon, Avon: Tieto, 175–94.

—— (1982). 'Inequality Decomposition by Factor Components', *Econometrica*, 50: 193–211.

—— (1983). 'The Impact of Income Components on the Distribution of Family Incomes', *Quarterly Journal of Economics*, 98: 311–26.

—— (2004). 'Inequality and Welfare Evaluation of Heterogeneous Income Distributions', *Journal of Economic Inequality*, 2: 193–218.

Smith, N. and Middleton, S. (2007). *A Review of Poverty Dynamics Research in the UK*. York: York Publishing Services for the Joseph Rowntree Foundation. <http://www.jrf.org.uk/sites/files/jrf/2040-poverty-dynamics-review.pdf>.

Statistics Canada (n.d.). 'The LifePaths Microsimulation Model: An Overview'. Unpublished paper. Ottawa: Statistics Canada. <http://www.statcan.gc.ca/microsimulation/pdf/lifepaths-overview-vuedensemble-eng.pdf>.

Stevens, A. H. (1994). 'Persistence in Poverty and Welfare: The Dynamics of Poverty Spells: Updating Bane and Ellwood', *American Economic Review (Papers and Proceedings)*, 82: 34–7.

—— (1995). 'Climbing Out of Poverty, Falling Back In: Measuring the Persistence of Poverty over Multiple Spells'. NBER Working Paper 5390. Cambridge, Mass.: National Bureau of Economic Research. <http://www.nber.org/papers/w5390.pdf>.

—— (1999). 'Climbing Out of Poverty, Falling Back In: Measuring the Persistence of Poverty over Multiple Spells', *Journal of Human Resources*, 34: 557–88.

Stewart, M. B. (1999). 'Low Pay, No Pay Dynamics', in *Persistent Poverty and Lifetime Inequality: The Evidence*. Proceedings of a Workshop held at HM Treasury, 17–18 November 1998. CASEreport 5. London: Centre for the Analysis of Social Exclusion, London School of Economics, 3–8. <http://eprints.lse.ac.uk/28299/1/casereport5.pdf>.

—— (2007). 'The Interrelated Dynamics of Unemployment and Low Pay', *Journal of Applied Econometrics*, 22: 511–31.

—— and Swaffield, J. K. (1999). 'Low Pay Dynamics and Transition Probabilities', *Economica* 66: 23–42.

Sutherland, H. and Wilson, M. (1995). 'Using the FES to Simulate Income Tax in POLIMOD'. Microsimulation Unit Research Note MU/RN/15. Cambridge: Department of Applied Economics, University of Cambridge.

Swihart, B. J., Caffo, B., James, B. D., Strand, M., Schwartz, B. S., and Punjabi, N. M. (2010). 'Lasagna Plots: A Saucy Alternative to Spaghetti Plots', *Epidemiology*, 21: 621–5.

Townsend, P. (1979). *Poverty in the United Kingdom*. Harmondsworth: Penguin.

HM Treasury (1999), 'Tackling Poverty and Extending Opportunity'. The Modernisation of Britain's Tax and Benefit System Paper No. 4. London: HM Treasury.

Uhrig, S. C. N. (2008). 'The Nature and Causes of Attrition in the British Household Panel Study'. ISER Working Paper 2008–05. Colchester: Institute for Social and Economic Research, University of Essex. <http://www.iser.essex.ac.uk/publications/working-papers/iser/2008-05.pdf>.

Ulrick, S. W. (2008). 'Using Semi-Parametric Methods in an Analysis of Earnings Mobility', *Econometric Journal*, 11: 478–98.

Valletta, R. G. (2006). 'The Ins and Outs of Poverty in Advanced Economies: Government Policy and Poverty Dynamics in Canada, Germany, Great Britain, and the United States', *Review of Income and Wealth*, 52: 261–84.

Van den Berg, G. J. and Lindeboom, M. (1998). 'Attrition in Panel Survey Data and the Estimation of Multi-State Labor Market Models', *Journal of Human Resources*, 33: 458–78.

—— —— and Ridder, G. (1994). 'Attrition in Longitudinal Panel Data and the Empirical Analysis of Labor Market Behaviour', *Journal of Applied Econometrics*, 9: 421–35.

Van Kerm, P. (2003). 'An Anatomy of Household Income Volatility in European Countries'. CHER Working Paper 16. Differdange, Luxembourg: CEPS/INSTEAD. <http://www.ceps.lu/unites_de_recherche/erdi/publications_erdi/?p=5#>.

—— (2009). 'Income Mobility Profiles', *Economics Letters*, 102: 93–5.

Van Praag, B. and Ferrer-i-Carbonell, A. (2009). 'Inequality and Happiness', in W. Salverda, B. Nolan, and T. M. Smeeding (eds), *The Oxford Handbook on Economic Inequality*. Oxford: Oxford University Press, 364–83.

Vogler, C. (1989). 'Labour Market Change and Patterns of Financial Allocation within Households', in M. Anderson, F. Bechhofer, and J. Gershuny (eds), *The Social and Political Economy of the Household*. Oxford: Oxford University Press, 225–66.

Waldfogel, J. (2010). *Britain's War against Poverty*. New York: Russell Sage Foundation.

Walker, I. and Zhu, Y. (2003). 'Education, Earnings, and Productivity: Recent UK Evidence', *Labour Market Trends*, 111: 145–52.

Walker, R. (2005). *Social Security and Welfare: Concepts and Comparisons*. Milton Keynes: Open University Press/McGraw-Hill.

—— in association with Ashworth, K. (1994). *Poverty Dynamics: Issues and Examples*. Aldershot: Avebury Press.

Watson, D. (2003). 'Sample Attrition between Waves 1 and 5 in the European Community Household Panel', *European Sociological Review*, 19: 361–78.

Watson, N. and Wooden, M. (2006). 'Modelling Longitudinal Survey Response: The Experience of the HILDA Survey'. HILDA Discussion Paper series No. 2/06.

Melbourne: Melbourne Institute, University of Melbourne. <http://www.melbour-neinstitute.com/hilda/hdps/HILDA%20DP%202.06.pdf>.

Webb, S. (1995). *Poverty Dynamics in Great Britain: Preliminary Analysis from the British Household Panel Survey*. IFS Commentary No. 48. London: Institute for Fiscal Studies. <http://www.ifs.org.uk/comms/comm48.pdf>.

Winship, C. and Radbill, L. (1998). 'Sampling Weights and Regression Analysis'. *Sociological Methods and Research*, 23: 230–57.

Wooldridge, J. M. (2002a). 'Inverse Probability Weighted M-Estimators for Sample Selection, Attrition, and Stratification', *Portugese Economic Journal*, 1: 117–39.

—— (2002b). *Econometric Analysis of Cross-Sectional and Panel Data*. Cambridge, Mass.: MIT Press.

Worts, D., Sacker, A., and McDonough, P. (2010). 'Re-assessing Poverty Dynamics and State Protections in Britain and the US: The Role of Measurement Error', *Social Indicators Research*, 97: 419–38.

Wren-Lewis, L., Muriel, A., and Brewer, M. (2009), 'Accounting for Changes in Inequality since 1968: Decomposition Analyses for Great Britain'. Report to the National Equality Panel. London: Institute for Fiscal Studies. <http://www.equalities.gov.uk/pdf/Accounting%20for%20changes%20in%20inequality.pdf>.

Zantomio, F., Pudney, S. E., and Hancock, R. M. (2010). 'Estimating the Impact of a Policy Reform on Welfare Participation: The 2001 Extension to the Minimum Income Guarantee for UK pensioners, *Economica*, 77: 234–54.

Zellner, A. (1992). 'Statistics, Science and Public Policy', *Journal of the American Statistical Association*, 87: 1–6.

Author Index

393

Subject Index

Page numbers in italics refer to tables.